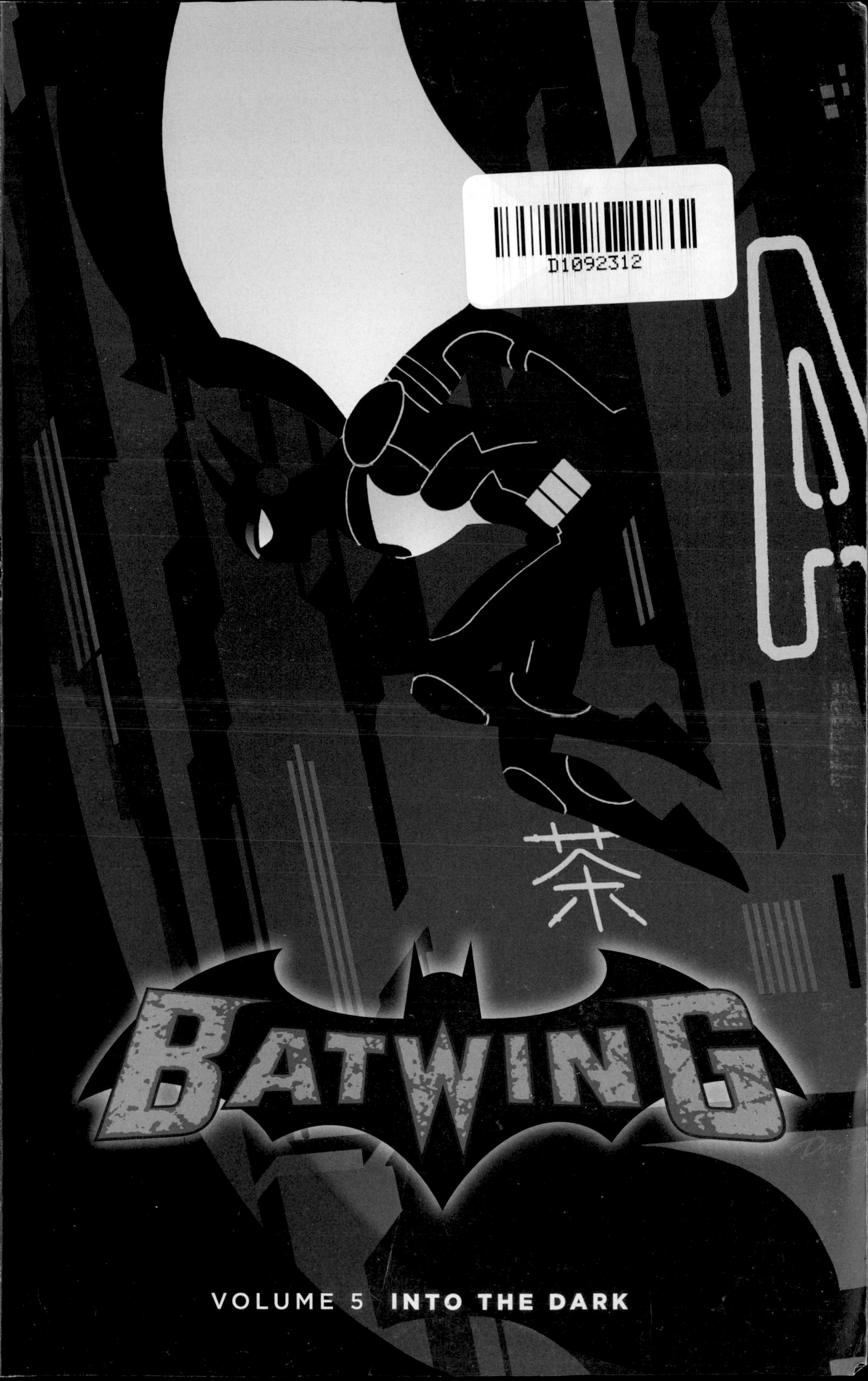
茶
BATWING
VOLUME 5 INTO THE DARK

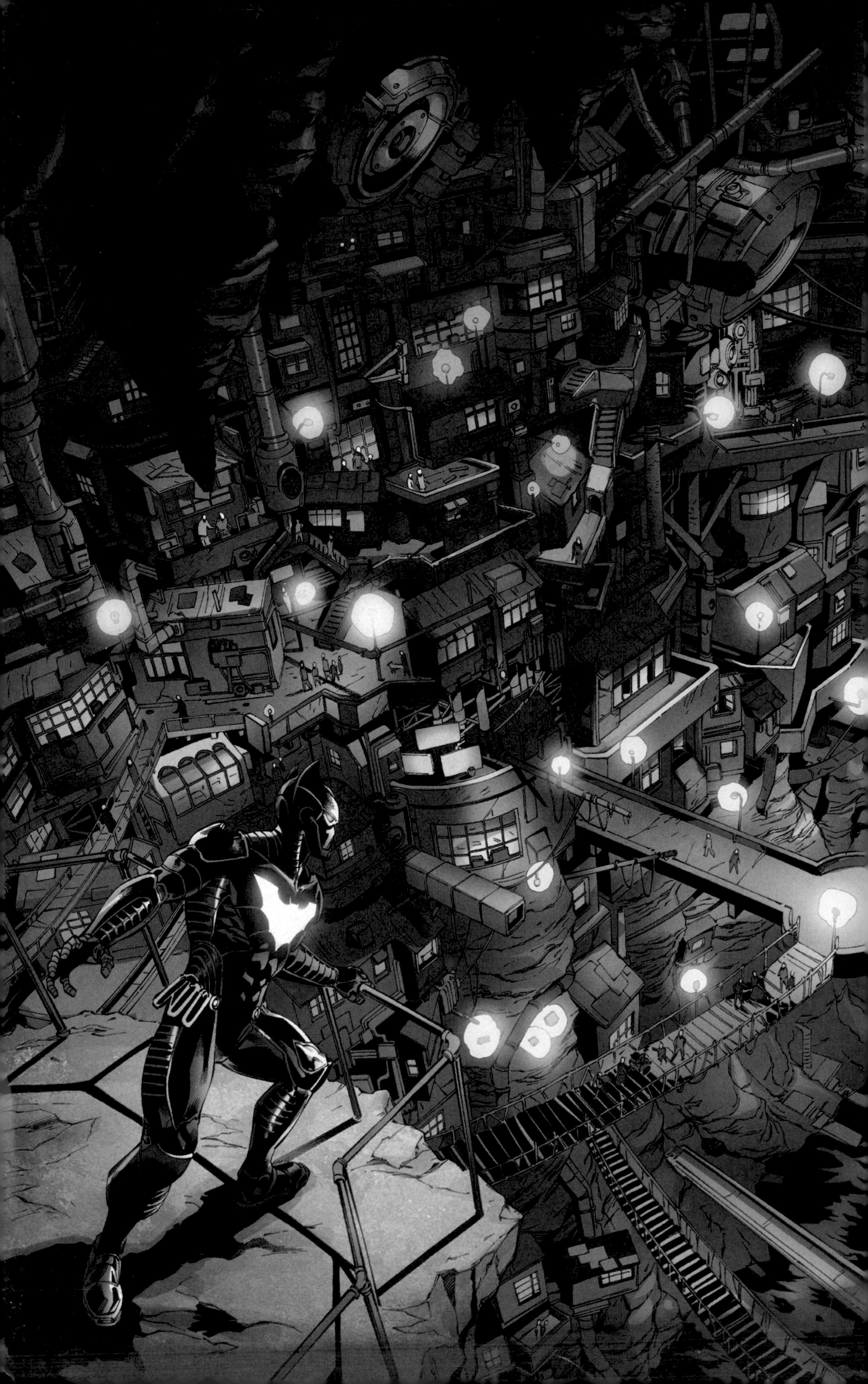

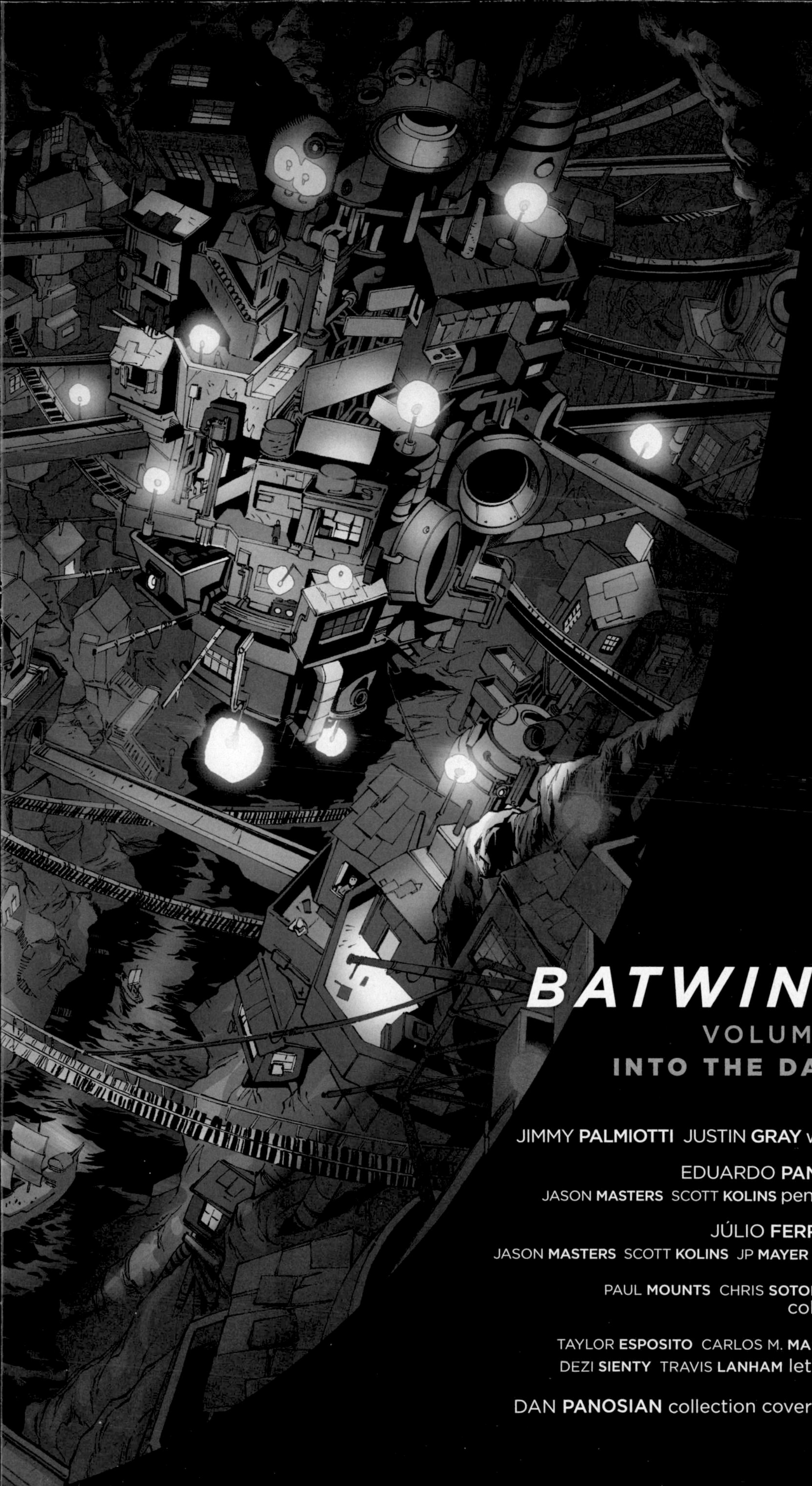

BATWING

VOLUME 5
INTO THE DARK

JIMMY **PALMIOTTI** JUSTIN **GRAY** writers

EDUARDO **PANSICA**
JASON **MASTERS** SCOTT **KOLINS** pencillers

JÚLIO **FERREIRA**
JASON **MASTERS** SCOTT **KOLINS** JP **MAYER** inkers

PAUL **MOUNTS** CHRIS **SOTOMAYOR**
colorists

TAYLOR **ESPOSITO** CARLOS M. **MANGUAL**
DEZI **SIENTY** TRAVIS **LANHAM** letterers

DAN **PANOSIAN** collection cover artist

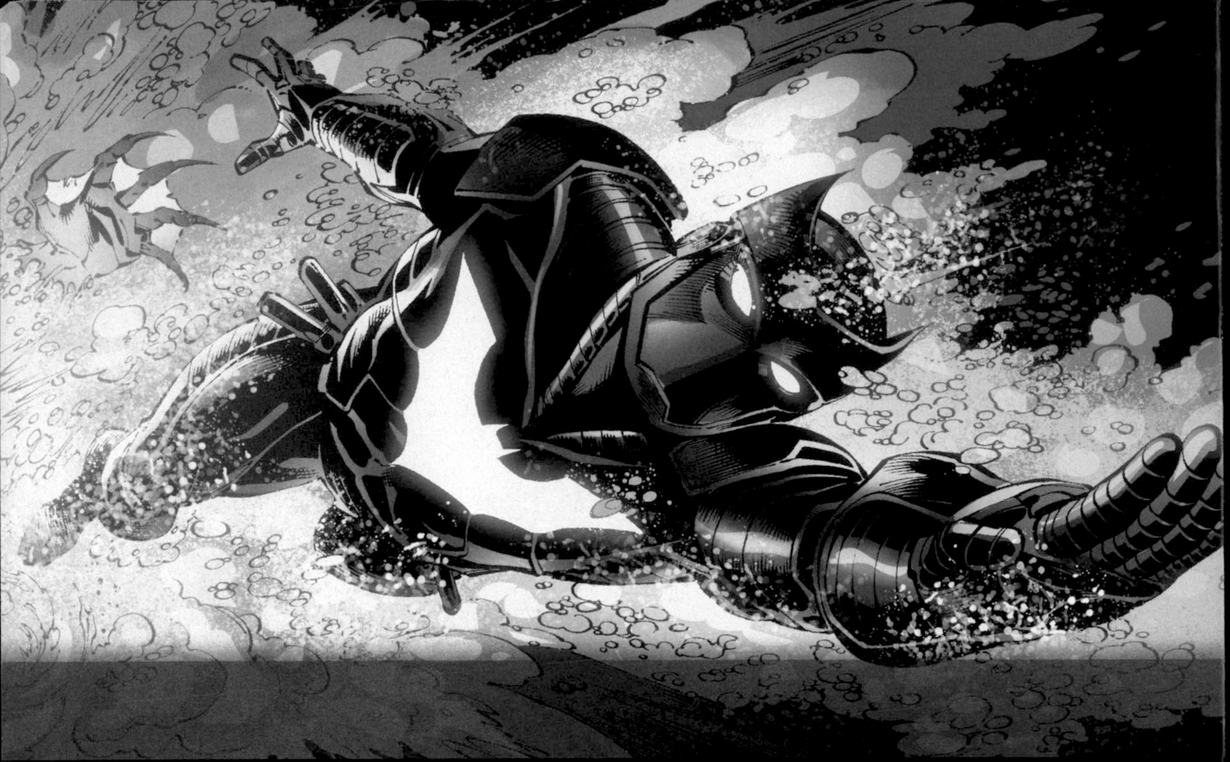

RACHEL GLUCKSTERN Editor – Original Series DARREN SHAN DAVE WIELGOSZ Assistant Editors – Original Series
JEREMY BENT Editor ROBBIN BROSTERMAN Design Director – Books ROBBIE BIEDERMAN Publication Design

BOB HARRAS Senior VP – Editor-in-Chief, DC Comics

DIANE NELSON President DAN DIDIO and JIM LEE Co-Publishers GEOFF JOHNS Chief Creative Officer
AMIT DESAI Senior VP – Marketing and Franchise Management
AMY GENKINS Senior VP – Business and Legal Affairs NAIRI GARDINER Senior VP – Finance
JEFF BOISON VP – Publishing Planning MARK CHIARELLO VP – Art Direction and Design
JOHN CUNNINGHAM VP – Marketing TERRI CUNNINGHAM VP – Editorial Administration
LARRY GANEM VP – Talent Relations and Services ALISON GILL Senior VP – Manufacturing and Operations
HANK KANALZ Senior VP – Vertigo and Integrated Publishing JAY KOGAN VP – Business and Legal Affairs, Publishing
JACK MAHAN VP – Business Affairs, Talent NICK NAPOLITANO VP – Manufacturing Administration SUE POHJA VP – Book Sales
FRED RUIZ VP – Manufacturing Operations COURTNEY SIMMONS Senior VP – Publicity BOB WAYNE Senior VP – Sales

BATWING VOLUME 5: INTO THE DARK

DC Comics, 1700 Broadway, New York, NY 10019
A Warner Bros. Entertainment Company.
Printed by RR Donnelley, Owensville, MO, USA. 1/23/15. First Printing.
ISBN: 978-1-4012-5081-2

SUSTAINABLE FORESTRY INITIATIVE
Certified Chain of Custody
20% Certified Forest Content,
80% Certified Sourcing
www.sfiprogram.org
SFI-01042
APPLIES TO TEXT STOCK ONLY

Library of Congress Cataloging-in-Publication Data

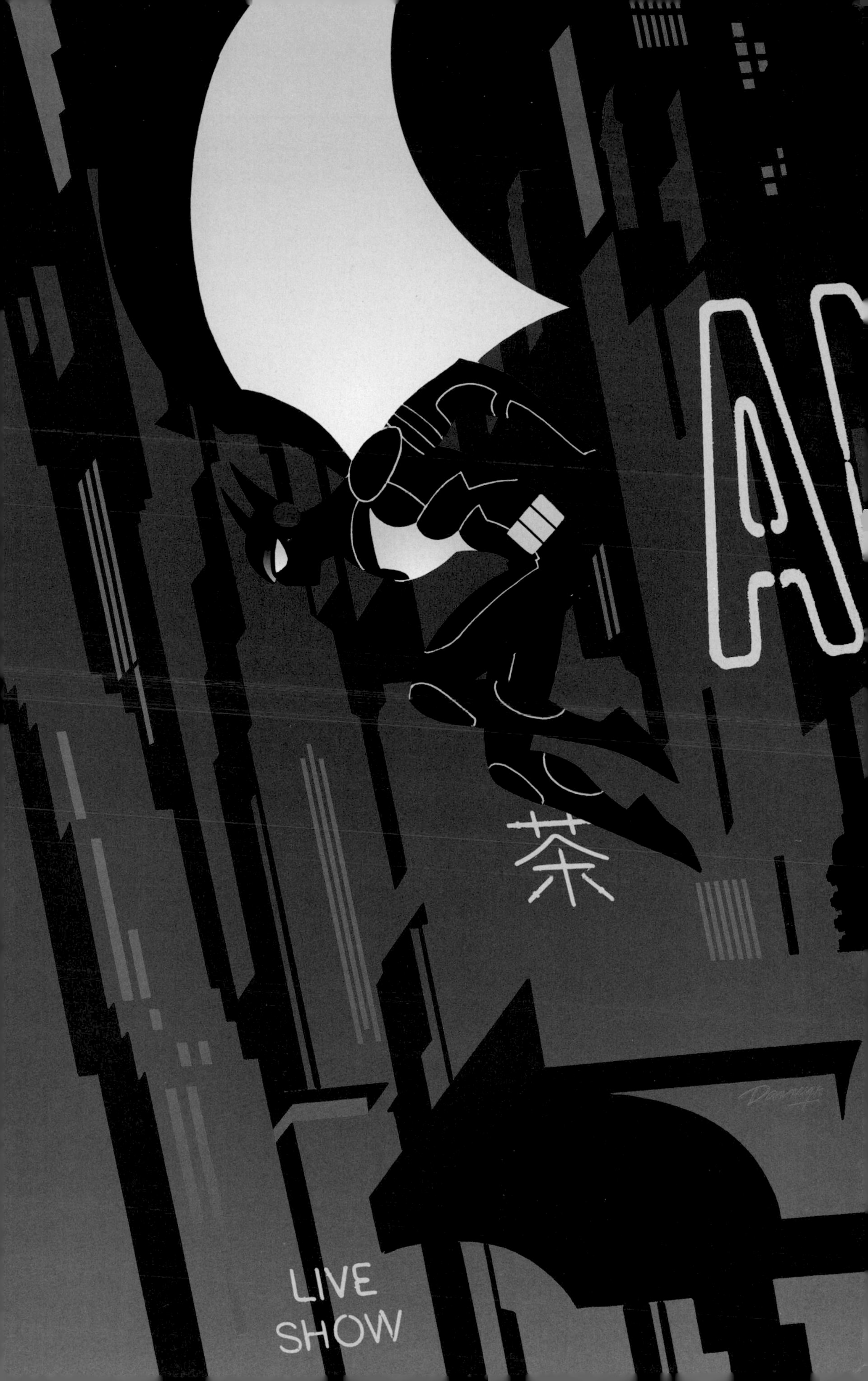
茶
LIVE
SHOW

NOT ALL THAT GLITTERS

JIMMY PALMIOTTI
JUSTIN GRAY
writers

JASON MASTERS
SCOTT KOLINS
artists

CHRIS SOTOMAYOR
colorist

TAYLOR ESPOSITO
letterer

cover art by
DARWYN COOKE

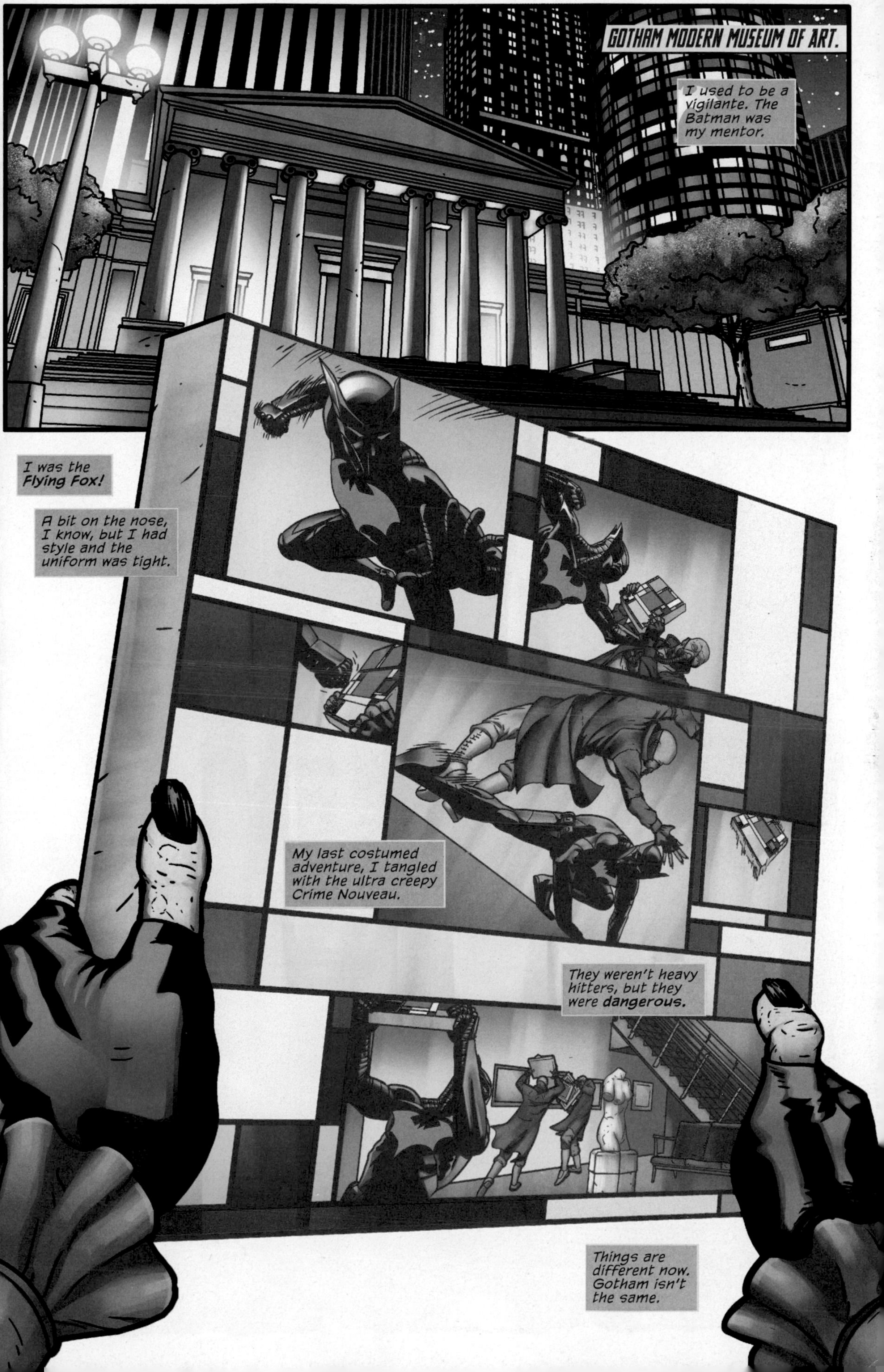
GOTHAM MODERN MUSEUM OF ART.
I used to be a vigilante. The Batman was my mentor.
I was the **Flying Fox!**
A bit on the nose, I know, but I had style and the uniform was tight.
My last costumed adventure, I tangled with the ultra creepy Crime Nouveau.
They weren't heavy hitters, but they were **dangerous.**
Things are different now. Gotham isn't the same.

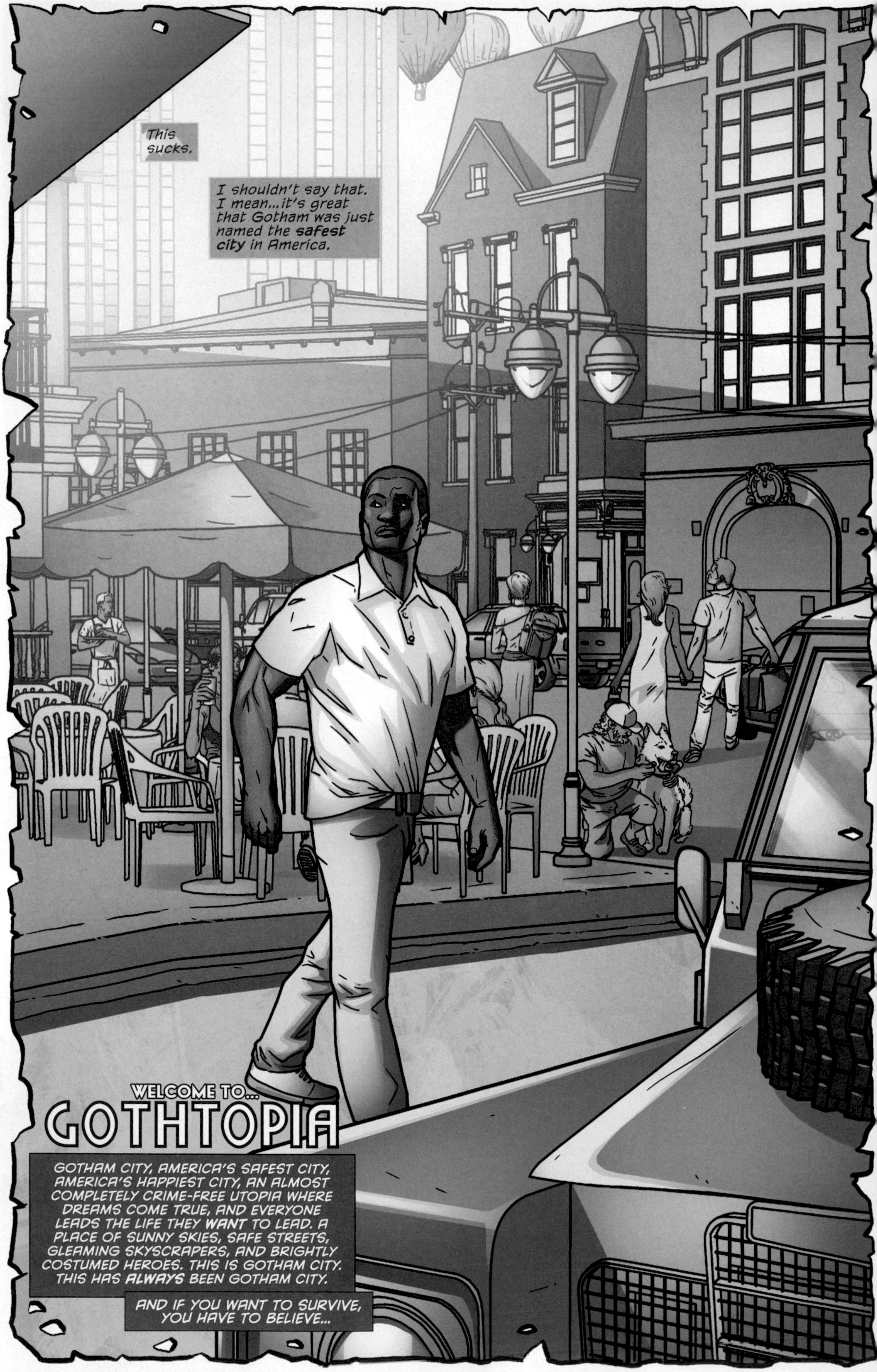
This sucks.
I shouldn't say that. I mean...it's great that Gotham was just named the **safest city** in America.
WELCOME TO...
GOTHTOPIA
GOTHAM CITY, AMERICA'S SAFEST CITY, AMERICA'S HAPPIEST CITY, AN ALMOST COMPLETELY CRIME-FREE UTOPIA WHERE DREAMS COME TRUE, AND EVERYONE LEADS THE LIFE THEY **WANT** TO LEAD. A PLACE OF SUNNY SKIES, SAFE STREETS, GLEAMING SKYSCRAPERS, AND BRIGHTLY COSTUMED HEROES. THIS IS GOTHAM CITY. THIS HAS **ALWAYS** BEEN GOTHAM CITY.
AND IF YOU WANT TO SURVIVE, YOU HAVE TO BELIEVE...

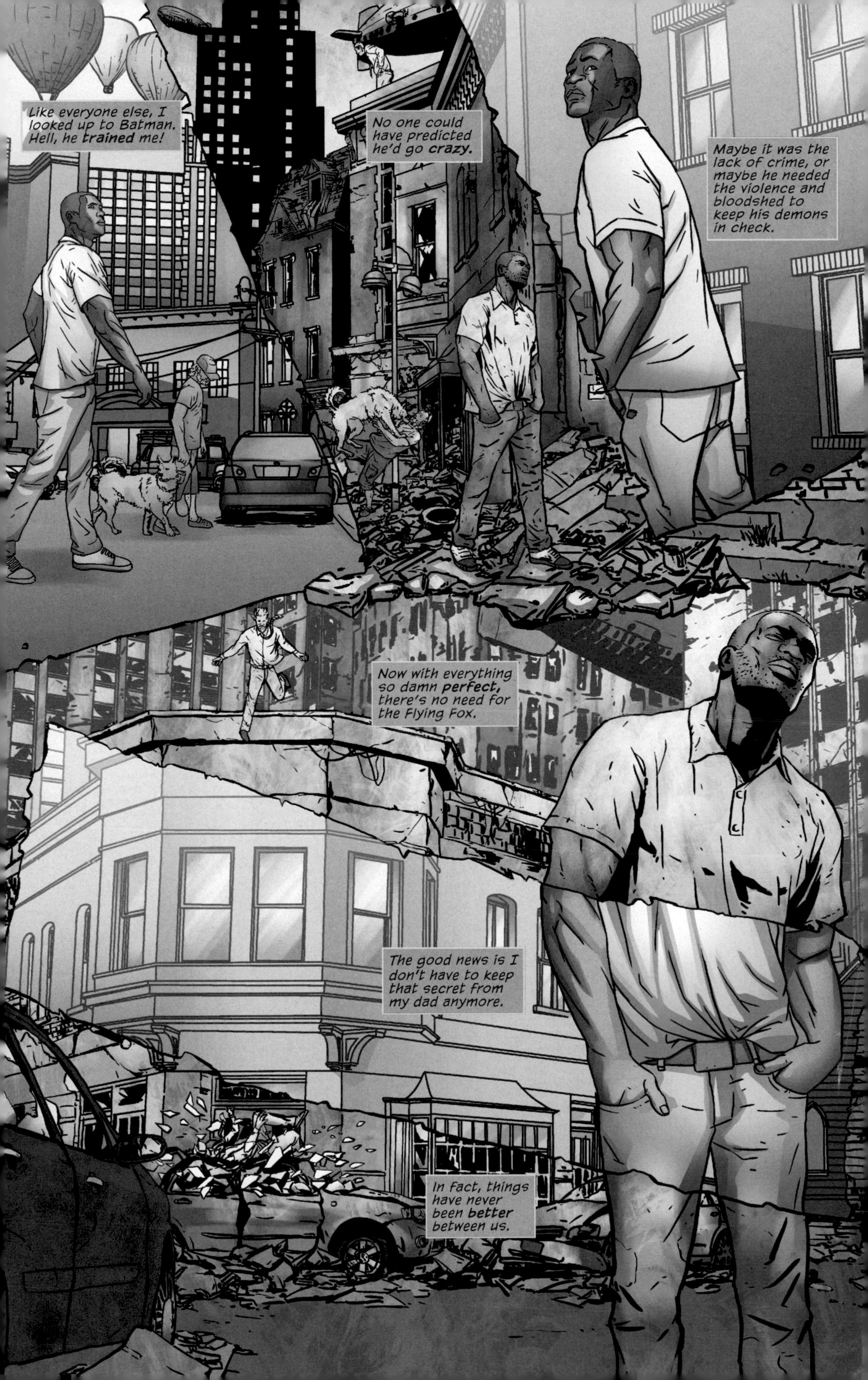
Like everyone else, I looked up to Batman. Hell, he trained me!
No one could have predicted he'd go crazy.
Maybe it was the lack of crime, or maybe he needed the violence and bloodshed to keep his demons in check.
Now with everything so damn perfect, there's no need for the Flying Fox.
The good news is I don't have to keep that secret from my dad anymore.
In fact, things have never been better between us.

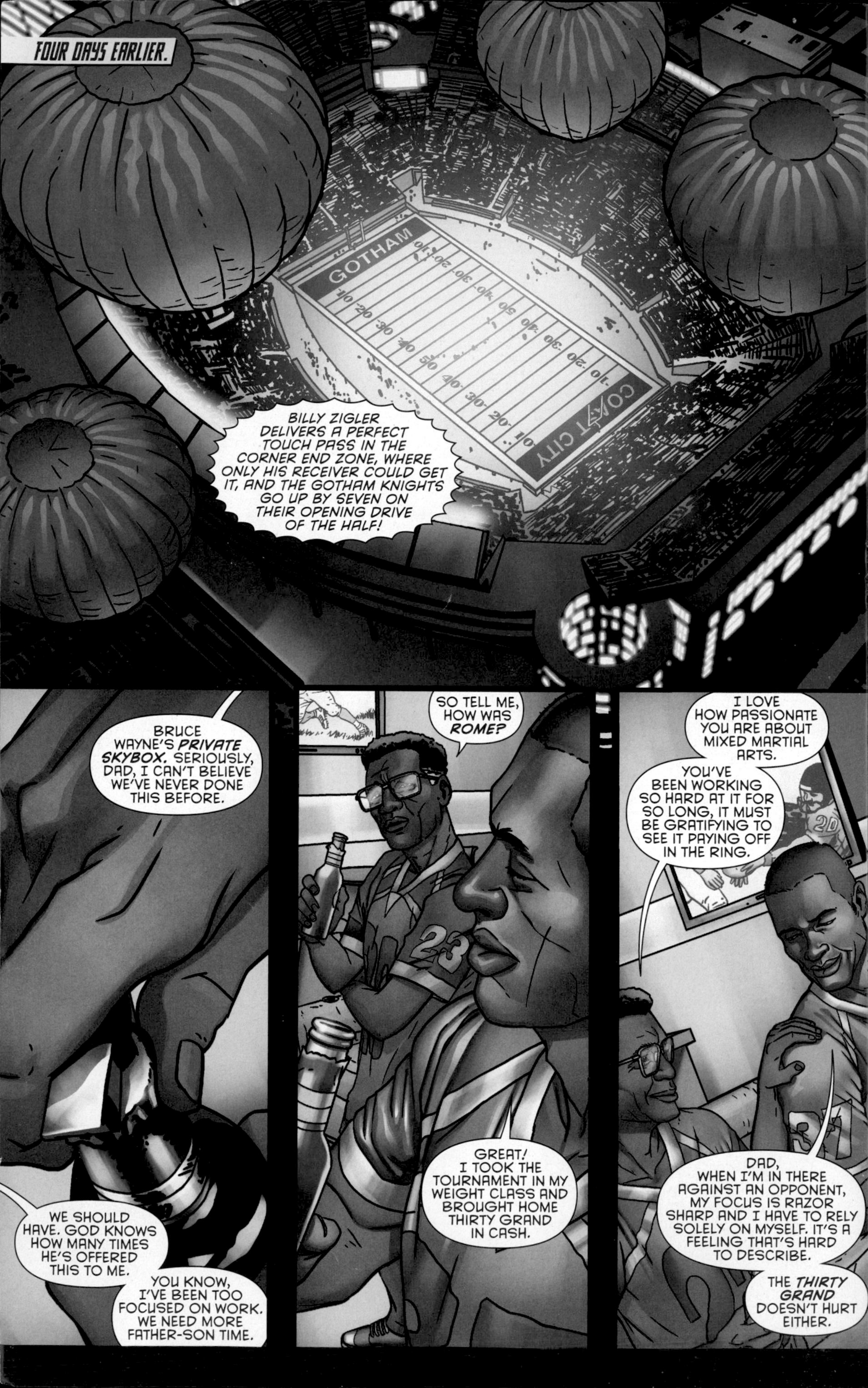

FOUR DAYS EARLIER.
GOTHAM
COAST CITY
BILLY ZIGLER DELIVERS A PERFECT TOUCH PASS IN THE CORNER END ZONE, WHERE ONLY HIS RECEIVER COULD GET IT, AND THE GOTHAM KNIGHTS GO UP BY SEVEN ON THEIR OPENING DRIVE OF THE HALF!
BRUCE WAYNE'S *PRIVATE SKYBOX.* SERIOUSLY, DAD, I CAN'T BELIEVE WE'VE NEVER DONE THIS BEFORE.
WE SHOULD HAVE. GOD KNOWS HOW MANY TIMES HE'S OFFERED THIS TO ME.
YOU KNOW, I'VE BEEN TOO FOCUSED ON WORK. WE NEED MORE FATHER-SON TIME.
SO TELL ME, HOW WAS *ROME?*
GREAT! I TOOK THE TOURNAMENT IN MY WEIGHT CLASS AND BROUGHT HOME THIRTY GRAND IN CASH.
I LOVE HOW PASSIONATE YOU ARE ABOUT MIXED MARTIAL ARTS.
YOU'VE BEEN WORKING SO HARD AT IT FOR SO LONG, IT MUST BE GRATIFYING TO SEE IT PAYING OFF IN THE RING.
DAD, WHEN I'M IN THERE AGAINST AN OPPONENT, MY FOCUS IS RAZOR SHARP AND I HAVE TO RELY SOLELY ON MYSELF. IT'S A FEELING THAT'S HARD TO DESCRIBE.
THE *THIRTY GRAND* DOESN'T HURT EITHER.

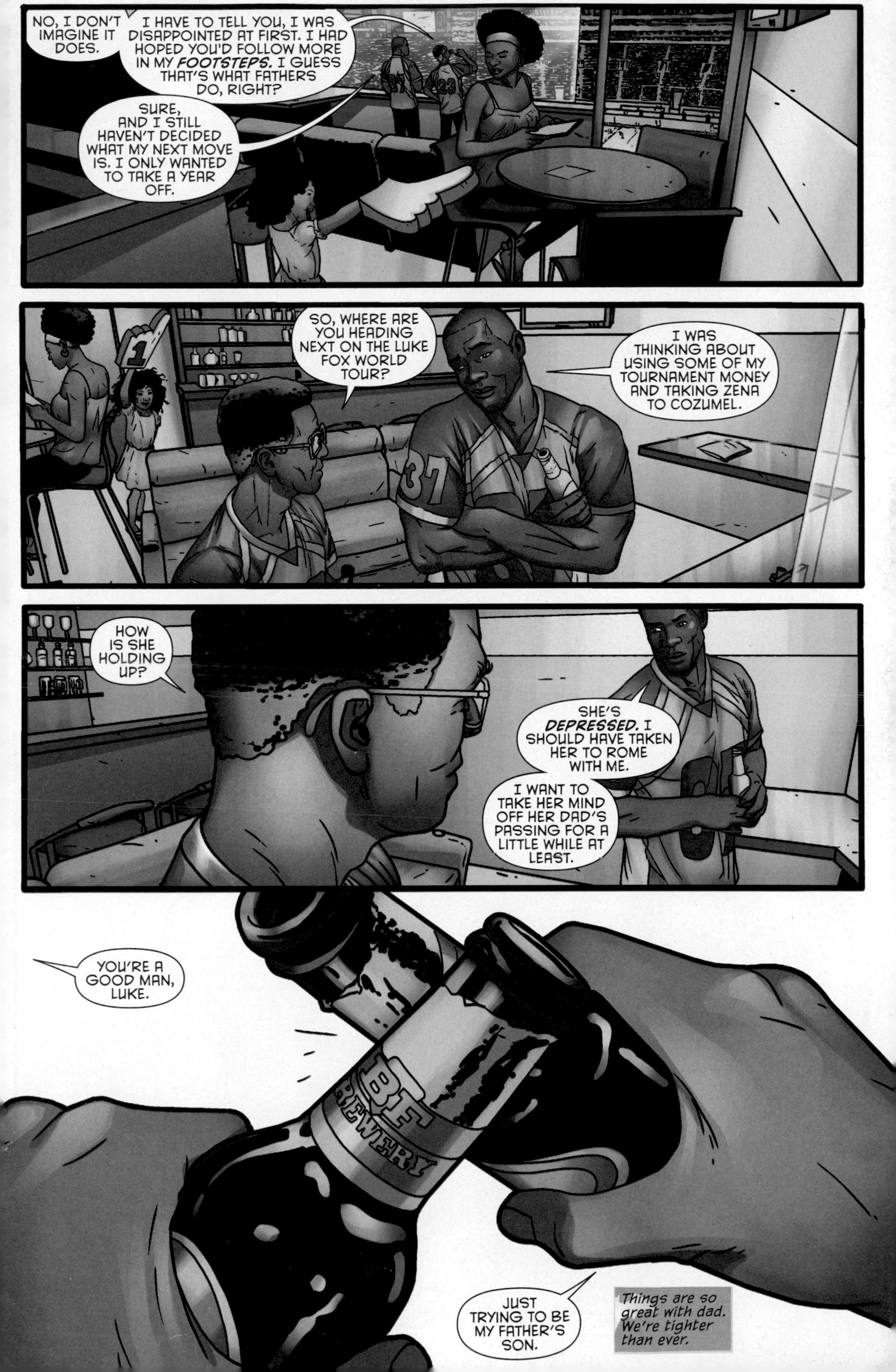
NO, I DON'T IMAGINE IT DOES.
I HAVE TO TELL YOU, I WAS DISAPPOINTED AT FIRST. I HAD HOPED YOU'D FOLLOW MORE IN MY FOOTSTEPS. I GUESS THAT'S WHAT FATHERS DO, RIGHT?
SURE, AND I STILL HAVEN'T DECIDED WHAT MY NEXT MOVE IS. I ONLY WANTED TO TAKE A YEAR OFF.
SO, WHERE ARE YOU HEADING NEXT ON THE LUKE FOX WORLD TOUR?
I WAS THINKING ABOUT USING SOME OF MY TOURNAMENT MONEY AND TAKING ZENA TO COZUMEL.
HOW IS SHE HOLDING UP?
SHE'S DEPRESSED. I SHOULD HAVE TAKEN HER TO ROME WITH ME.
I WANT TO TAKE HER MIND OFF HER DAD'S PASSING FOR A LITTLE WHILE AT LEAST.
YOU'RE A GOOD MAN, LUKE.
JUST TRYING TO BE MY FATHER'S SON.
Things are so great with dad. We're tighter than ever.

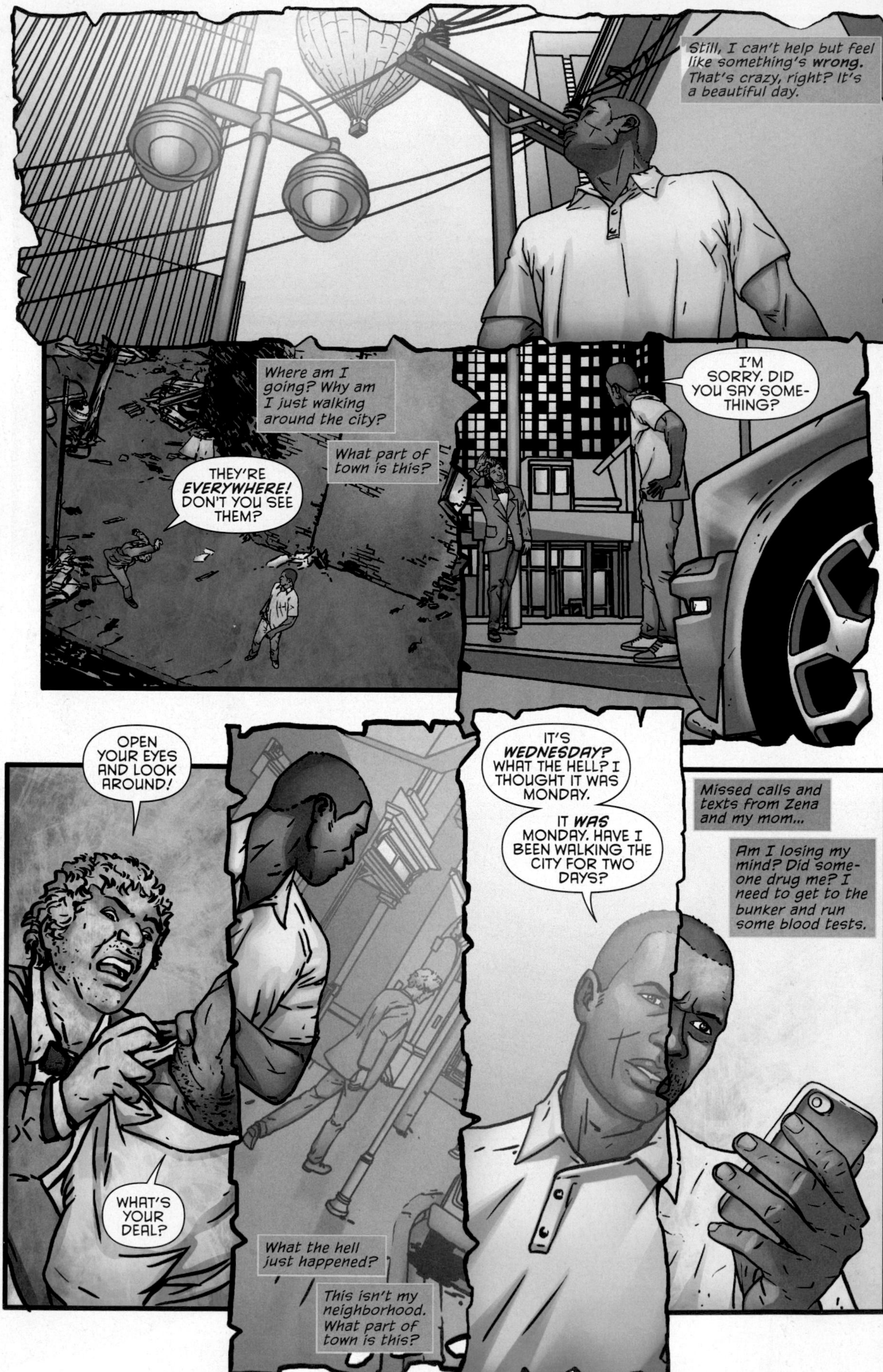
Still, I can't help but feel like something's **wrong.** That's crazy, right? It's a beautiful day.
Where am I going? Why am I just walking around the city?
What part of town is this?
THEY'RE ***EVERYWHERE!*** DON'T YOU SEE THEM?
I'M SORRY. DID YOU SAY SOMETHING?
OPEN YOUR EYES AND LOOK AROUND!
WHAT'S YOUR DEAL?
What the hell just happened?
This isn't my neighborhood. What part of town is this?
IT'S ***WEDNESDAY?*** WHAT THE HELL? I THOUGHT IT WAS MONDAY.
IT ***WAS*** MONDAY. HAVE I BEEN WALKING THE CITY FOR TWO DAYS?
Missed calls and texts from Zena and my mom...
Am I losing my mind? Did someone drug me? I need to get to the bunker and run some blood tests.

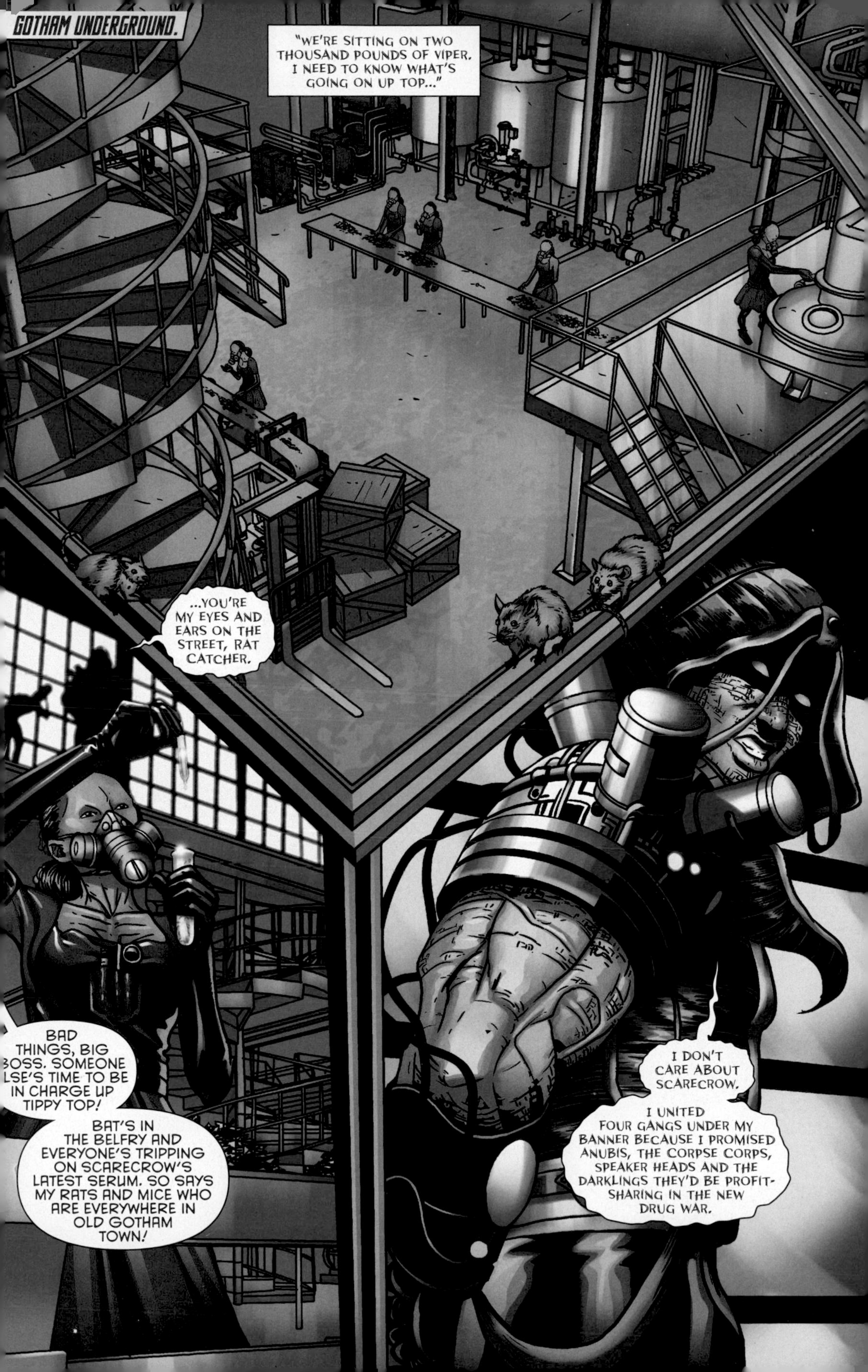
GOTHAM UNDERGROUND.
"WE'RE SITTING ON TWO THOUSAND POUNDS OF VIPER. I NEED TO KNOW WHAT'S GOING ON UP TOP..."
...YOU'RE MY EYES AND EARS ON THE STREET, RAT CATCHER.
BAD THINGS, BIG BOSS. SOMEONE LSE'S TIME TO BE IN CHARGE UP TIPPY TOP!
BAT'S IN THE BELFRY AND EVERYONE'S TRIPPING ON SCARECROW'S LATEST SERUM. SO SAYS MY RATS AND MICE WHO ARE EVERYWHERE IN OLD GOTHAM TOWN!
I DON'T CARE ABOUT SCARECROW.
I UNITED FOUR GANGS UNDER MY BANNER BECAUSE I PROMISED ANUBIS, THE CORPSE CORPS, SPEAKER HEADS AND THE DARKLINGS THEY'D BE PROFIT-SHARING IN THE NEW DRUG WAR.

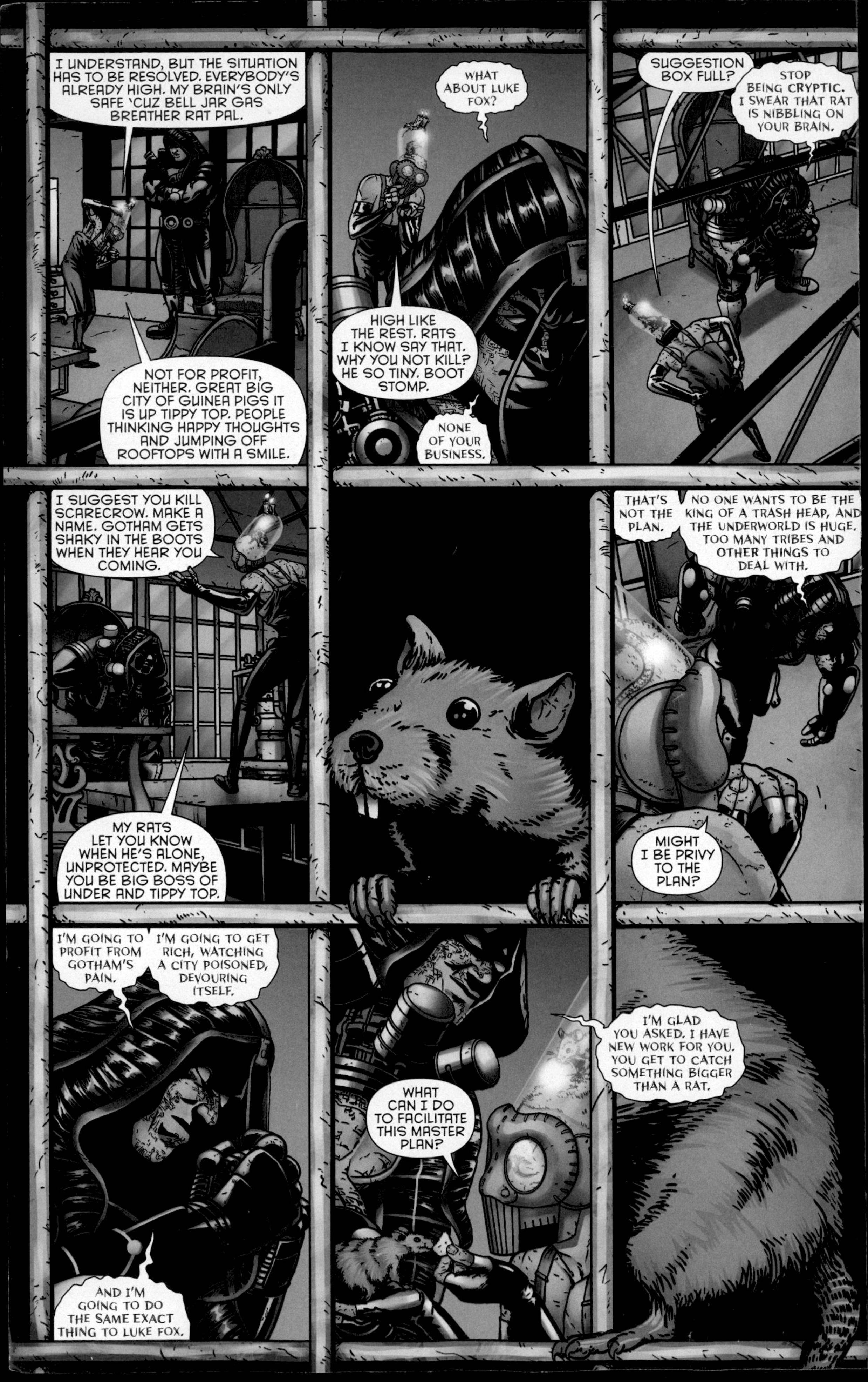
I UNDERSTAND, BUT THE SITUATION HAS TO BE RESOLVED. EVERYBODY'S ALREADY HIGH. MY BRAIN'S ONLY SAFE 'CUZ BELL JAR GAS BREATHER RAT PAL.
NOT FOR PROFIT, NEITHER. GREAT BIG CITY OF GUINEA PIGS IT IS UP TIPPY TOP. PEOPLE THINKING HAPPY THOUGHTS AND JUMPING OFF ROOFTOPS WITH A SMILE.
WHAT ABOUT LUKE FOX?
HIGH LIKE THE REST. RATS I KNOW SAY THAT. WHY YOU NOT KILL? HE SO TINY. BOOT STOMP.
NONE OF YOUR BUSINESS.
SUGGESTION BOX FULL?
STOP BEING CRYPTIC. I SWEAR THAT RAT IS NIBBLING ON YOUR BRAIN.
I SUGGEST YOU KILL SCARECROW. MAKE A NAME. GOTHAM GETS SHAKY IN THE BOOTS WHEN THEY HEAR YOU COMING.
MY RATS LET YOU KNOW WHEN HE'S ALONE, UNPROTECTED. MAYBE YOU BE BIG BOSS OF UNDER AND TIPPY TOP.
THAT'S NOT THE PLAN.
NO ONE WANTS TO BE THE KING OF A TRASH HEAP, AND THE UNDERWORLD IS HUGE. TOO MANY TRIBES AND OTHER THINGS TO DEAL WITH.
MIGHT I BE PRIVY TO THE PLAN?
I'M GOING TO PROFIT FROM GOTHAM'S PAIN.
I'M GOING TO GET RICH, WATCHING A CITY POISONED, DEVOURING ITSELF.
AND I'M GOING TO DO THE SAME EXACT THING TO LUKE FOX.
WHAT CAN I DO TO FACILITATE THIS MASTER PLAN?
I'M GLAD YOU ASKED. I HAVE NEW WORK FOR YOU. YOU GET TO CATCH SOMETHING BIGGER THAN A RAT.

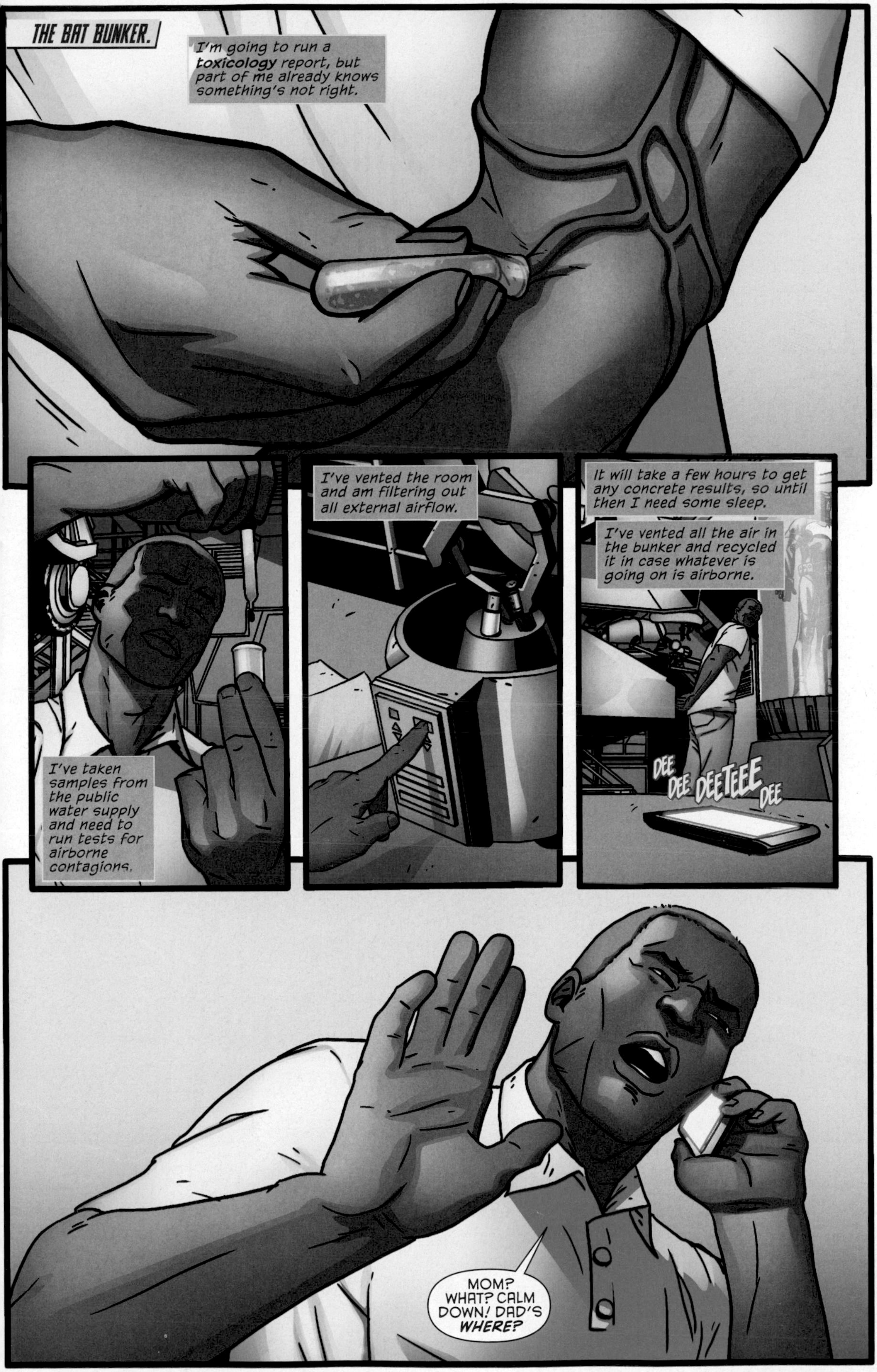
THE BAT BUNKER.
I'm going to run a toxicology report, but part of me already knows something's not right.
I've taken samples from the public water supply and need to run tests for airborne contagions.
I've vented the room and am filtering out all external airflow.
It will take a few hours to get any concrete results, so until then I need some sleep.
I've vented all the air in the bunker and recycled it in case whatever is going on is airborne.
DEE DEE DEETEEE DEE
MOM? WHAT? CALM DOWN! DAD'S WHERE?

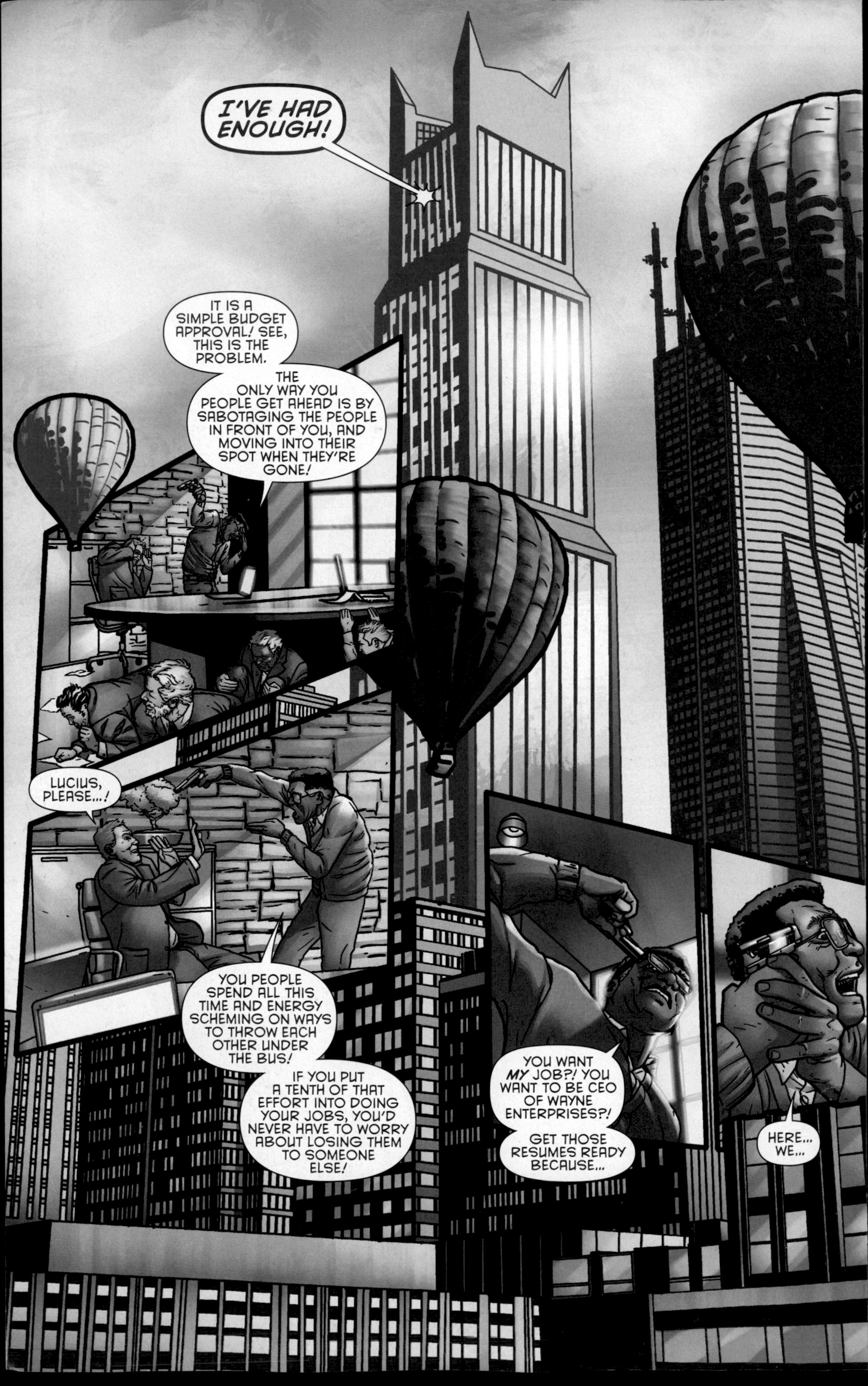
I'VE HAD ENOUGH!
IT IS A SIMPLE BUDGET APPROVAL! SEE, THIS IS THE PROBLEM.
THE ONLY WAY YOU PEOPLE GET AHEAD IS BY SABOTAGING THE PEOPLE IN FRONT OF YOU, AND MOVING INTO THEIR SPOT WHEN THEY'RE GONE!
LUCIUS, PLEASE...!
YOU PEOPLE SPEND ALL THIS TIME AND ENERGY SCHEMING ON WAYS TO THROW EACH OTHER UNDER THE BUS!
IF YOU PUT A TENTH OF THAT EFFORT INTO DOING YOUR JOBS, YOU'D NEVER HAVE TO WORRY ABOUT LOSING THEM TO SOMEONE ELSE!
YOU WANT MY JOB?! YOU WANT TO BE CEO OF WAYNE ENTERPRISES?!
GET THOSE RESUMES READY BECAUSE...
HERE... WE...

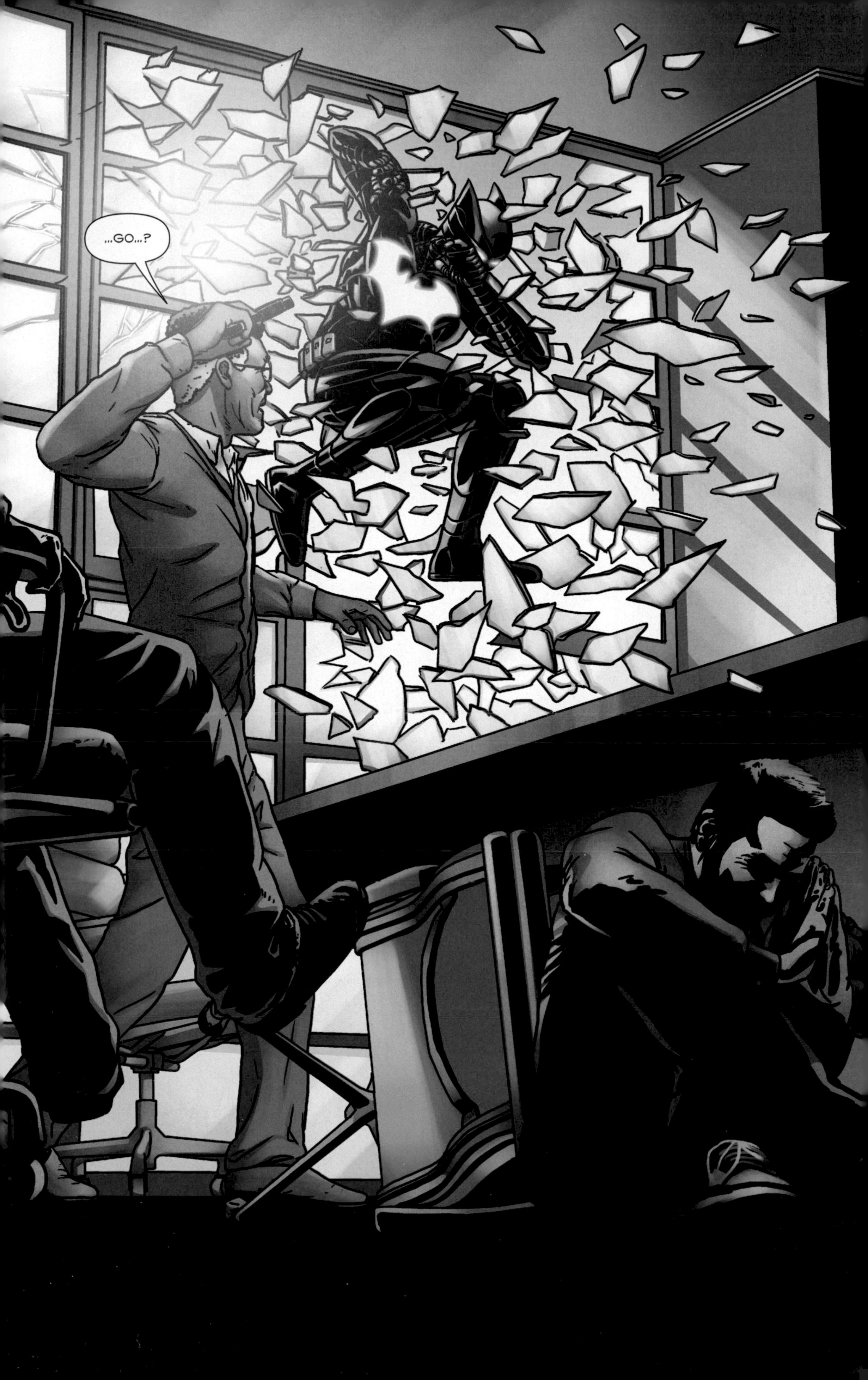
...GO...?

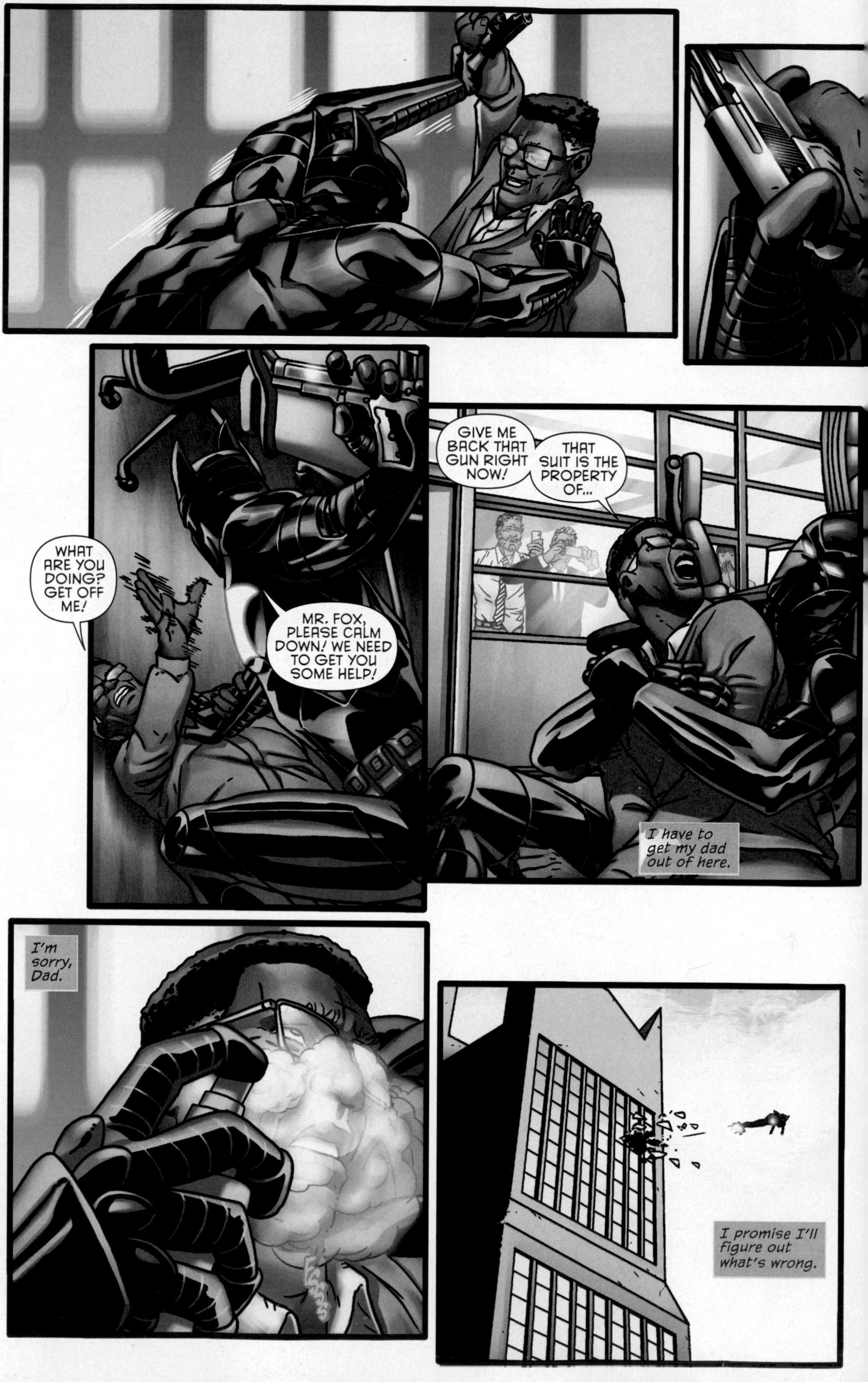
WHAT ARE YOU DOING? GET OFF ME!
MR. FOX, PLEASE CALM DOWN! WE NEED TO GET YOU SOME HELP!
GIVE ME BACK THAT GUN RIGHT NOW!
THAT SUIT IS THE PROPERTY OF...
I have to get my dad out of here.
I'm sorry, Dad.
I promise I'll figure out what's wrong.

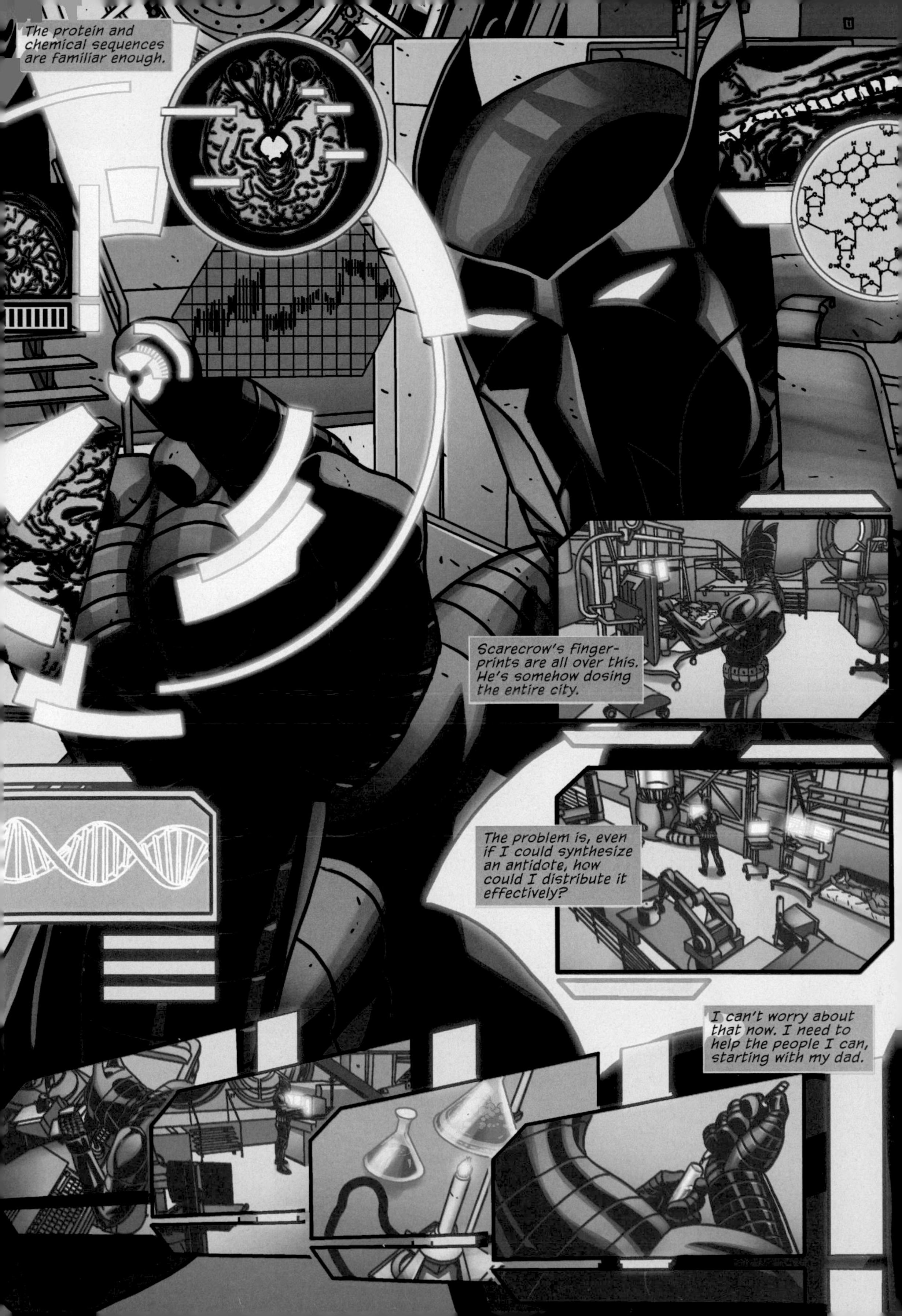
The protein and chemical sequences are familiar enough.
Scarecrow's finger-prints are all over this. He's somehow dosing the entire city.
The problem is, even if I could synthesize an antidote, how could I distribute it effectively?
I can't worry about that now. I need to help the people I can, starting with my dad.

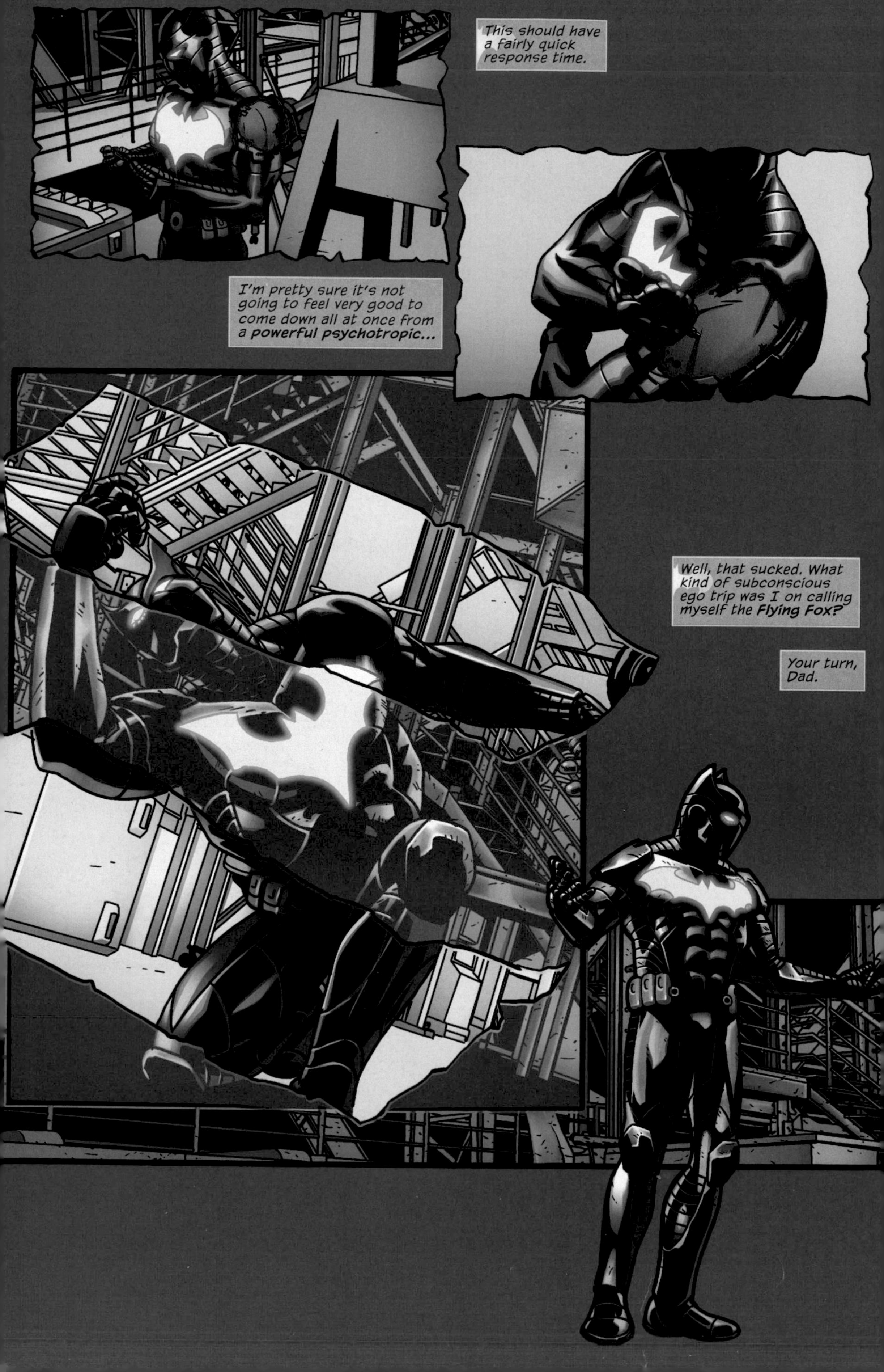
This should have a fairly quick response time.
I'm pretty sure it's not going to feel very good to come down all at once from a **powerful psychotropic...**
Well, that sucked. What kind of subconscious ego trip was I on calling myself the ***Flying Fox?***
Your turn, Dad.

HOW ARE YOU FEELING, MR. FOX?

WHERE *AM* I?

YOU'RE SAFE. YOU WERE EXPOSED TO A KIND OF HALLUCINOGENIC DRUG, BUT I'VE DEVELOPED A NANO-ANTITOXIN THAT I BELIEVE WILL PROTECT YOU FROM FURTHER CONTAMINATION.

YOU'RE THAT NEW BATWING?

YES, SIR, I AM. I HAVE PRODUCED ENOUGH OF THE ANTITOXIN FOR YOU TO INOCULATE YOUR FAMILY.

THAT SHOULD KEEP THEM SAFE, BUT I WOULD RECOMMEND STAYING HOME UNTIL THE SITUATION HAS BEEN RESOLVED.

AND HOW EXACTLY IS THE SITUATION GOING TO BE RESOLVED?

I HAVE FAITH THAT WE CAN STOP THIS.

"WE"?

BATMAN AND OTHERS LIKE MYSELF.

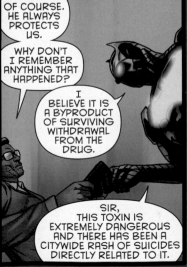

OF COURSE. HE ALWAYS PROTECTS US.

WHY DON'T I REMEMBER ANYTHING THAT HAPPENED?

I BELIEVE IT IS A BYPRODUCT OF SURVIVING WITHDRAWAL FROM THE DRUG.

SIR, THIS TOXIN IS EXTREMELY DANGEROUS AND THERE HAS BEEN A CITYWIDE RASH OF SUICIDES DIRECTLY RELATED TO IT.

I CAN'T MANUFACTURE ENOUGH TO CURE THE CITY, SO I HIGHLY RECOMMEND YOU INOCULATE YOUR LOVED ONES AS SOON AS POSSIBLE.

HOW DID YOU KNOW HOW MANY SHOTS I WOULD NEED?

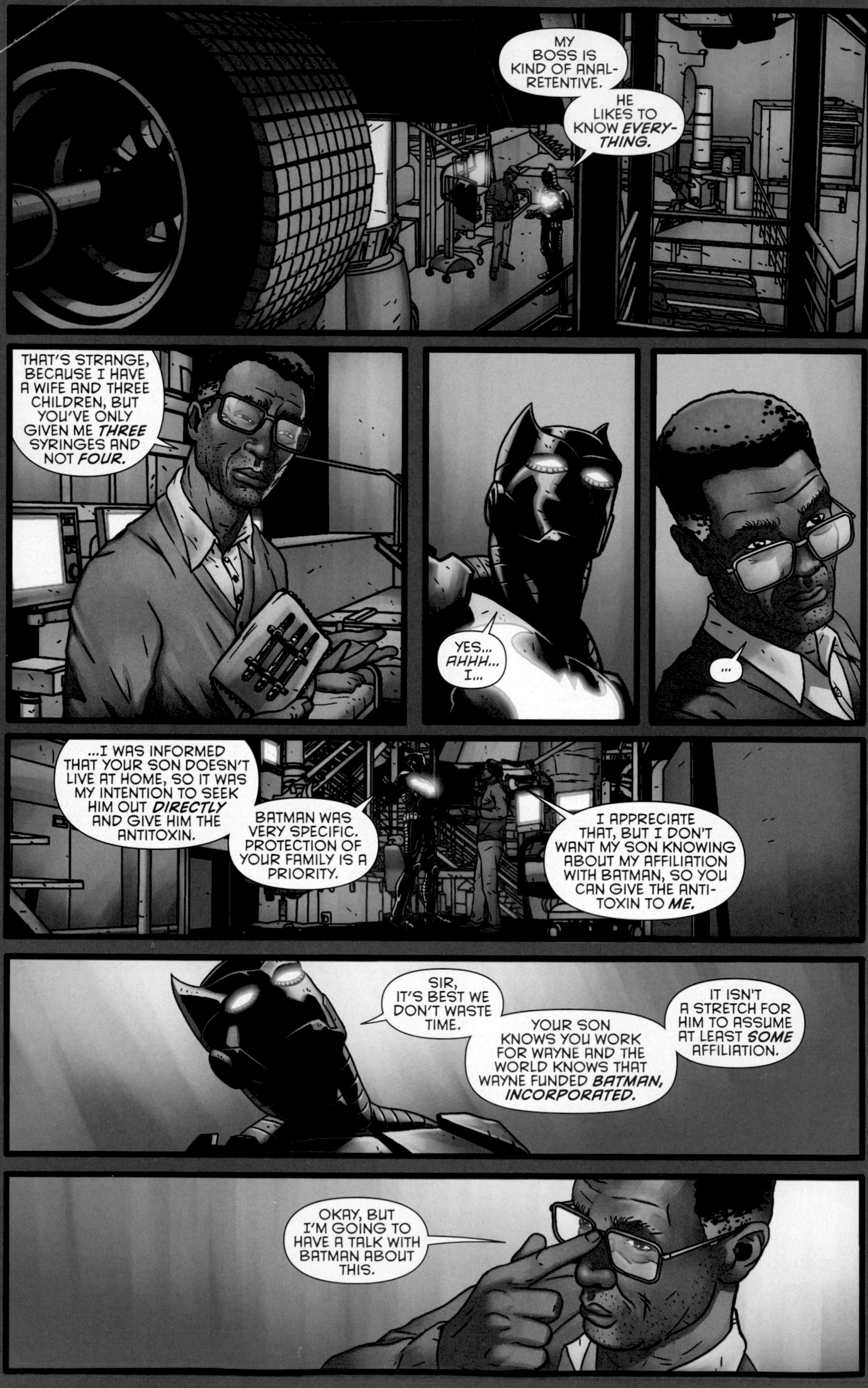

MY BOSS IS KIND OF ANAL-RETENTIVE.
HE LIKES TO KNOW *EVERY-THING.*
THAT'S STRANGE, BECAUSE I HAVE A WIFE AND THREE CHILDREN, BUT YOU'VE ONLY GIVEN ME *THREE* SYRINGES AND NOT *FOUR.*
YES... AHHH... I...
...
...I WAS INFORMED THAT YOUR SON DOESN'T LIVE AT HOME, SO IT WAS MY INTENTION TO SEEK HIM OUT *DIRECTLY* AND GIVE HIM THE ANTITOXIN.
BATMAN WAS VERY SPECIFIC. PROTECTION OF YOUR FAMILY IS A PRIORITY.
I APPRECIATE THAT, BUT I DON'T WANT MY SON KNOWING ABOUT MY AFFILIATION WITH BATMAN, SO YOU CAN GIVE THE ANTI-TOXIN TO *ME.*
SIR, IT'S BEST WE DON'T WASTE TIME.
YOUR SON KNOWS YOU WORK FOR WAYNE AND THE WORLD KNOWS THAT WAYNE FUNDED *BATMAN, INCORPORATED.*
IT ISN'T A STRETCH FOR HIM TO ASSUME AT LEAST *SOME* AFFILIATION.
OKAY, BUT I'M GOING TO HAVE A TALK WITH BATMAN ABOUT THIS.

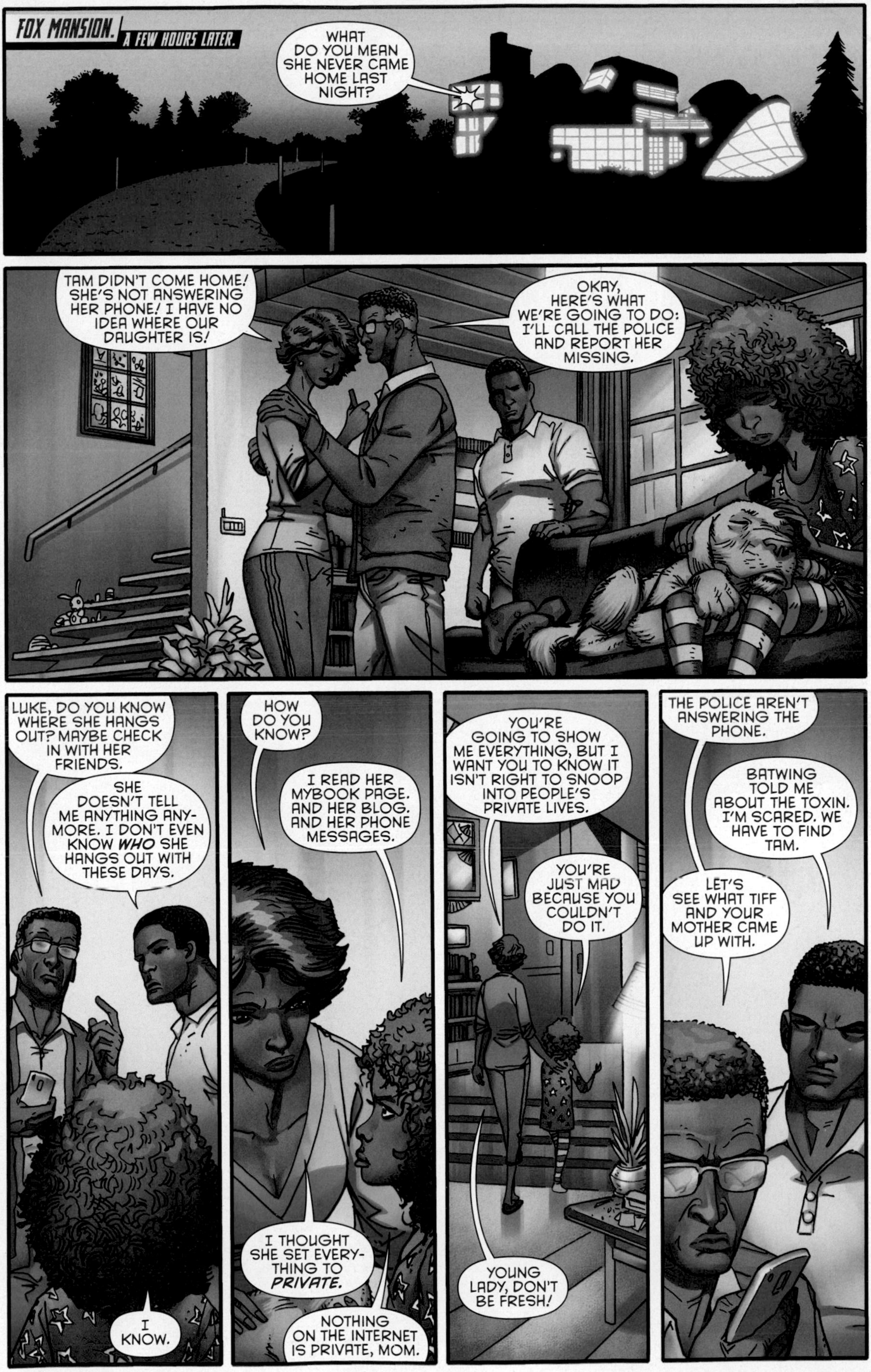
FOX MANSION.
A FEW HOURS LATER.
WHAT DO YOU MEAN SHE NEVER CAME HOME LAST NIGHT?
TAM DIDN'T COME HOME! SHE'S NOT ANSWERING HER PHONE! I HAVE NO IDEA WHERE OUR DAUGHTER IS!
OKAY, HERE'S WHAT WE'RE GOING TO DO: I'LL CALL THE POLICE AND REPORT HER MISSING.
LUKE, DO YOU KNOW WHERE SHE HANGS OUT? MAYBE CHECK IN WITH HER FRIENDS.
SHE DOESN'T TELL ME ANYTHING ANY-MORE. I DON'T EVEN KNOW *WHO* SHE HANGS OUT WITH THESE DAYS.
I KNOW.
HOW DO YOU KNOW?
I READ HER MYBOOK PAGE. AND HER BLOG. AND HER PHONE MESSAGES.
I THOUGHT SHE SET EVERY-THING TO *PRIVATE.*
NOTHING ON THE INTERNET IS PRIVATE, MOM.
YOU'RE GOING TO SHOW ME EVERYTHING, BUT I WANT YOU TO KNOW IT ISN'T RIGHT TO SNOOP INTO PEOPLE'S PRIVATE LIVES.
YOU'RE JUST MAD BECAUSE YOU COULDN'T DO IT.
YOUNG LADY, DON'T BE FRESH!
THE POLICE AREN'T ANSWERING THE PHONE.
BATWING TOLD ME ABOUT THE TOXIN. I'M SCARED. WE HAVE TO FIND TAM.
LET'S SEE WHAT TIFF AND YOUR MOTHER CAME UP WITH.

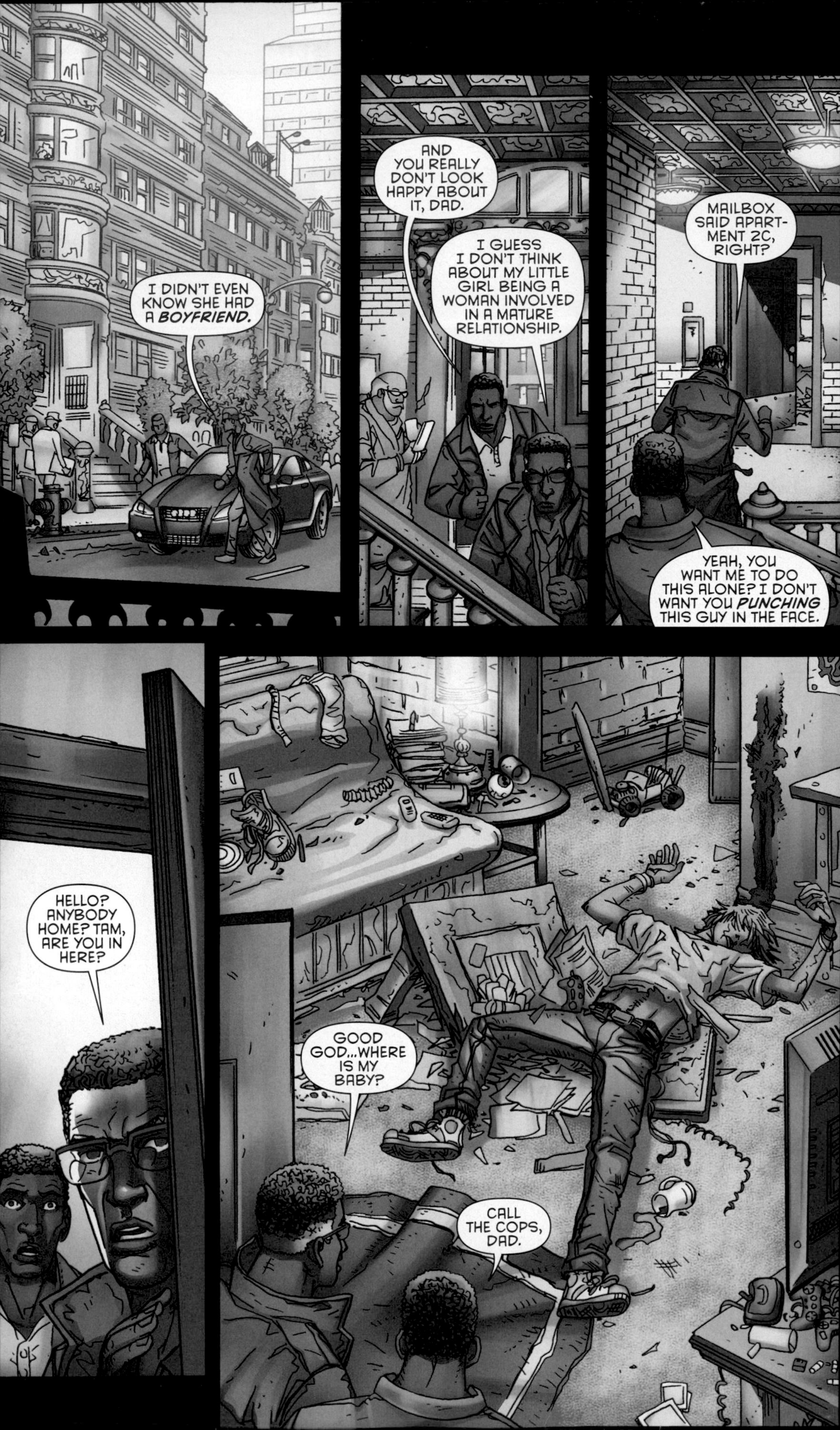
I DIDN'T EVEN KNOW SHE HAD A *BOYFRIEND.*
AND YOU REALLY DON'T LOOK HAPPY ABOUT IT, DAD.
I GUESS I DON'T THINK ABOUT MY LITTLE GIRL BEING A WOMAN INVOLVED IN A MATURE RELATIONSHIP.
MAILBOX SAID APARTMENT 2C, RIGHT?
YEAH, YOU WANT ME TO DO THIS ALONE? I DON'T WANT YOU *PUNCHING* THIS GUY IN THE FACE.
HELLO? ANYBODY HOME? TAM, ARE YOU IN HERE?
GOOD GOD...WHERE IS MY BABY?
CALL THE COPS, DAD.

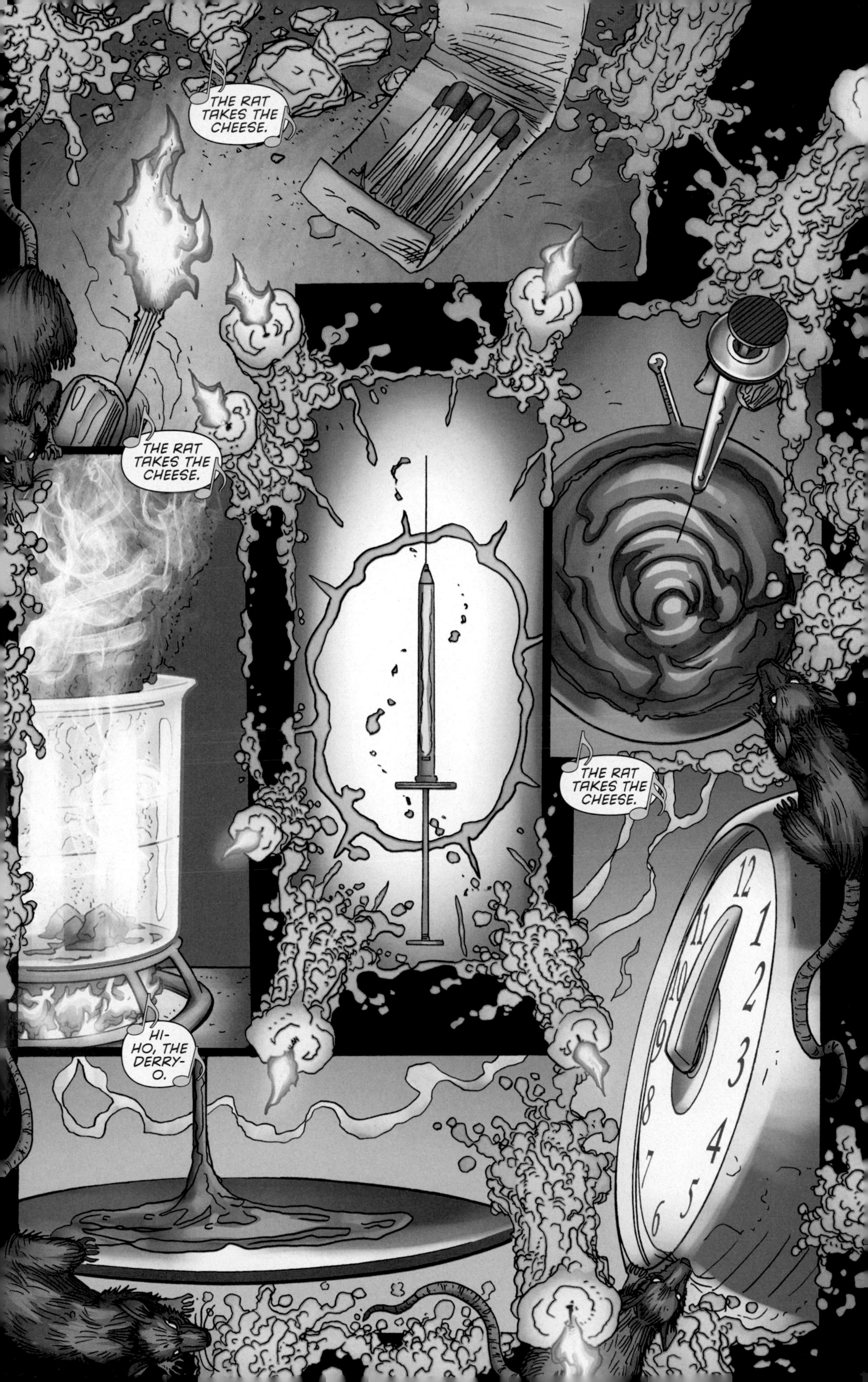
THE RAT TAKES THE CHEESE.
THE RAT TAKES THE CHEESE.
THE RAT TAKES THE CHEESE.
HI-HO, THE DERRY-O.

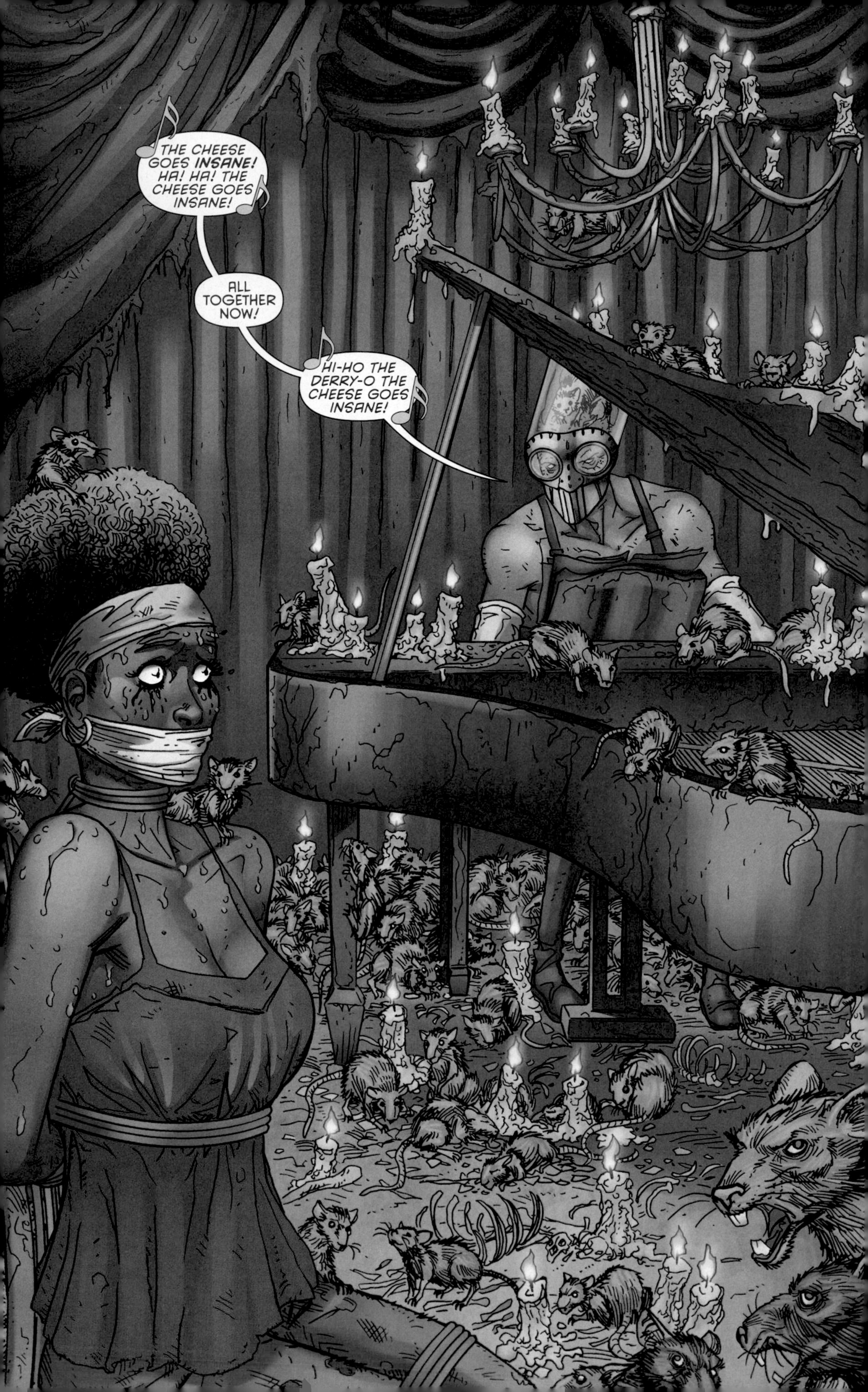
THE CHEESE GOES INSANE! HA! HA! THE CHEESE GOES INSANE!
ALL TOGETHER NOW!
HI-HO THE DERRY-O THE CHEESE GOES INSANE!

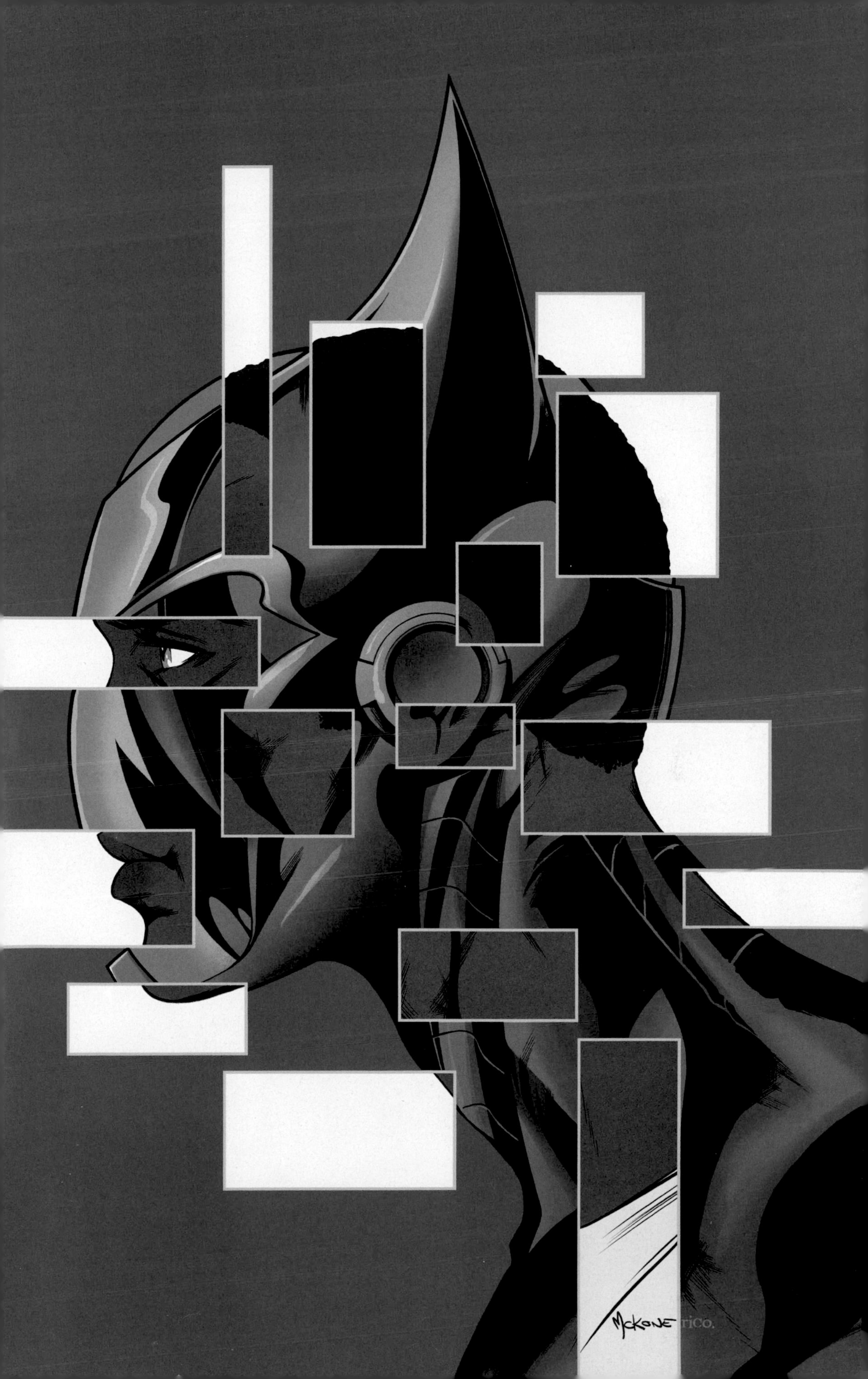
MCKONE rico.

LOST, BUT NOT FOUND

JIMMY PALMIOTTI
JUSTIN GRAY
writers

EDUARDO PANSICA
penciller

JÚLIO FERREIRA
inker

PAUL MOUNTS
colorist

CARLOS M. MANGUAL
letterer

cover art by
MIKE MCKONE and RICO RENZI

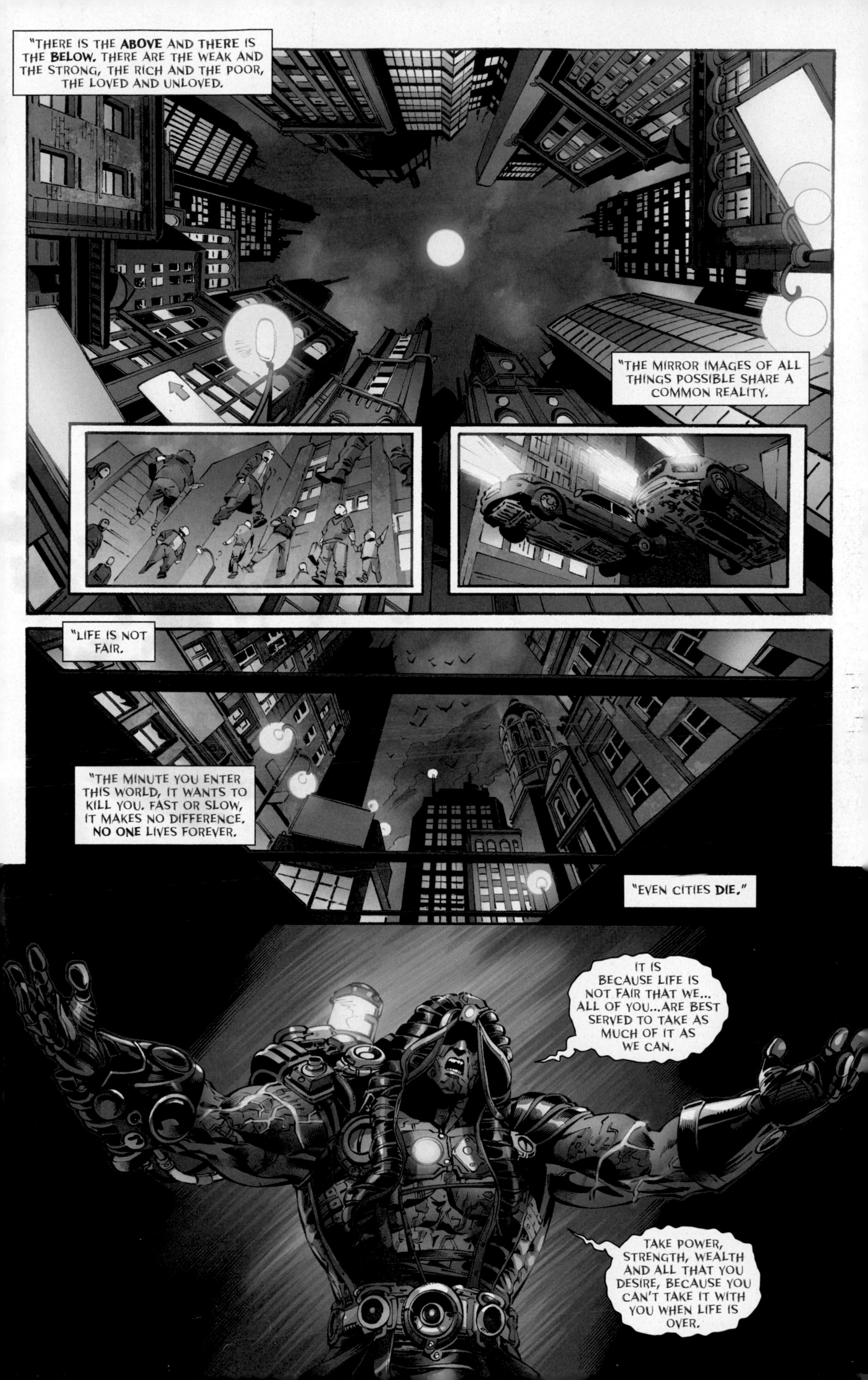
"THERE IS THE ABOVE AND THERE IS THE BELOW. THERE ARE THE WEAK AND THE STRONG, THE RICH AND THE POOR, THE LOVED AND UNLOVED.
"THE MIRROR IMAGES OF ALL THINGS POSSIBLE SHARE A COMMON REALITY.
"LIFE IS NOT FAIR.
"THE MINUTE YOU ENTER THIS WORLD, IT WANTS TO KILL YOU. FAST OR SLOW, IT MAKES NO DIFFERENCE. NO ONE LIVES FOREVER.
"EVEN CITIES DIE."
IT IS BECAUSE LIFE IS NOT FAIR THAT WE... ALL OF YOU...ARE BEST SERVED TO TAKE AS MUCH OF IT AS WE CAN.
TAKE POWER, STRENGTH, WEALTH AND ALL THAT YOU DESIRE, BECAUSE YOU CAN'T TAKE IT WITH YOU WHEN LIFE IS OVER.

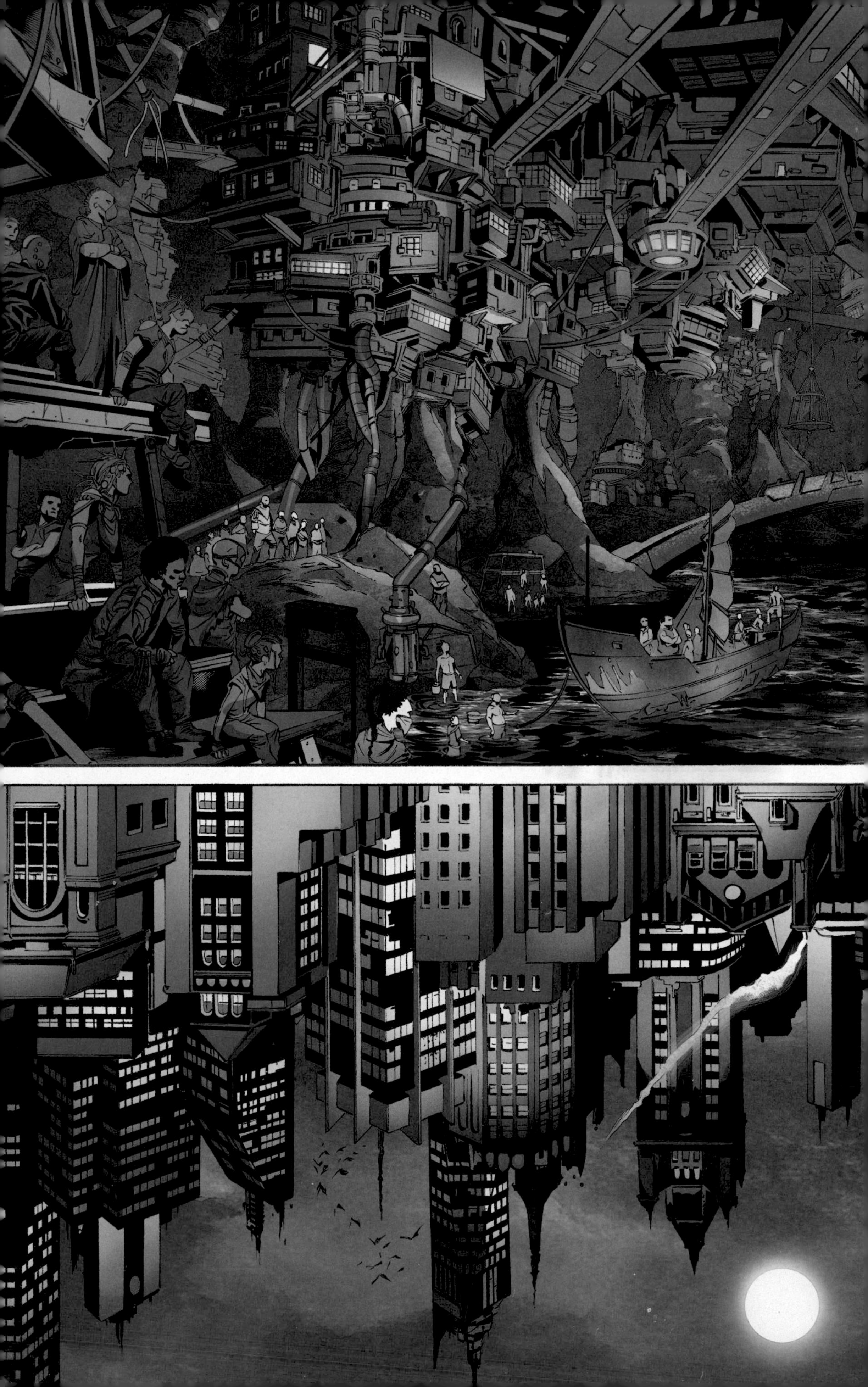

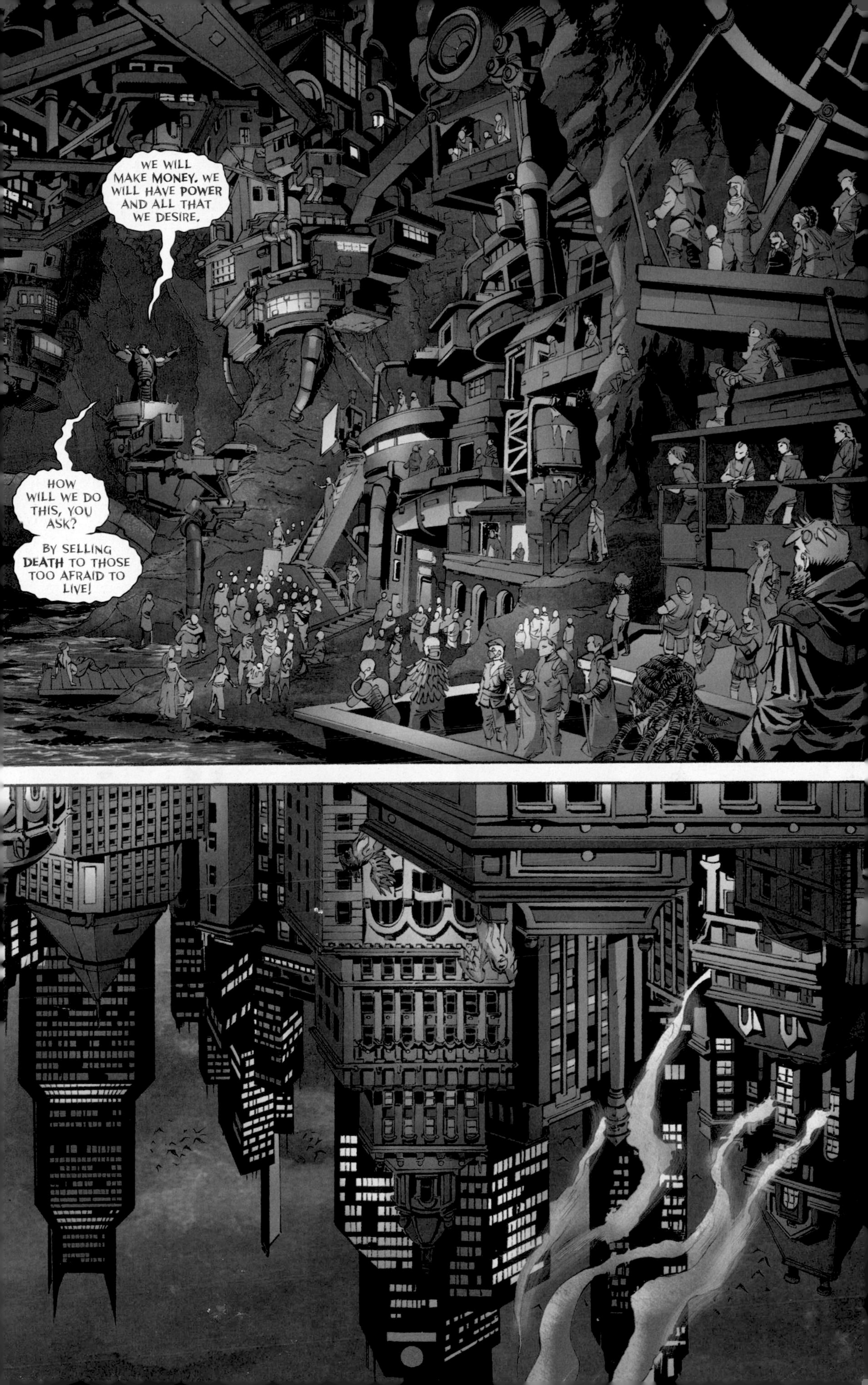
WE WILL MAKE MONEY. WE WILL HAVE POWER AND ALL THAT WE DESIRE.
HOW WILL WE DO THIS, YOU ASK?
BY SELLING DEATH TO THOSE TOO AFRAID TO LIVE!

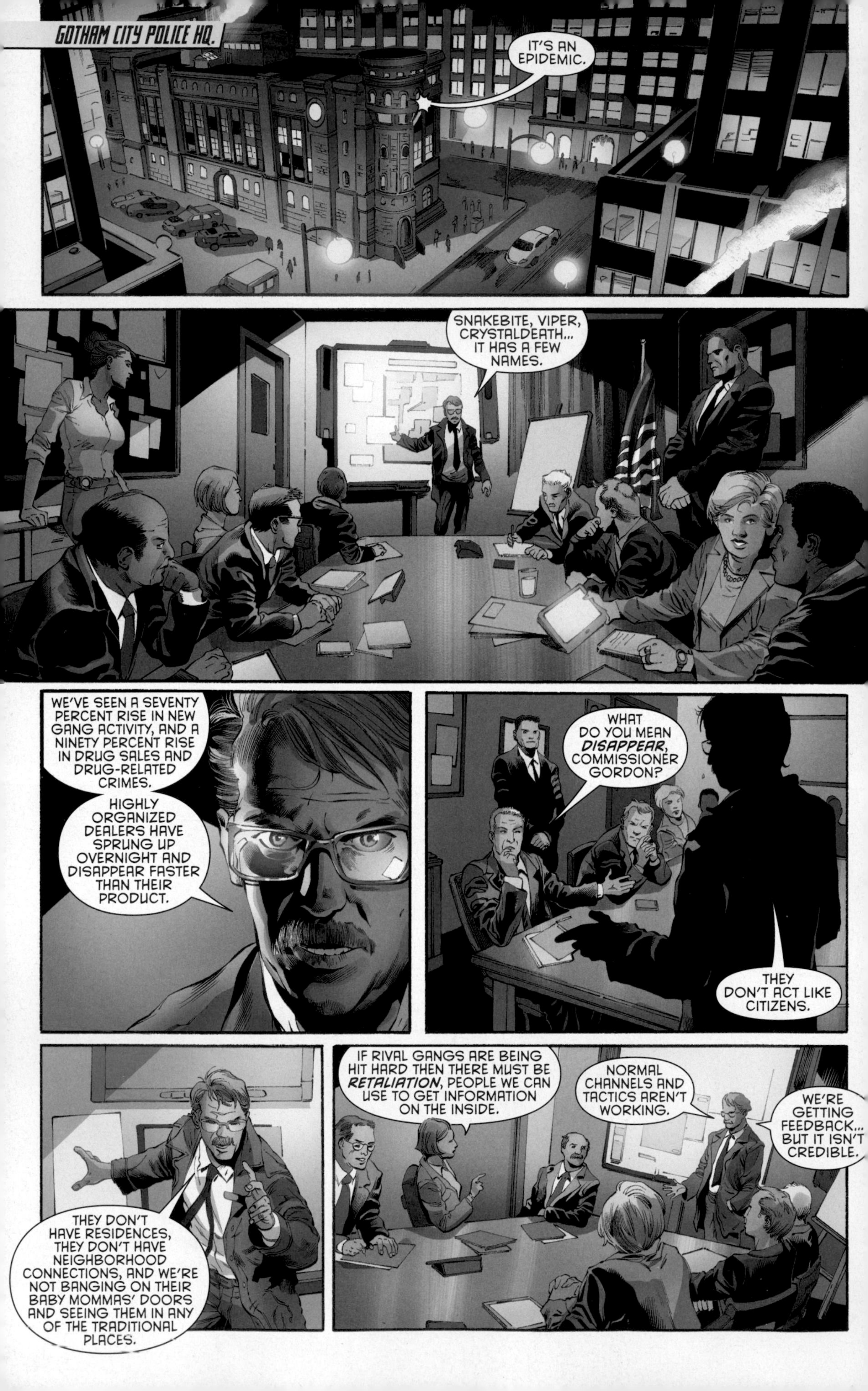
GOTHAM CITY POLICE HQ.
IT'S AN EPIDEMIC.
SNAKEBITE, VIPER, CRYSTALDEATH... IT HAS A FEW NAMES.
WE'VE SEEN A SEVENTY PERCENT RISE IN NEW GANG ACTIVITY, AND A NINETY PERCENT RISE IN DRUG SALES AND DRUG-RELATED CRIMES.
HIGHLY ORGANIZED DEALERS HAVE SPRUNG UP OVERNIGHT AND DISAPPEAR FASTER THAN THEIR PRODUCT.
WHAT DO YOU MEAN *DISAPPEAR*, COMMISSIONER GORDON?
THEY DON'T ACT LIKE CITIZENS.
THEY DON'T HAVE RESIDENCES, THEY DON'T HAVE NEIGHBORHOOD CONNECTIONS, AND WE'RE NOT BANGING ON THEIR BABY MOMMAS' DOORS AND SEEING THEM IN ANY OF THE TRADITIONAL PLACES.
IF RIVAL GANGS ARE BEING HIT HARD THEN THERE MUST BE *RETALIATION*, PEOPLE WE CAN USE TO GET INFORMATION ON THE INSIDE.
NORMAL CHANNELS AND TACTICS AREN'T WORKING.
WE'RE GETTING FEEDBACK... BUT IT ISN'T CREDIBLE.

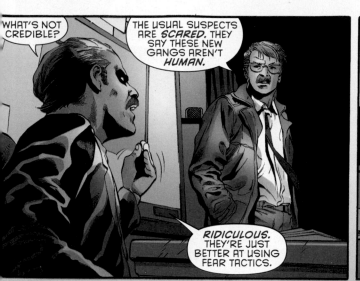

WHAT'S NOT CREDIBLE?

THE USUAL SUSPECTS ARE *SCARED.* THEY SAY THESE NEW GANGS AREN'T *HUMAN.*

RIDICULOUS. THEY'RE JUST BETTER AT USING FEAR TACTICS.

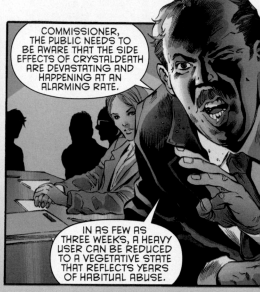

COMMISSIONER, THE PUBLIC NEEDS TO BE AWARE THAT THE SIDE EFFECTS OF CRYSTALDEATH ARE DEVASTATING AND HAPPENING AT AN ALARMING RATE.

IN AS FEW AS THREE WEEKS, A HEAVY USER CAN BE REDUCED TO A VEGETATIVE STATE THAT REFLECTS YEARS OF HABITUAL ABUSE.

I HAVE THE REPORTS OF EVERYONE IN THIS ROOM, AND I'M TELLING YOU WE NEED A RADICALLY *DIFFERENT* APPROACH.

WE'RE FACING A NEW GENERATION OF CRIMINAL ENTERPRISES OPERATING WITH NEW CHANNELS OF DISTRIBUTION.

WHY CAN'T YOU PUT PEOPLE INTO DEEP COVER SCENARIOS?!

SO THERE HAVE BEEN *NO* ARRESTS AT ALL?

HAVE YOU NOT HEARD ANYTHING I'VE SAID?!

THEY ARE *IMPOSSIBLE* TO LOCATE OR TRACE AND HAVE NO RECORDS OF ANY KIND!

IT'S LIKE THEY'RE NOT EVEN LIVING IN GOTHAM CITY!

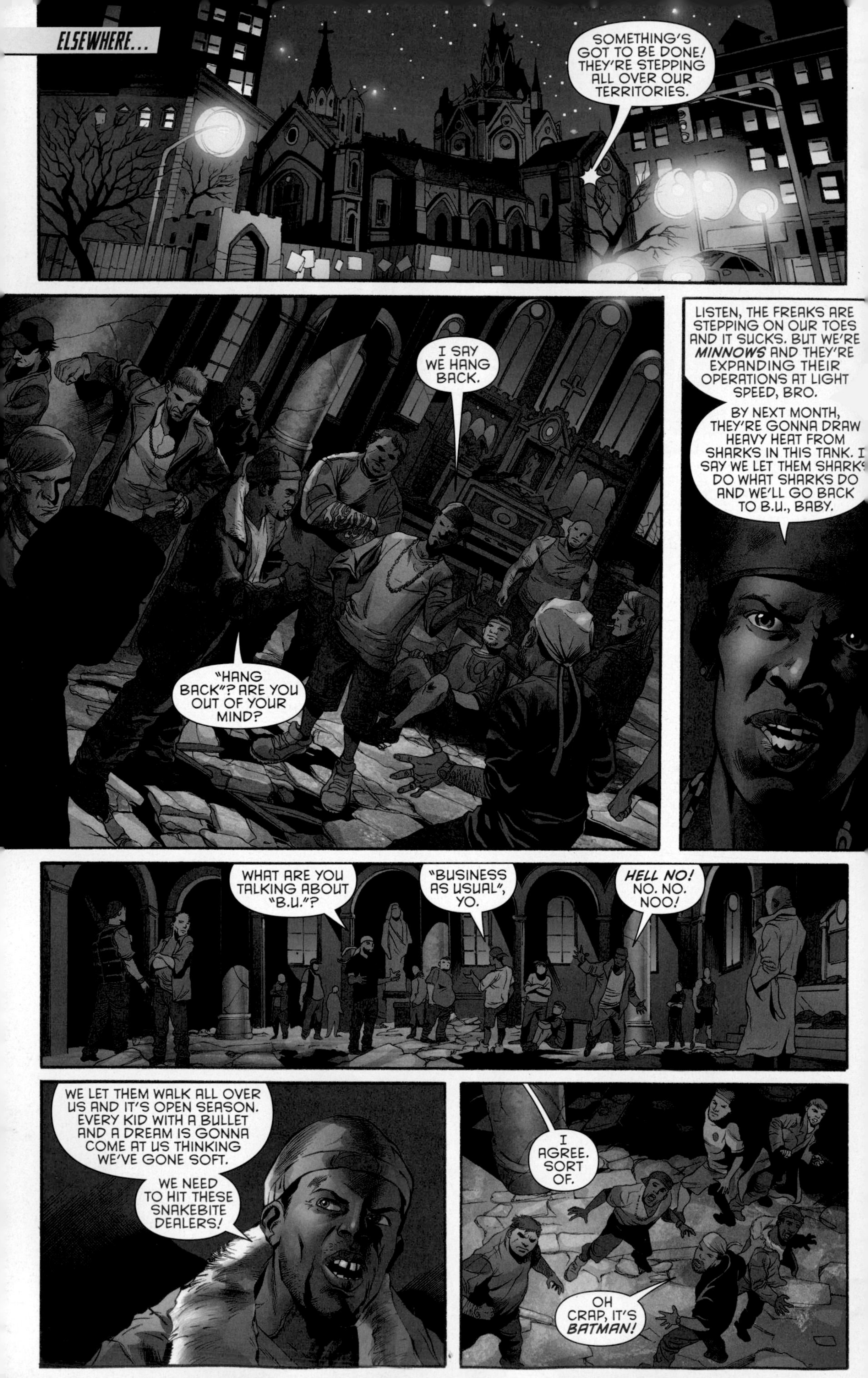
ELSEWHERE...
SOMETHING'S GOT TO BE DONE! THEY'RE STEPPING ALL OVER OUR TERRITORIES.
I SAY WE HANG BACK.
"HANG BACK"? ARE YOU OUT OF YOUR MIND?
LISTEN, THE FREAKS ARE STEPPING ON OUR TOES AND IT SUCKS. BUT WE'RE MINNOWS AND THEY'RE EXPANDING THEIR OPERATIONS AT LIGHT SPEED, BRO.
BY NEXT MONTH, THEY'RE GONNA DRAW HEAVY HEAT FROM SHARKS IN THIS TANK. I SAY WE LET THEM SHARKS DO WHAT SHARKS DO AND WE'LL GO BACK TO B.U., BABY.
WHAT ARE YOU TALKING ABOUT "B.U."?
"BUSINESS AS USUAL", YO.
HELL NO! NO. NO. NOO!
WE LET THEM WALK ALL OVER US AND IT'S OPEN SEASON. EVERY KID WITH A BULLET AND A DREAM IS GONNA COME AT US THINKING WE'VE GONE SOFT.
WE NEED TO HIT THESE SNAKEBITE DEALERS!
I AGREE. SORT OF.
OH CRAP, IT'S BATMAN!

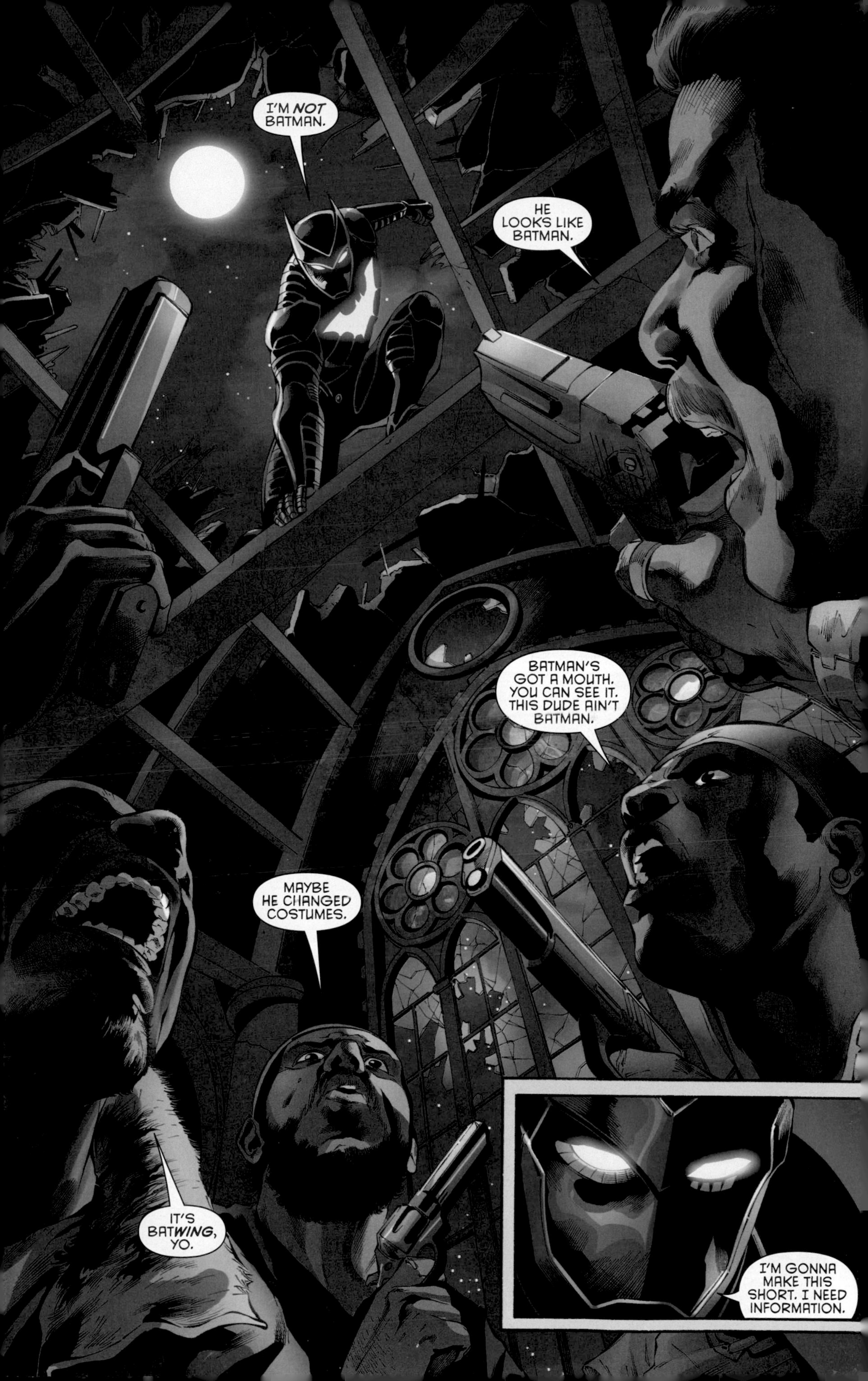
I'M NOT BATMAN.
HE LOOKS LIKE BATMAN.
BATMAN'S GOT A MOUTH. YOU CAN SEE IT. THIS DUDE AIN'T BATMAN.
MAYBE HE CHANGED COSTUMES.
IT'S BATWING, YO.
I'M GONNA MAKE THIS SHORT. I NEED INFORMATION.

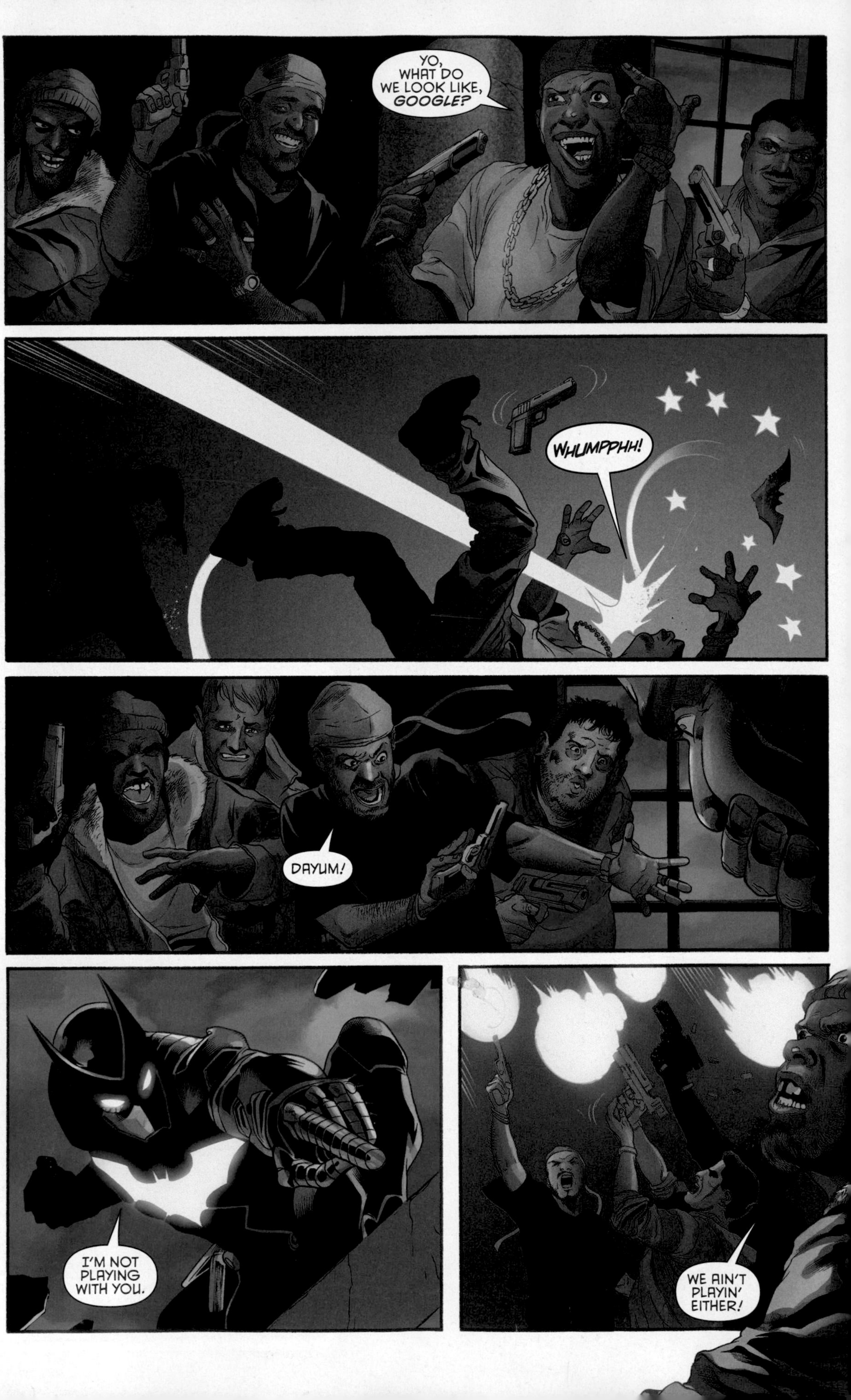
YO, WHAT DO WE LOOK LIKE, GOOGLE?
WHUMPPHH!
DAYUM!
I'M NOT PLAYING WITH YOU.
WE AIN'T PLAYIN' EITHER!

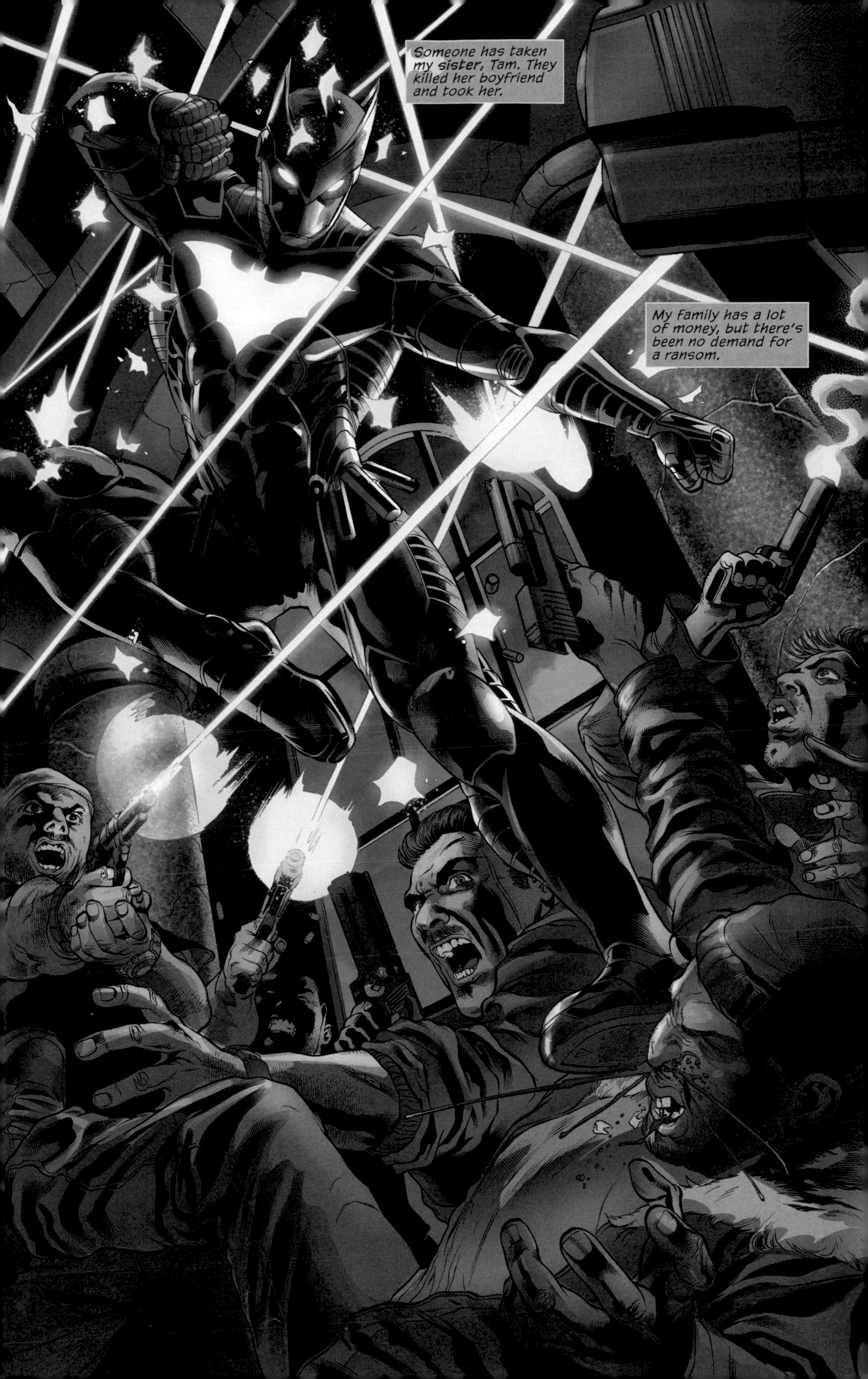
Someone has taken my sister, Tam. They killed her boyfriend and took her.
My family has a lot of money, but there's been no demand for a ransom.

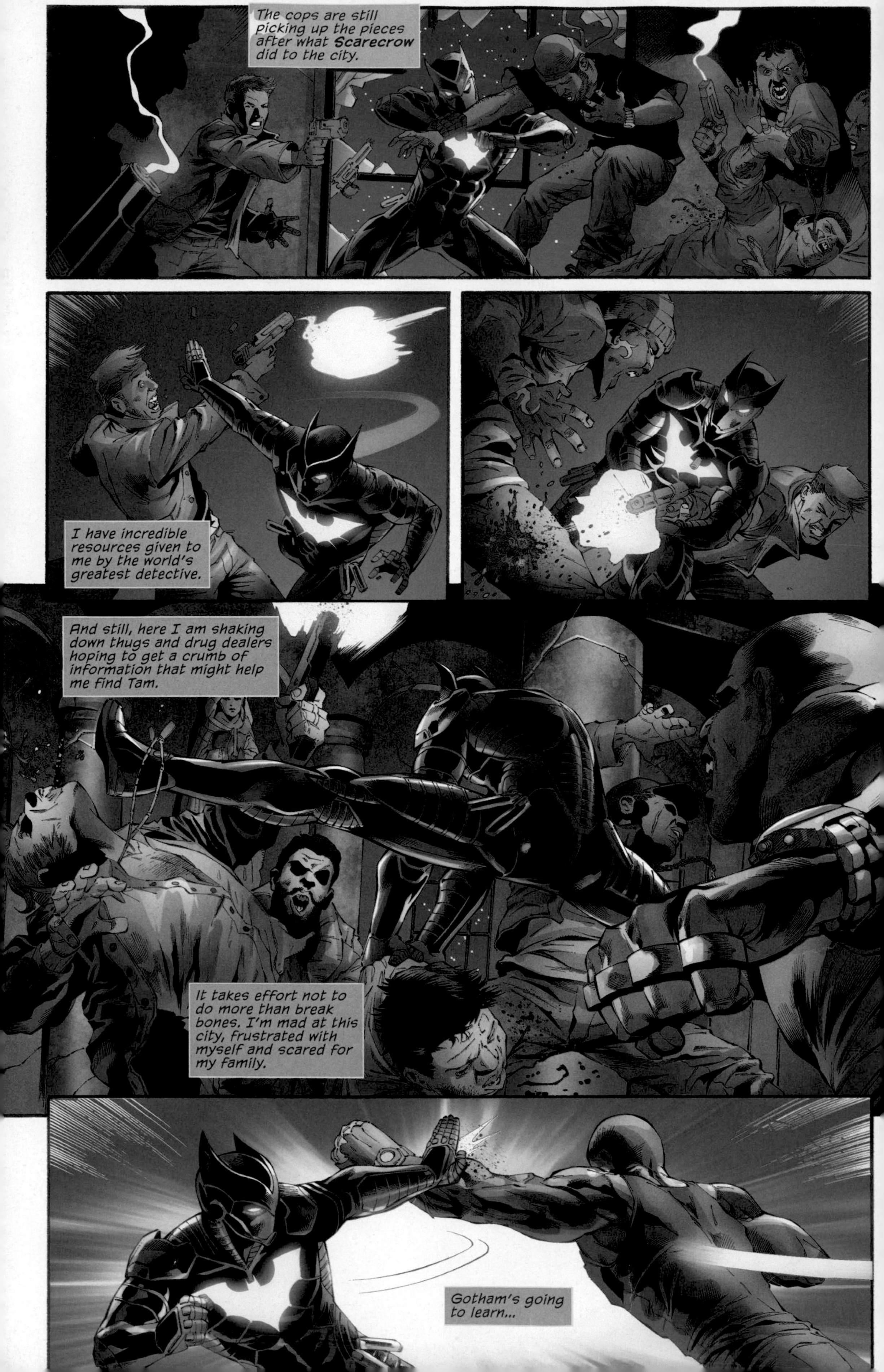
The cops are still picking up the pieces after what Scarecrow did to the city.
I have incredible resources given to me by the world's greatest detective.
And still, here I am shaking down thugs and drug dealers hoping to get a crumb of information that might help me find Tam.
It takes effort not to do more than break bones. I'm mad at this city, frustrated with myself and scared for my family.
Gotham's going to learn...

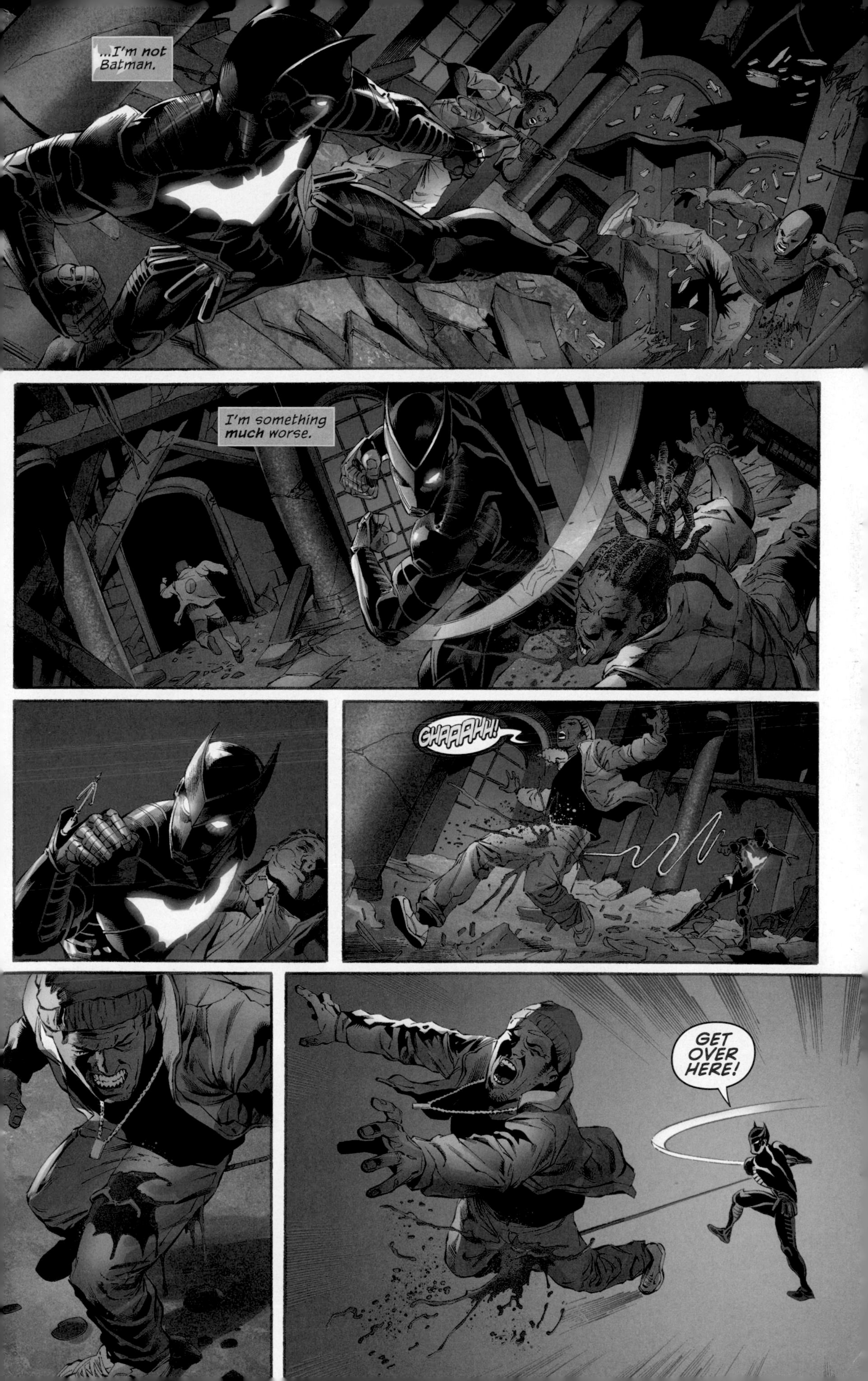
...I'm not Batman.
I'm something much worse.
GHAAAHH!
GET OVER HERE!

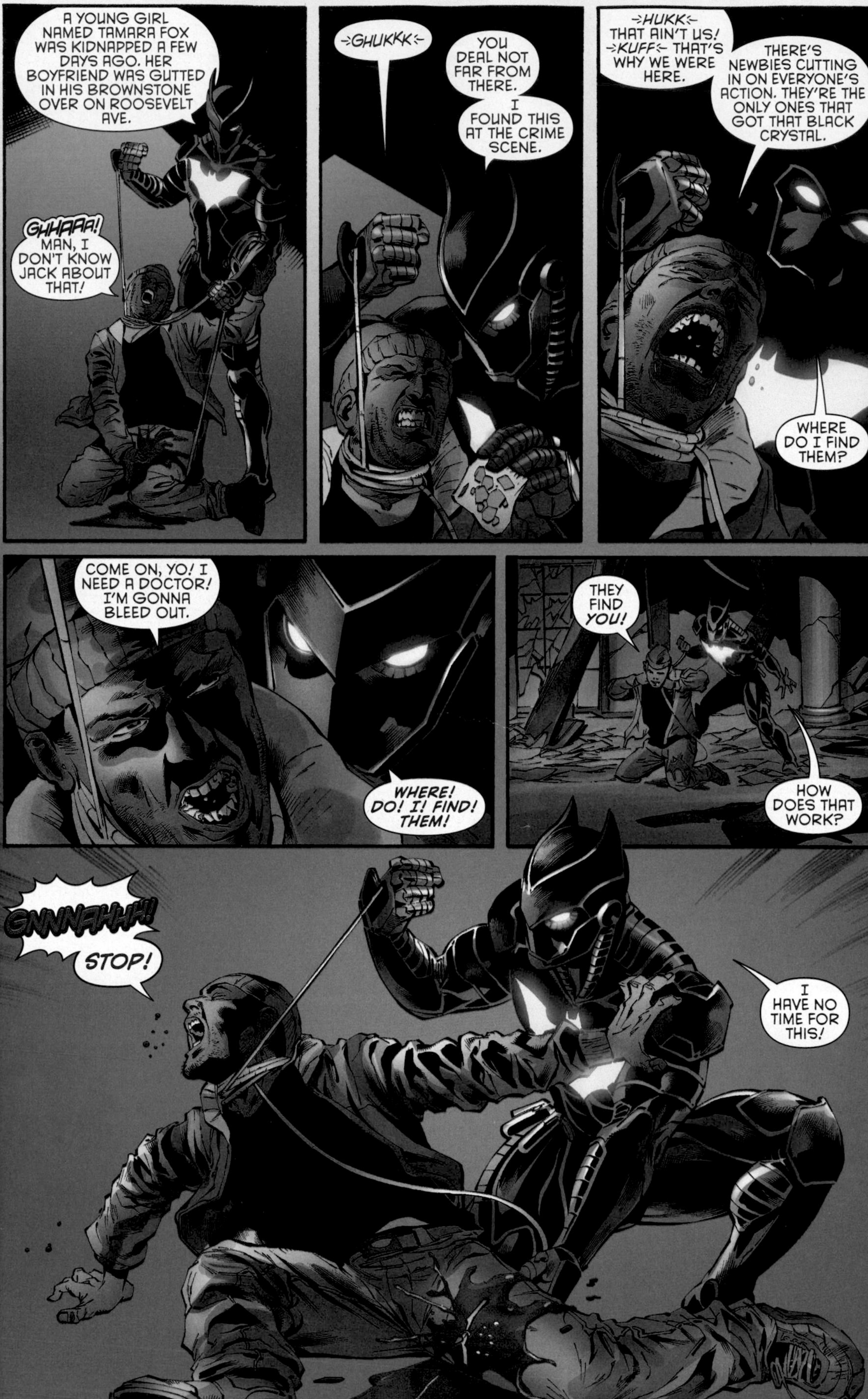
A YOUNG GIRL NAMED TAMARA FOX WAS KIDNAPPED A FEW DAYS AGO. HER BOYFRIEND WAS GUTTED IN HIS BROWNSTONE OVER ON ROOSEVELT AVE.
GHHAAA! MAN, I DON'T KNOW JACK ABOUT THAT!
-GHUKKK-
YOU DEAL NOT FAR FROM THERE.
I FOUND THIS AT THE CRIME SCENE.
-HUKK- THAT AIN'T US! -KUFF- THAT'S WHY WE WERE HERE.
THERE'S NEWBIES CUTTING IN ON EVERYONE'S ACTION. THEY'RE THE ONLY ONES THAT GOT THAT BLACK CRYSTAL.
WHERE DO I FIND THEM?
COME ON, YO! I NEED A DOCTOR! I'M GONNA BLEED OUT.
WHERE! DO! I! FIND! THEM!
THEY FIND YOU!
HOW DOES THAT WORK?
GNNNAHHH!
STOP!
I HAVE NO TIME FOR THIS!

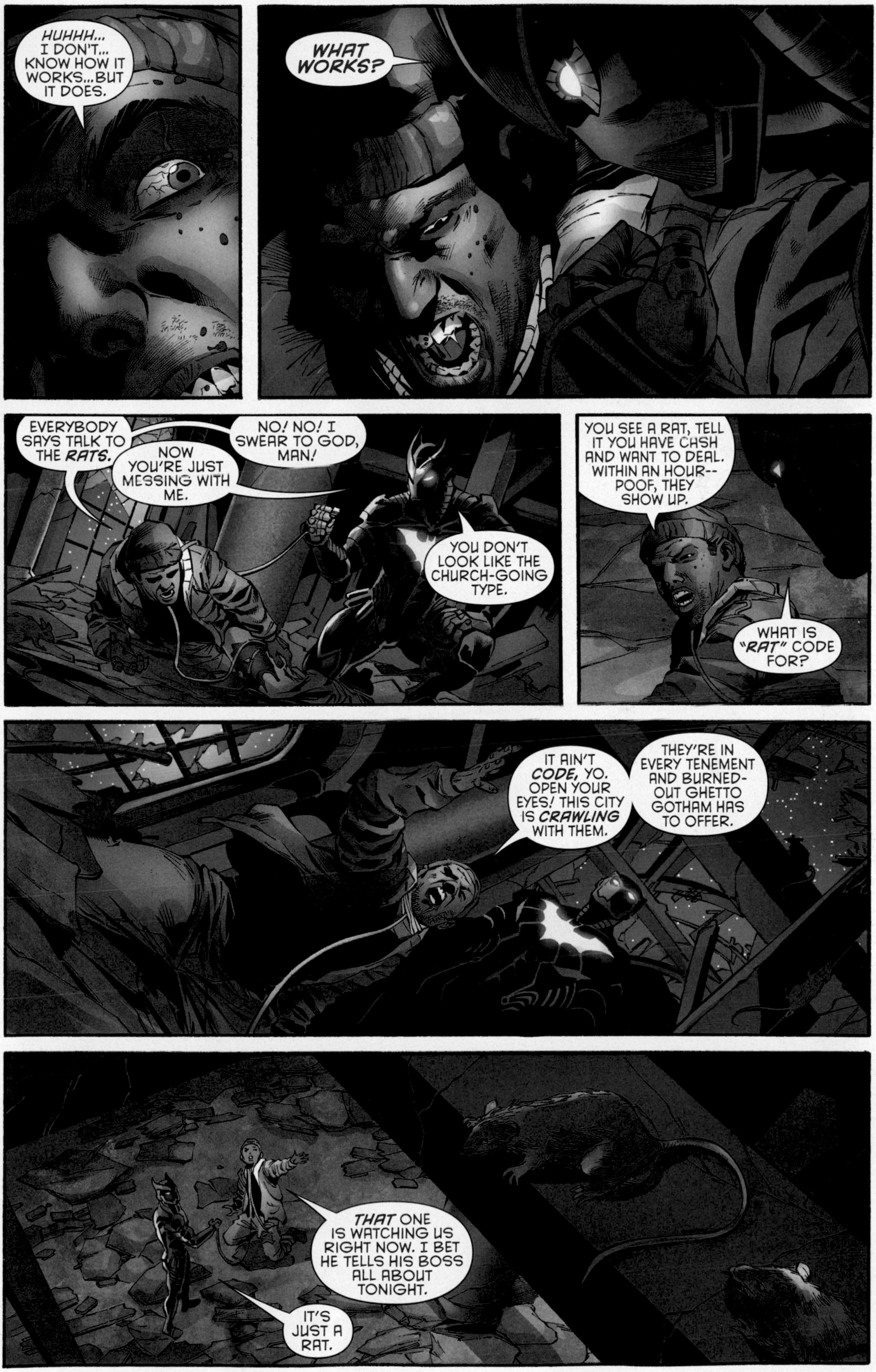
HUHHH... I DON'T... KNOW HOW IT WORKS...BUT IT DOES.
WHAT WORKS?
EVERYBODY SAYS TALK TO THE RATS.
NOW YOU'RE JUST MESSING WITH ME.
NO! NO! I SWEAR TO GOD, MAN!
YOU DON'T LOOK LIKE THE CHURCH-GOING TYPE.
YOU SEE A RAT, TELL IT YOU HAVE CASH AND WANT TO DEAL. WITHIN AN HOUR-- POOF, THEY SHOW UP.
WHAT IS "RAT" CODE FOR?
IT AIN'T CODE, YO. OPEN YOUR EYES! THIS CITY IS CRAWLING WITH THEM.
THEY'RE IN EVERY TENEMENT AND BURNED-OUT GHETTO GOTHAM HAS TO OFFER.
THAT ONE IS WATCHING US RIGHT NOW. I BET HE TELLS HIS BOSS ALL ABOUT TONIGHT.
IT'S JUST A RAT.

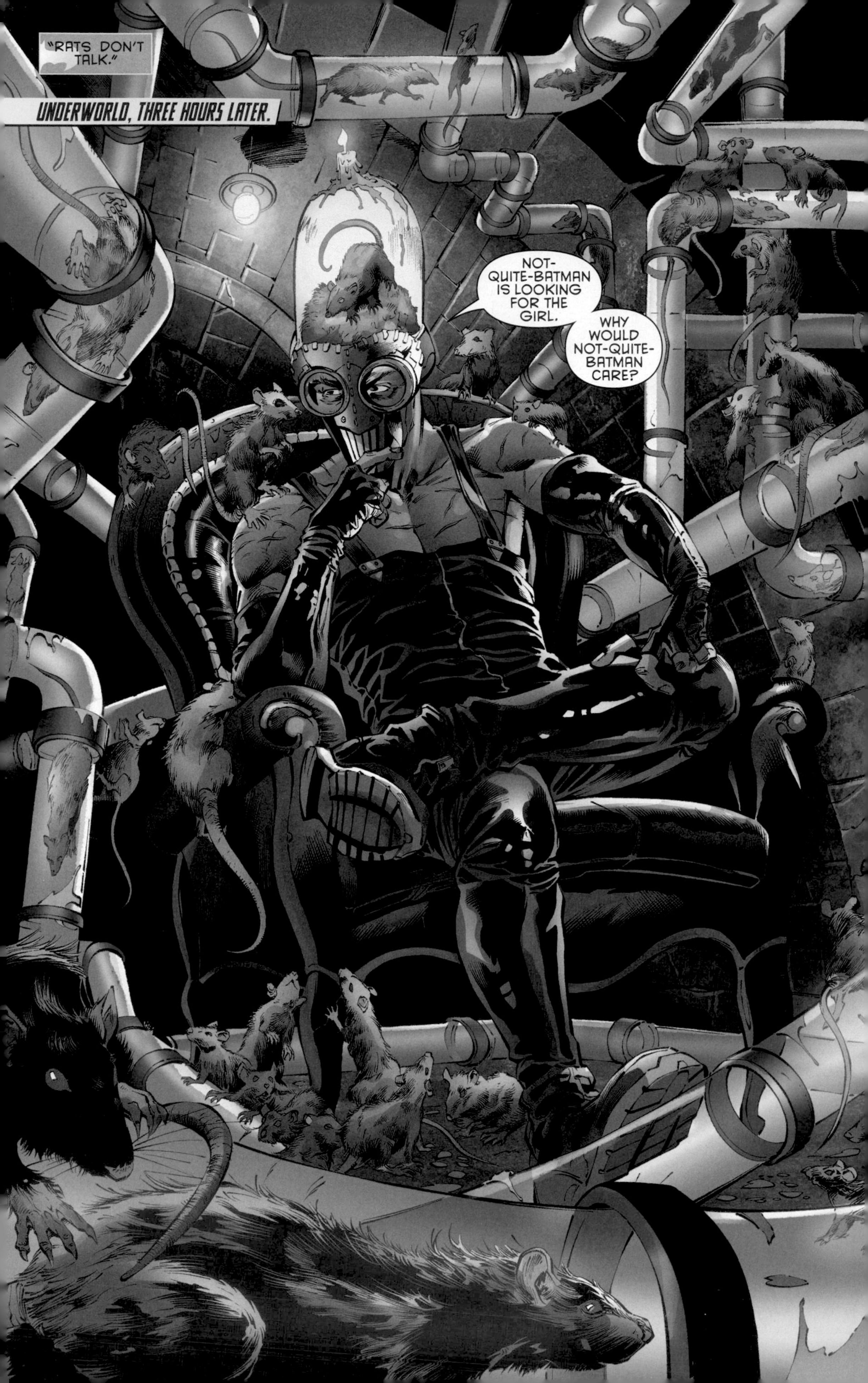
"RATS DON'T TALK."
UNDERWORLD, THREE HOURS LATER.
NOT-QUITE-BATMAN IS LOOKING FOR THE GIRL.
WHY WOULD NOT-QUITE-BATMAN CARE?

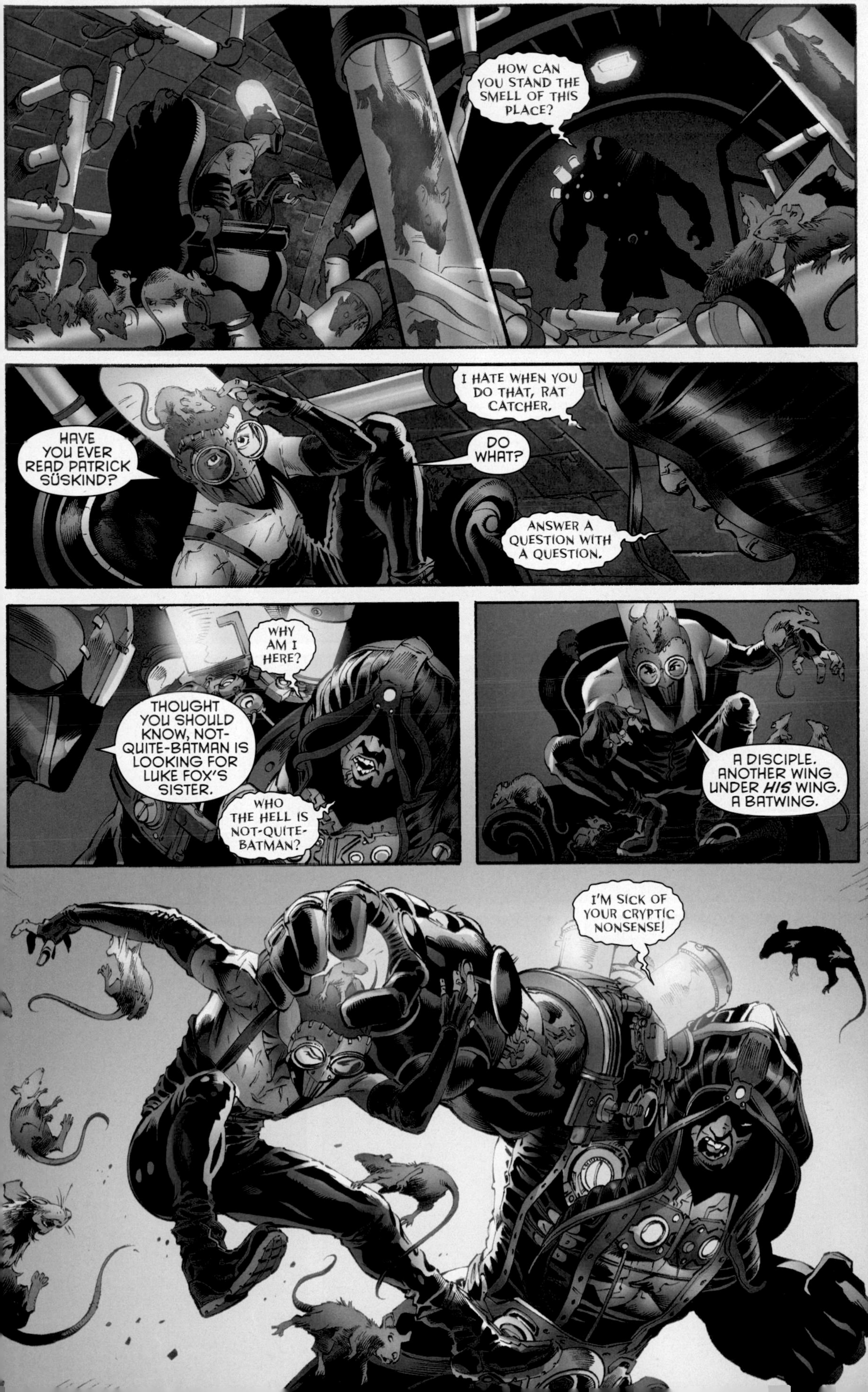
HOW CAN YOU STAND THE SMELL OF THIS PLACE?
HAVE YOU EVER READ PATRICK SÜSKIND?
I HATE WHEN YOU DO THAT, RAT CATCHER.
DO WHAT?
ANSWER A QUESTION WITH A QUESTION.
WHY AM I HERE?
THOUGHT YOU SHOULD KNOW, NOT-QUITE-BATMAN IS LOOKING FOR LUKE FOX'S SISTER.
WHO THE HELL IS NOT-QUITE-BATMAN?
A DISCIPLE. ANOTHER WING UNDER *HIS* WING. A BATWING.
I'M SICK OF YOUR CRYPTIC NONSENSE!

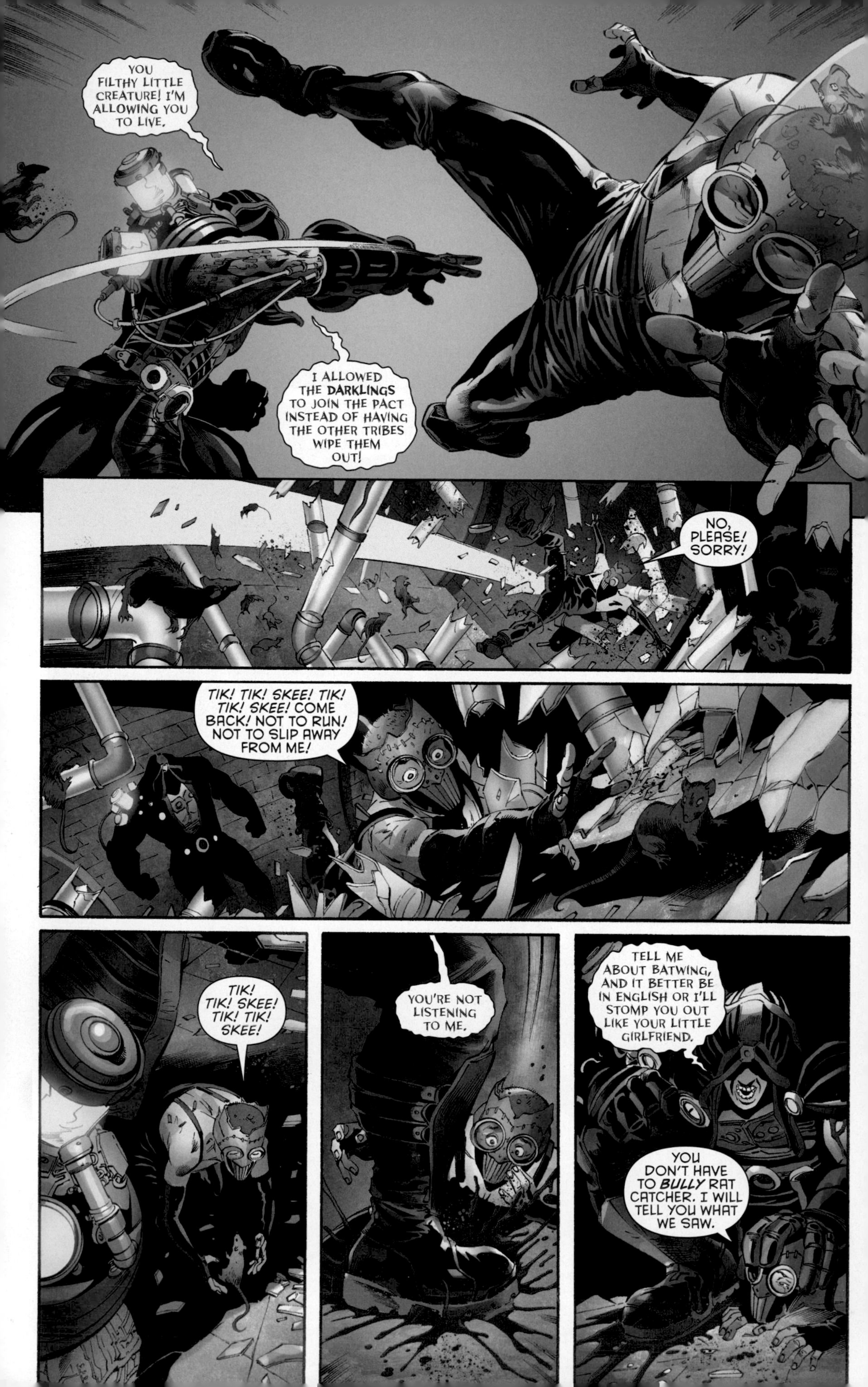
YOU FILTHY LITTLE CREATURE! I'M ALLOWING YOU TO LIVE.
I ALLOWED THE DARKLINGS TO JOIN THE PACT INSTEAD OF HAVING THE OTHER TRIBES WIPE THEM OUT!
NO, PLEASE! SORRY!
TIK! TIK! SKEE! TIK! TIK! SKEE! COME BACK! NOT TO RUN! NOT TO SLIP AWAY FROM ME!
TIK! TIK! SKEE! TIK! TIK! SKEE!
YOU'RE NOT LISTENING TO ME.
TELL ME ABOUT BATWING, AND IT BETTER BE IN ENGLISH OR I'LL STOMP YOU OUT LIKE YOUR LITTLE GIRLFRIEND.
YOU DON'T HAVE TO BULLY RAT CATCHER. I WILL TELL YOU WHAT WE SAW.

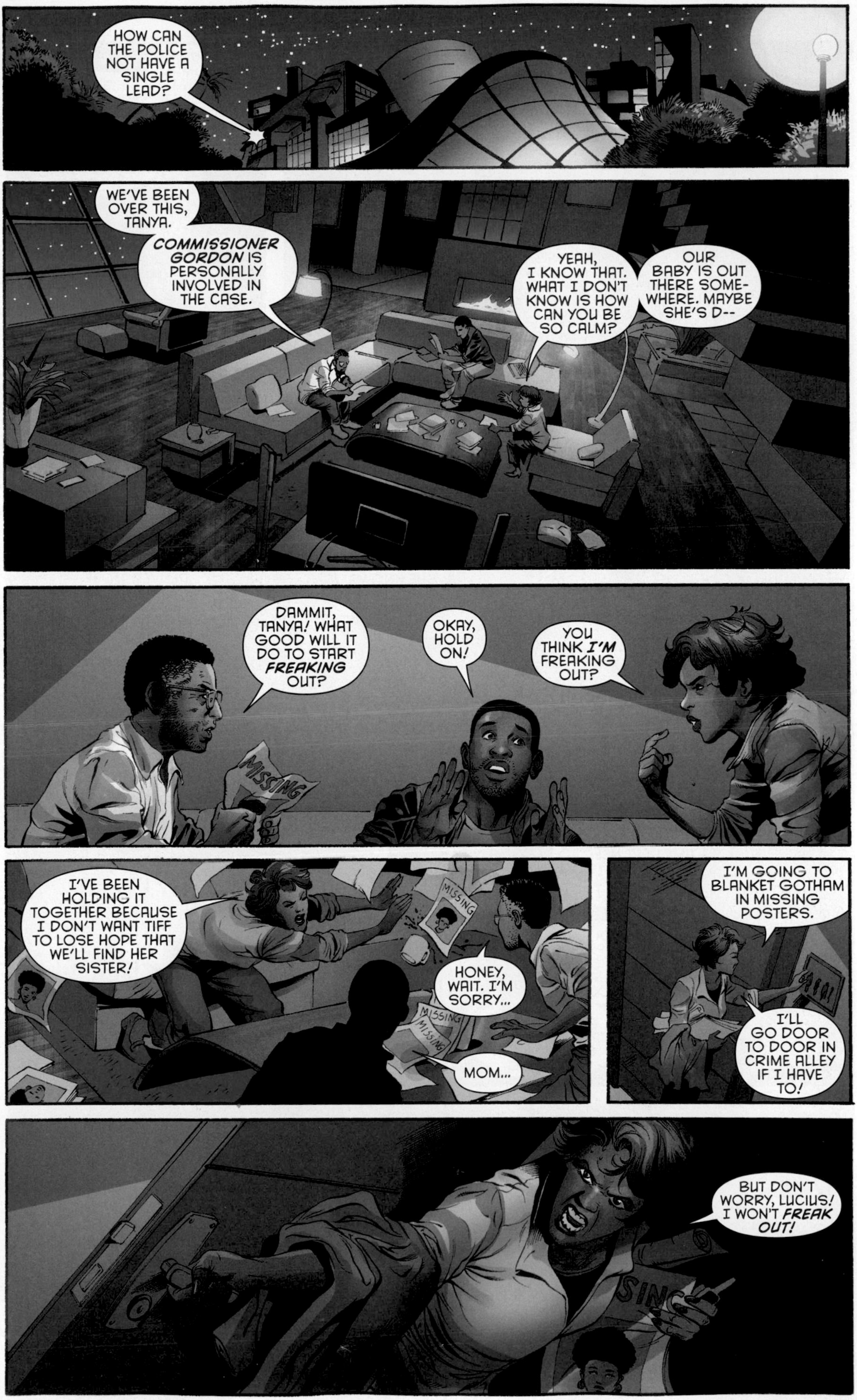
HOW CAN THE POLICE NOT HAVE A SINGLE LEAD?
WE'VE BEEN OVER THIS, TANYA.
COMMISSIONER GORDON IS PERSONALLY INVOLVED IN THE CASE.
YEAH, I KNOW THAT. WHAT I DON'T KNOW IS HOW CAN YOU BE SO CALM?
OUR BABY IS OUT THERE SOME-WHERE. MAYBE SHE'S D--
DAMMIT, TANYA! WHAT GOOD WILL IT DO TO START FREAKING OUT?
OKAY, HOLD ON!
YOU THINK I'M FREAKING OUT?
MISSING
I'VE BEEN HOLDING IT TOGETHER BECAUSE I DON'T WANT TIFF TO LOSE HOPE THAT WE'LL FIND HER SISTER!
MISSING
HONEY, WAIT. I'M SORRY...
MISSING
MISSING
MOM...
I'M GOING TO BLANKET GOTHAM IN MISSING POSTERS.
I'LL GO DOOR TO DOOR IN CRIME ALLEY IF I HAVE TO!
BUT DON'T WORRY, LUCIUS! I WON'T FREAK OUT!

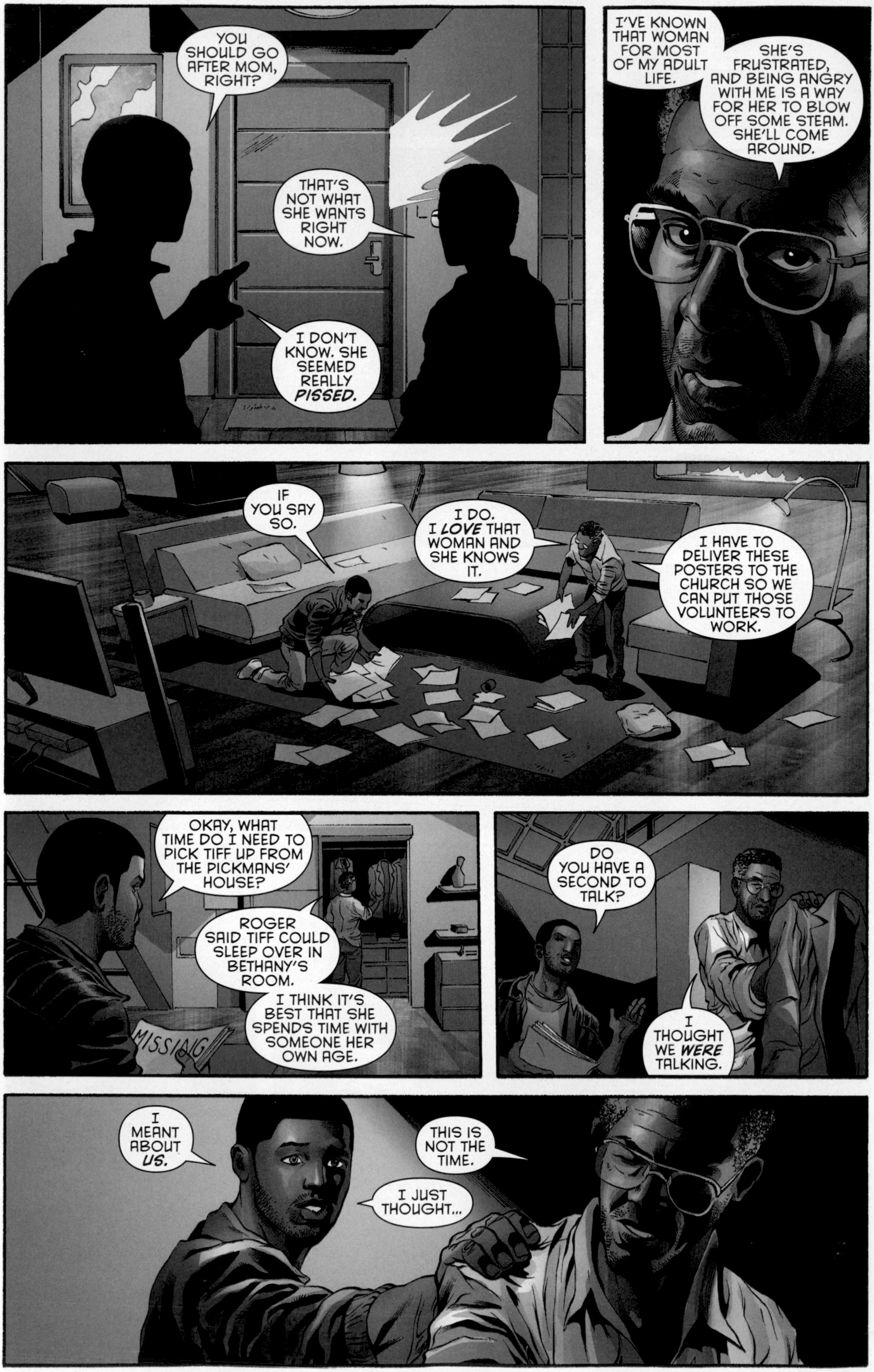
YOU SHOULD GO AFTER MOM, RIGHT?
THAT'S NOT WHAT SHE WANTS RIGHT NOW.
I DON'T KNOW. SHE SEEMED REALLY *PISSED.*
I'VE KNOWN THAT WOMAN FOR MOST OF MY ADULT LIFE.
SHE'S FRUSTRATED, AND BEING ANGRY WITH ME IS A WAY FOR HER TO BLOW OFF SOME STEAM. SHE'LL COME AROUND.
IF YOU SAY SO.
I DO. I *LOVE* THAT WOMAN AND SHE KNOWS IT.
I HAVE TO DELIVER THESE POSTERS TO THE CHURCH SO WE CAN PUT THOSE VOLUNTEERS TO WORK.
OKAY, WHAT TIME DO I NEED TO PICK TIFF UP FROM THE PICKMANS' HOUSE?
ROGER SAID TIFF COULD SLEEP OVER IN BETHANY'S ROOM.
I THINK IT'S BEST THAT SHE SPENDS TIME WITH SOMEONE HER OWN AGE.
DO YOU HAVE A SECOND TO TALK?
I THOUGHT WE *WERE* TALKING.
I MEANT ABOUT *US.*
THIS IS NOT THE TIME.
I JUST THOUGHT...

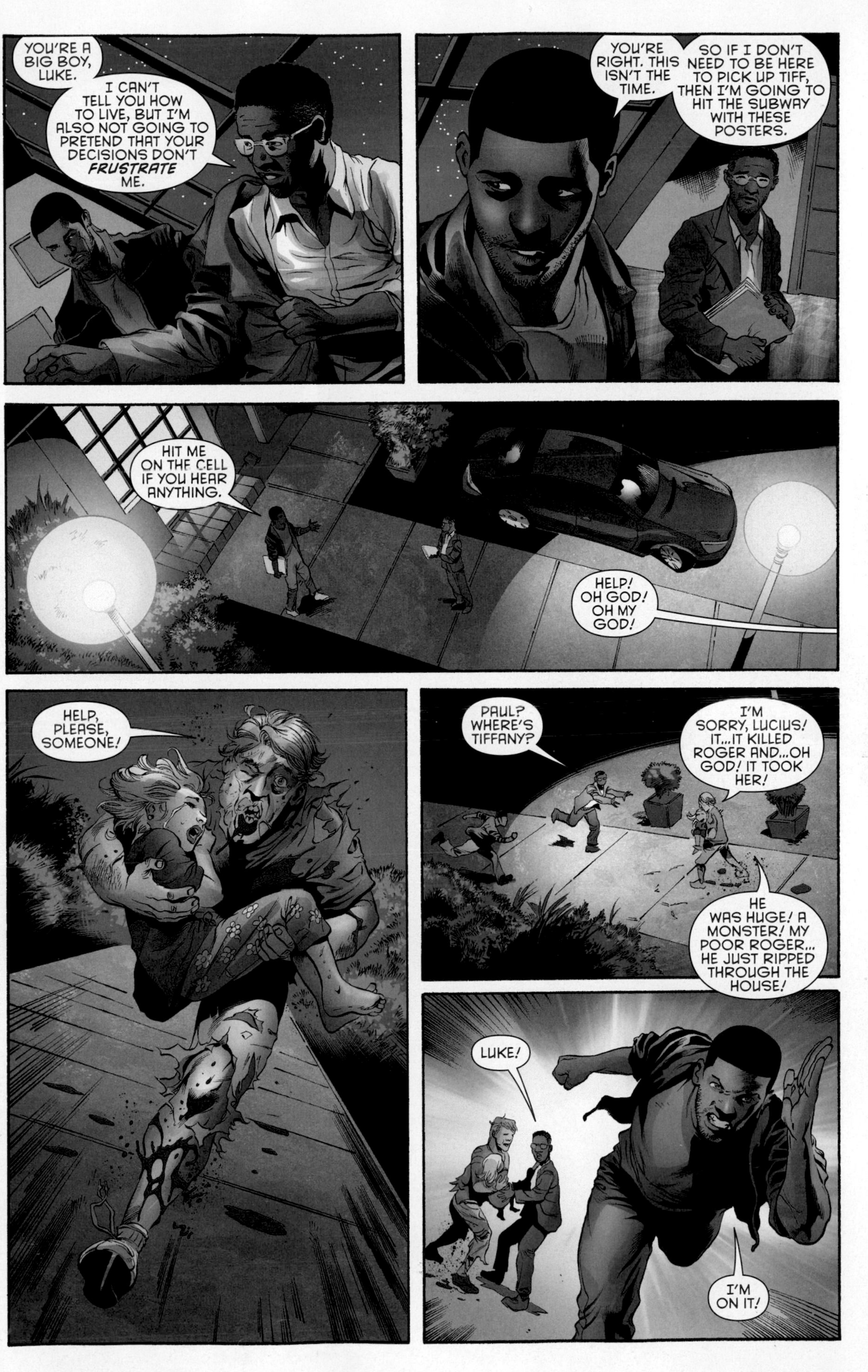
YOU'RE A BIG BOY, LUKE.
I CAN'T TELL YOU HOW TO LIVE, BUT I'M ALSO NOT GOING TO PRETEND THAT YOUR DECISIONS DON'T *FRUSTRATE* ME.
YOU'RE RIGHT. THIS ISN'T THE TIME.
SO IF I DON'T NEED TO BE HERE TO PICK UP TIFF, THEN I'M GOING TO HIT THE SUBWAY WITH THESE POSTERS.
HIT ME ON THE CELL IF YOU HEAR ANYTHING.
HELP! OH GOD! OH MY GOD!
HELP, PLEASE, SOMEONE!
PAUL? WHERE'S TIFFANY?
I'M SORRY, LUCIUS! IT...IT KILLED ROGER AND...OH GOD! IT TOOK HER!
HE WAS HUGE! A MONSTER! MY POOR ROGER... HE JUST RIPPED THROUGH THE HOUSE!
LUKE!
I'M ON IT!

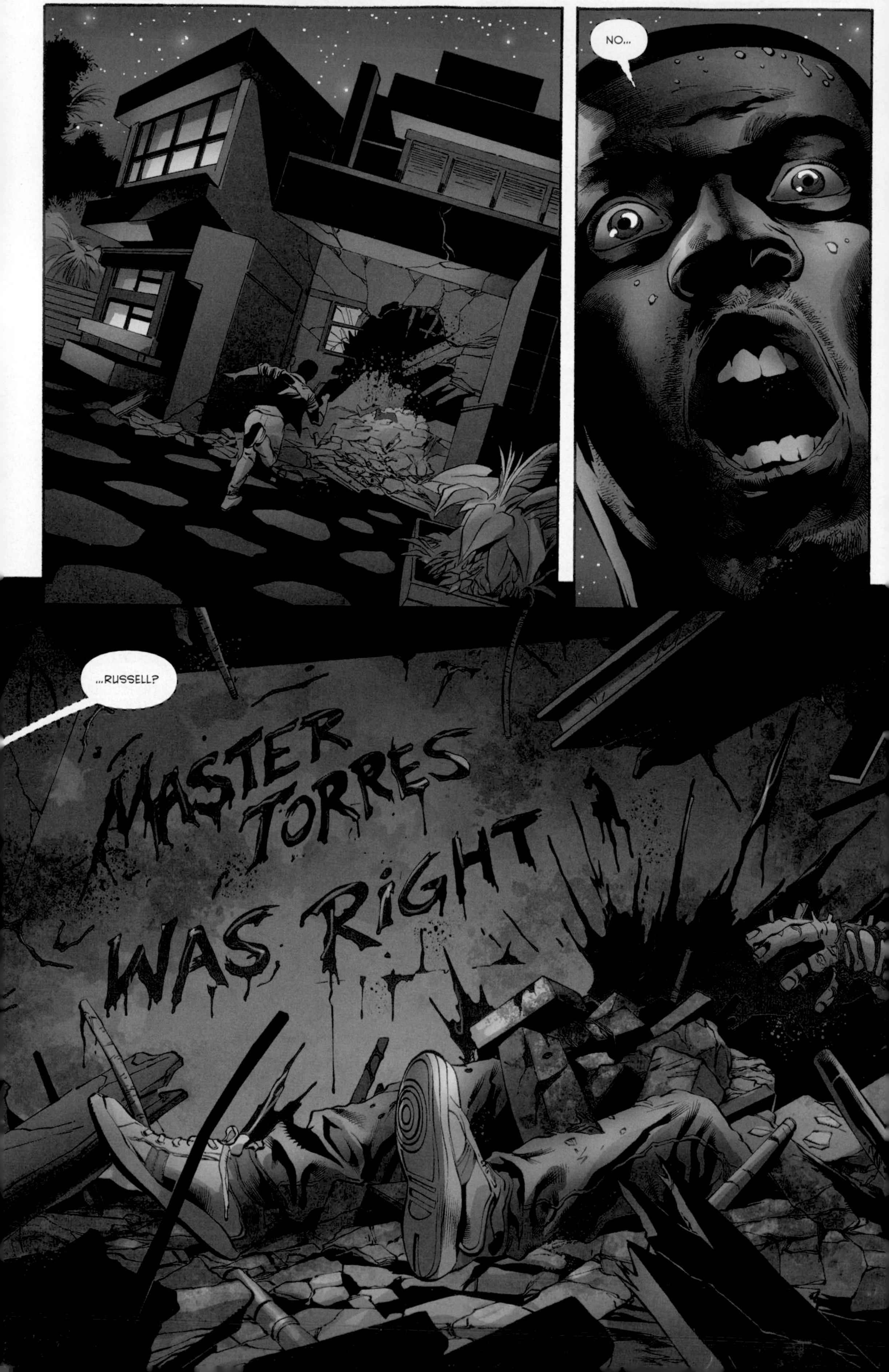
NO...
...RUSSELL?
MASTER TORRES WAS RIGHT

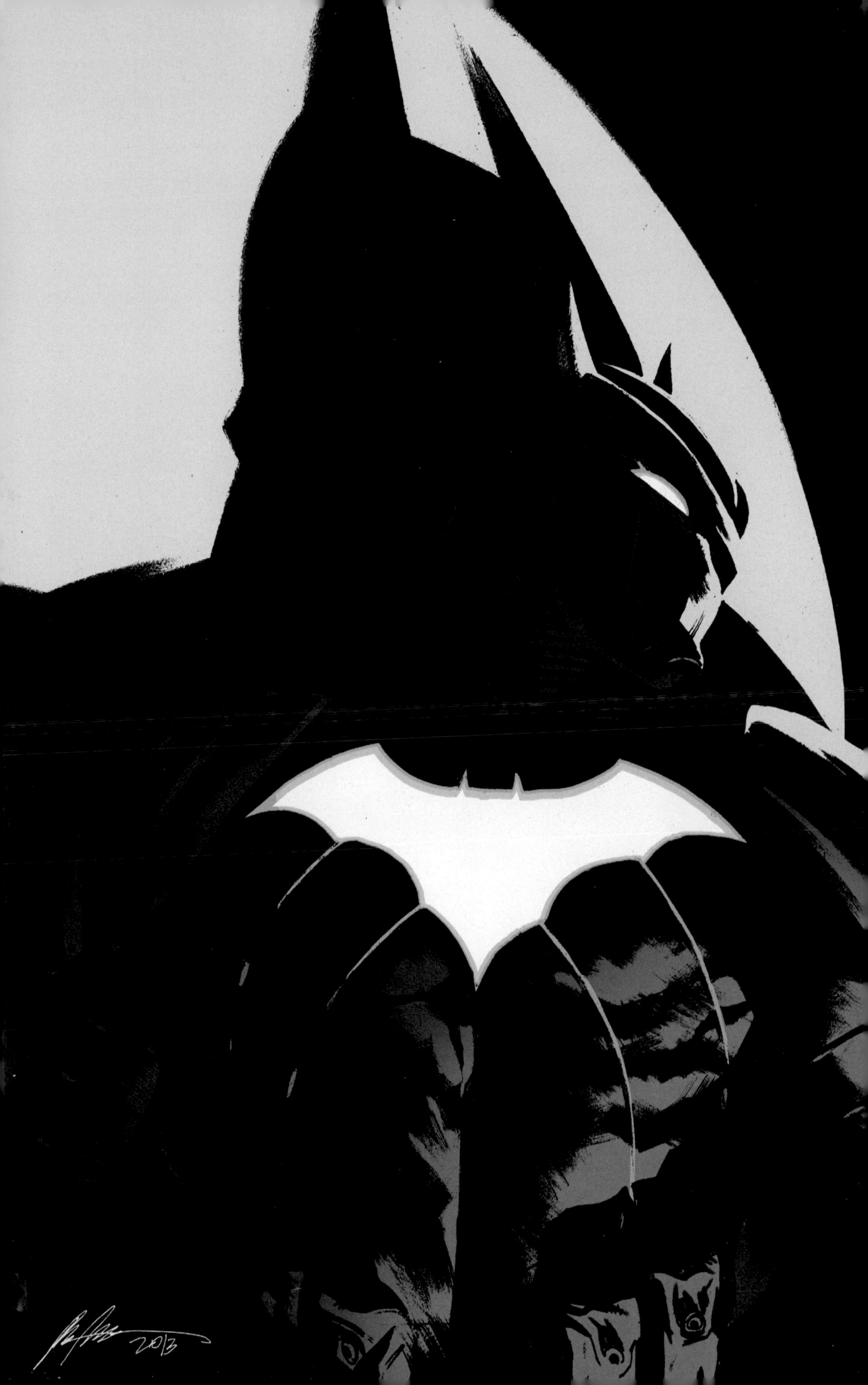

GOING DOWN TO THE UNDERGROUND

JIMMY PALMIOTTI
JUSTIN GRAY
writers

EDUARDO PANSICA
penciller

JÚLIO FERREIRA
inker

PAUL MOUNTS
colorist

TAYLOR ESPOSITO
letterer

cover art by
RAFAEL ALBUQUERQUE

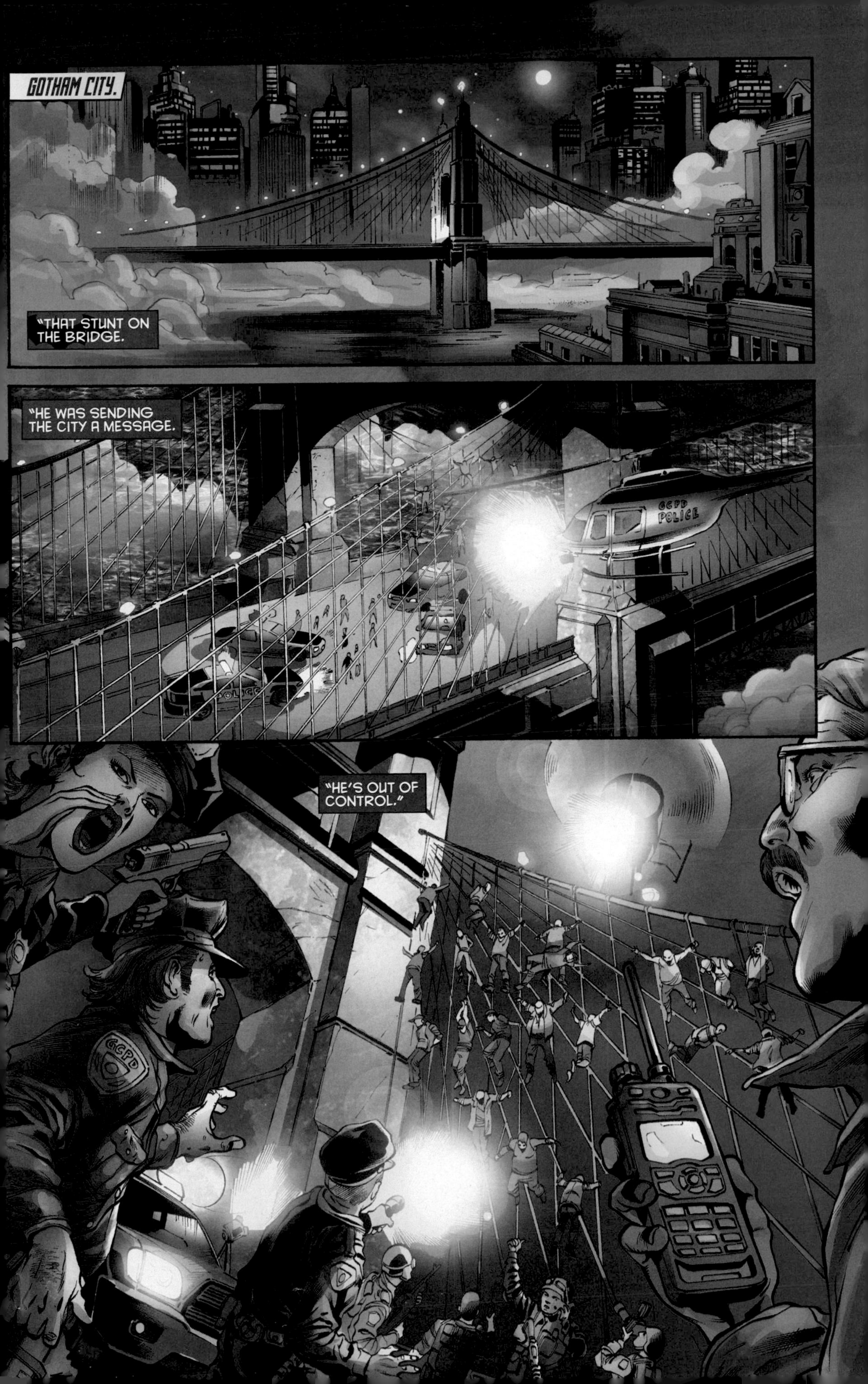
GOTHAM CITY.
"THAT STUNT ON THE BRIDGE.
"HE WAS SENDING THE CITY A MESSAGE.
GCPD POLICE
POLICE
"HE'S OUT OF CONTROL."
GCPD

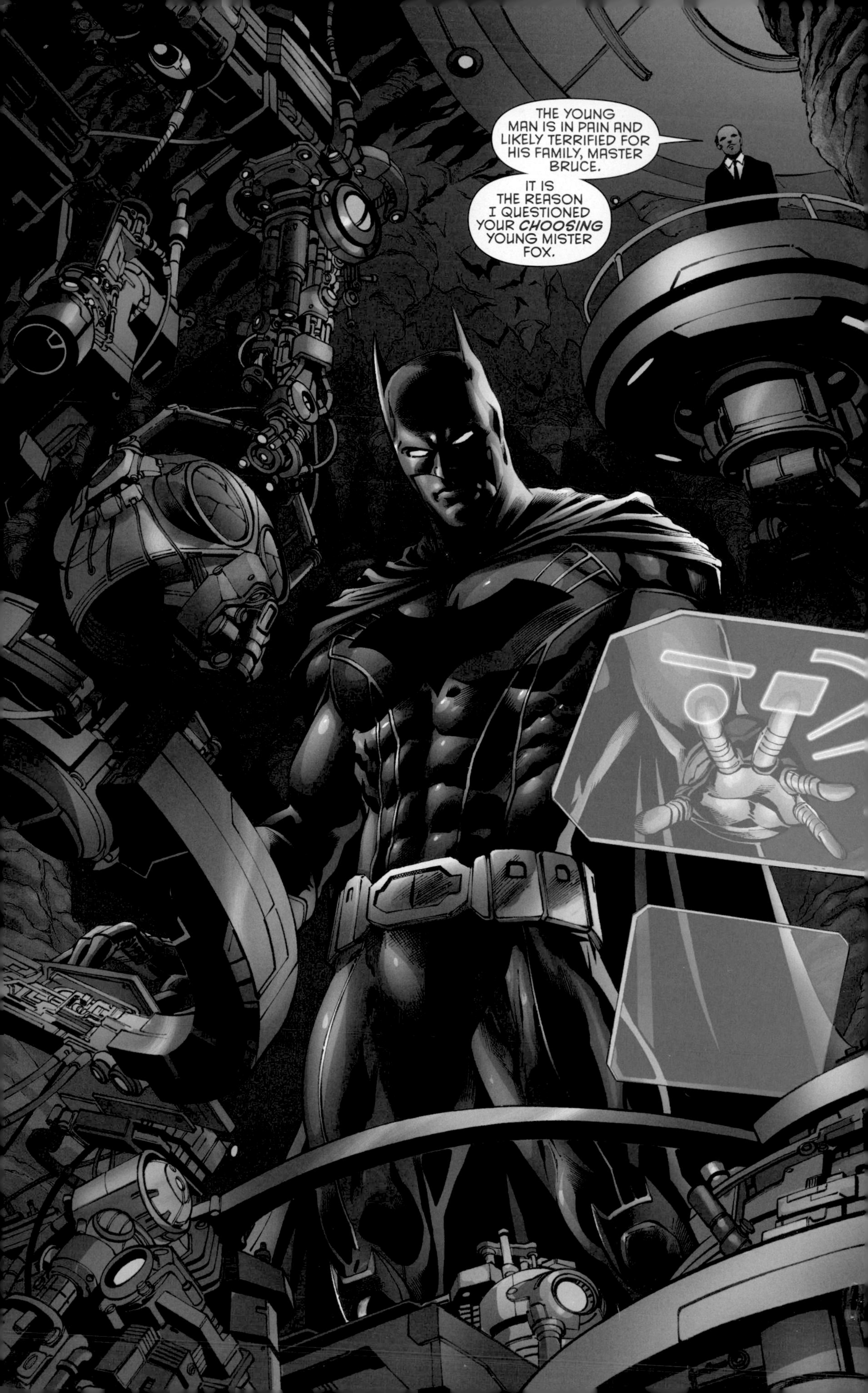
THE YOUNG MAN IS IN PAIN AND LIKELY TERRIFIED FOR HIS FAMILY, MASTER BRUCE.
IT IS THE REASON I QUESTIONED YOUR *CHOOSING* YOUNG MISTER FOX.

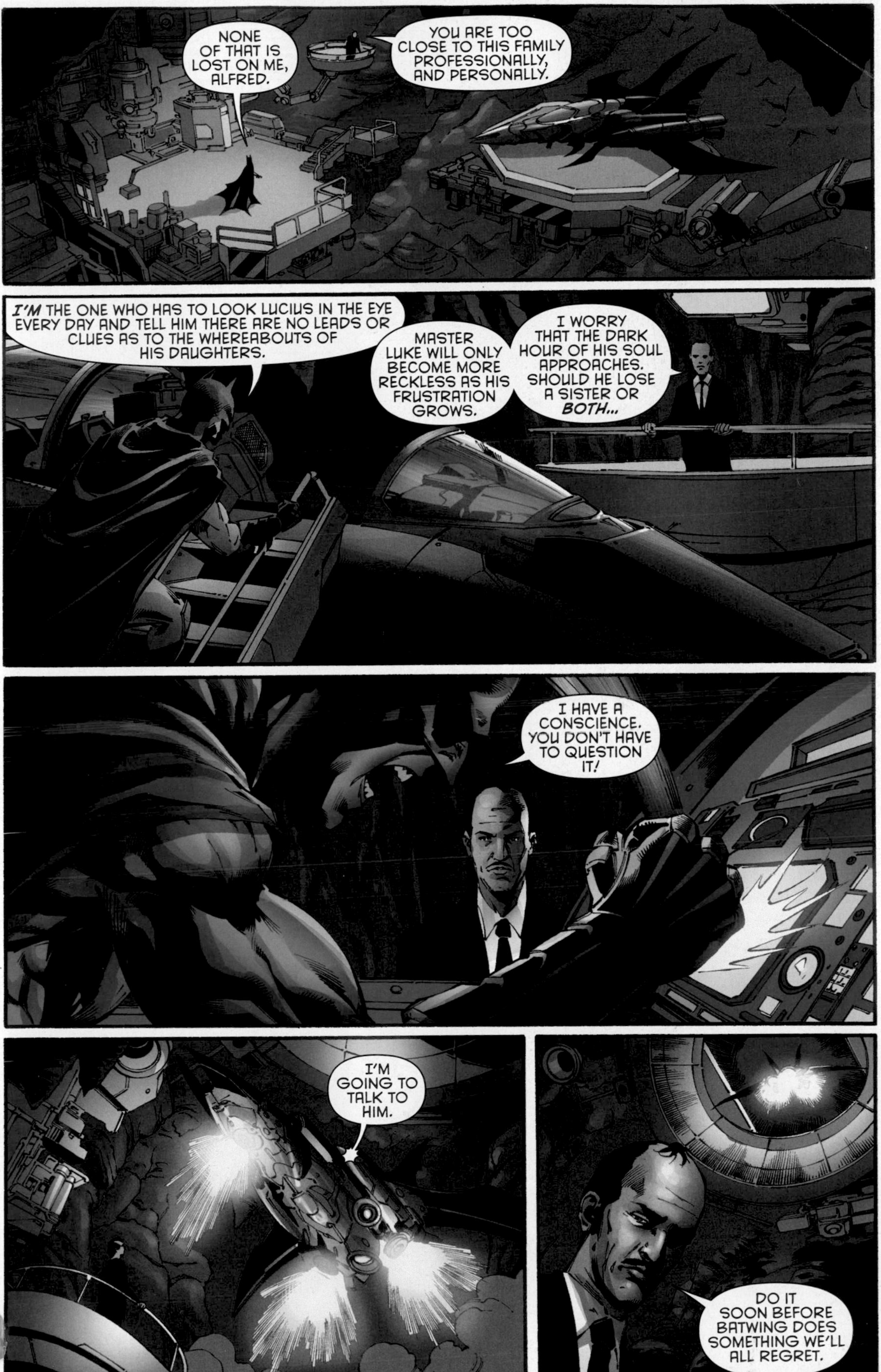
NONE OF THAT IS LOST ON ME, ALFRED.
YOU ARE TOO CLOSE TO THIS FAMILY PROFESSIONALLY, AND PERSONALLY.
I'M THE ONE WHO HAS TO LOOK LUCIUS IN THE EYE EVERY DAY AND TELL HIM THERE ARE NO LEADS OR CLUES AS TO THE WHEREABOUTS OF HIS DAUGHTERS.
MASTER LUKE WILL ONLY BECOME MORE RECKLESS AS HIS FRUSTRATION GROWS.
I WORRY THAT THE DARK HOUR OF HIS SOUL APPROACHES. SHOULD HE LOSE A SISTER OR BOTH...
I HAVE A CONSCIENCE. YOU DON'T HAVE TO QUESTION IT!
I'M GOING TO TALK TO HIM.
DO IT SOON BEFORE BATWING DOES SOMETHING WE'LL ALL REGRET.

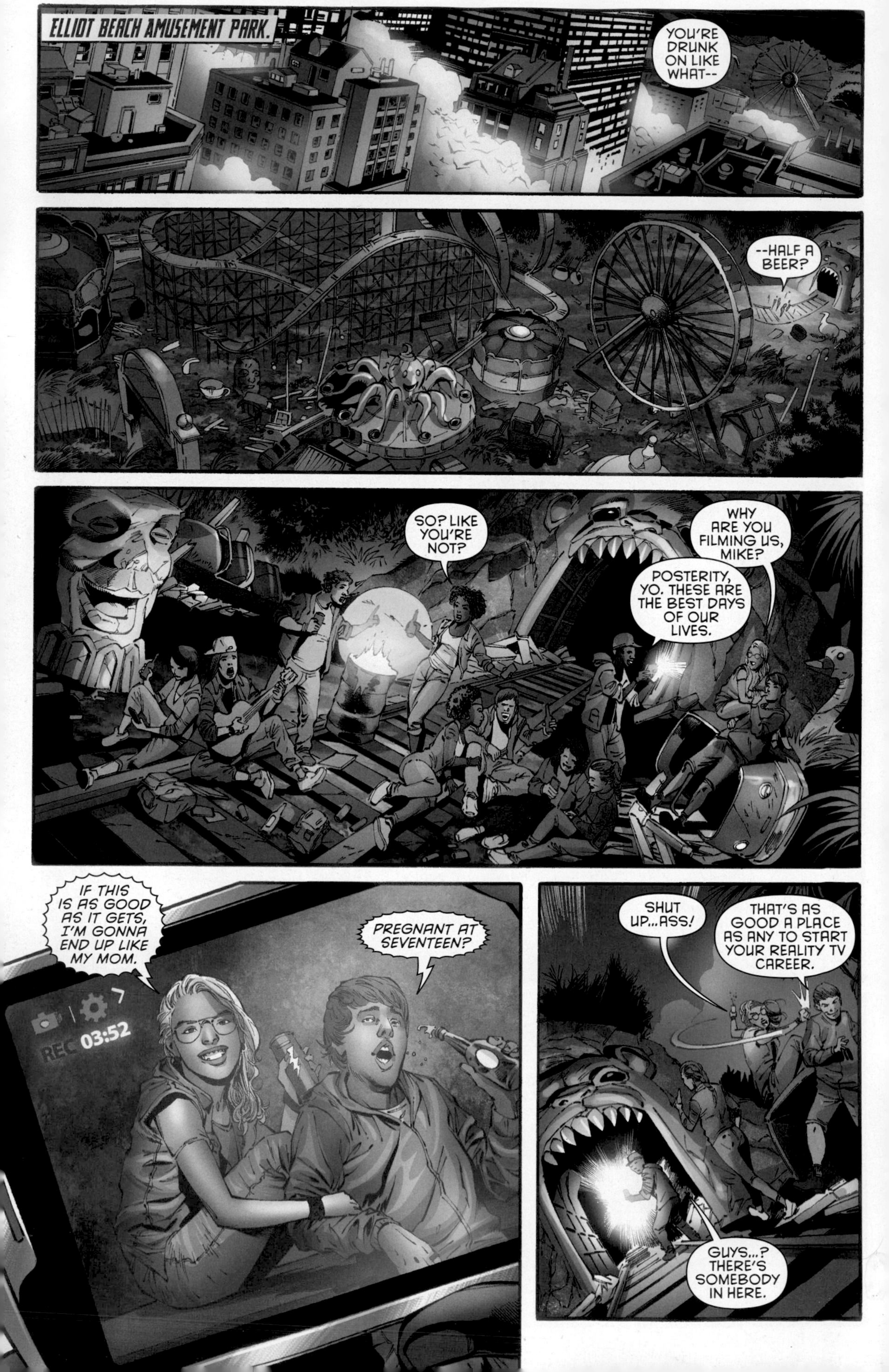
ELLIOT BEACH AMUSEMENT PARK.
YOU'RE DRUNK ON LIKE WHAT--
--HALF A BEER?
SO? LIKE YOU'RE NOT?
WHY ARE YOU FILMING US, MIKE?
POSTERITY, YO. THESE ARE THE BEST DAYS OF OUR LIVES.
IF THIS IS AS GOOD AS IT GETS, I'M GONNA END UP LIKE MY MOM.
PREGNANT AT SEVENTEEN?
REC 03:52
SHUT UP...ASS!
THAT'S AS GOOD A PLACE AS ANY TO START YOUR REALITY TV CAREER.
GUYS...? THERE'S SOMEBODY IN HERE.

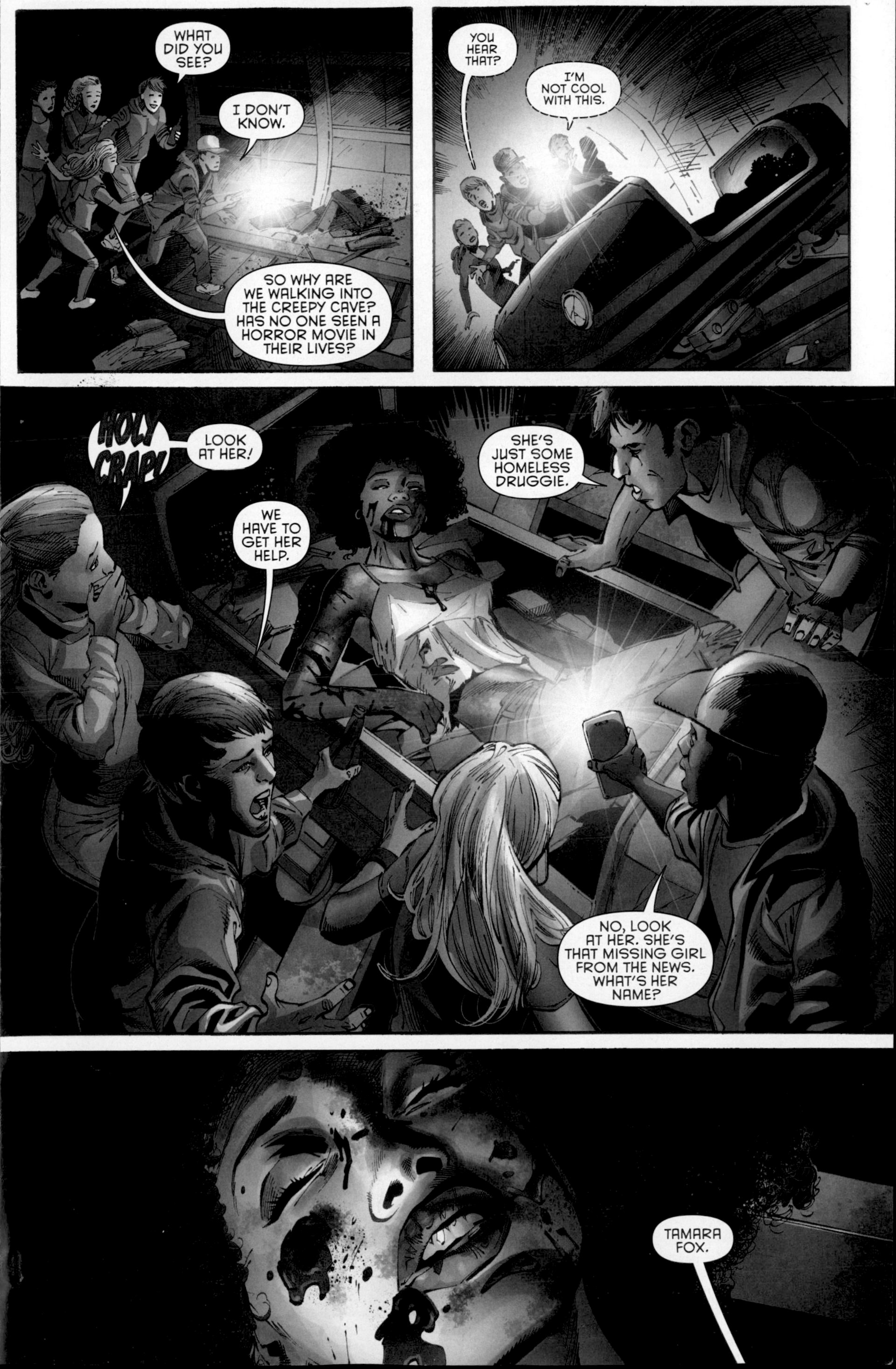
WHAT DID YOU SEE?
I DON'T KNOW.
SO WHY ARE WE WALKING INTO THE CREEPY CAVE? HAS NO ONE SEEN A HORROR MOVIE IN THEIR LIVES?
YOU HEAR THAT?
I'M NOT COOL WITH THIS.
HOLY CRAP!
LOOK AT HER!
WE HAVE TO GET HER HELP.
SHE'S JUST SOME HOMELESS DRUGGIE.
NO, LOOK AT HER. SHE'S THAT MISSING GIRL FROM THE NEWS. WHAT'S HER NAME?
TAMARA FOX.

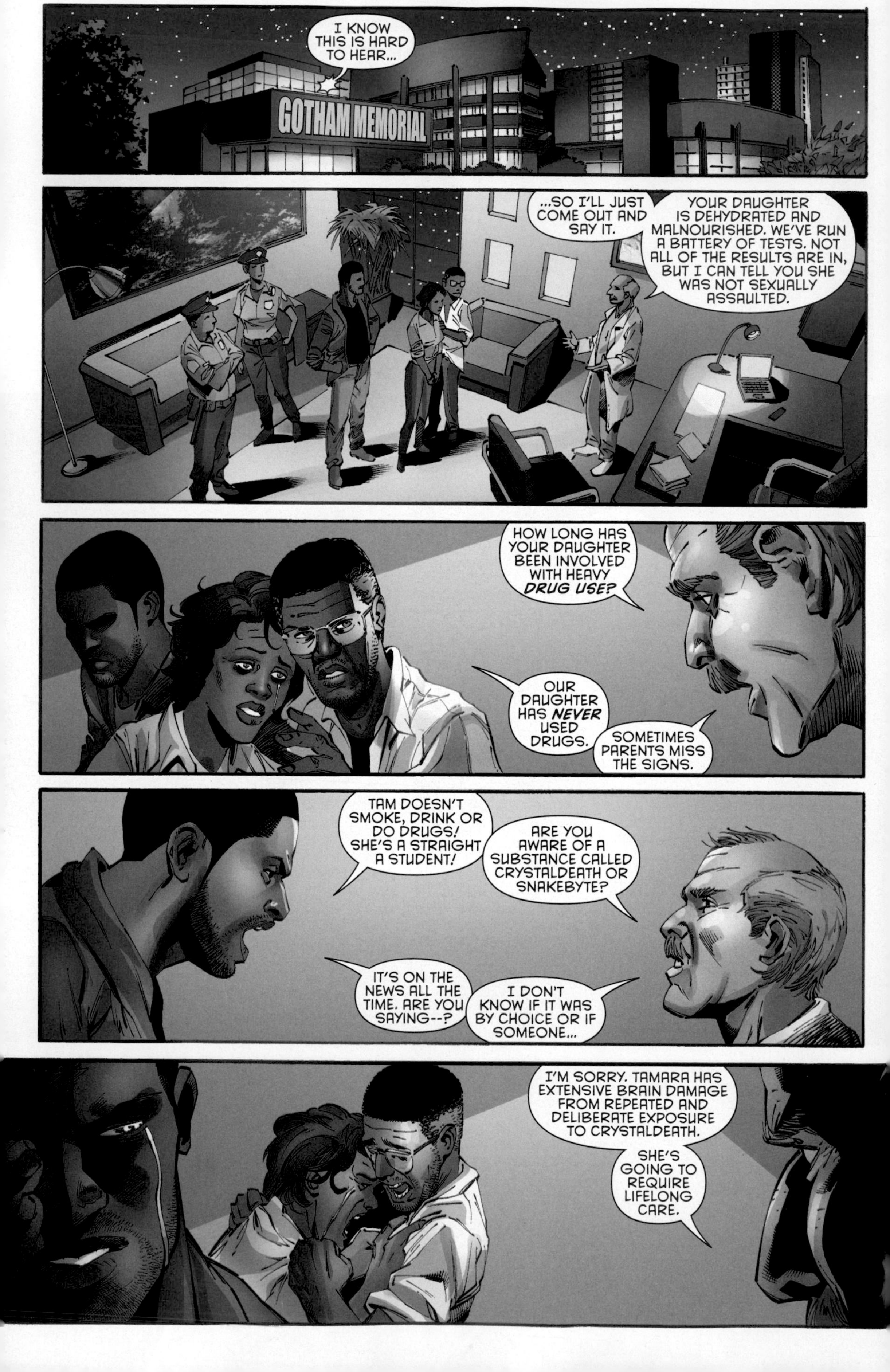
I KNOW THIS IS HARD TO HEAR...
GOTHAM MEMORIAL
...SO I'LL JUST COME OUT AND SAY IT.
YOUR DAUGHTER IS DEHYDRATED AND MALNOURISHED. WE'VE RUN A BATTERY OF TESTS. NOT ALL OF THE RESULTS ARE IN, BUT I CAN TELL YOU SHE WAS NOT SEXUALLY ASSAULTED.
HOW LONG HAS YOUR DAUGHTER BEEN INVOLVED WITH HEAVY DRUG USE?
OUR DAUGHTER HAS NEVER USED DRUGS.
SOMETIMES PARENTS MISS THE SIGNS.
TAM DOESN'T SMOKE, DRINK OR DO DRUGS! SHE'S A STRAIGHT A STUDENT!
ARE YOU AWARE OF A SUBSTANCE CALLED CRYSTALDEATH OR SNAKEBYTE?
IT'S ON THE NEWS ALL THE TIME. ARE YOU SAYING--?
I DON'T KNOW IF IT WAS BY CHOICE OR IF SOMEONE...
I'M SORRY. TAMARA HAS EXTENSIVE BRAIN DAMAGE FROM REPEATED AND DELIBERATE EXPOSURE TO CRYSTALDEATH.
SHE'S GOING TO REQUIRE LIFELONG CARE.

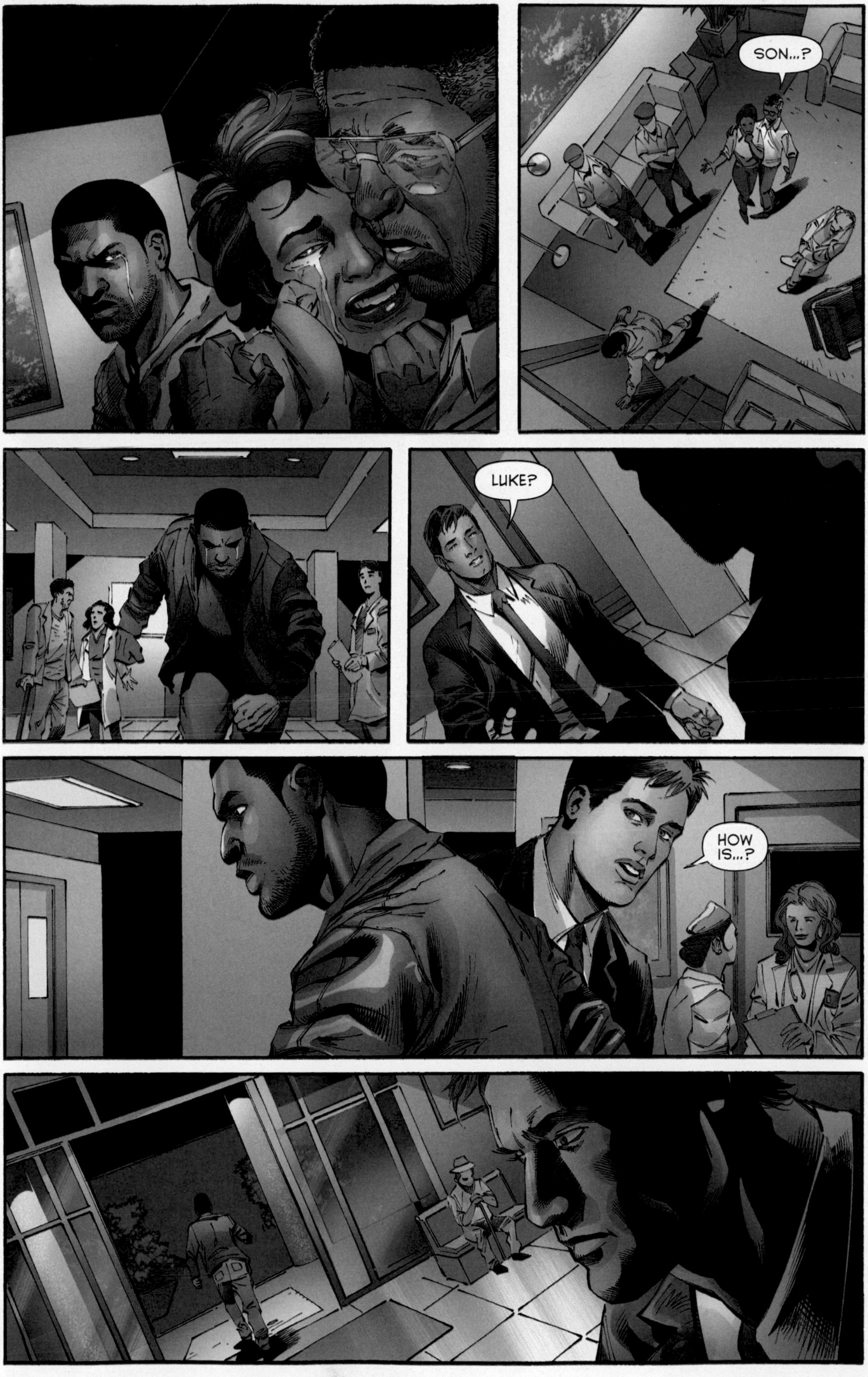
SON...?
LUKE?
HOW IS...?

LATER...

I'm so angry. I have to act. Just can't sit still.

The police won't find anything useful. They don't have the right equipment.

But me, I can go to the dark places.

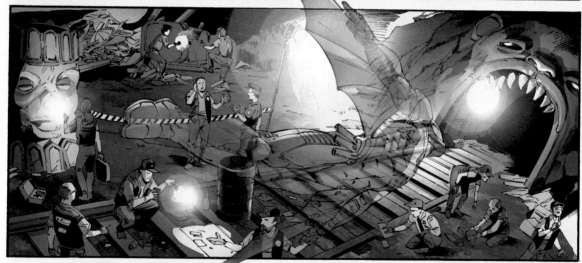

Down the hatch.

I don't want to insult anyone, but these guys wouldn't find any clue right under their noses.

I guess I just see things a little differently.

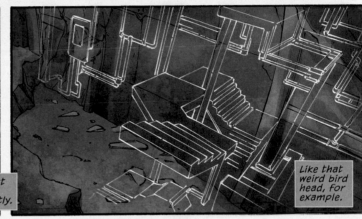

Like that weird bird head, for example.

If I just press--

...whoa.

No turning back, I guess.

Ready or not...

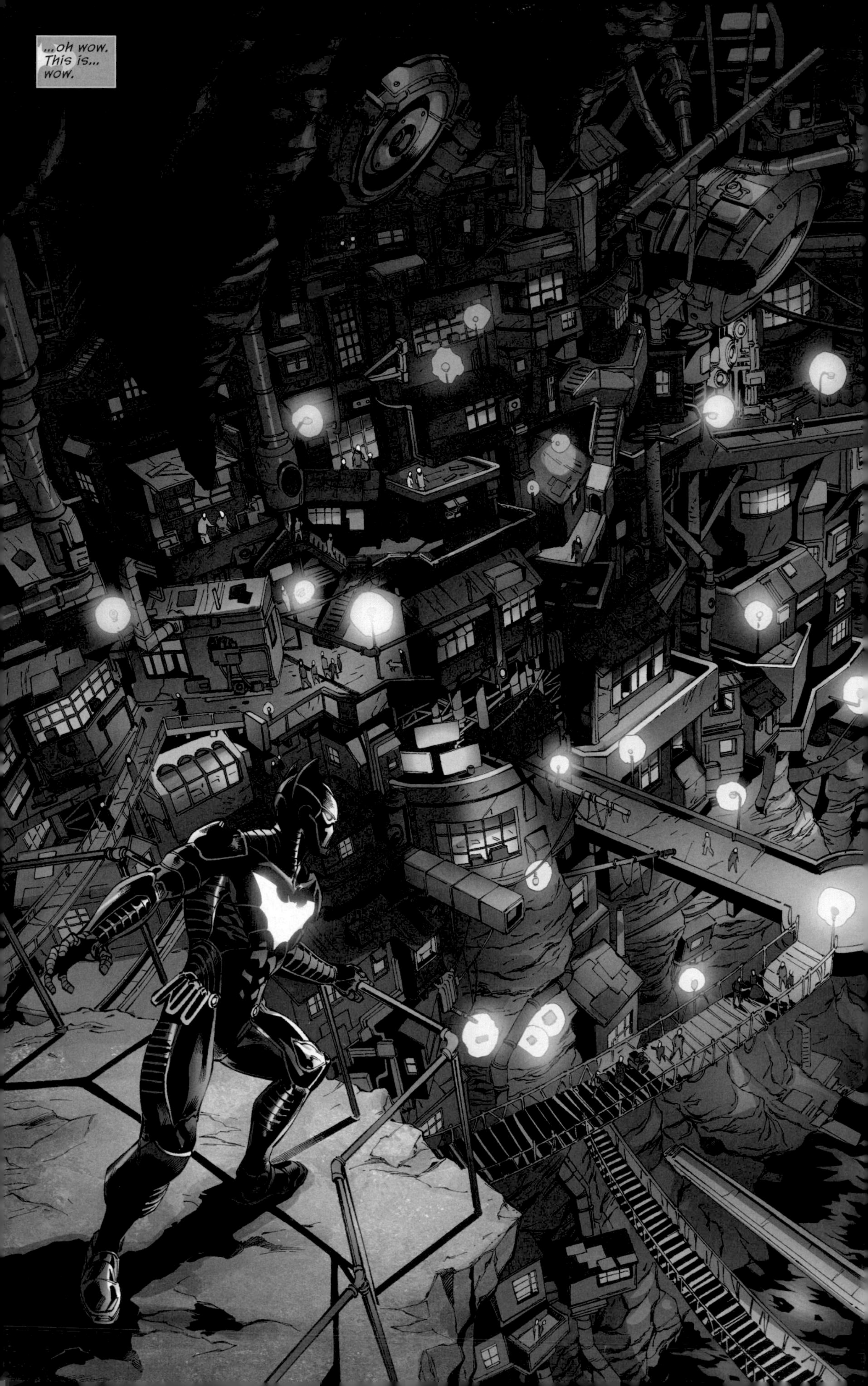
...oh wow. This is... wow.

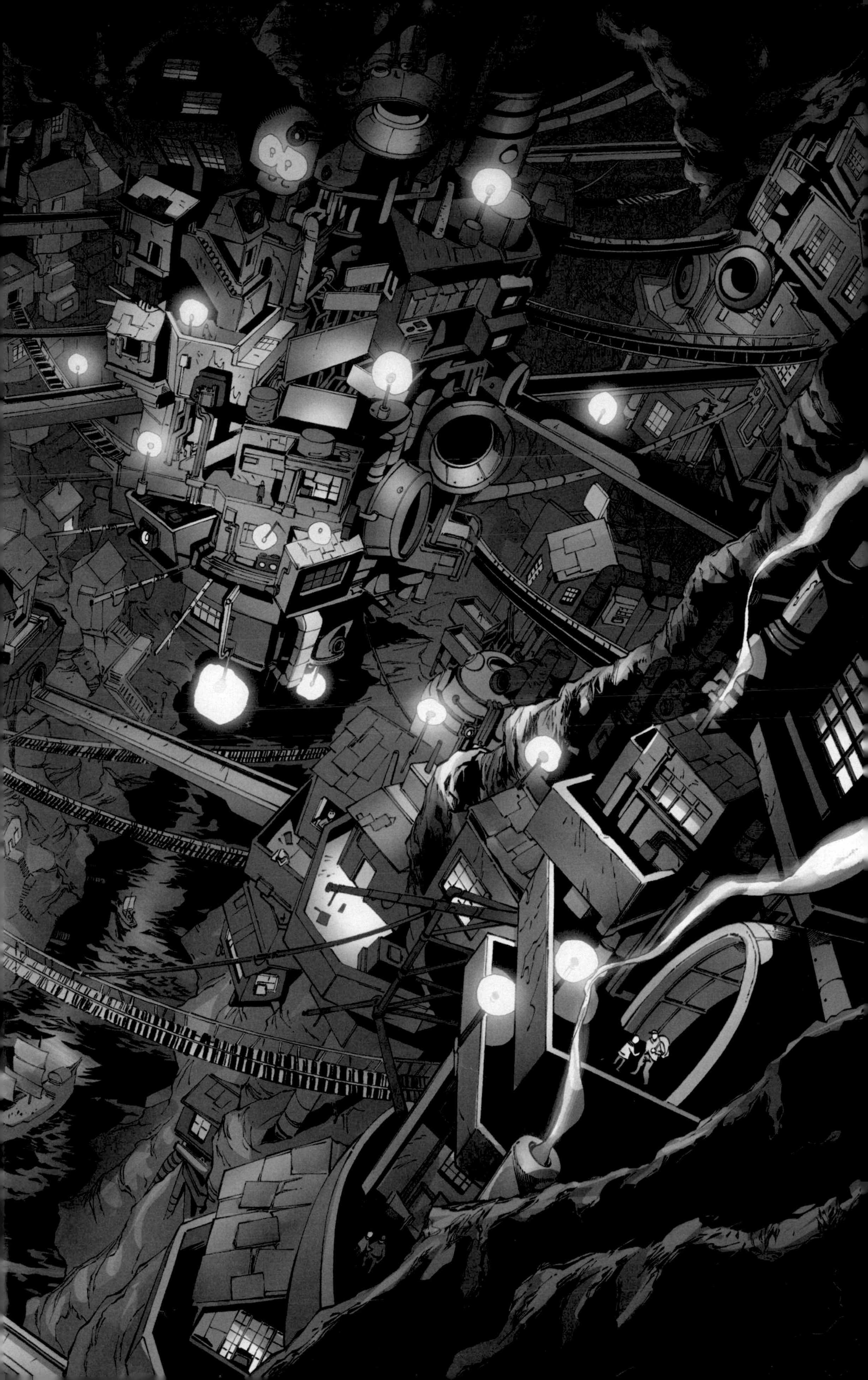

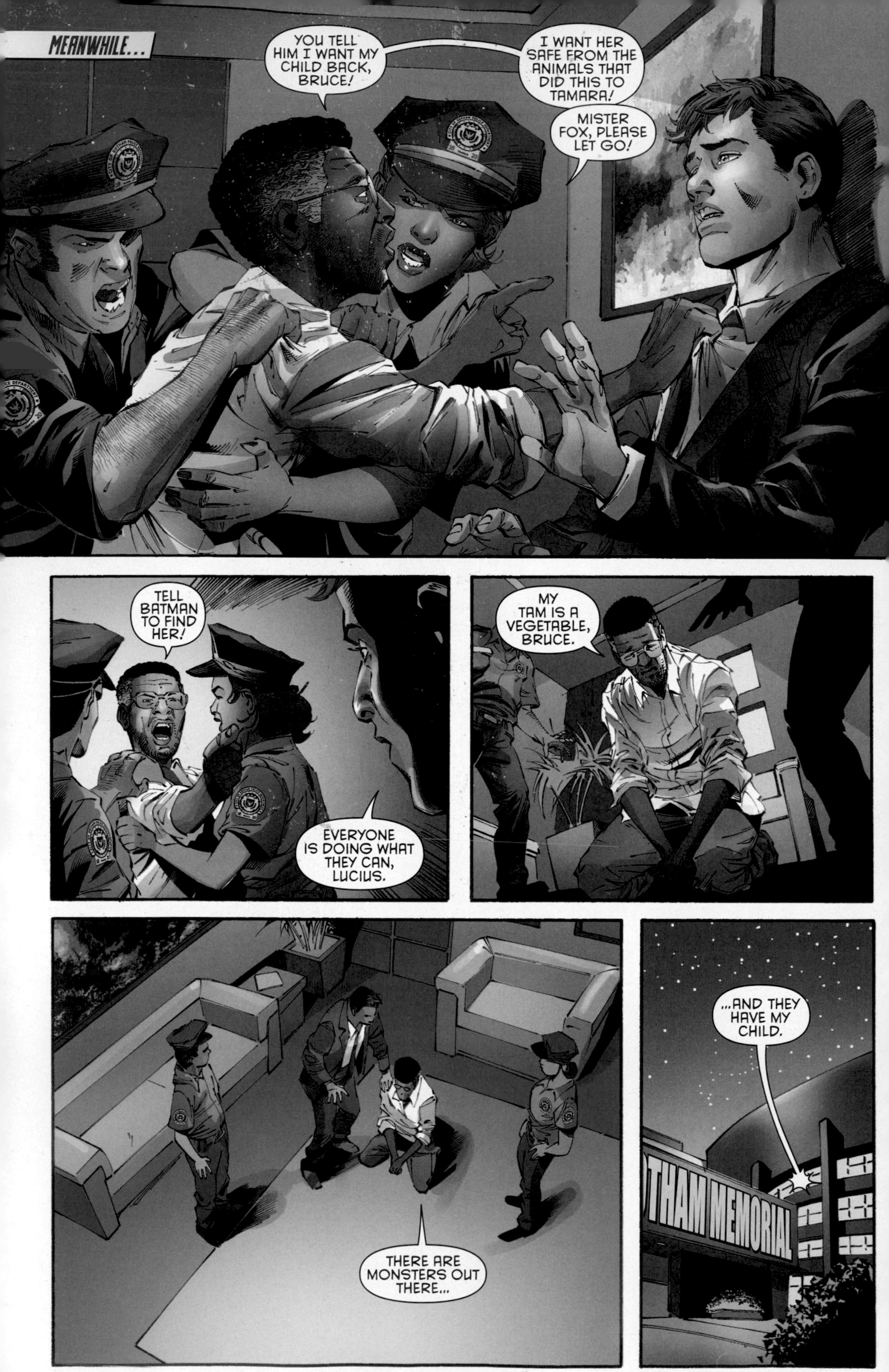
MEANWHILE...
YOU TELL HIM I WANT MY CHILD BACK, BRUCE!
I WANT HER SAFE FROM THE ANIMALS THAT DID THIS TO TAMARA!
MISTER FOX, PLEASE LET GO!
TELL BATMAN TO FIND HER!
EVERYONE IS DOING WHAT THEY CAN, LUCIUS.
MY TAM IS A VEGETABLE, BRUCE.
THERE ARE MONSTERS OUT THERE...
...AND THEY HAVE MY CHILD.
THAM MEMORIAL

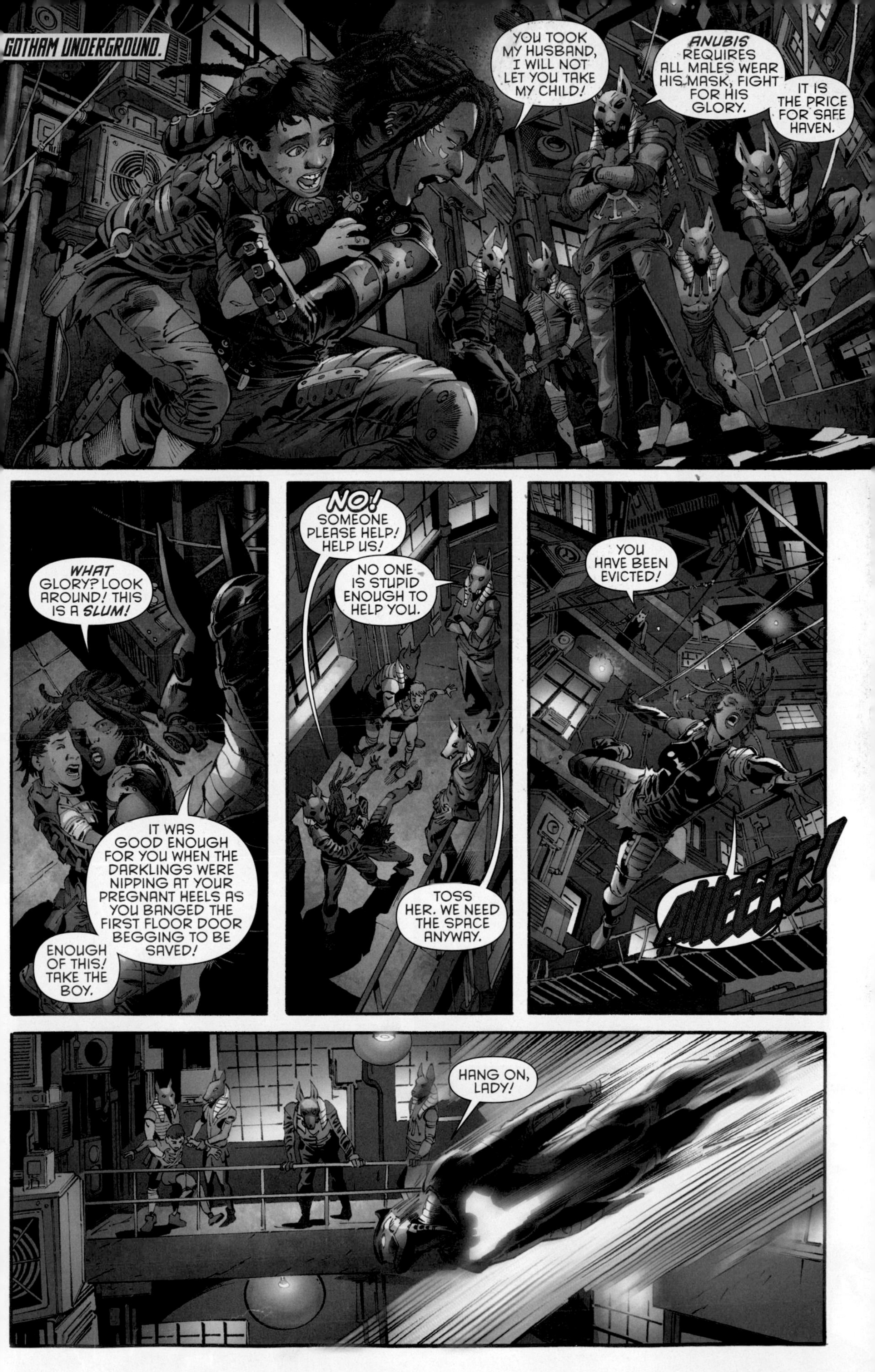
GOTHAM UNDERGROUND.
YOU TOOK MY HUSBAND, I WILL NOT LET YOU TAKE MY CHILD!
ANUBIS REQUIRES ALL MALES WEAR HIS MASK, FIGHT FOR HIS GLORY.
IT IS THE PRICE FOR SAFE HAVEN.
WHAT GLORY? LOOK AROUND! THIS IS A SLUM!
IT WAS GOOD ENOUGH FOR YOU WHEN THE DARKLINGS WERE NIPPING AT YOUR PREGNANT HEELS AS YOU BANGED THE FIRST FLOOR DOOR BEGGING TO BE SAVED!
ENOUGH OF THIS! TAKE THE BOY.
NO! SOMEONE PLEASE HELP! HELP US!
NO ONE IS STUPID ENOUGH TO HELP YOU.
TOSS HER. WE NEED THE SPACE ANYWAY.
YOU HAVE BEEN EVICTED!
AIIEEEE!
HANG ON, LADY!

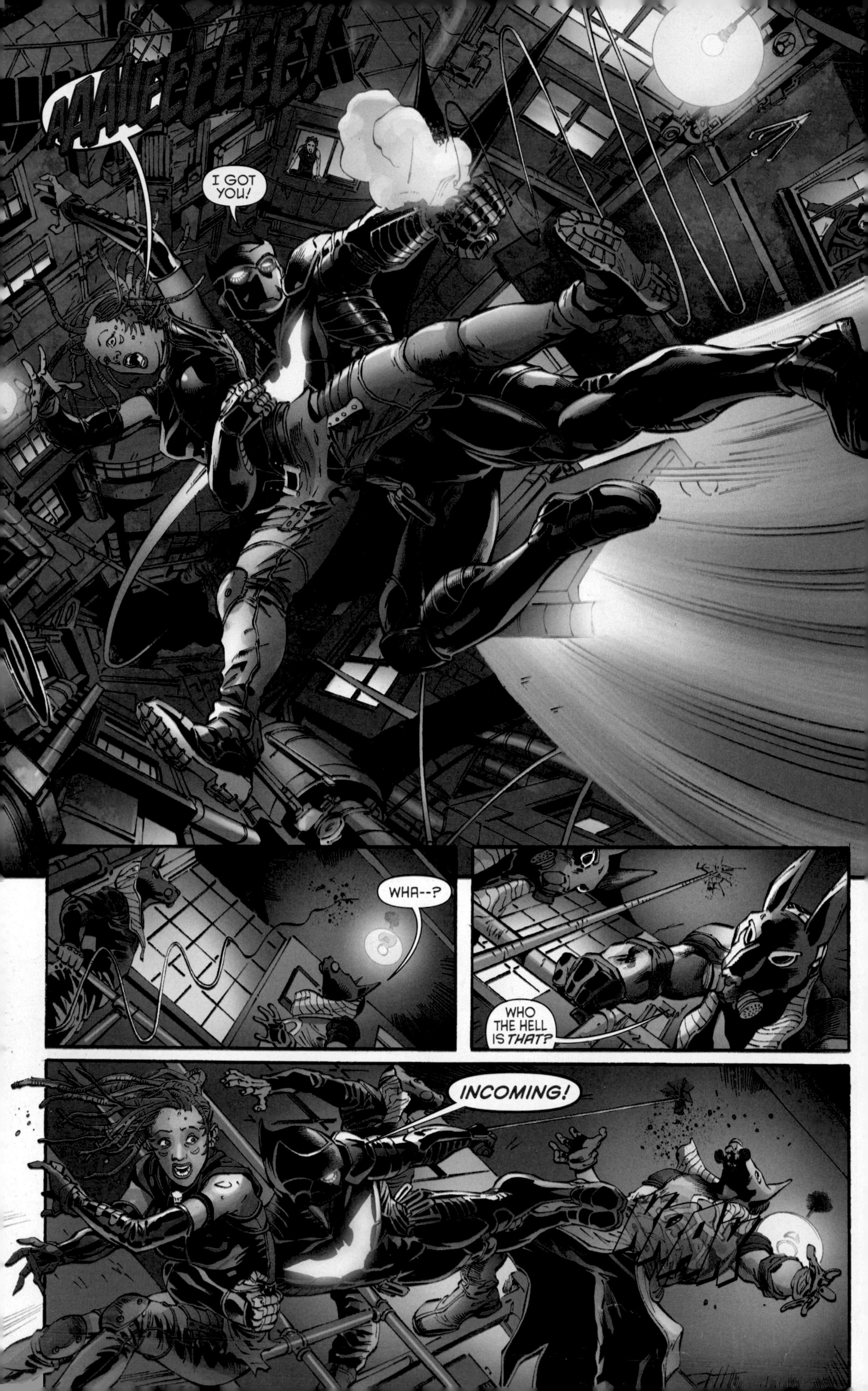
AAAIIEEEEEEE!
I GOT YOU!
WHA--?
WHO THE HELL IS THAT?
INCOMING!

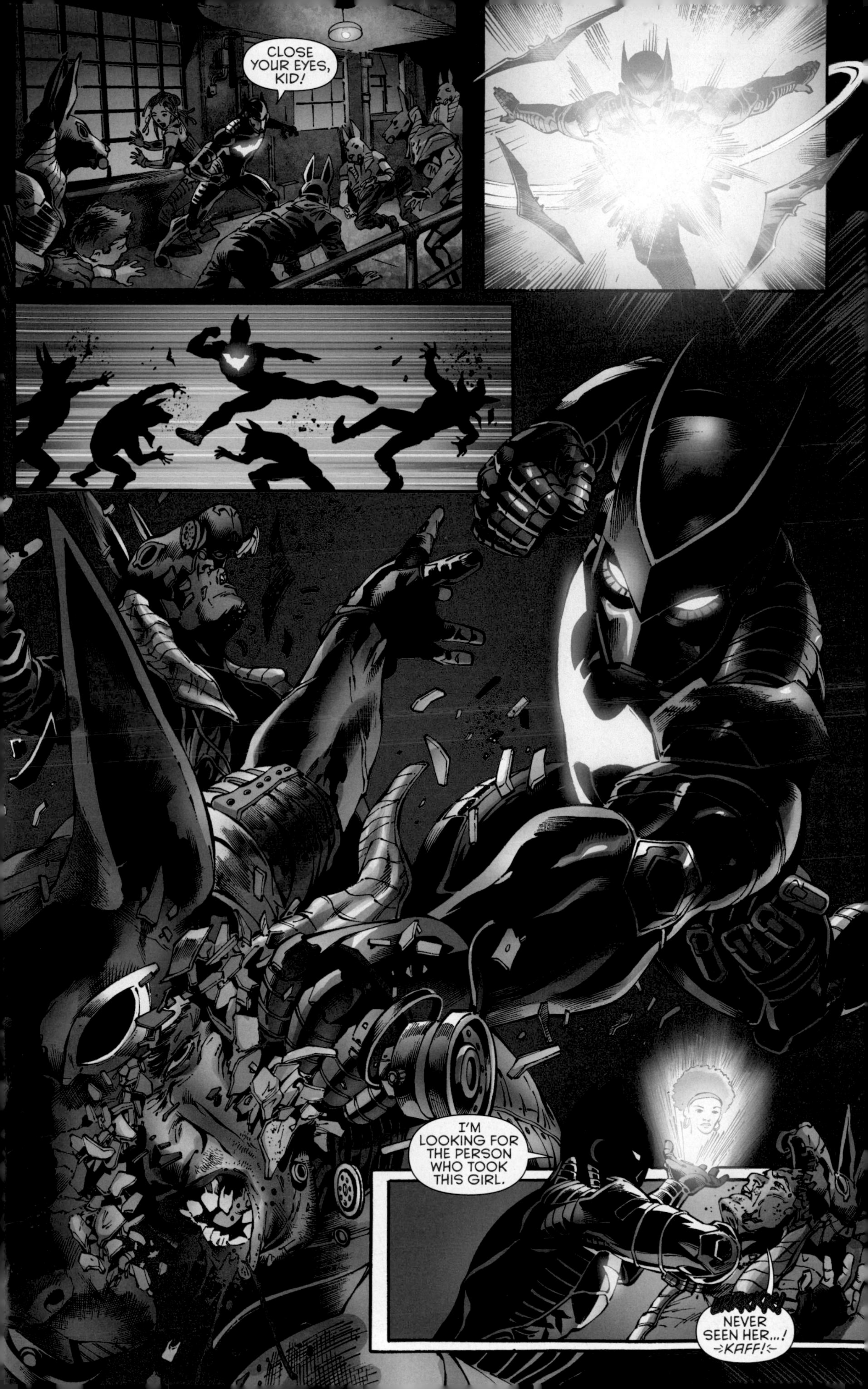
CLOSE YOUR EYES, KID!
I'M LOOKING FOR THE PERSON WHO TOOK THIS GIRL.
NEVER SEEN HER...! -KAFF!-

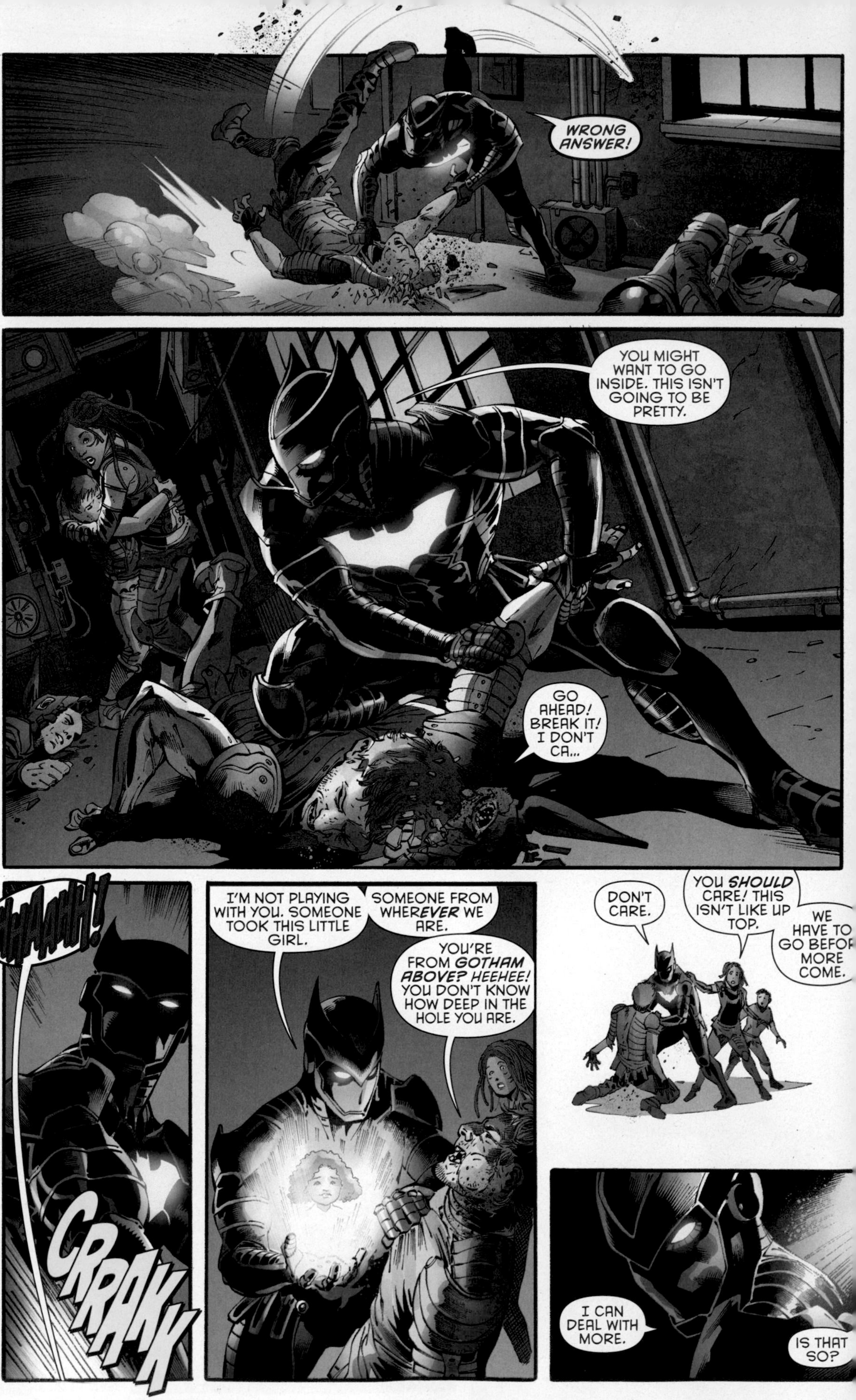
WRONG ANSWER!
YOU MIGHT WANT TO GO INSIDE. THIS ISN'T GOING TO BE PRETTY.
GO AHEAD! BREAK IT! I DON'T CA...
CRRAKK
I'M NOT PLAYING WITH YOU. SOMEONE TOOK THIS LITTLE GIRL.
SOMEONE FROM WHEREVER WE ARE.
YOU'RE FROM GOTHAM ABOVE? HEEHEE! YOU DON'T KNOW HOW DEEP IN THE HOLE YOU ARE.
DON'T CARE.
YOU SHOULD CARE! THIS ISN'T LIKE UP TOP.
WE HAVE TO GO BEFOR MORE COME.
I CAN DEAL WITH MORE.
IS THAT SO?

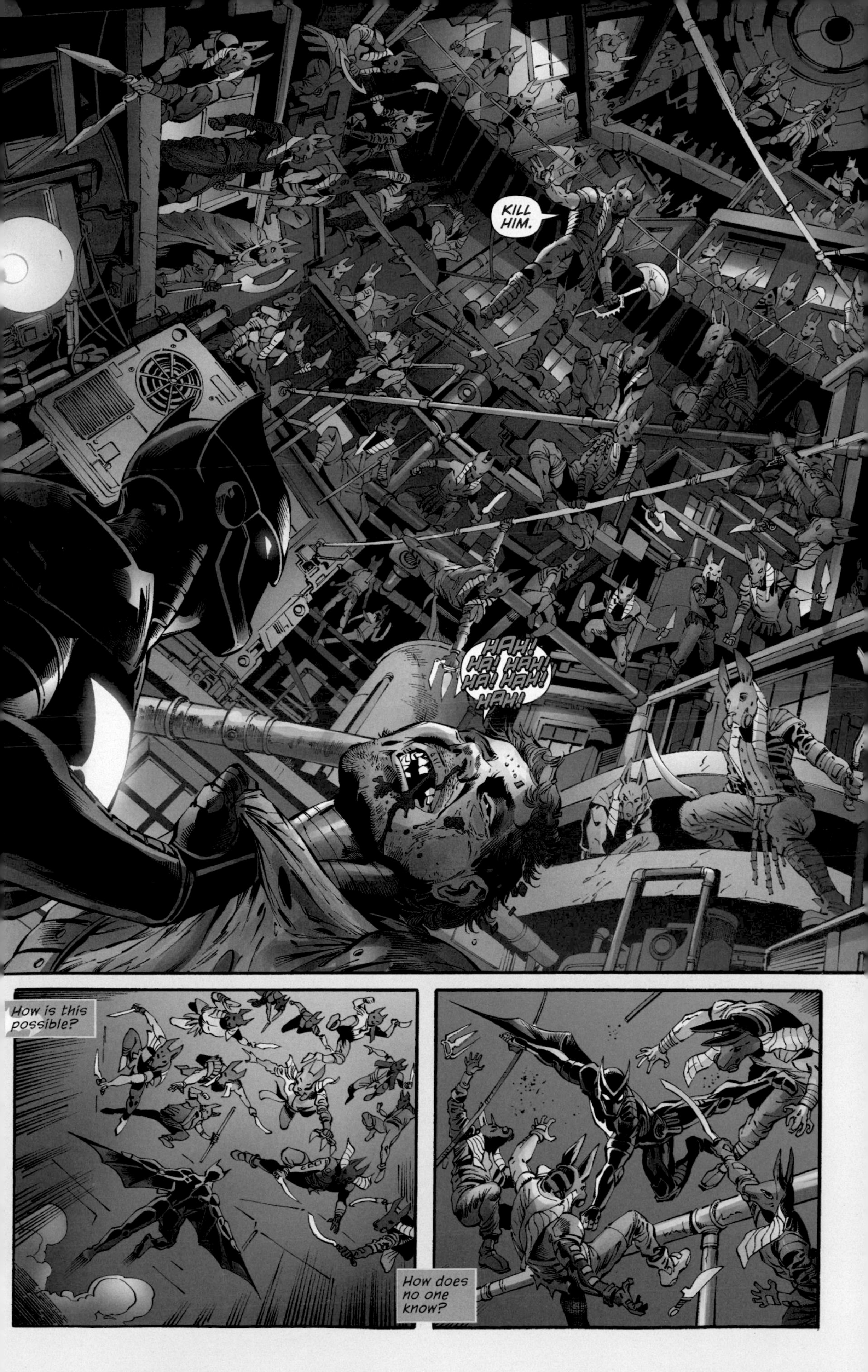

KILL HIM.
HAH! HA! HAH! HA! HAH! HAH!
How is this possible?
How does no one know?

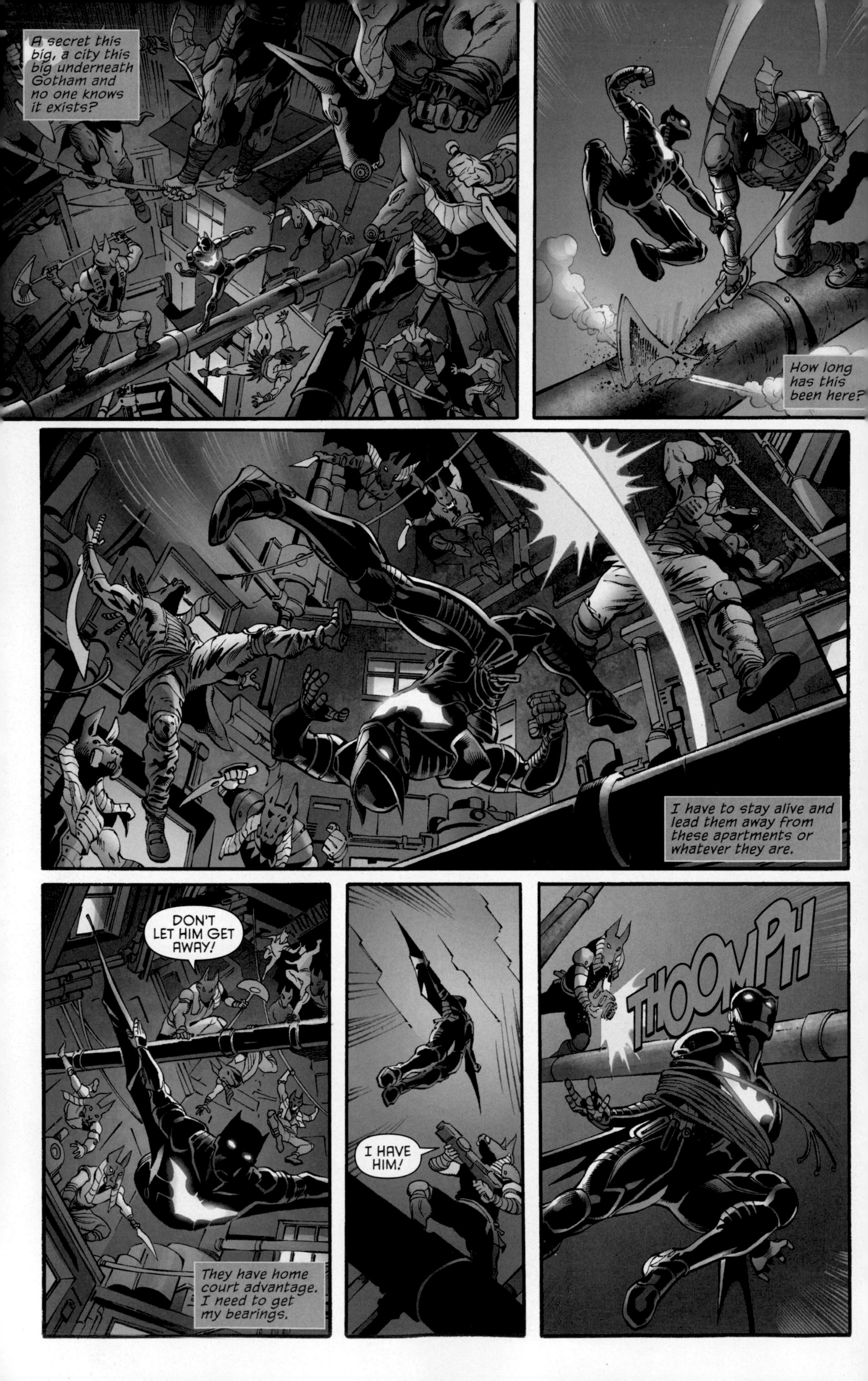
A secret this big, a city this big underneath Gotham and no one knows it exists?
How long has this been here?
I have to stay alive and lead them away from these apartments or whatever they are.
DON'T LET HIM GET AWAY!
They have home court advantage. I need to get my bearings.
I HAVE HIM!
THOOMPH

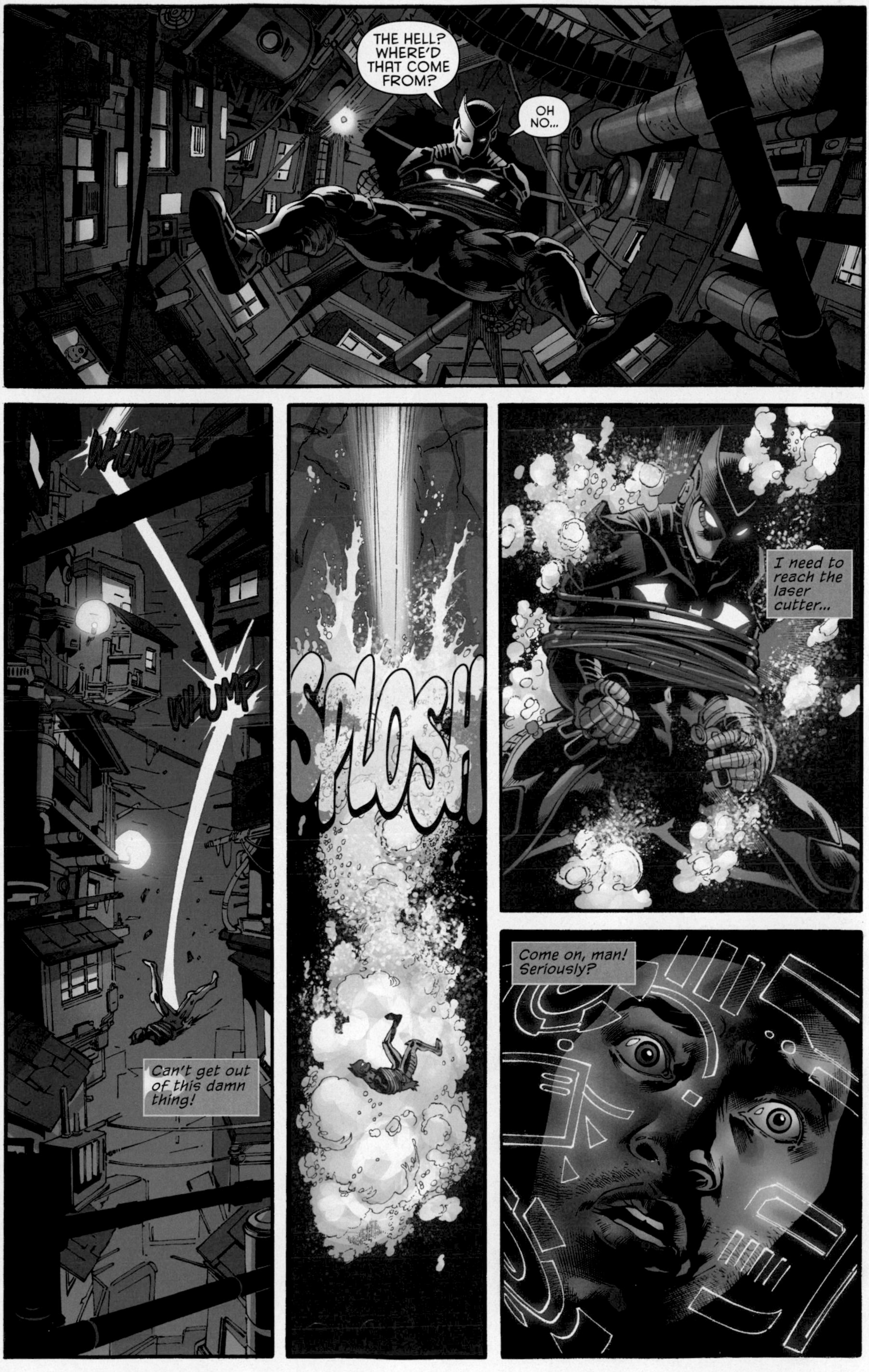
THE HELL? WHERE'D THAT COME FROM?
OH NO...
WHUMP
WHUMP
Can't get out of this damn thing!
SPLOSH
I need to reach the laser cutter...
Come on, man! Seriously?

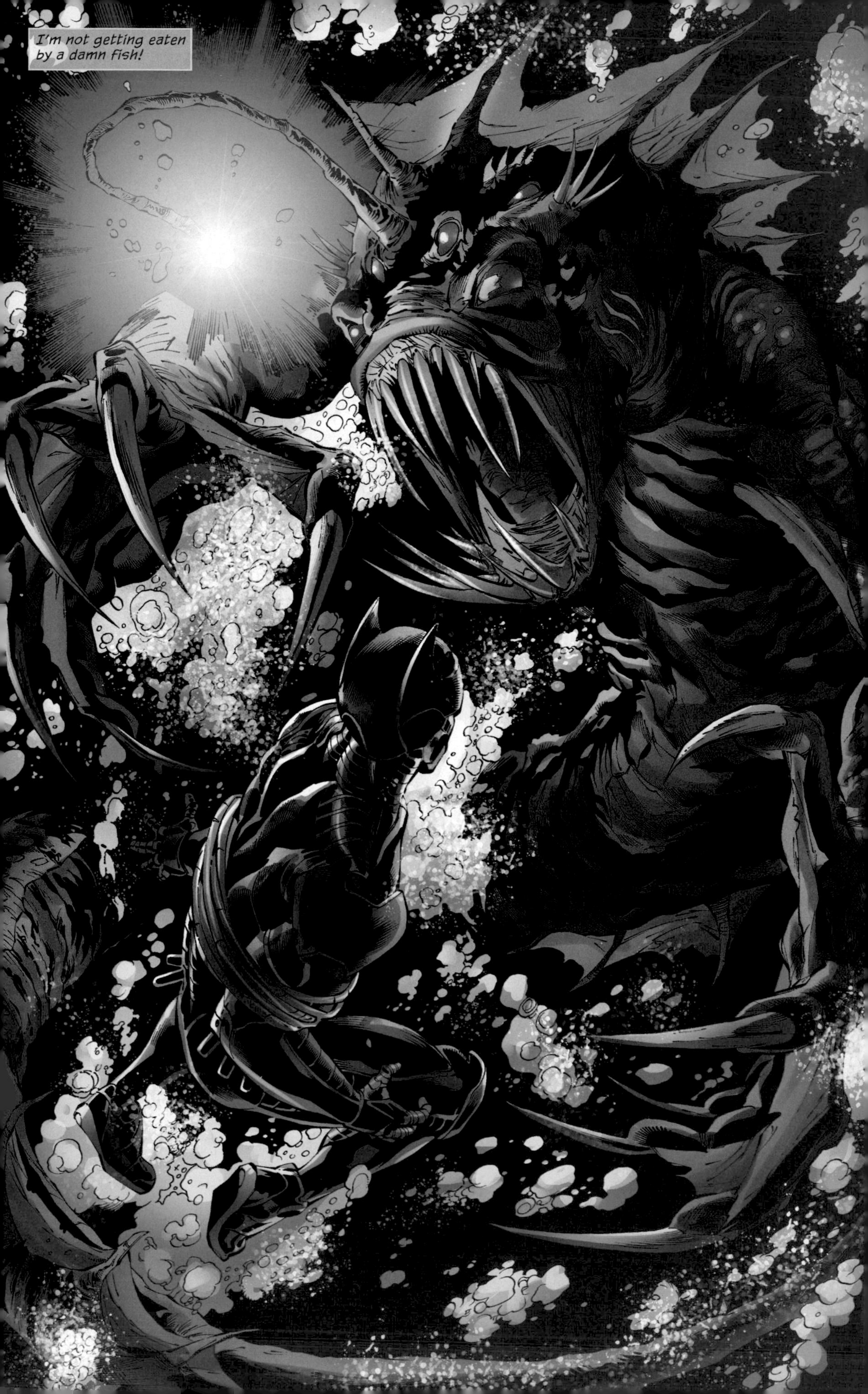
I'm not getting eaten by a damn fish!

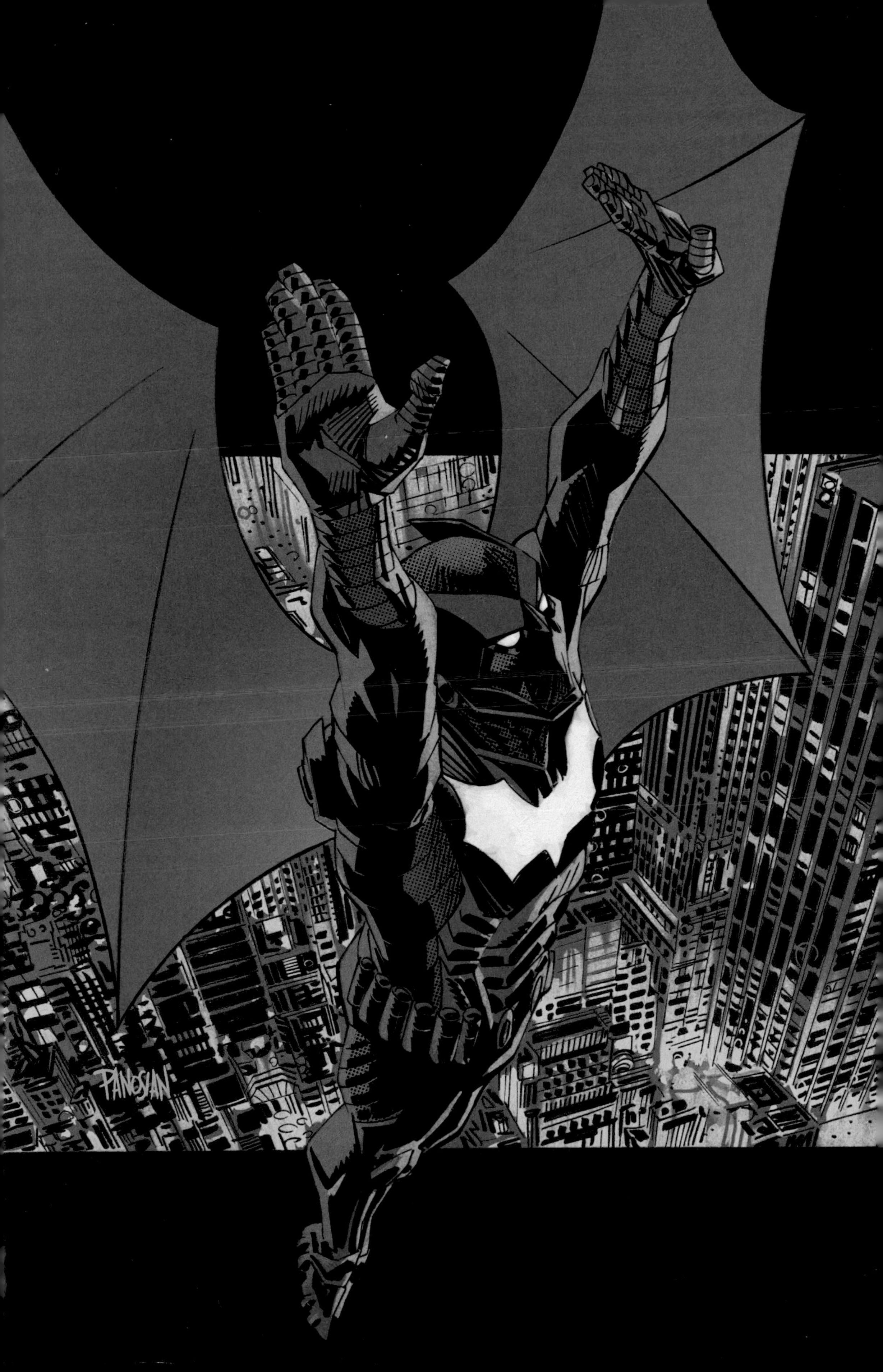
PANOSIAN

UNDERBELLY

JIMMY PALMIOTTI
JUSTIN GRAY
writers

EDUARDO PANSICA
penciller

JÚLIO FERREIRA
inker

PAUL MOUNTS
colorist

TAYLOR ESPOSITO
letterer

cover art by
DAN PANOSIAN

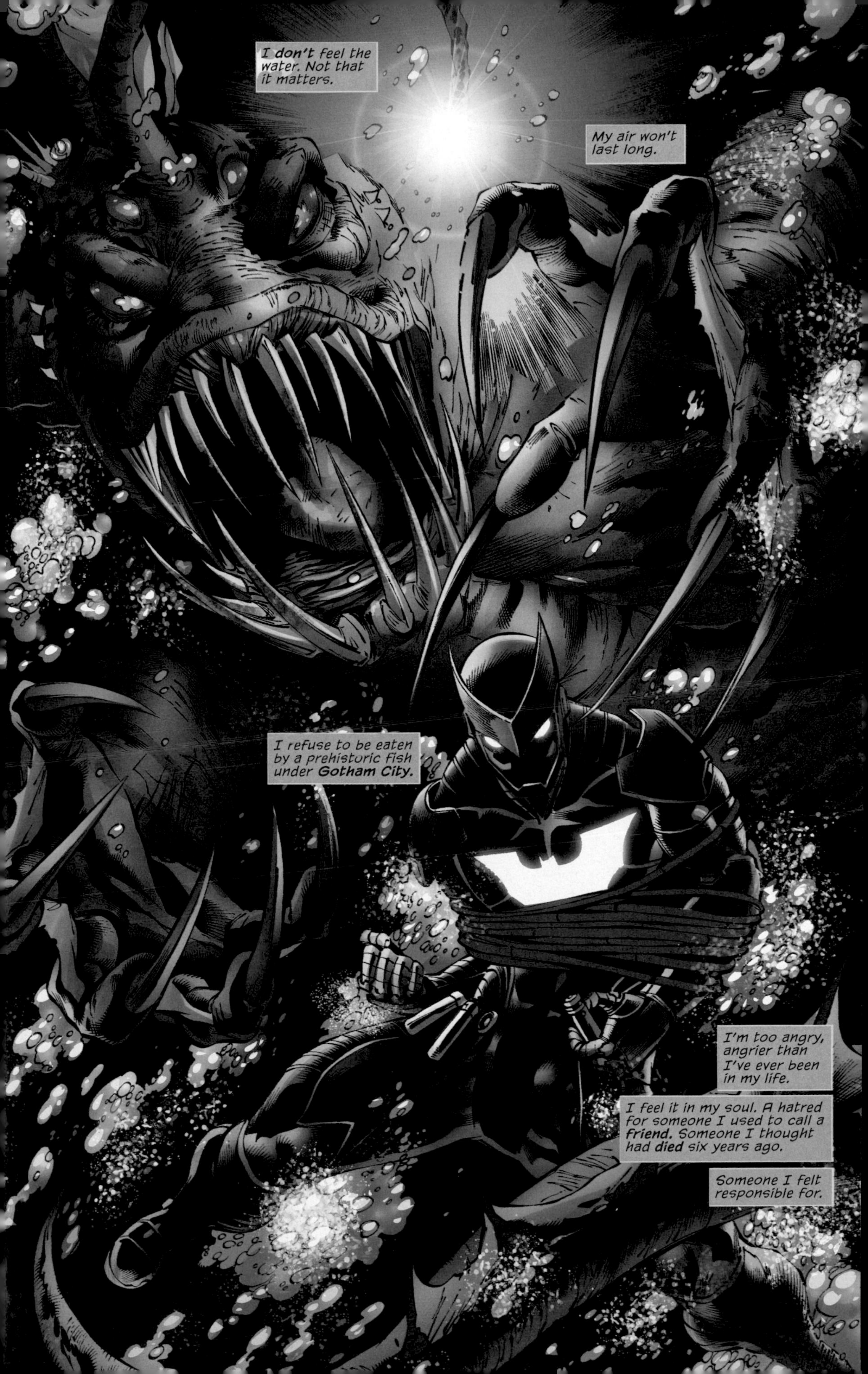
I don't feel the water. Not that it matters.
My air won't last long.
I refuse to be eaten by a prehistoric fish under Gotham City.
I'm too angry, angrier than I've ever been in my life.
I feel it in my soul. A hatred for someone I used to call a friend. Someone I thought had died six years ago.
Someone I felt responsible for.

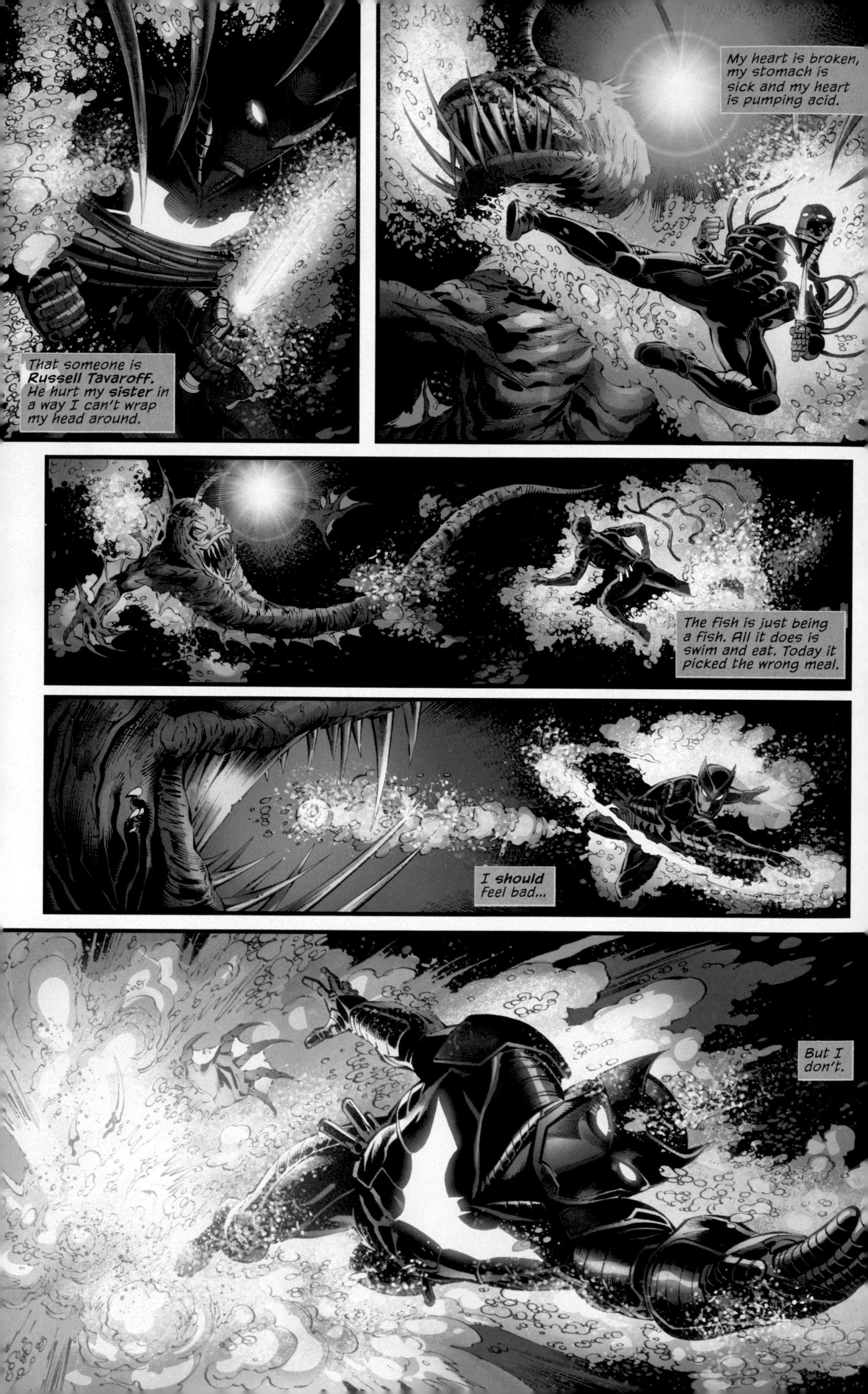
That someone is **Russell Tavaroff.** He hurt my **sister** in a way I can't wrap my head around.
My heart is broken, my stomach is sick and my heart is pumping acid.
The fish is just being a fish. All it does is swim and eat. Today it picked the wrong meal.
I should feel bad...
But I don't.

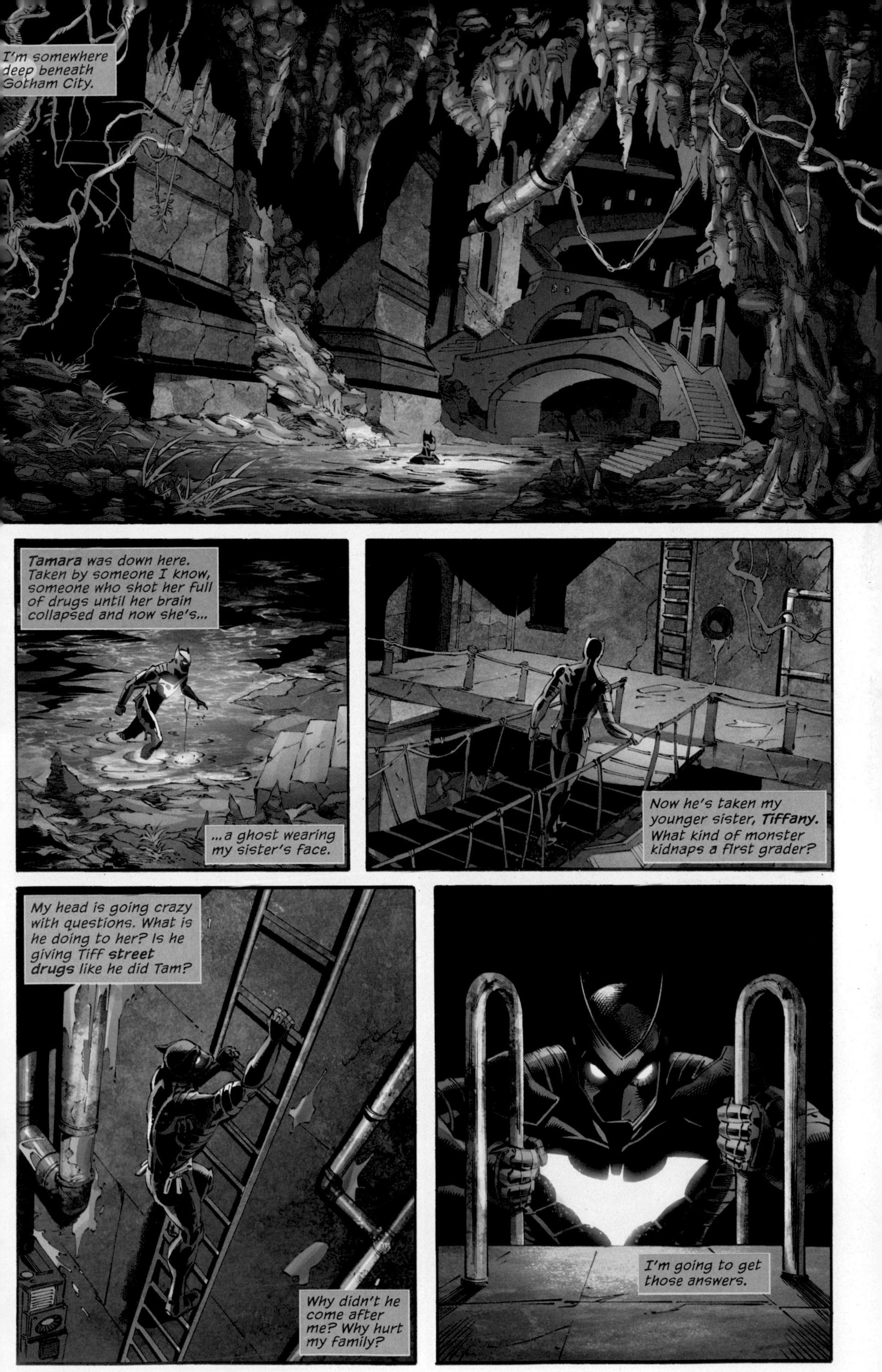

I'm somewhere deep beneath Gotham City.
Tamara was down here. Taken by someone I know, someone who shot her full of drugs until her brain collapsed and now she's...
...a ghost wearing my sister's face.
Now he's taken my younger sister, Tiffany. What kind of monster kidnaps a first grader?
My head is going crazy with questions. What is he doing to her? Is he giving Tiff street drugs like he did Tam?
Why didn't he come after me? Why hurt my family?
I'm going to get those answers.

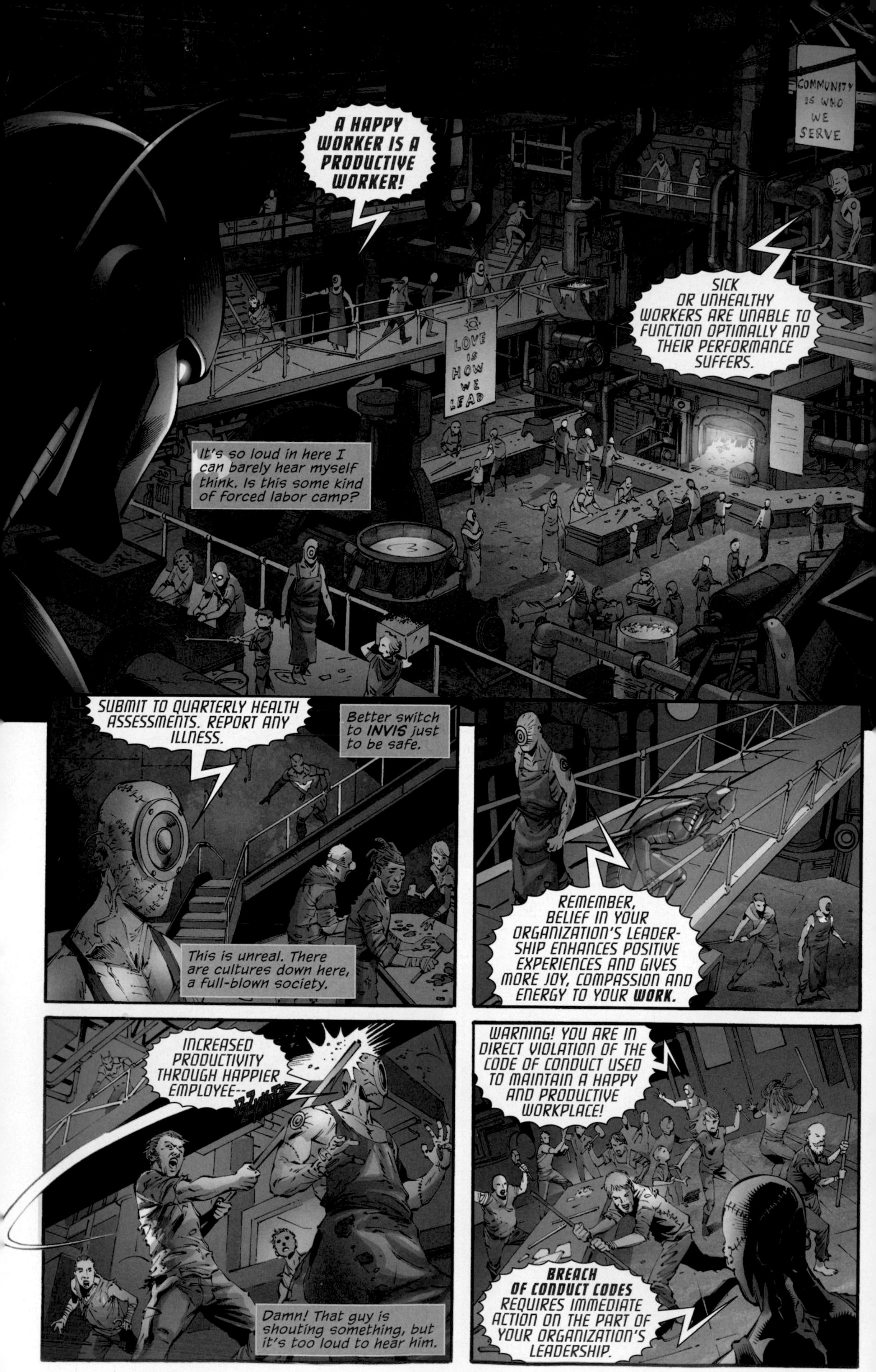
COMMUNITY IS WHO WE SERVE
A HAPPY WORKER IS A PRODUCTIVE WORKER!
SICK OR UNHEALTHY WORKERS ARE UNABLE TO FUNCTION OPTIMALLY AND THEIR PERFORMANCE SUFFERS.
LOVE IS HOW WE LEAD
It's so loud in here I can barely hear myself think. Is this some kind of forced labor camp?
SUBMIT TO QUARTERLY HEALTH ASSESSMENTS. REPORT ANY ILLNESS.
Better switch to INVIS just to be safe.
This is unreal. There are cultures down here, a full-blown society.
REMEMBER, BELIEF IN YOUR ORGANIZATION'S LEADERSHIP ENHANCES POSITIVE EXPERIENCES AND GIVES MORE JOY, COMPASSION AND ENERGY TO YOUR WORK.
INCREASED PRODUCTIVITY THROUGH HAPPIER EMPLOYEE--
Damn! That guy is shouting something, but it's too loud to hear him.
WARNING! YOU ARE IN DIRECT VIOLATION OF THE CODE OF CONDUCT USED TO MAINTAIN A HAPPY AND PRODUCTIVE WORKPLACE!
BREACH OF CONDUCT CODES REQUIRES IMMEDIATE ACTION ON THE PART OF YOUR ORGANIZATION'S LEADERSHIP.

They're killing them with **sound!**

The suit's audio dampeners are working well enough.

Still, there's no reason to risk a direct **sonic blast** from these freaks.

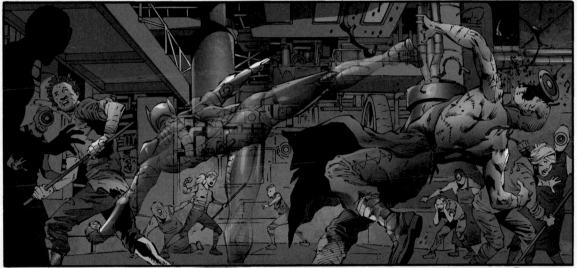

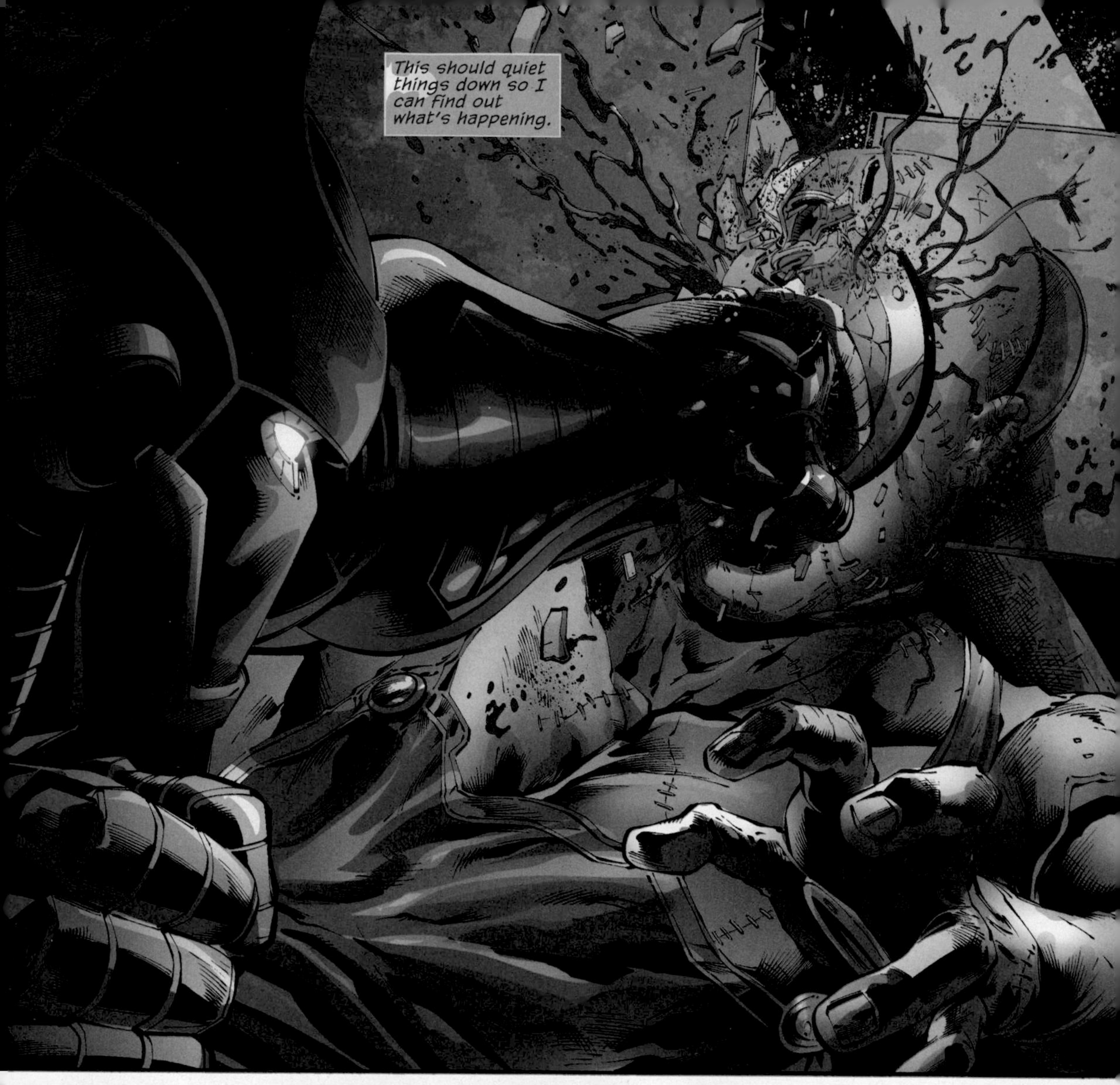
This should quiet things down so I can find out what's happening.

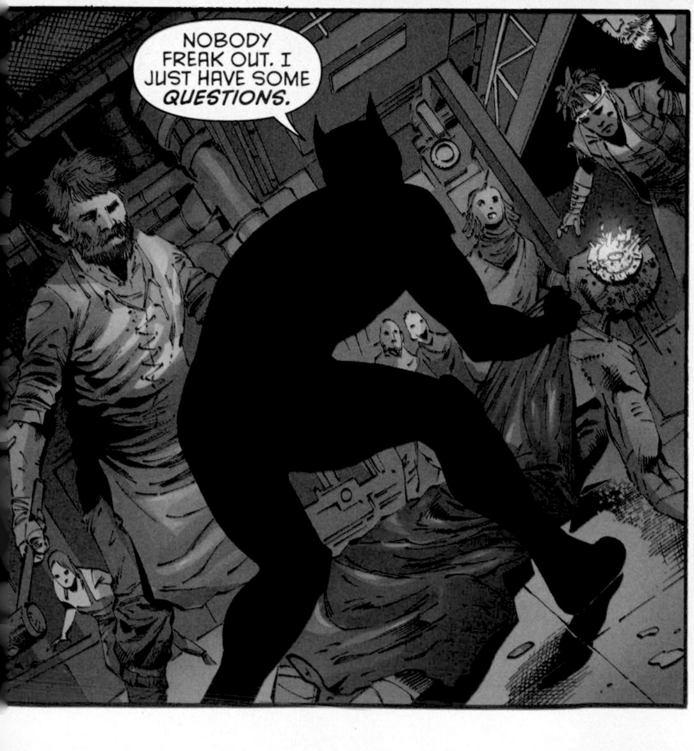
NOBODY FREAK OUT. I JUST HAVE SOME *QUESTIONS.*

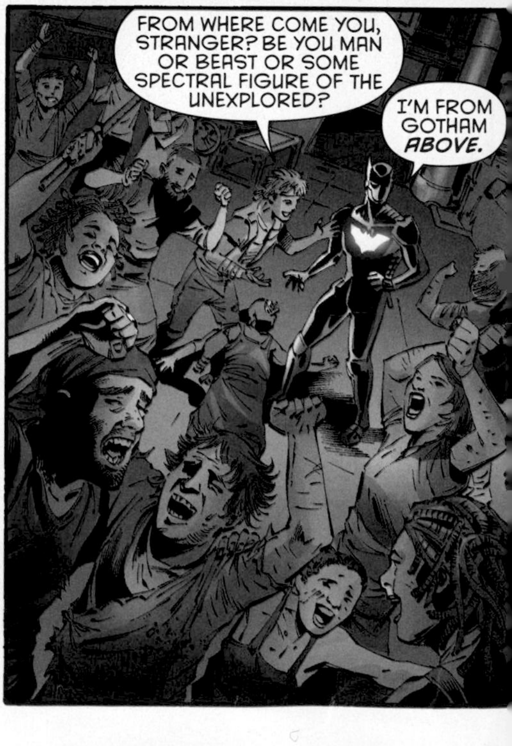
FROM WHERE COME YOU, STRANGER? BE YOU MAN OR BEAST OR SOME SPECTRAL FIGURE OF THE UNEXPLORED?
I'M FROM GOTHAM *ABOVE.*

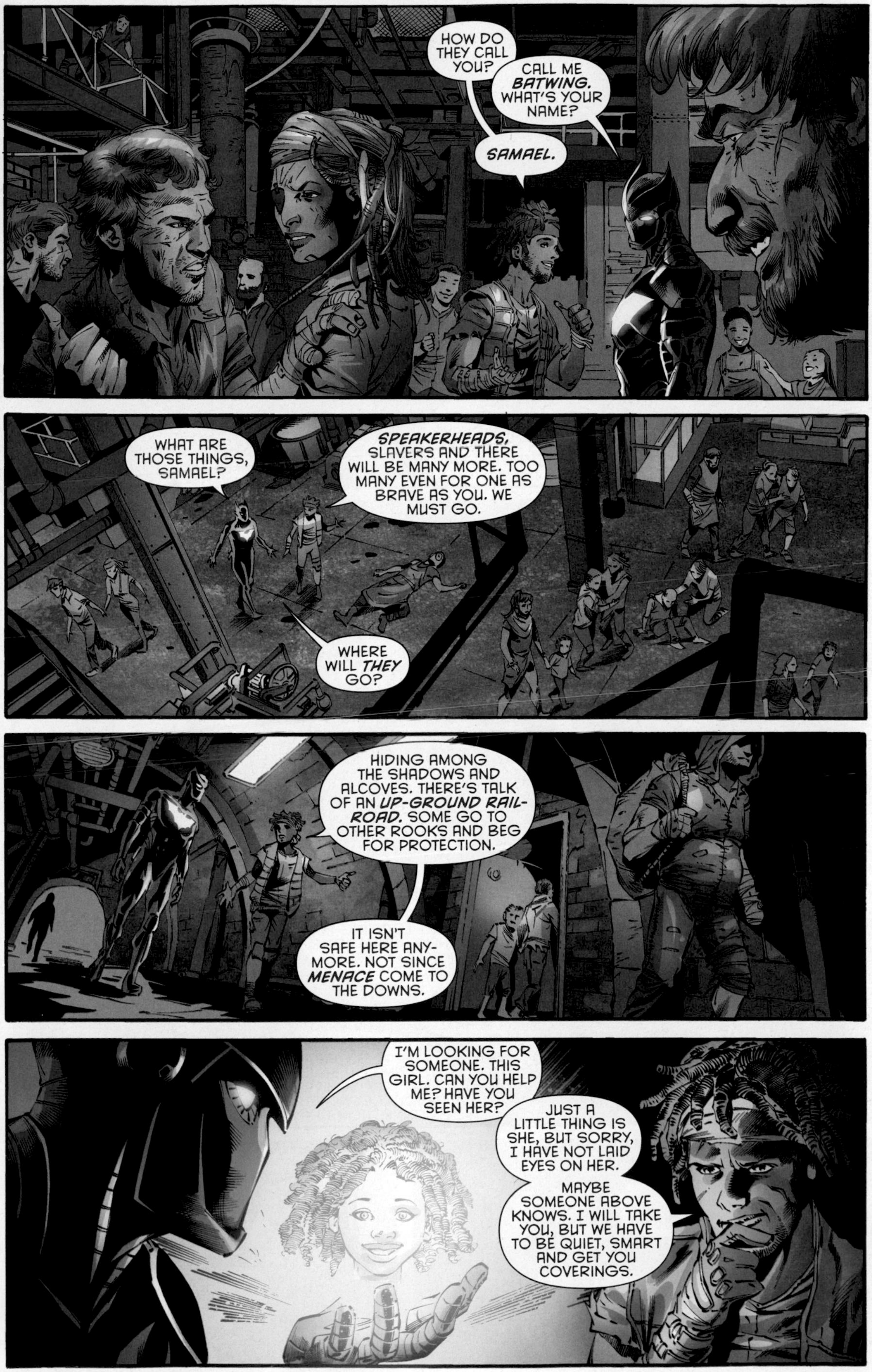
HOW DO THEY CALL YOU?
CALL ME BATWING. WHAT'S YOUR NAME?
SAMAEL.
WHAT ARE THOSE THINGS, SAMAEL?
SPEAKERHEADS, SLAVERS AND THERE WILL BE MANY MORE. TOO MANY EVEN FOR ONE AS BRAVE AS YOU. WE MUST GO.
WHERE WILL THEY GO?
HIDING AMONG THE SHADOWS AND ALCOVES. THERE'S TALK OF AN UP-GROUND RAIL-ROAD. SOME GO TO OTHER ROOKS AND BEG FOR PROTECTION.
IT ISN'T SAFE HERE ANY-MORE. NOT SINCE MENACE COME TO THE DOWNS.
I'M LOOKING FOR SOMEONE. THIS GIRL. CAN YOU HELP ME? HAVE YOU SEEN HER?
JUST A LITTLE THING IS SHE, BUT SORRY, I HAVE NOT LAID EYES ON HER.
MAYBE SOMEONE ABOVE KNOWS. I WILL TAKE YOU, BUT WE HAVE TO BE QUIET, SMART AND GET YOU COVERINGS.

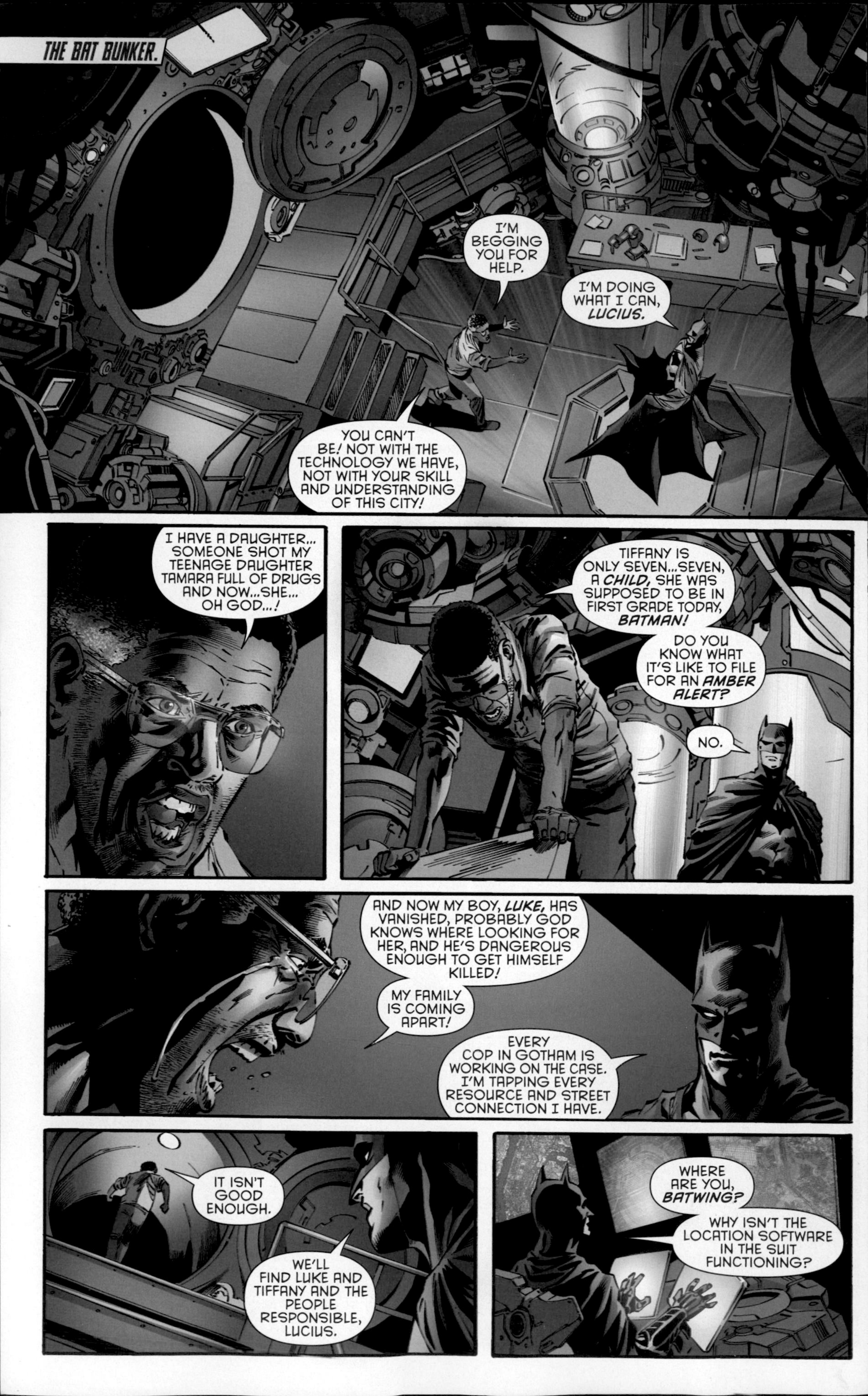
THE BAT BUNKER.
I'M BEGGING YOU FOR HELP.
I'M DOING WHAT I CAN, LUCIUS.
YOU CAN'T BE! NOT WITH THE TECHNOLOGY WE HAVE, NOT WITH YOUR SKILL AND UNDERSTANDING OF THIS CITY!
I HAVE A DAUGHTER... SOMEONE SHOT MY TEENAGE DAUGHTER TAMARA FULL OF DRUGS AND NOW...SHE... OH GOD...!
TIFFANY IS ONLY SEVEN...SEVEN, A CHILD, SHE WAS SUPPOSED TO BE IN FIRST GRADE TODAY, BATMAN!
DO YOU KNOW WHAT IT'S LIKE TO FILE FOR AN AMBER ALERT?
NO.
AND NOW MY BOY, LUKE, HAS VANISHED, PROBABLY GOD KNOWS WHERE LOOKING FOR HER, AND HE'S DANGEROUS ENOUGH TO GET HIMSELF KILLED!
MY FAMILY IS COMING APART!
EVERY COP IN GOTHAM IS WORKING ON THE CASE. I'M TAPPING EVERY RESOURCE AND STREET CONNECTION I HAVE.
IT ISN'T GOOD ENOUGH.
WE'LL FIND LUKE AND TIFFANY AND THE PEOPLE RESPONSIBLE, LUCIUS.
WHERE ARE YOU, BATWING?
WHY ISN'T THE LOCATION SOFTWARE IN THE SUIT FUNCTIONING?

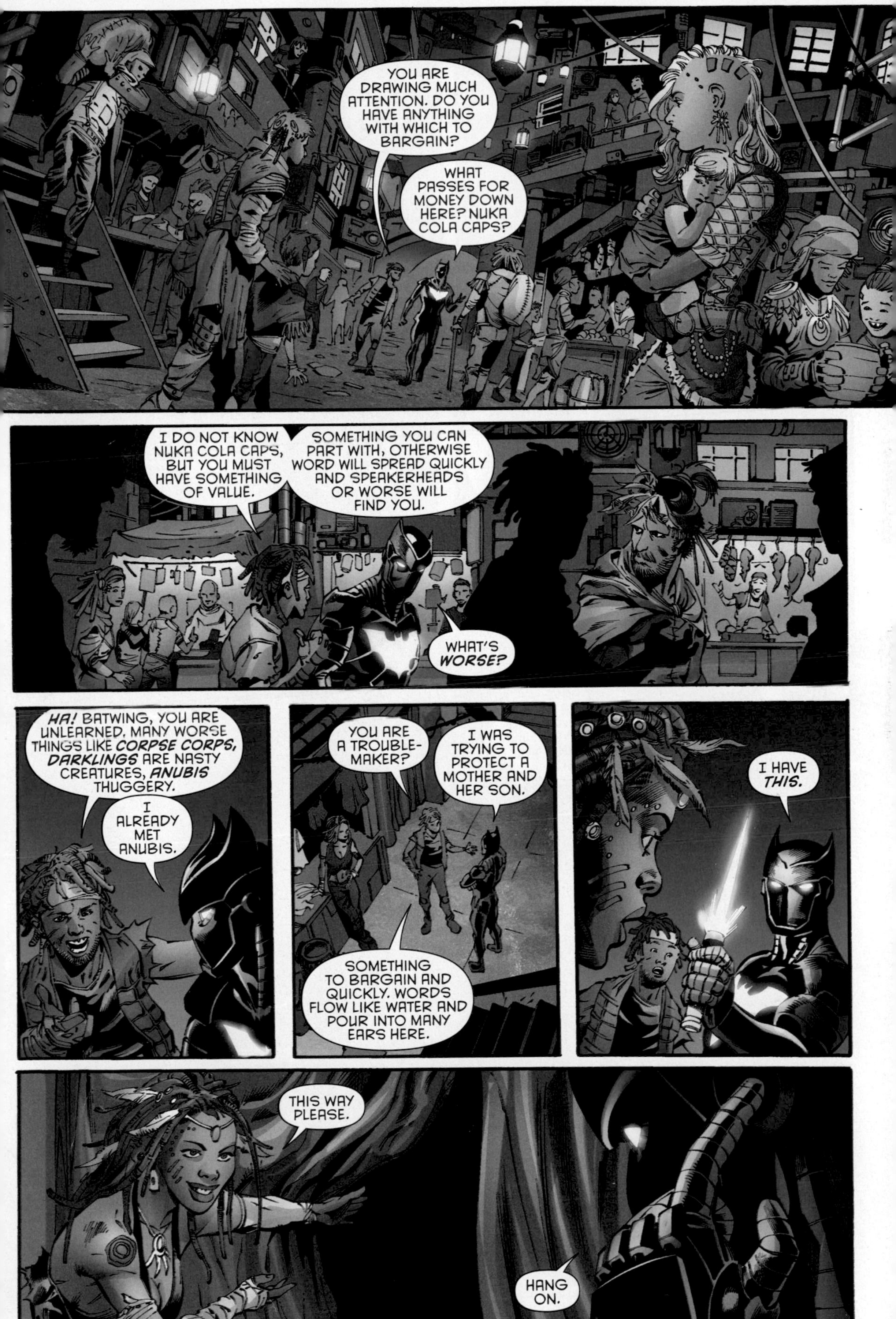
YOU ARE DRAWING MUCH ATTENTION. DO YOU HAVE ANYTHING WITH WHICH TO BARGAIN?
WHAT PASSES FOR MONEY DOWN HERE? NUKA COLA CAPS?
I DO NOT KNOW NUKA COLA CAPS, BUT YOU MUST HAVE SOMETHING OF VALUE.
SOMETHING YOU CAN PART WITH, OTHERWISE WORD WILL SPREAD QUICKLY AND SPEAKERHEADS OR WORSE WILL FIND YOU.
WHAT'S *WORSE?*
HA! BATWING, YOU ARE UNLEARNED. MANY WORSE THINGS LIKE *CORPSE CORPS, DARKLINGS* ARE NASTY CREATURES, *ANUBIS* THUGGERY.
I ALREADY MET ANUBIS.
YOU ARE A TROUBLE-MAKER?
I WAS TRYING TO PROTECT A MOTHER AND HER SON.
SOMETHING TO BARGAIN AND QUICKLY. WORDS FLOW LIKE WATER AND POUR INTO MANY EARS HERE.
I HAVE *THIS.*
THIS WAY PLEASE.
HANG ON.

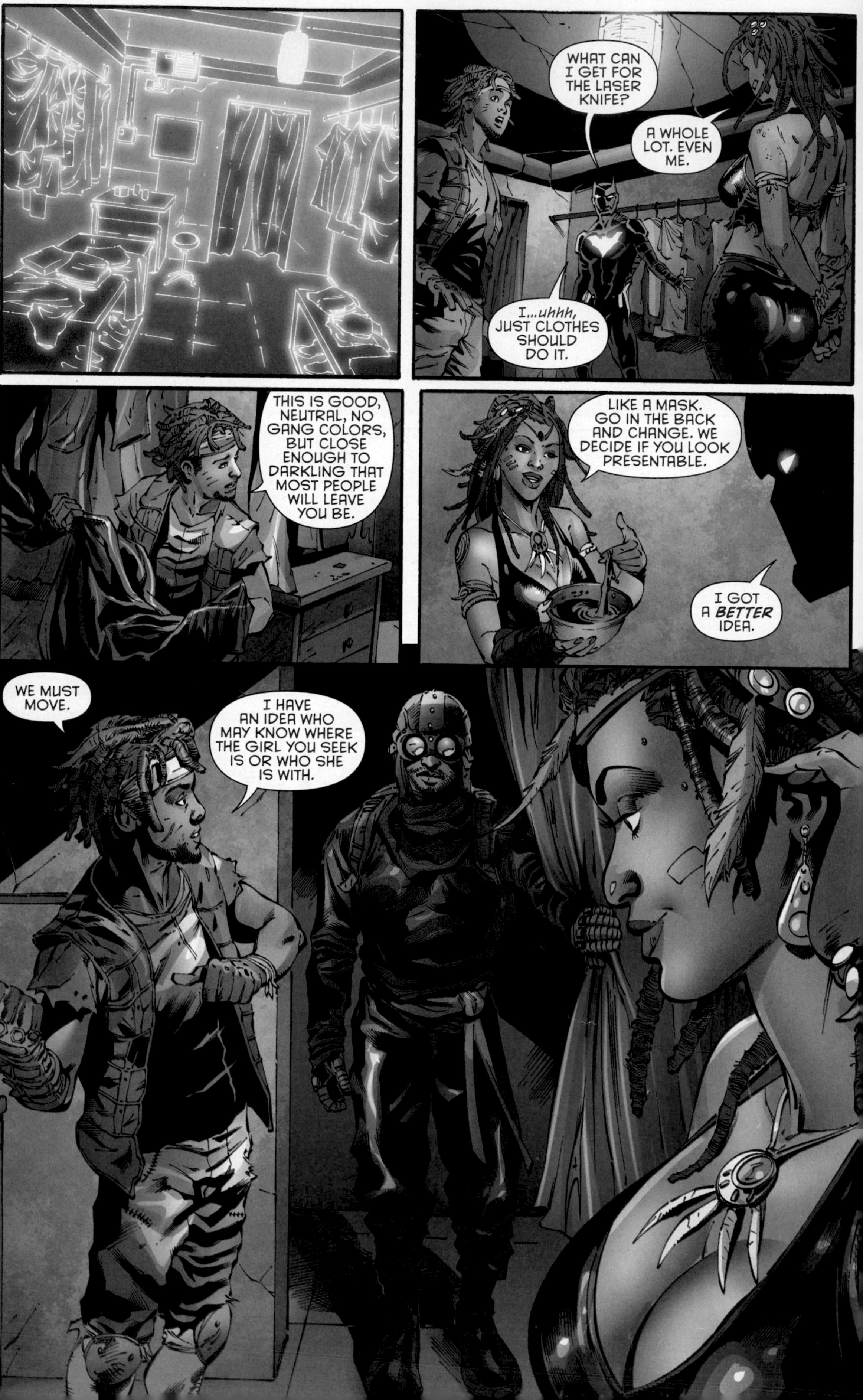
WHAT CAN I GET FOR THE LASER KNIFE?
A WHOLE LOT. EVEN ME.
I...uhhh, JUST CLOTHES SHOULD DO IT.
THIS IS GOOD, NEUTRAL, NO GANG COLORS, BUT CLOSE ENOUGH TO DARKLING THAT MOST PEOPLE WILL LEAVE YOU BE.
LIKE A MASK. GO IN THE BACK AND CHANGE. WE DECIDE IF YOU LOOK PRESENTABLE.
I GOT A *BETTER* IDEA.
WE MUST MOVE.
I HAVE AN IDEA WHO MAY KNOW WHERE THE GIRL YOU SEEK IS OR WHO SHE IS WITH.

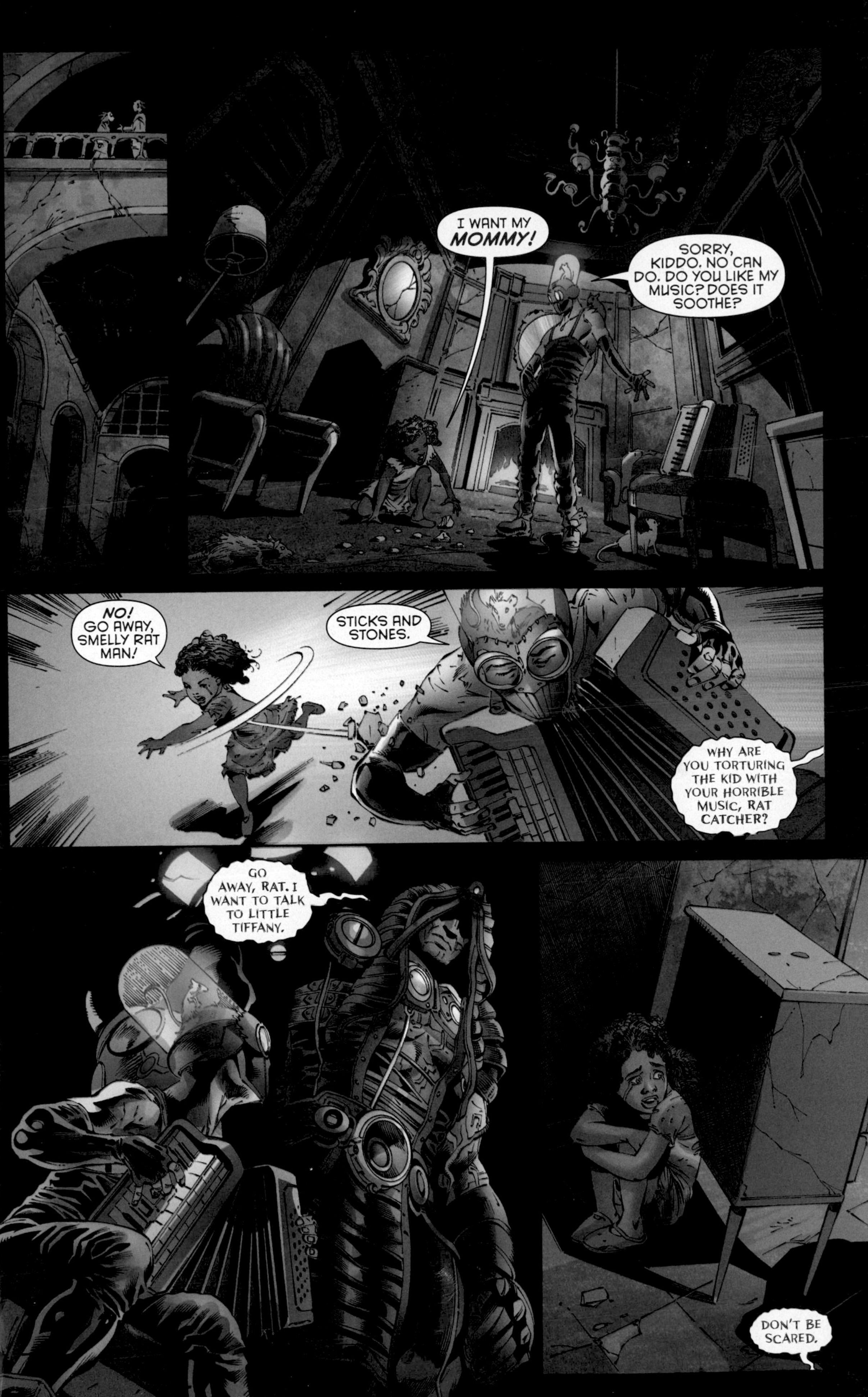
I WANT MY MOMMY!
SORRY, KIDDO. NO CAN DO. DO YOU LIKE MY MUSIC? DOES IT SOOTHE?
NO! GO AWAY, SMELLY RAT MAN!
STICKS AND STONES.
WHY ARE YOU TORTURING THE KID WITH YOUR HORRIBLE MUSIC, RAT CATCHER?
GO AWAY, RAT. I WANT TO TALK TO LITTLE TIFFANY.
DON'T BE SCARED.

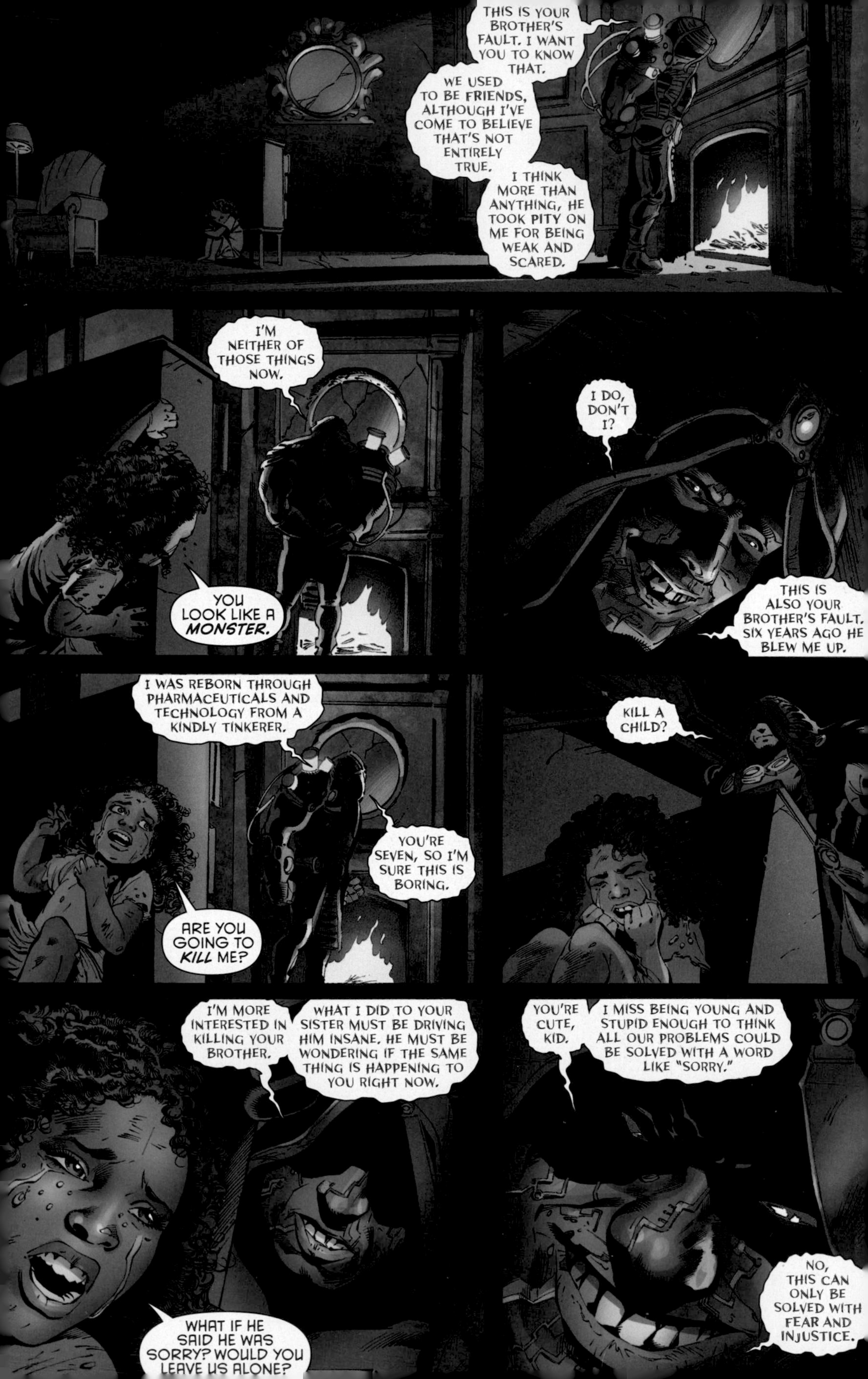
THIS IS YOUR BROTHER'S FAULT. I WANT YOU TO KNOW THAT.
WE USED TO BE FRIENDS, ALTHOUGH I'VE COME TO BELIEVE THAT'S NOT ENTIRELY TRUE.
I THINK MORE THAN ANYTHING, HE TOOK PITY ON ME FOR BEING WEAK AND SCARED.
I'M NEITHER OF THOSE THINGS NOW.
YOU LOOK LIKE A MONSTER.
I DO, DON'T I?
THIS IS ALSO YOUR BROTHER'S FAULT. SIX YEARS AGO HE BLEW ME UP.
I WAS REBORN THROUGH PHARMACEUTICALS AND TECHNOLOGY FROM A KINDLY TINKERER.
YOU'RE SEVEN, SO I'M SURE THIS IS BORING.
ARE YOU GOING TO KILL ME?
KILL A CHILD?
I'M MORE INTERESTED IN KILLING YOUR BROTHER.
WHAT I DID TO YOUR SISTER MUST BE DRIVING HIM INSANE. HE MUST BE WONDERING IF THE SAME THING IS HAPPENING TO YOU RIGHT NOW.
WHAT IF HE SAID HE WAS SORRY? WOULD YOU LEAVE US ALONE?
YOU'RE CUTE, KID.
I MISS BEING YOUNG AND STUPID ENOUGH TO THINK ALL OUR PROBLEMS COULD BE SOLVED WITH A WORD LIKE "SORRY."
NO, THIS CAN ONLY BE SOLVED WITH FEAR AND INJUSTICE.

THERE MUST BE THOUSANDS OF PEOPLE DOWN HERE. HOW IS THAT POSSIBLE?

HOW IS ANY PLACE POSSIBLE? PEOPLE LIVE, WORK, HAVE BABIES, DIE...

BUT HOW DO YOU KEEP SOMETHING LIKE THIS A SECRET?

NO ONE CARES. PEOPLE COME HERE TO DISAPPEAR FROM THE ABOVE WORLD.

SOME GO BACK. SOME DO NOT.

YOU'RE SIPHONING POWER FROM THE CITY?

ALL OVER, THE SMARTIES AND LECTRICS FOUND A WAY TO USE THE OVERHEAD TRAINS TO POWER THINGS TOO.

THEY DON'T KNOW IT ABOVE, IT JUST HAPPENS.

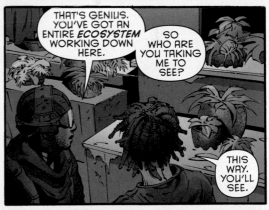

THAT'S GENIUS. YOU'VE GOT AN ENTIRE ECOSYSTEM WORKING DOWN HERE.

SO WHO ARE YOU TAKING ME TO SEE?

THIS WAY, YOU'LL SEE.

HOW DO THE SPEAKER-HEADS GET AWAY WITH FORCED LABOR?

PEOPLE NEED WHAT THEY PRODUCE AND SELL, SO PEOPLE LOOK THE OTHER WAY.

WON'T THEY COME LOOKING FOR YOU?

MOST DEFINITELY. I HAVE TO GET PROTECTION.

THAT WAY.

PROTECTION?

FROM PEOPLE THE SPEAKERHEADS FEAR.

LIKE WHO?

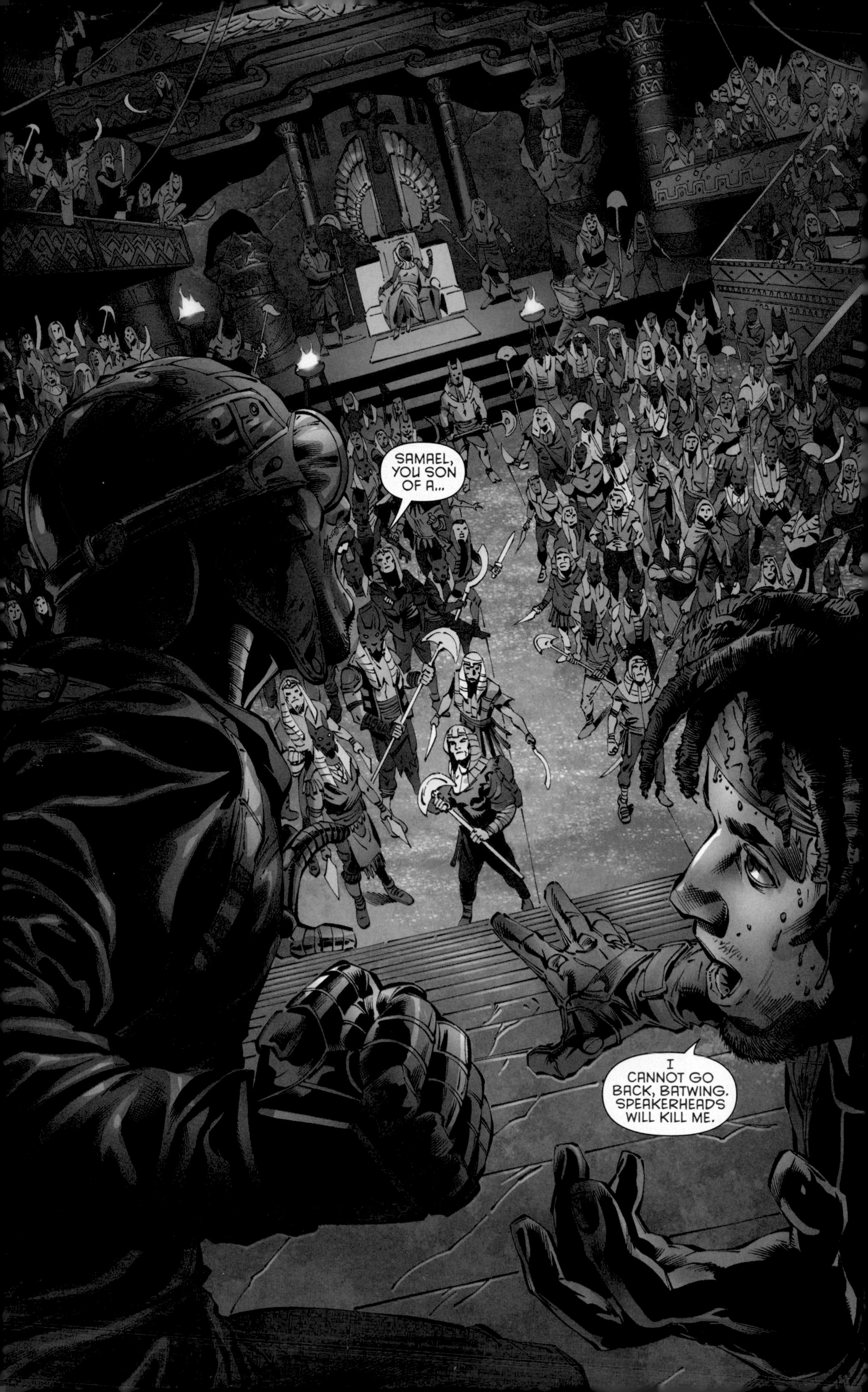
SAMAEL, YOU SON OF A...
I CANNOT GO BACK, BATWING. SPEAKERHEADS WILL KILL ME.

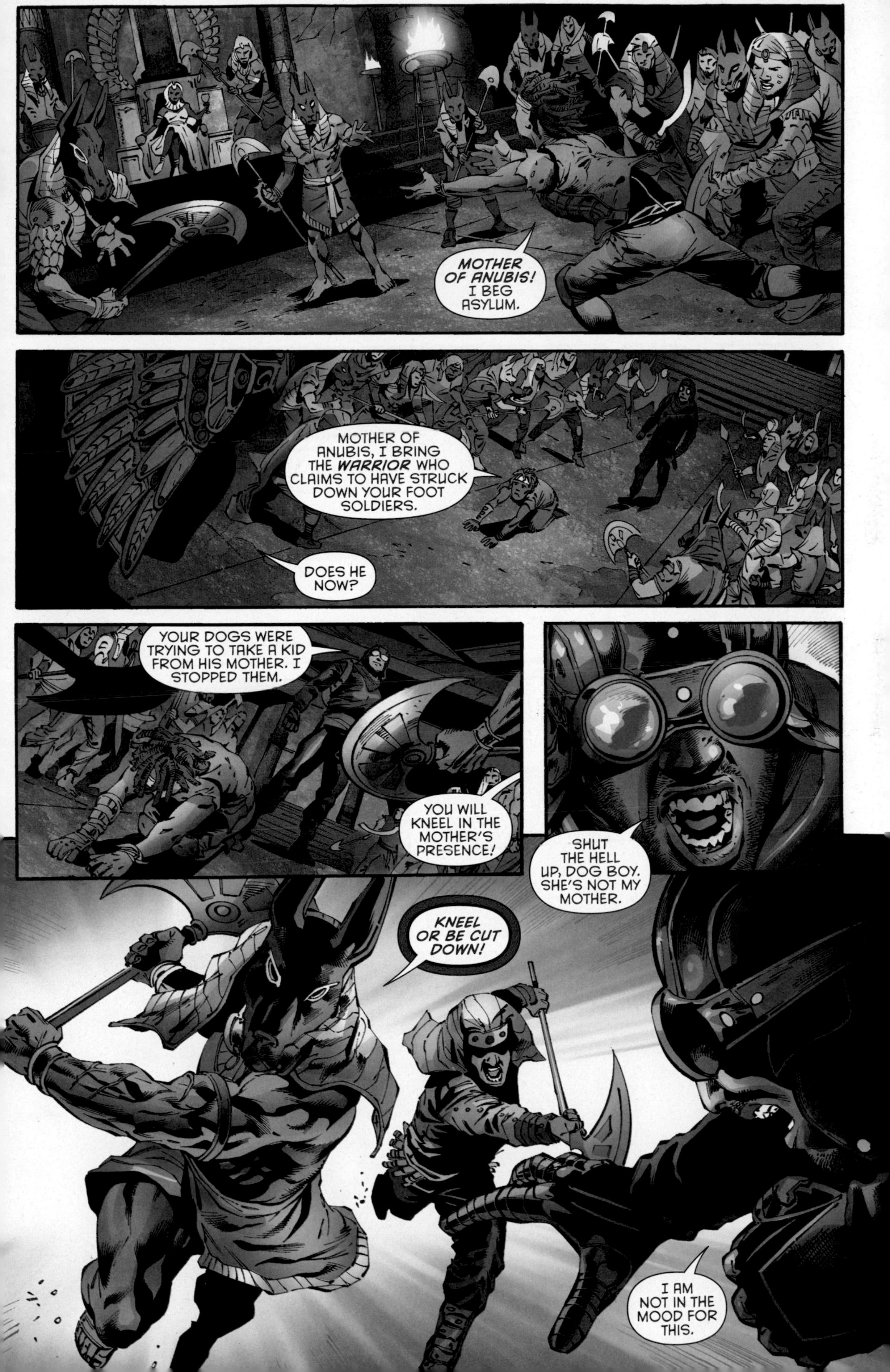

MOTHER OF ANUBIS! I BEG ASYLUM.
MOTHER OF ANUBIS, I BRING THE WARRIOR WHO CLAIMS TO HAVE STRUCK DOWN YOUR FOOT SOLDIERS.
DOES HE NOW?
YOUR DOGS WERE TRYING TO TAKE A KID FROM HIS MOTHER. I STOPPED THEM.
YOU WILL KNEEL IN THE MOTHER'S PRESENCE!
SHUT THE HELL UP, DOG BOY. SHE'S NOT MY MOTHER.
KNEEL OR BE CUT DOWN!
I AM NOT IN THE MOOD FOR THIS.

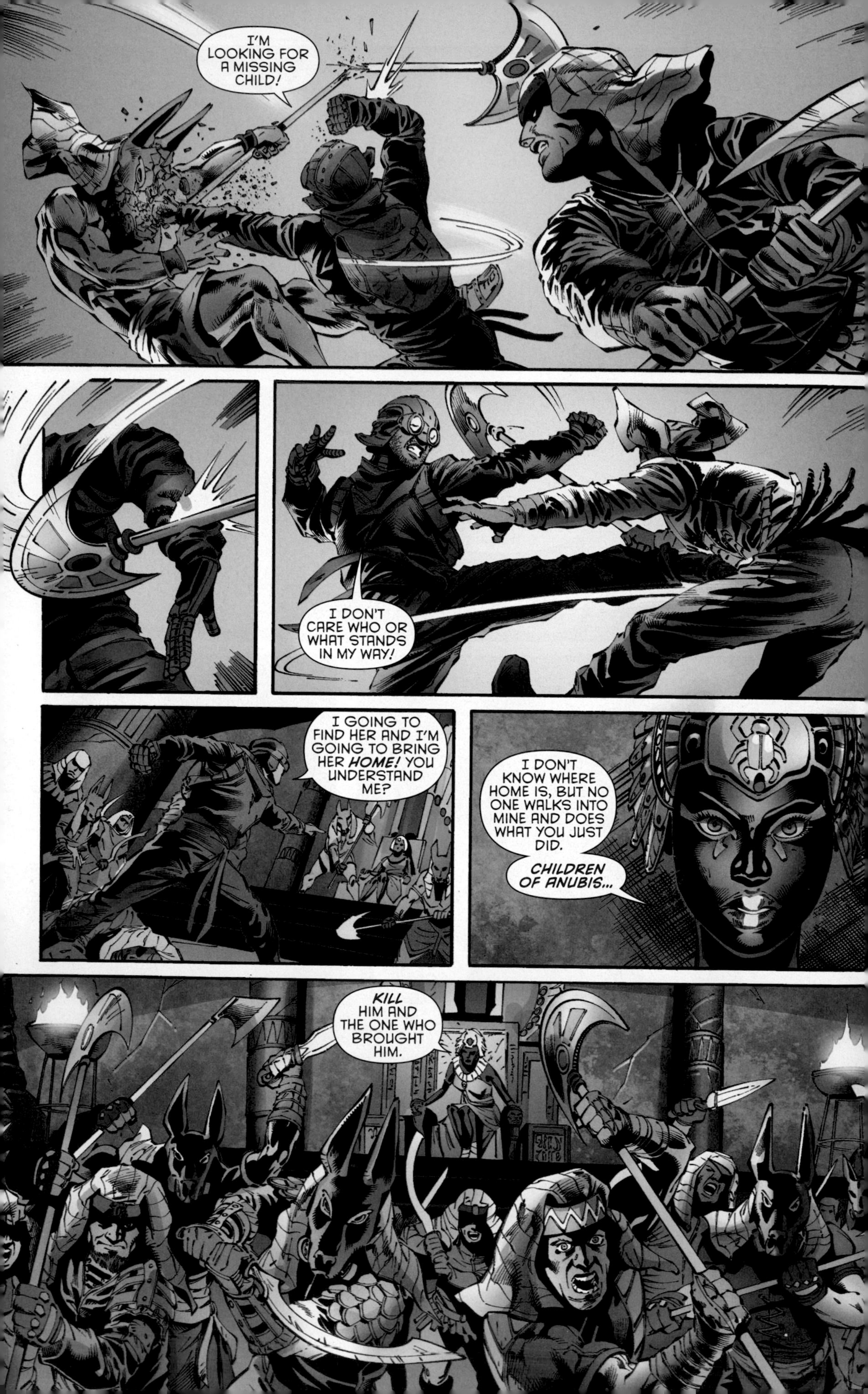
I'M LOOKING FOR A MISSING CHILD!
I DON'T CARE WHO OR WHAT STANDS IN MY WAY!
I GOING TO FIND HER AND I'M GOING TO BRING HER *HOME!* YOU UNDERSTAND ME?
I DON'T KNOW WHERE HOME IS, BUT NO ONE WALKS INTO MINE AND DOES WHAT YOU JUST DID.
CHILDREN OF ANUBIS...
KILL HIM AND THE ONE WHO BROUGHT HIM.

I'm trying not to get sucked into that dark place, but I welcome the rage in me. I embrace it.

I'm drunk on the heavy thud of my fists, the audible cracking of tooth and bone, the smell of their blood. I'm running on pure adrenaline and I know it won't last.

How does Batman do it? Does he cut off his emotions? Does he have no one he cares about?

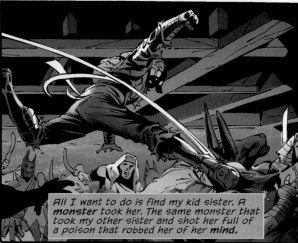

All I want to do is find my kid sister. A *monster* took her. The same monster that took my other sister and shot her full of a poison that robbed her of her *mind*.

I'm going to get tired soon. I might be used to five-minute rounds, but they come with breaks and water and smelling salts.

Fighting these Anubis *idiots* is a waste of time and energy.

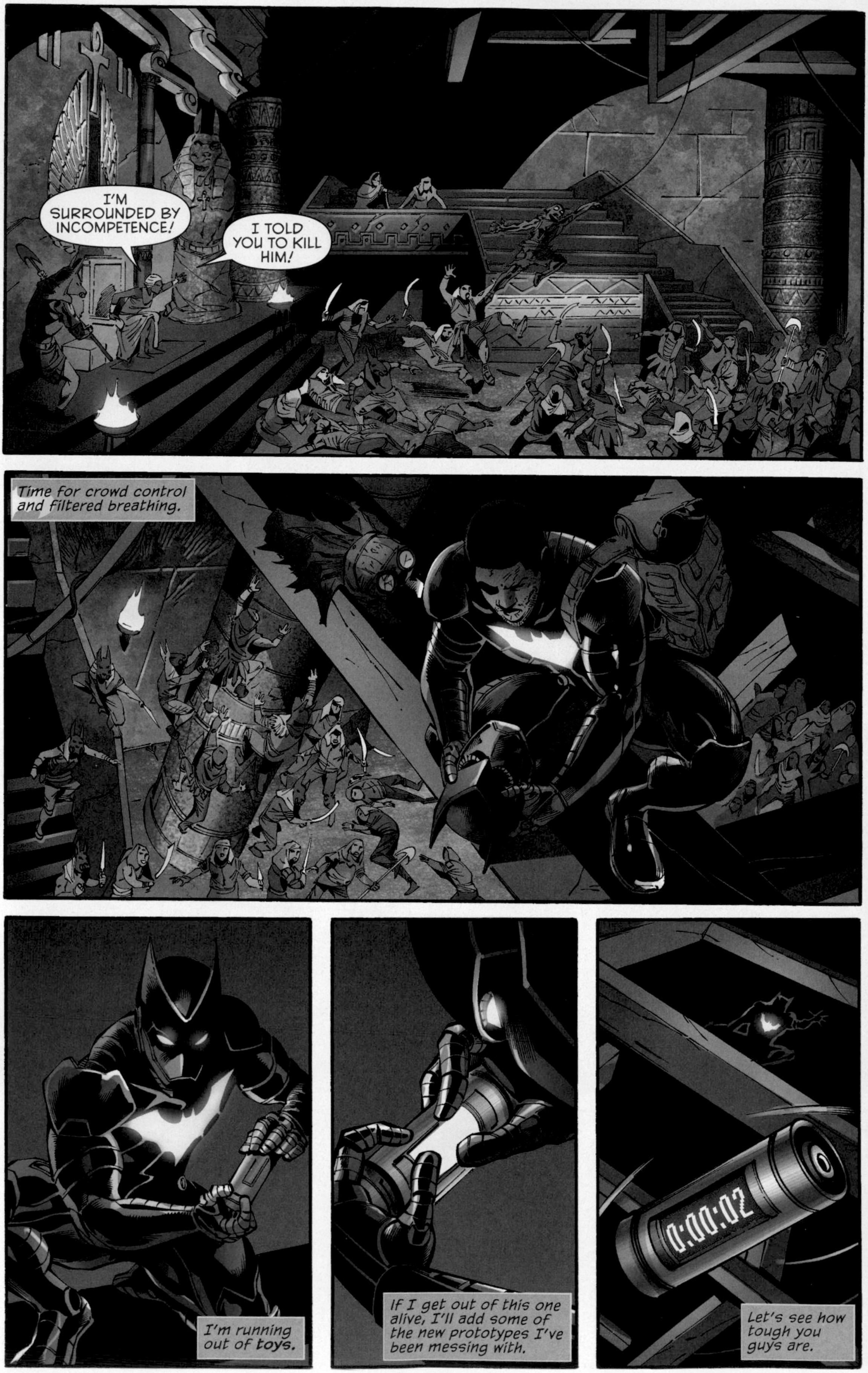
I'M SURROUNDED BY INCOMPETENCE!
I TOLD YOU TO KILL HIM!
Time for crowd control and filtered breathing.
I'm running out of toys.
If I get out of this one alive, I'll add some of the new prototypes I've been messing with.
0:00:02
Let's see how tough you guys are.

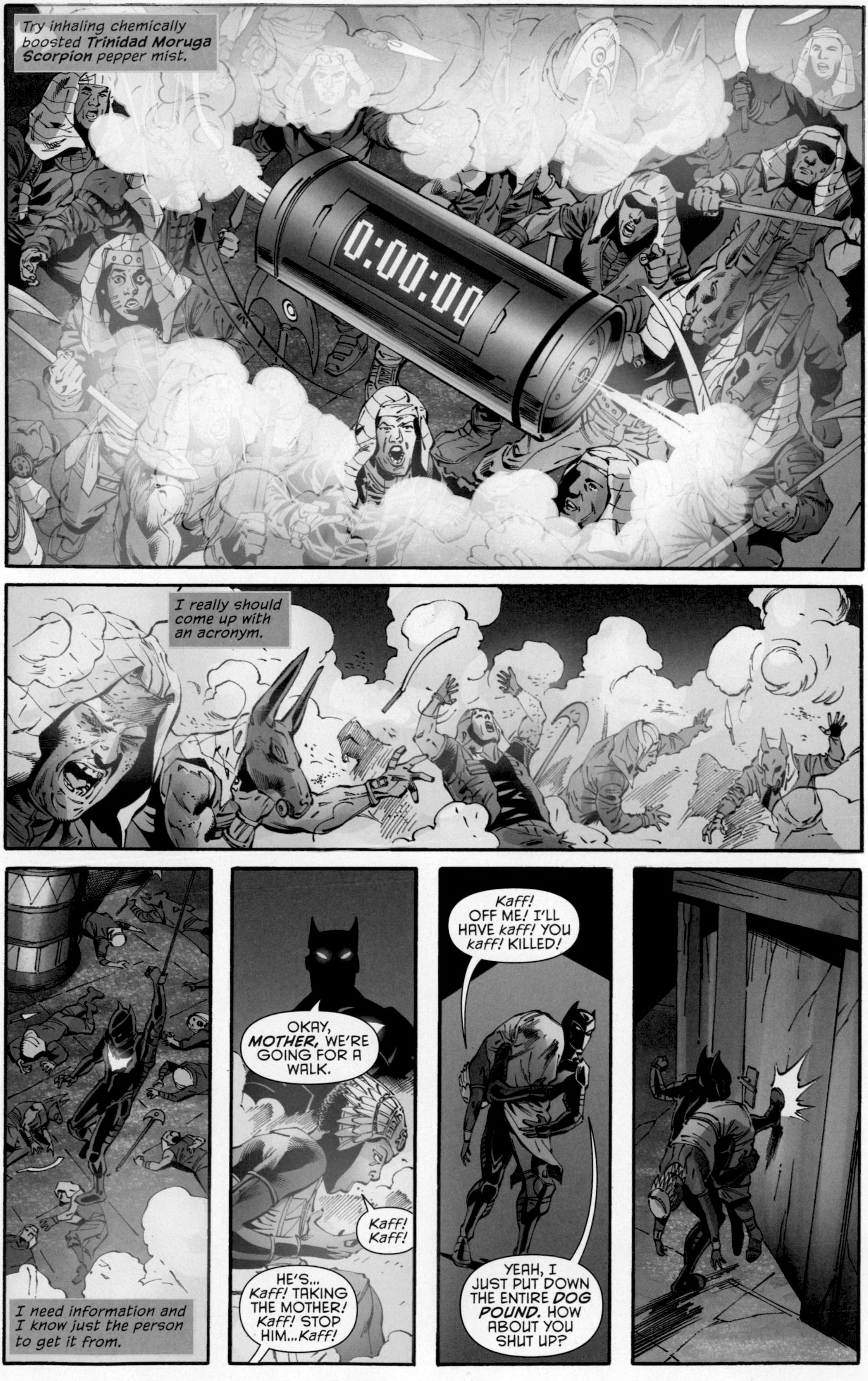
Try inhaling chemically boosted Trinidad Moruga Scorpion pepper mist.
0:00:00
I really should come up with an acronym.
I need information and I know just the person to get it from.
OKAY, MOTHER, WE'RE GOING FOR A WALK.
Kaff! Kaff!
HE'S... Kaff! TAKING THE MOTHER! Kaff! STOP HIM...Kaff!
Kaff! OFF ME! I'LL HAVE kaff! YOU kaff! KILLED!
YEAH, I JUST PUT DOWN THE ENTIRE DOG POUND. HOW ABOUT YOU SHUT UP?

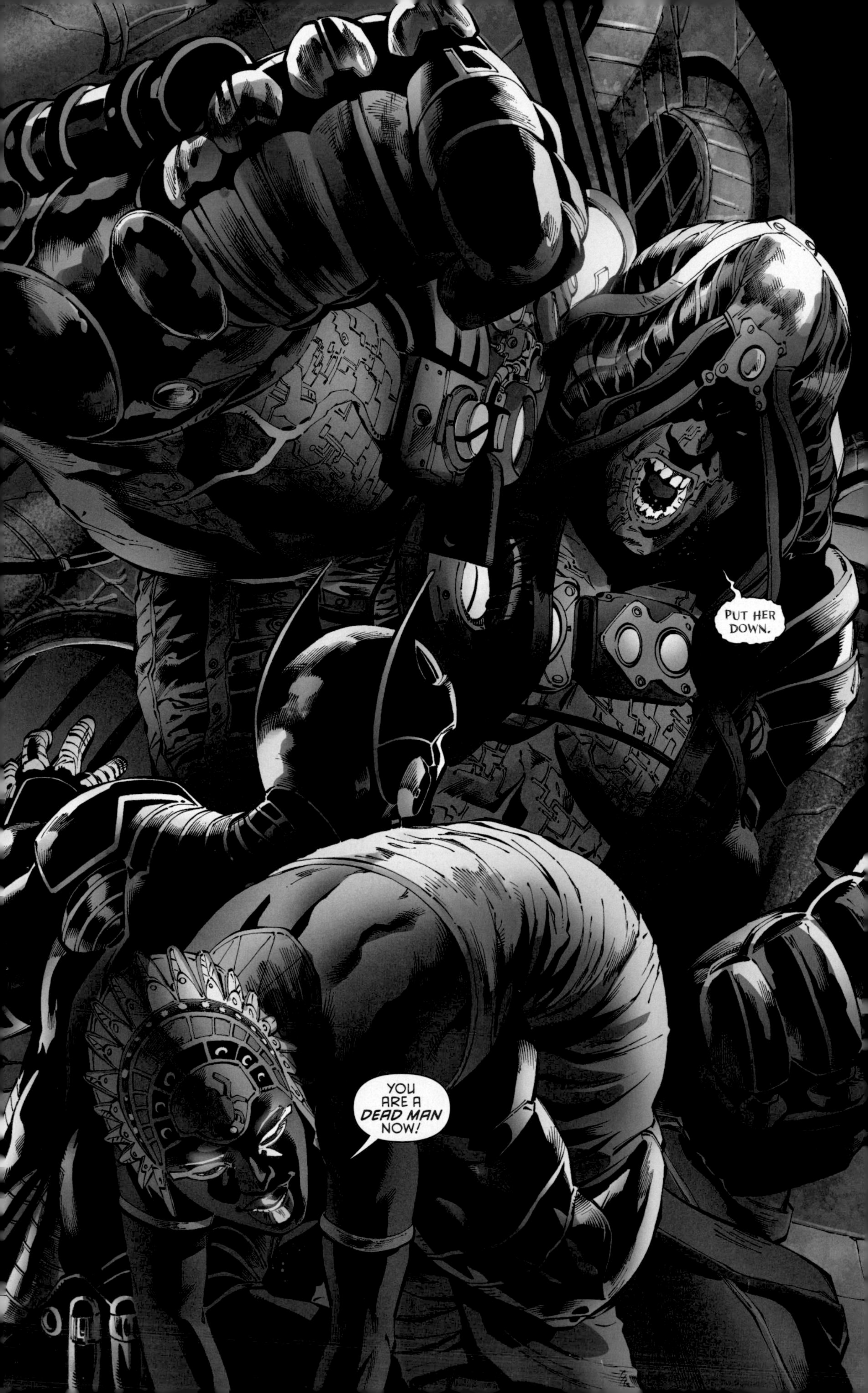
PUT HER DOWN.
YOU ARE A DEAD MAN NOW!

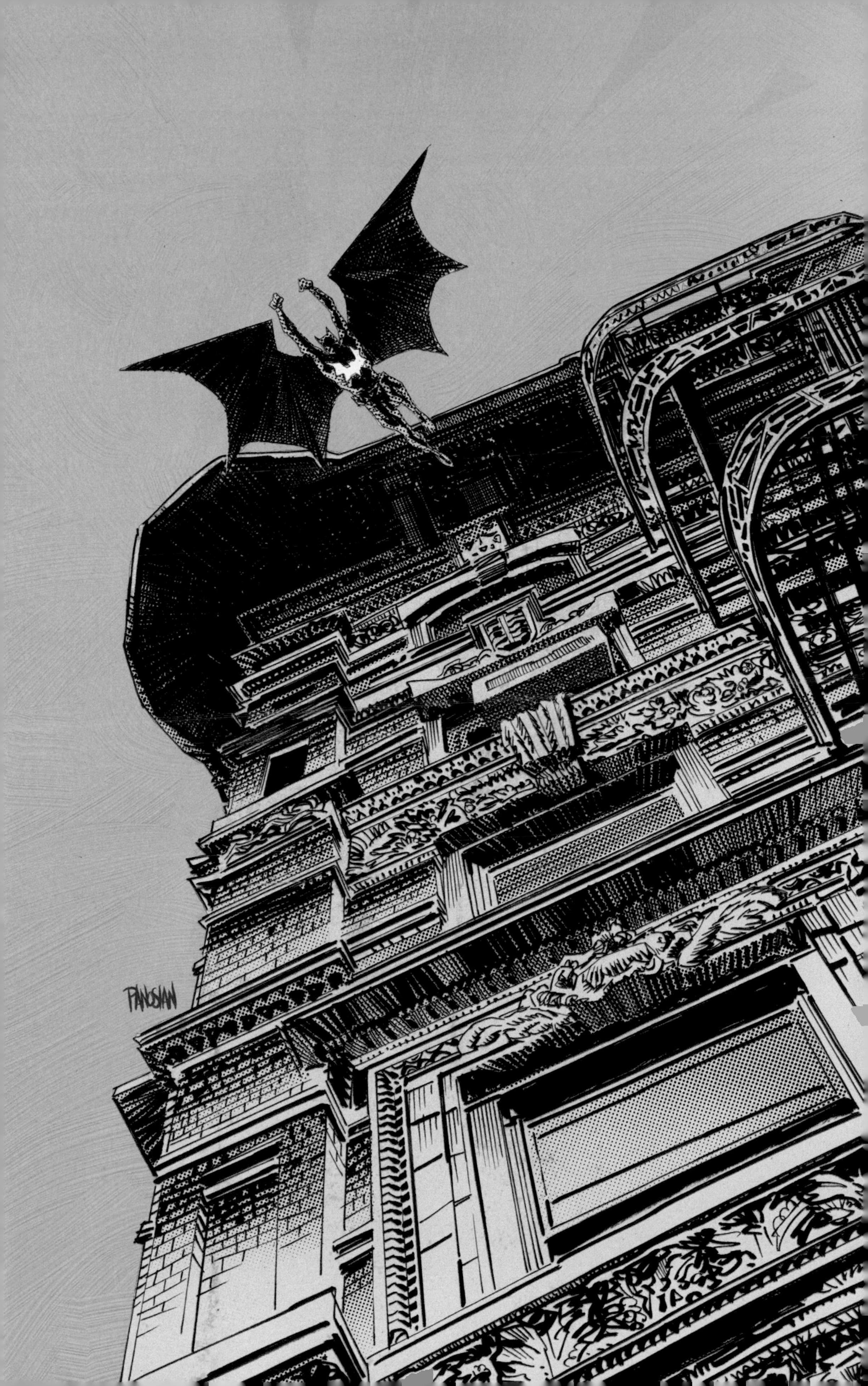
PANOSIAN

INTO THE DARK

JIMMY PALMIOTTI
JUSTIN GRAY
writers

EDUARDO PANSICA
penciller

JÚLIO FERREIRA
inker

PAUL MOUNTS
colorist

DEZI SIENTY
letterer

cover art by
DAN PANOSIAN

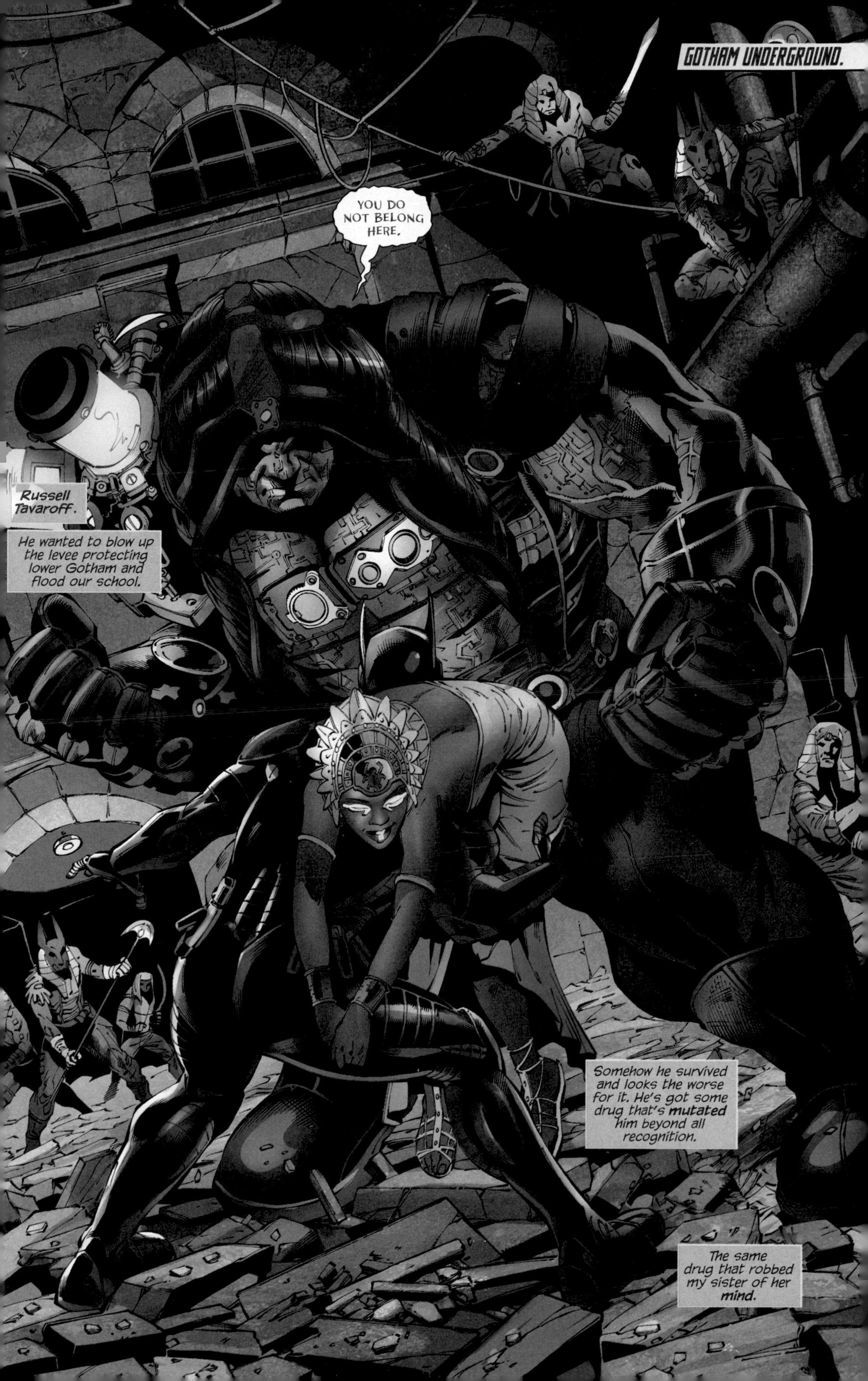
GOTHAM UNDERGROUND.
YOU DO NOT BELONG HERE.
Russell Tavaroff.
He wanted to blow up the levee protecting lower Gotham and flood our school.
Somehow he survived and looks the worse for it. He's got some drug that's **mutated** him beyond all recognition.
The same drug that robbed my sister of her **mind**.

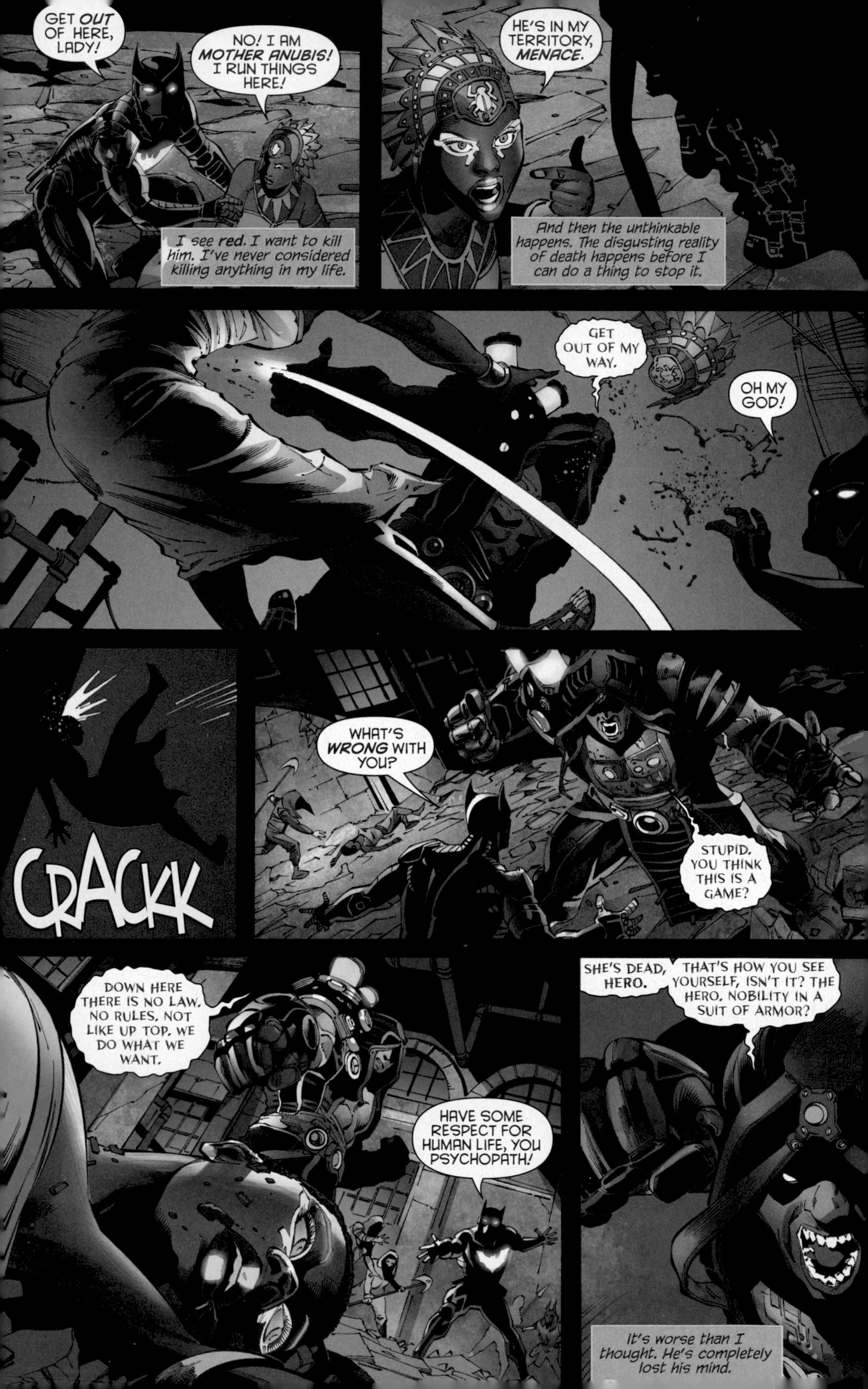
GET OUT OF HERE, LADY!
NO! I AM MOTHER ANUBIS! I RUN THINGS HERE!
I see red. I want to kill him. I've never considered killing anything in my life.
HE'S IN MY TERRITORY, MENACE.
And then the unthinkable happens. The disgusting reality of death happens before I can do a thing to stop it.
GET OUT OF MY WAY.
OH MY GOD!
CRACKK
WHAT'S WRONG WITH YOU?
STUPID. YOU THINK THIS IS A GAME?
DOWN HERE THERE IS NO LAW. NO RULES. NOT LIKE UP TOP. WE DO WHAT WE WANT.
HAVE SOME RESPECT FOR HUMAN LIFE, YOU PSYCHOPATH!
SHE'S DEAD, HERO.
THAT'S HOW YOU SEE YOURSELF, ISN'T IT? THE HERO. NOBILITY IN A SUIT OF ARMOR?
It's worse than I thought. He's completely lost his mind.

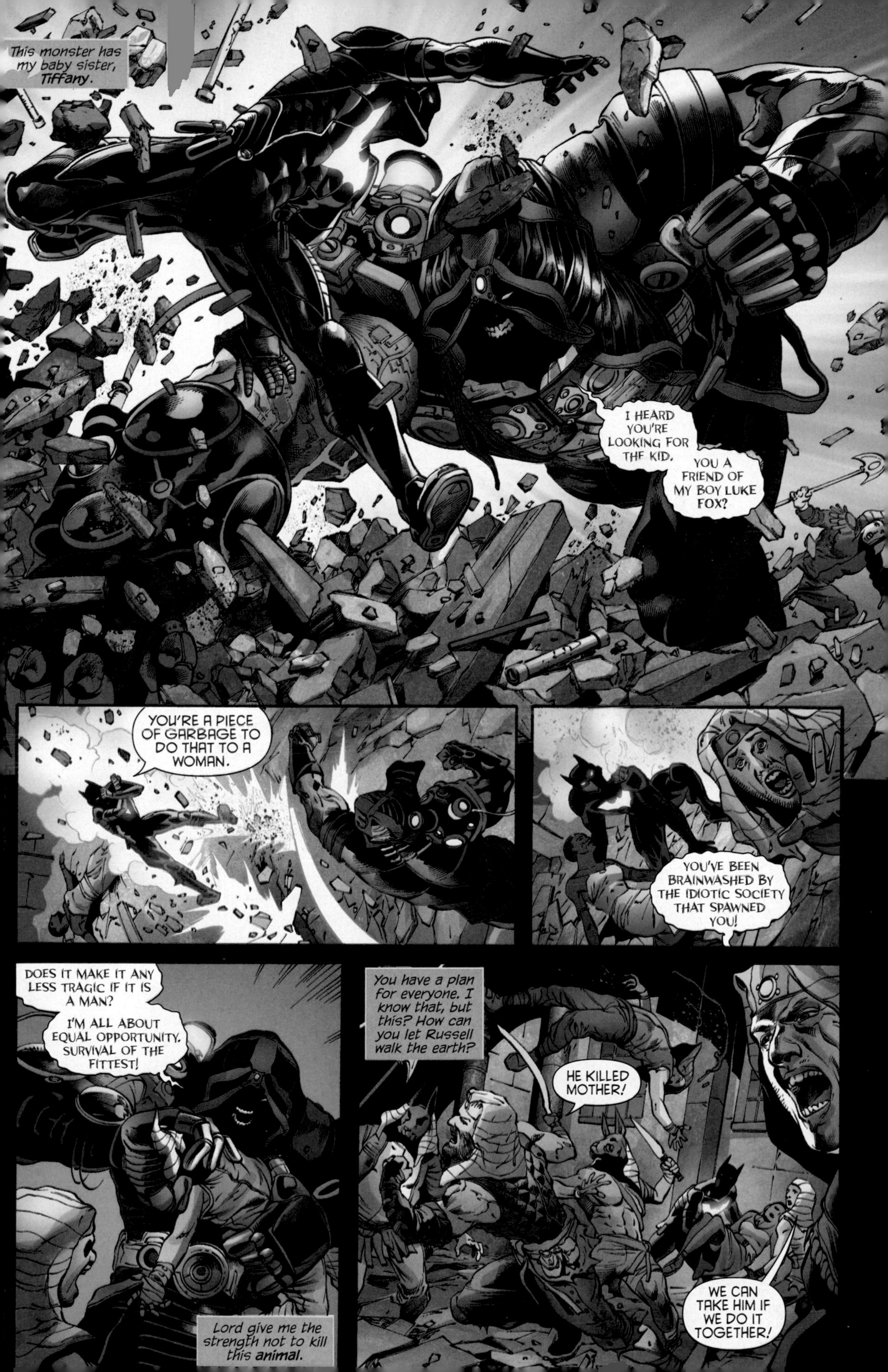
This monster has my baby sister, *Tiffany*.
I HEARD YOU'RE LOOKING FOR THE KID.
YOU A FRIEND OF MY BOY LUKE FOX?
YOU'RE A PIECE OF GARBAGE TO DO THAT TO A WOMAN.
YOU'VE BEEN BRAINWASHED BY THE IDIOTIC SOCIETY THAT SPAWNED YOU!
DOES IT MAKE IT ANY LESS TRAGIC IF IT IS A MAN?
I'M ALL ABOUT EQUAL OPPORTUNITY. SURVIVAL OF THE FITTEST!
Lord give me the strength not to kill this *animal*.
You have a plan for everyone. I know that, but this? How can you let Russell walk the earth?
HE KILLED MOTHER!
WE CAN TAKE HIM IF WE DO IT TOGETHER!

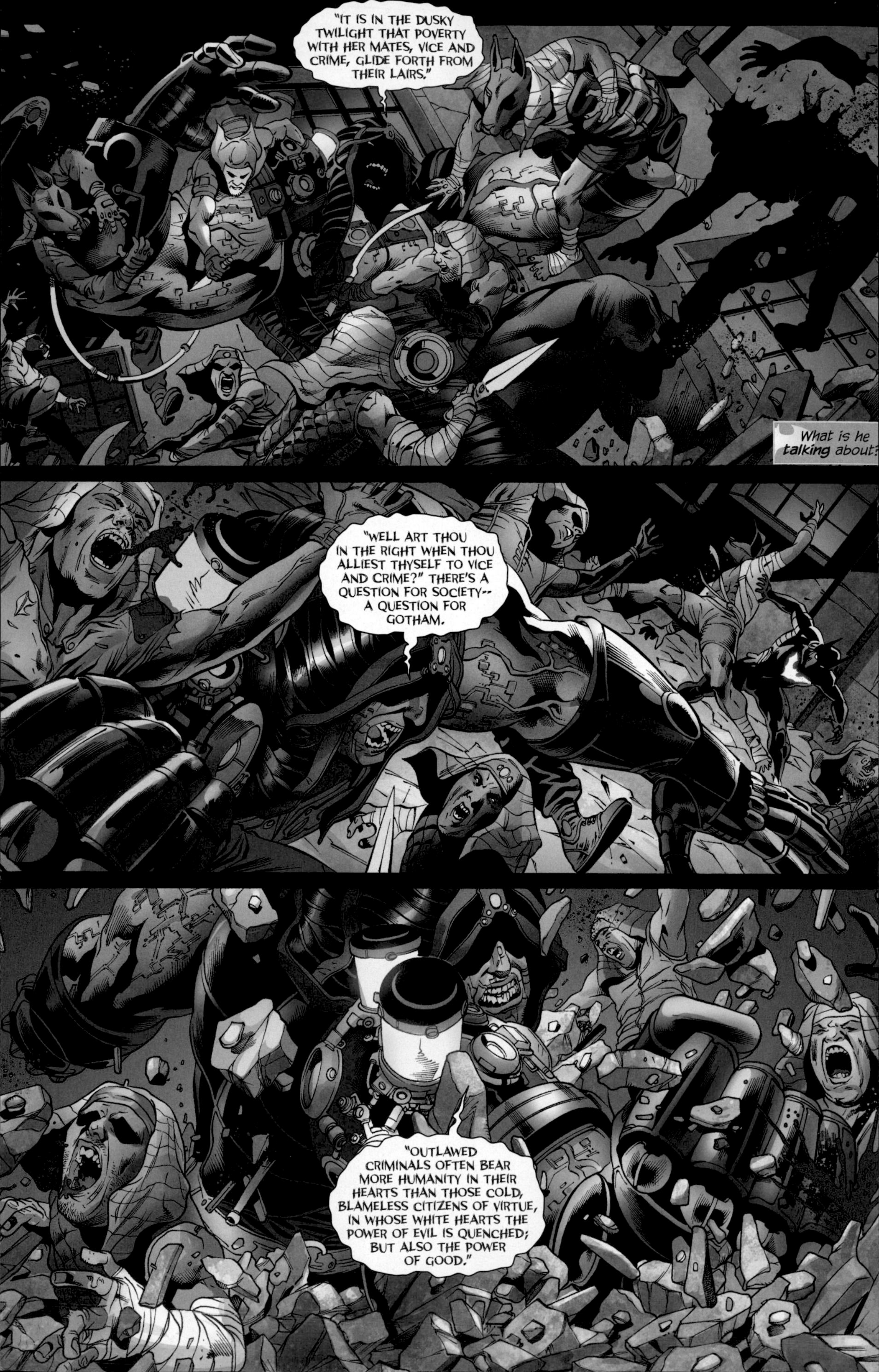
"IT IS IN THE DUSKY TWILIGHT THAT POVERTY WITH HER MATES, VICE AND CRIME, GLIDE FORTH FROM THEIR LAIRS."
What is he talking about?
"WELL ART THOU IN THE RIGHT WHEN THOU ALLIEST THYSELF TO VICE AND CRIME?" THERE'S A QUESTION FOR SOCIETY-- A QUESTION FOR GOTHAM.
"OUTLAWED CRIMINALS OFTEN BEAR MORE HUMANITY IN THEIR HEARTS THAN THOSE COLD, BLAMELESS CITIZENS OF VIRTUE, IN WHOSE WHITE HEARTS THE POWER OF EVIL IS QUENCHED; BUT ALSO THE POWER OF GOOD."

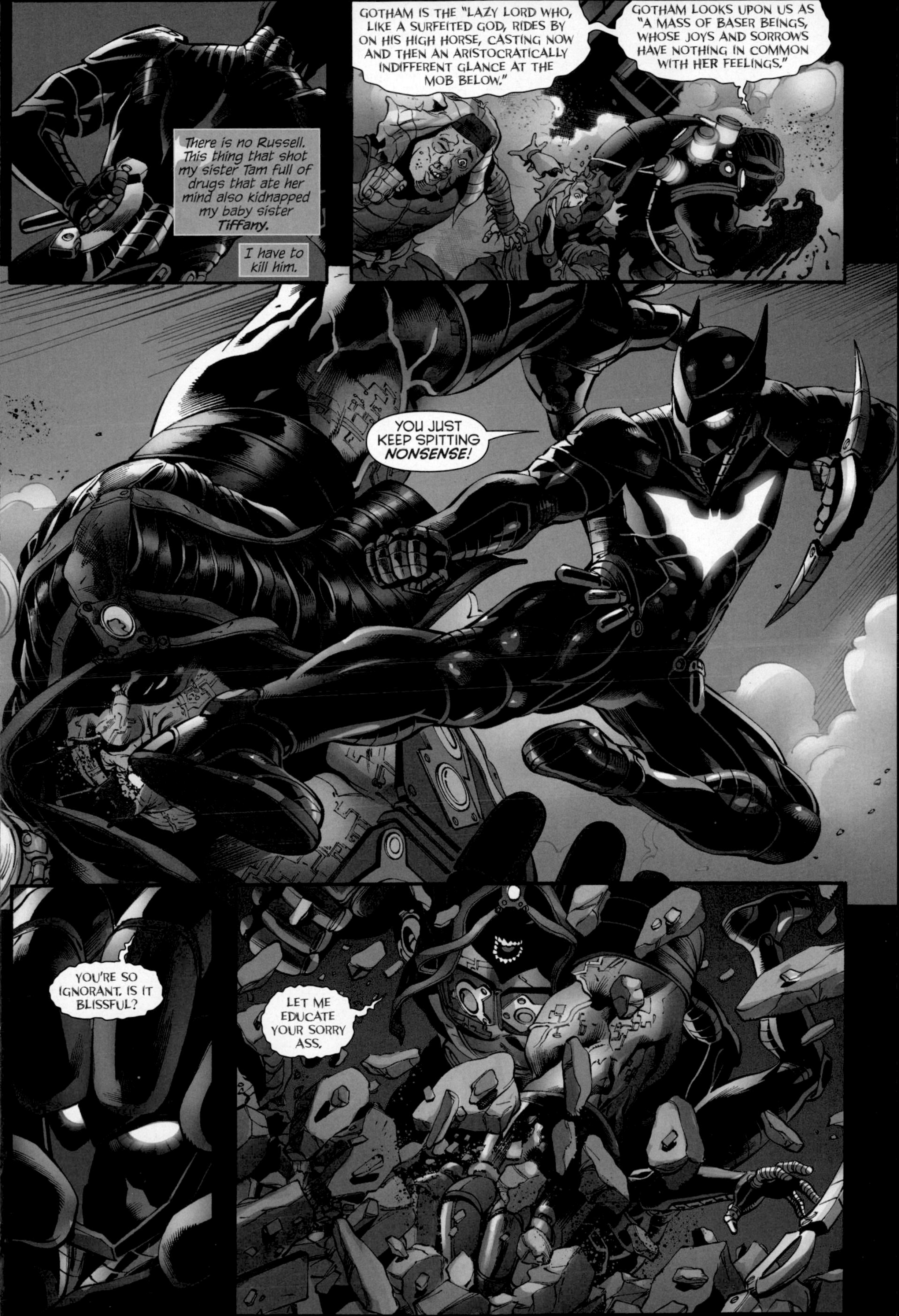
There is no Russell. This thing that shot my sister Tam full of drugs that ate her mind also kidnapped my baby sister *Tiffany*.
I have to kill him.
GOTHAM IS THE "LAZY LORD WHO, LIKE A SURFEITED GOD, RIDES BY ON HIS HIGH HORSE, CASTING NOW AND THEN AN ARISTOCRATICALLY INDIFFERENT GLANCE AT THE MOB BELOW."
GOTHAM LOOKS UPON US AS "A MASS OF BASER BEINGS, WHOSE JOYS AND SORROWS HAVE NOTHING IN COMMON WITH HER FEELINGS."
YOU JUST KEEP SPITTING *NONSENSE!*
YOU'RE SO IGNORANT. IS IT BLISSFUL?
LET ME EDUCATE YOUR SORRY ASS.

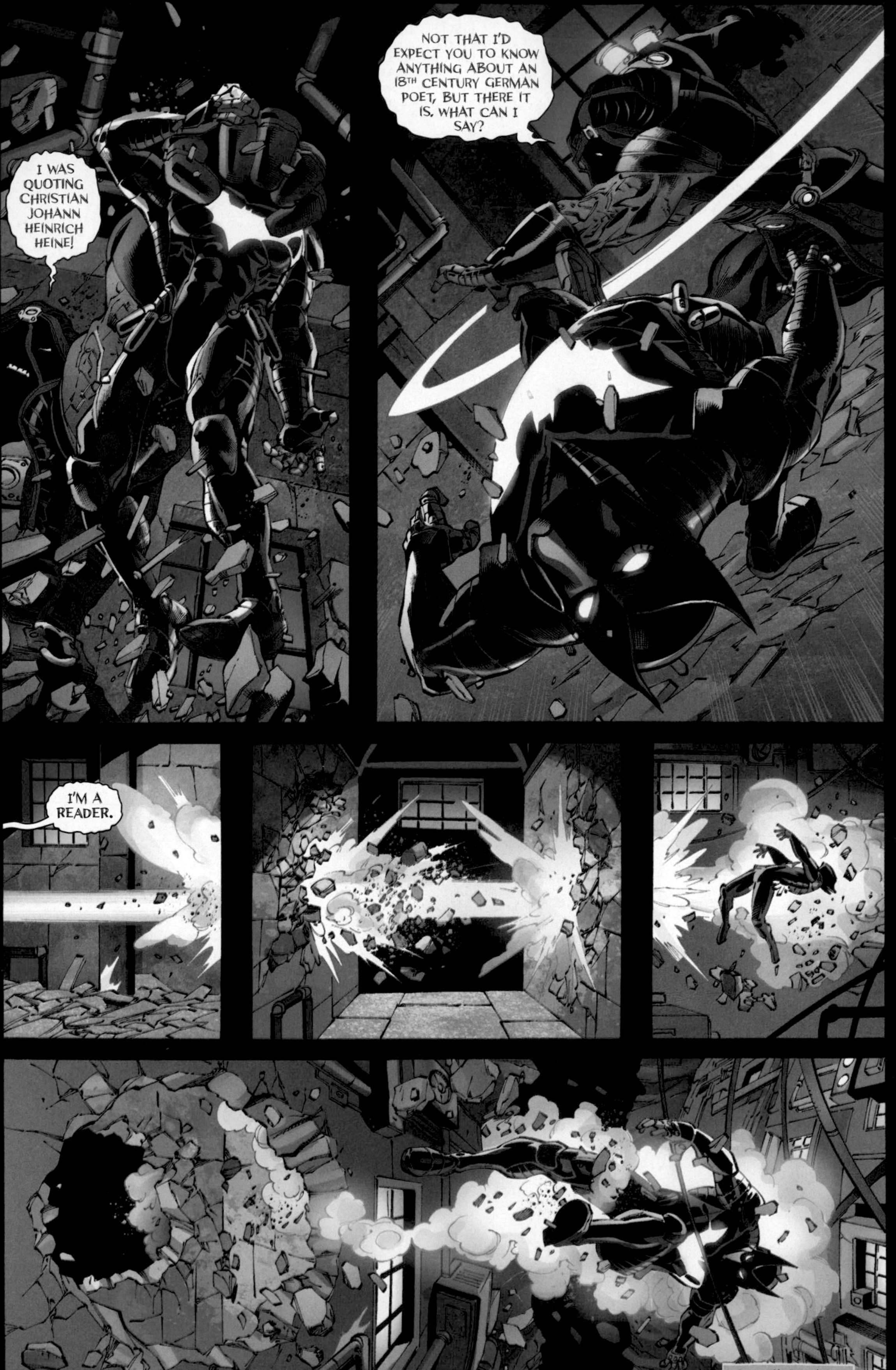
I WAS QUOTING CHRISTIAN JOHANN HEINRICH HEINE!
NOT THAT I'D EXPECT YOU TO KNOW ANYTHING ABOUT AN 18TH CENTURY GERMAN POET, BUT THERE IT IS. WHAT CAN I SAY?
I'M A READER.
I can't be doing this. I have to find Tiffany.

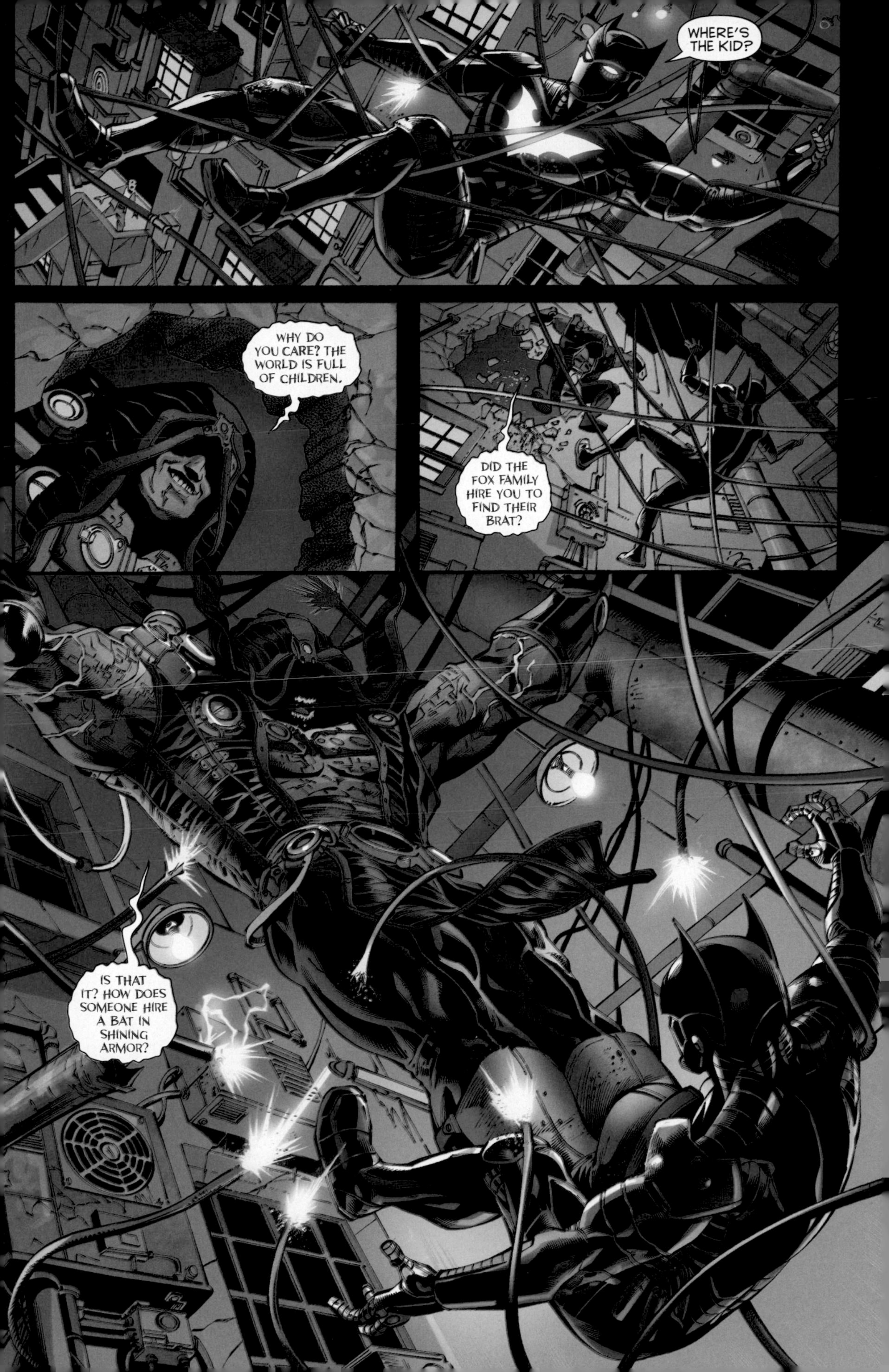
WHERE'S THE KID?
WHY DO YOU CARE? THE WORLD IS FULL OF CHILDREN.
DID THE FOX FAMILY HIRE YOU TO FIND THEIR BRAT?
IS THAT IT? HOW DOES SOMEONE HIRE A BAT IN SHINING ARMOR?

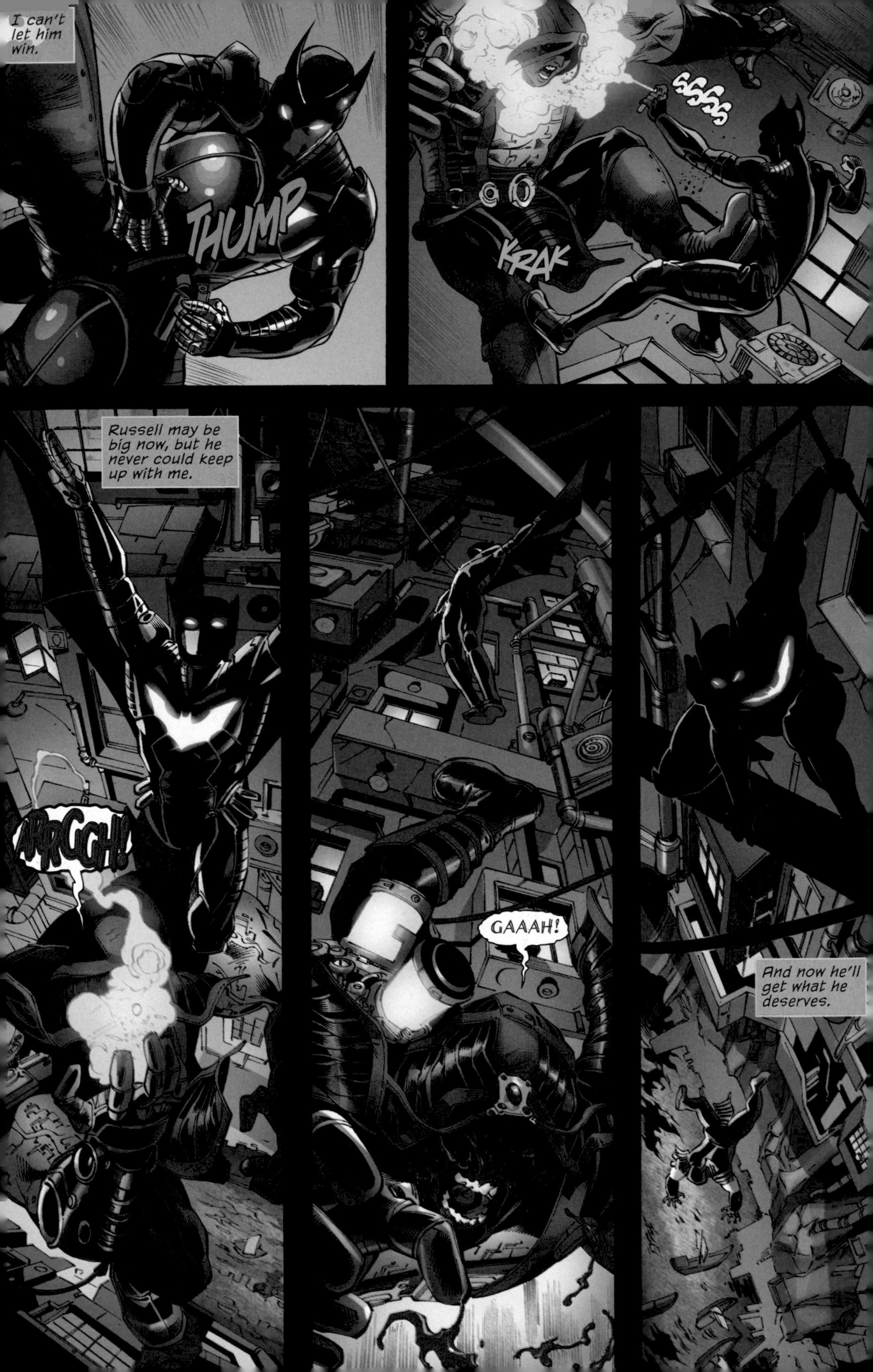
I can't let him win.
THUMP
SSSS
KRAK
Russell may be big now, but he never could keep up with me.
ARRRGGH!
GAAAH!
And now he'll get what he deserves.

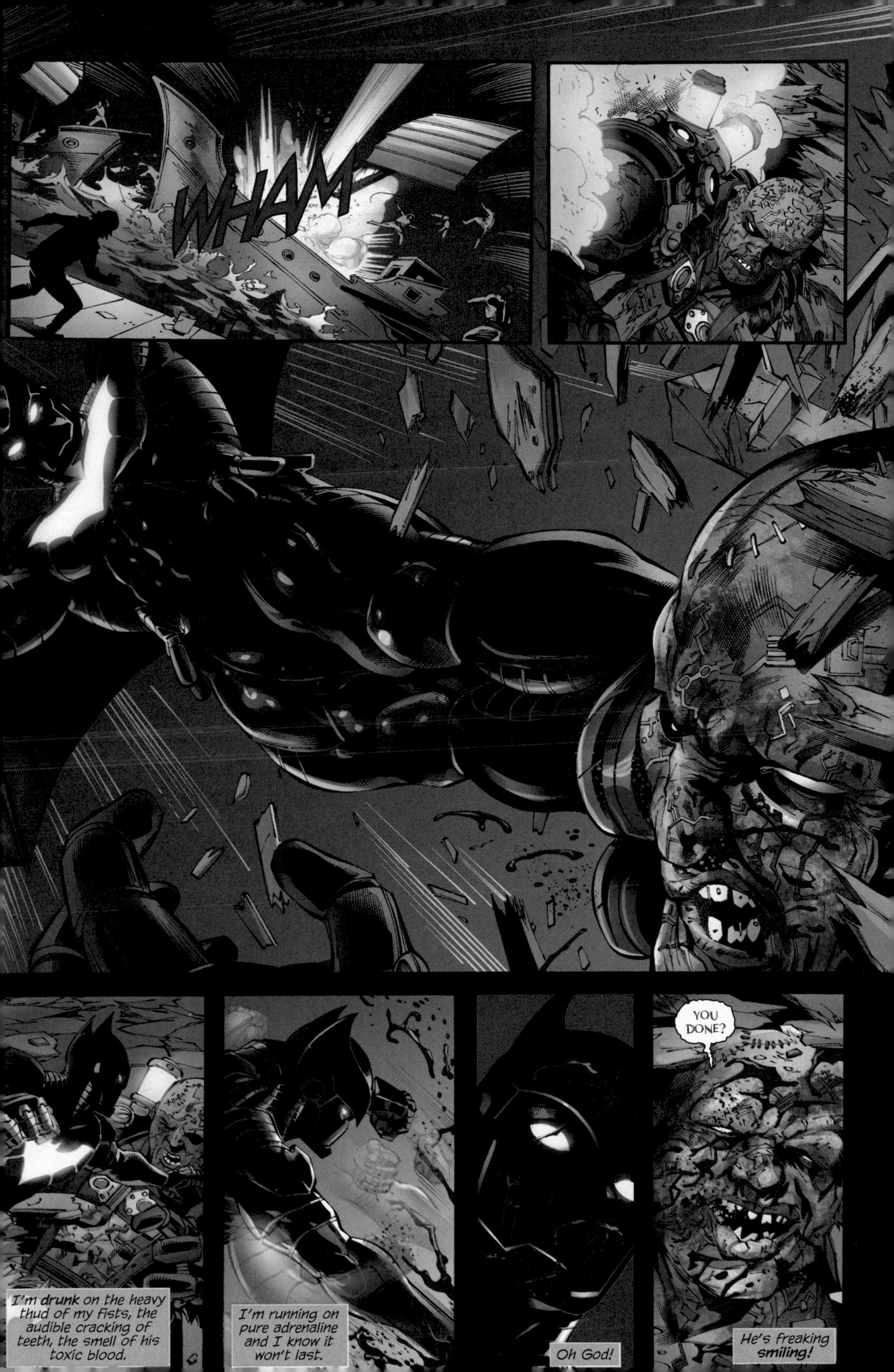
WHAM
I'm drunk on the heavy thud of my fists, the audible cracking of teeth, the smell of his toxic blood.
I'm running on pure adrenaline and I know it won't last.
Oh God!
YOU DONE?
He's freaking smiling!

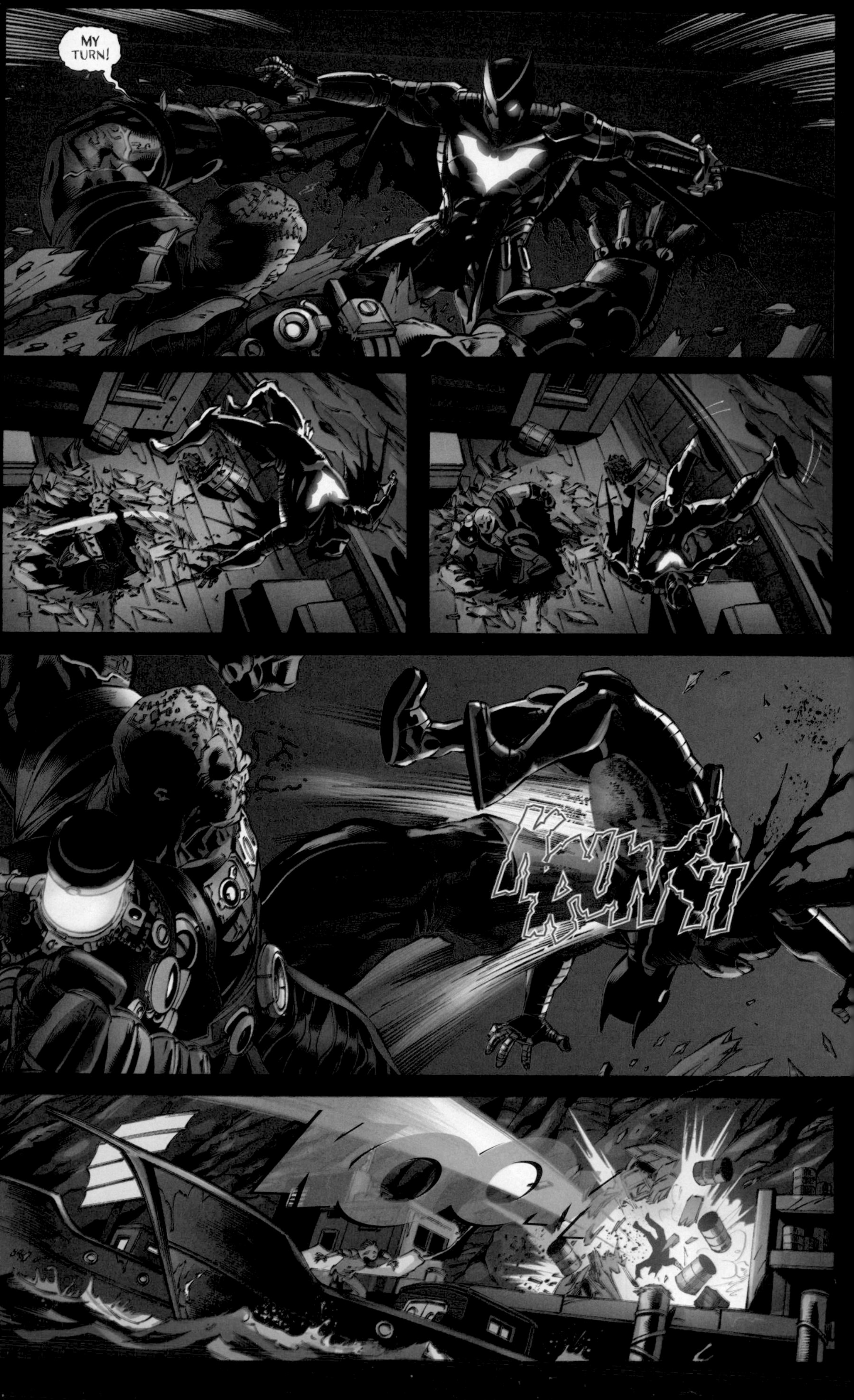
MY TURN!

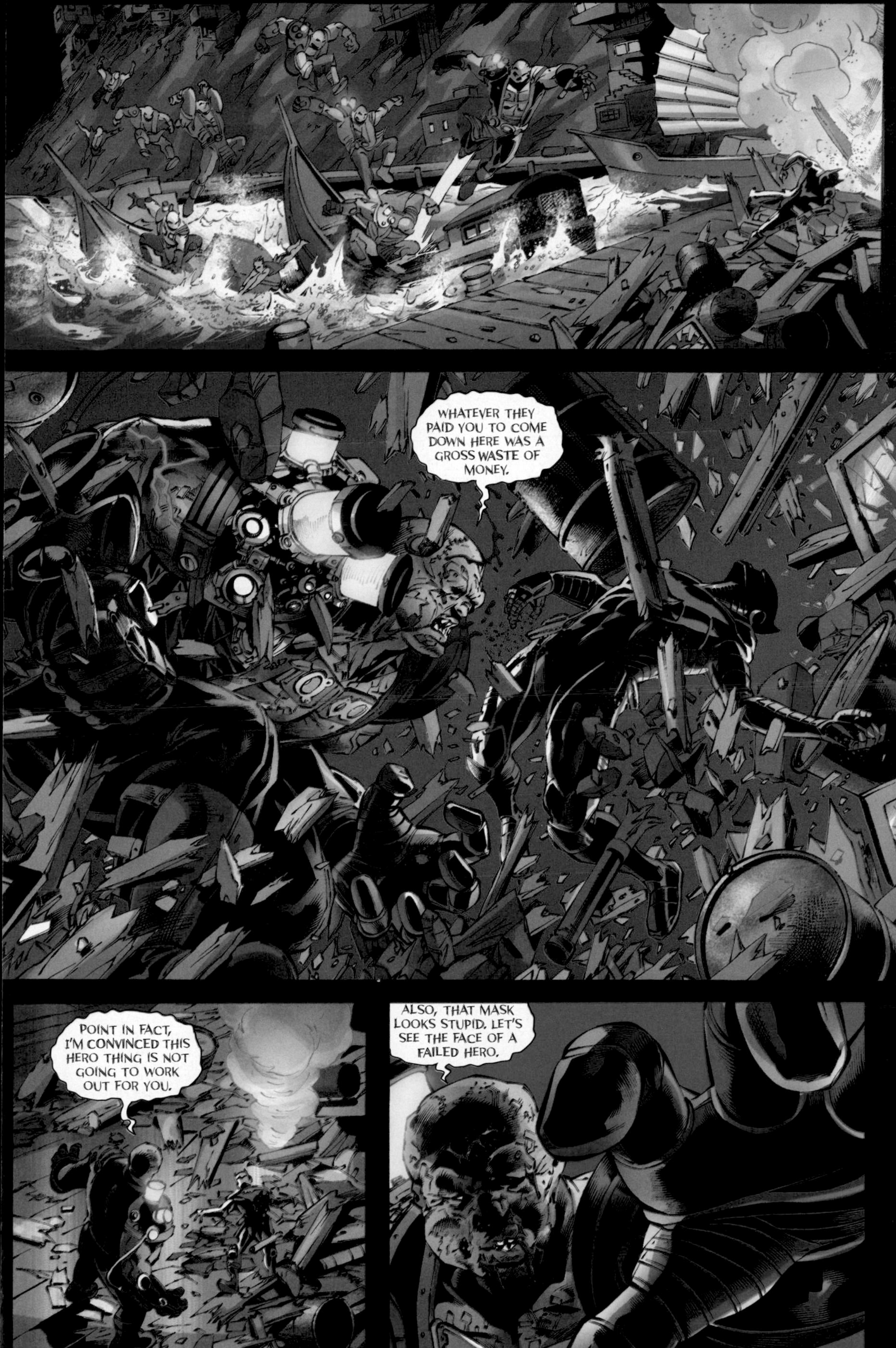
WHATEVER THEY PAID YOU TO COME DOWN HERE WAS A GROSS WASTE OF MONEY.
POINT IN FACT, I'M CONVINCED THIS HERO THING IS NOT GOING TO WORK OUT FOR YOU.
ALSO, THAT MASK LOOKS STUPID. LET'S SEE THE FACE OF A FAILED HERO.

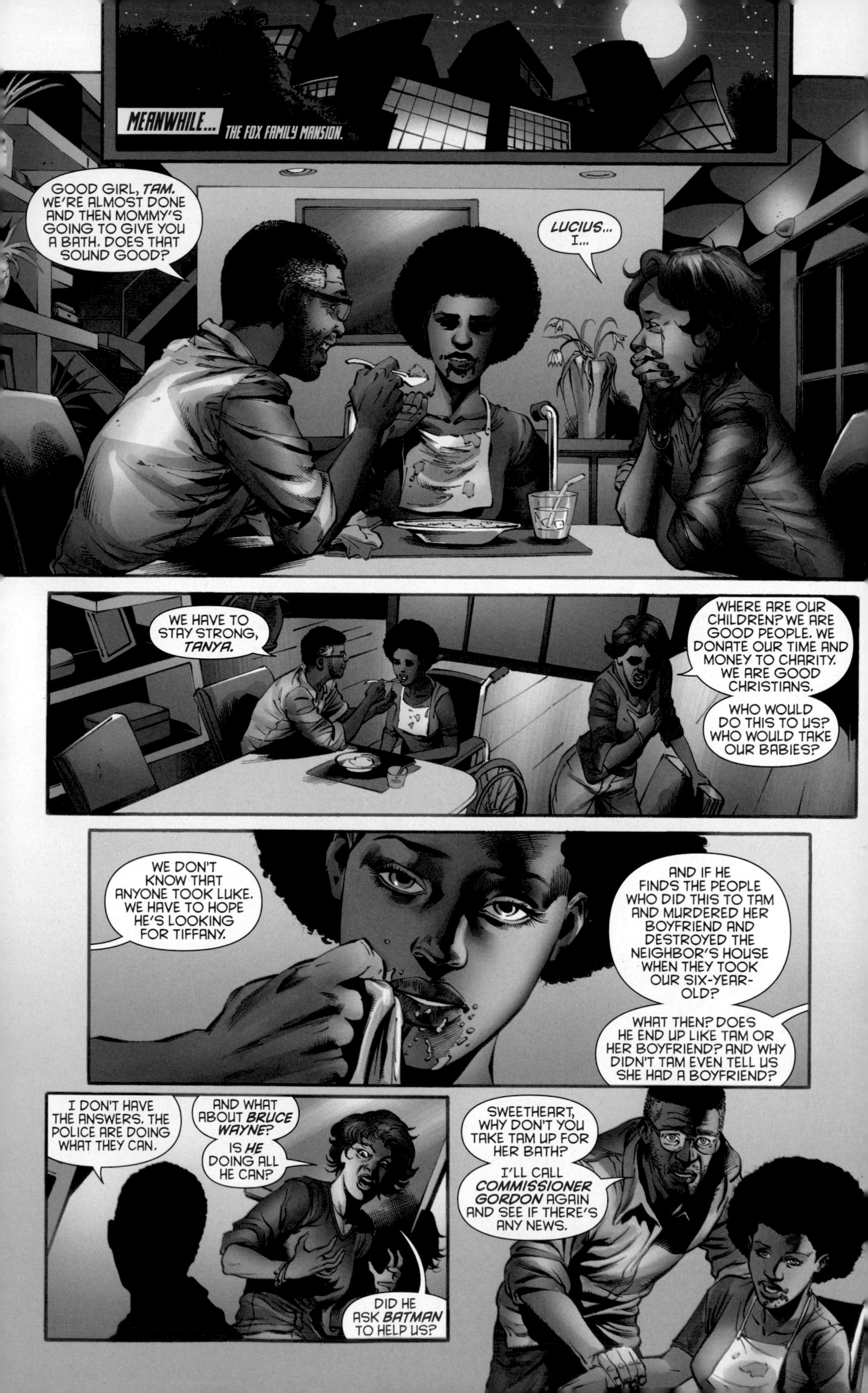
MEANWHILE... THE FOX FAMILY MANSION.
GOOD GIRL, TAM. WE'RE ALMOST DONE AND THEN MOMMY'S GOING TO GIVE YOU A BATH. DOES THAT SOUND GOOD?
LUCIUS... I...
WE HAVE TO STAY STRONG, TANYA.
WHERE ARE OUR CHILDREN? WE ARE GOOD PEOPLE. WE DONATE OUR TIME AND MONEY TO CHARITY. WE ARE GOOD CHRISTIANS.
WHO WOULD DO THIS TO US? WHO WOULD TAKE OUR BABIES?
WE DON'T KNOW THAT ANYONE TOOK LUKE. WE HAVE TO HOPE HE'S LOOKING FOR TIFFANY.
AND IF HE FINDS THE PEOPLE WHO DID THIS TO TAM AND MURDERED HER BOYFRIEND AND DESTROYED THE NEIGHBOR'S HOUSE WHEN THEY TOOK OUR SIX-YEAR-OLD?
WHAT THEN? DOES HE END UP LIKE TAM OR HER BOYFRIEND? AND WHY DIDN'T TAM EVEN TELL US SHE HAD A BOYFRIEND?
I DON'T HAVE THE ANSWERS. THE POLICE ARE DOING WHAT THEY CAN.
AND WHAT ABOUT BRUCE WAYNE?
IS HE DOING ALL HE CAN?
DID HE ASK BATMAN TO HELP US?
SWEETHEART, WHY DON'T YOU TAKE TAM UP FOR HER BATH?
I'LL CALL COMMISSIONER GORDON AGAIN AND SEE IF THERE'S ANY NEWS.

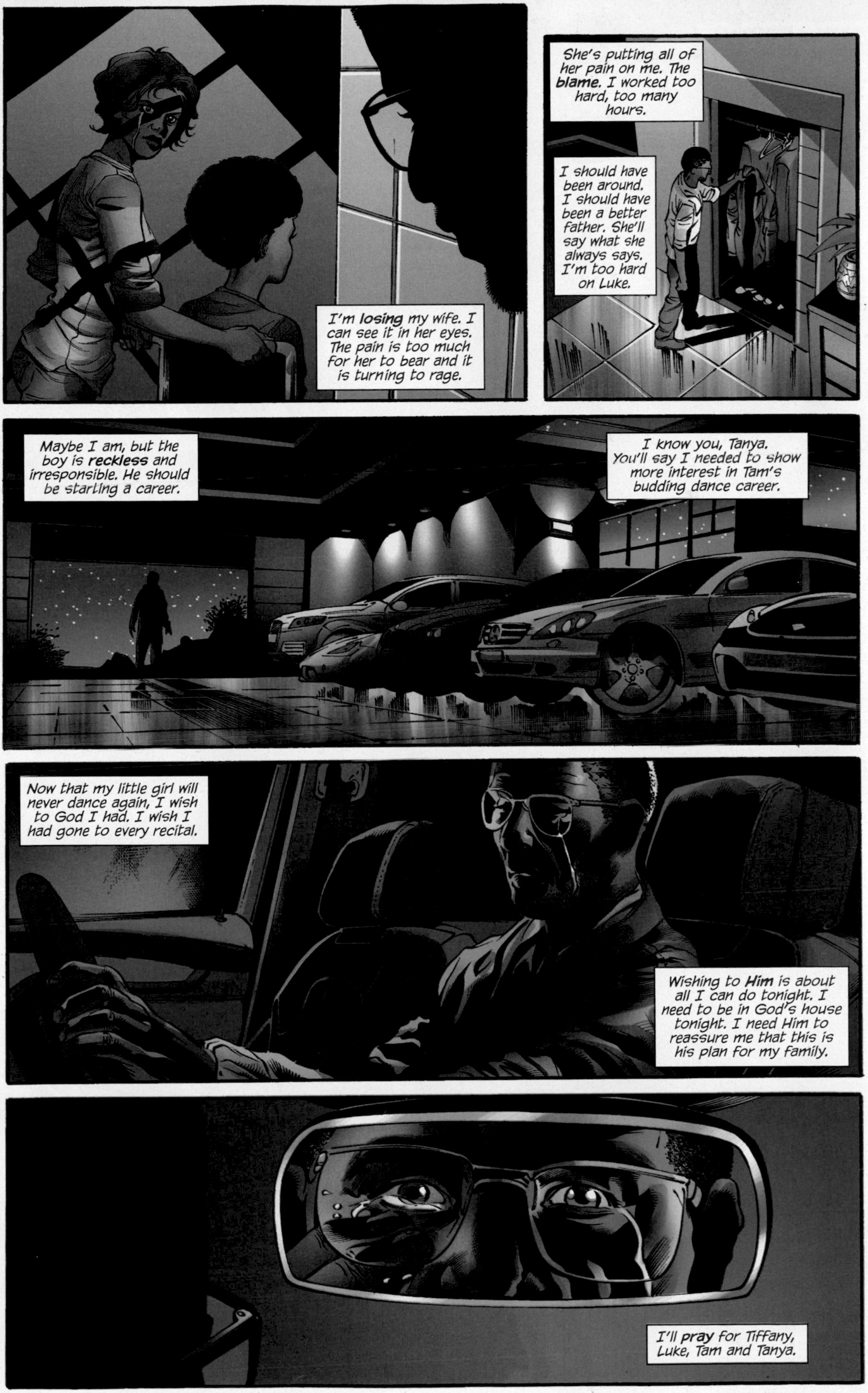
I'm **losing** my wife. I can see it in her eyes. The pain is too much for her to bear and it is turning to rage.
She's putting all of her pain on me. The **blame**. I worked too hard, too many hours.
I should have been around. I should have been a better father. She'll say what she always says. I'm too hard on Luke.
Maybe I am, but the boy is **reckless** and irresponsible. He should be starting a career.
I know you, Tanya. You'll say I needed to show more interest in Tam's budding dance career.
Now that my little girl will never dance again, I wish to God I had. I wish I had gone to every recital.
Wishing to **Him** is about all I can do tonight. I need to be in God's house tonight. I need Him to reassure me that this is his plan for my family.
I'll **pray** for Tiffany, Luke, Tam and Tanya.

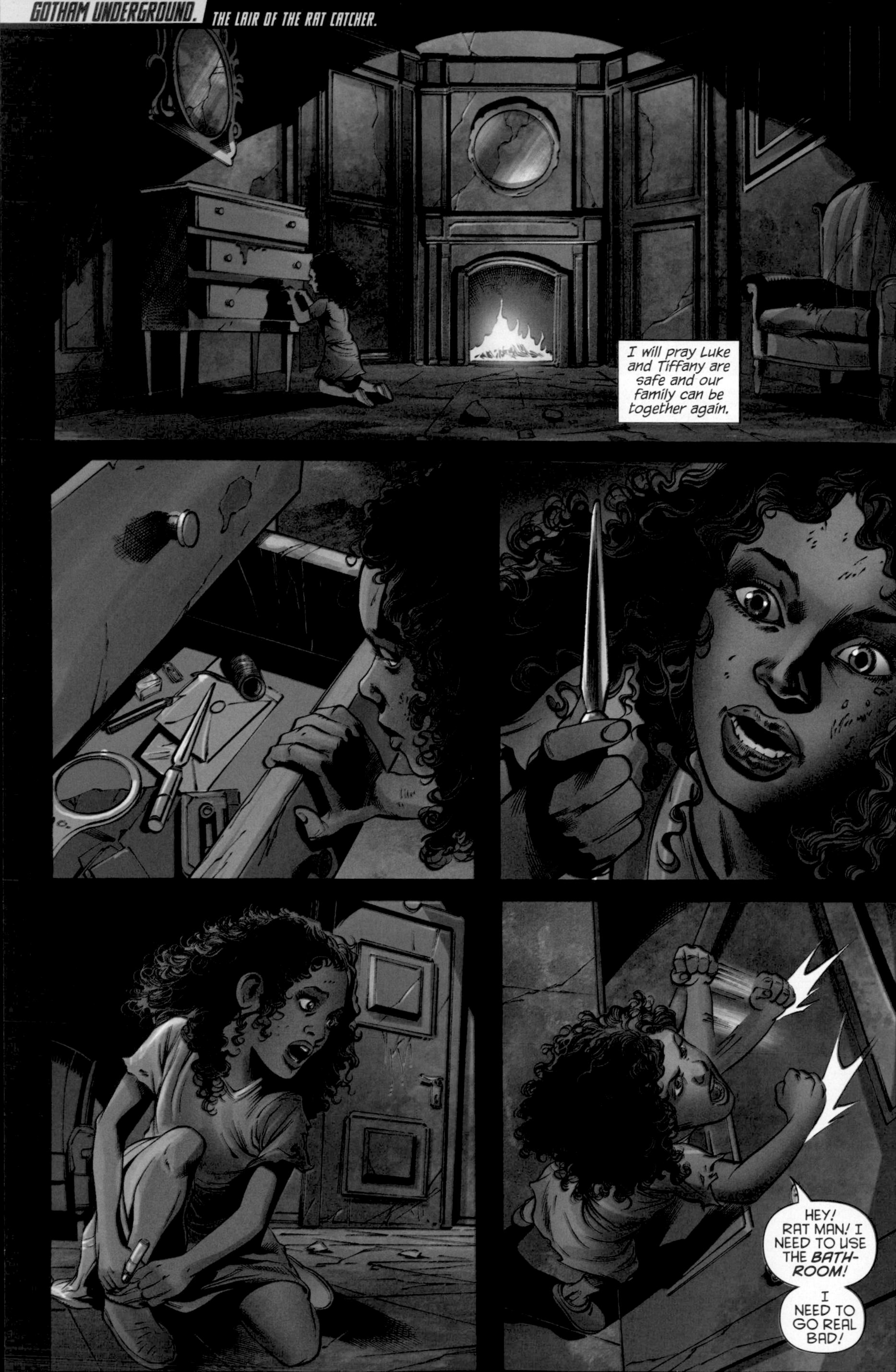
GOTHAM UNDERGROUND.
THE LAIR OF THE RAT CATCHER.
I will pray Luke and Tiffany are safe and our family can be together again.
HEY! RAT MAN! I NEED TO USE THE BATH-ROOM!
I NEED TO GO REAL BAD!

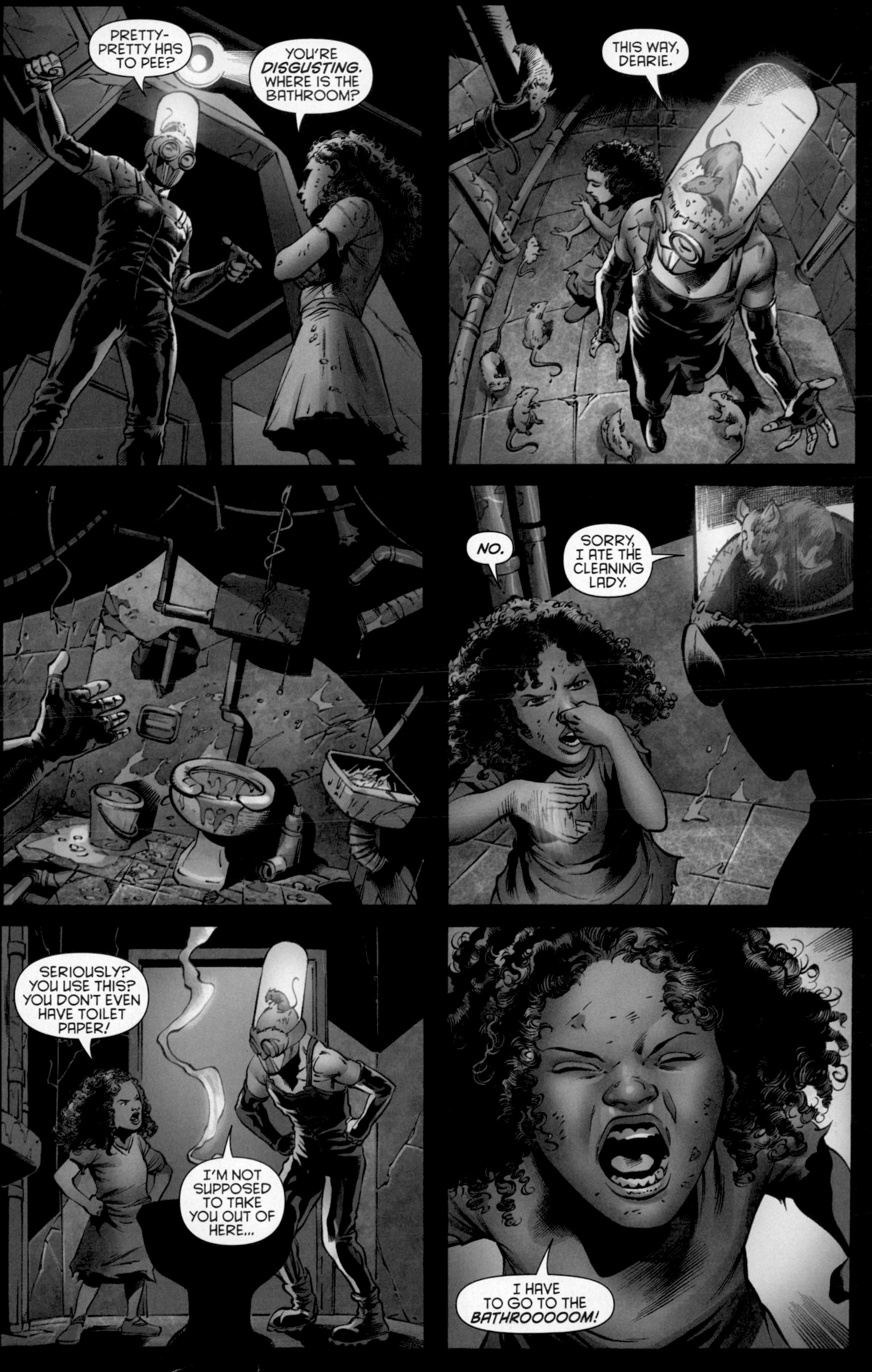
PRETTY-PRETTY HAS TO PEE?
YOU'RE *DISGUSTING.* WHERE IS THE BATHROOM?
THIS WAY, DEARIE.
NO.
SORRY, I ATE THE CLEANING LADY.
SERIOUSLY? YOU USE THIS? YOU DON'T EVEN HAVE TOILET PAPER!
I'M NOT SUPPOSED TO TAKE YOU OUT OF HERE...
I HAVE TO GO TO THE *BATHROOOOOM!*

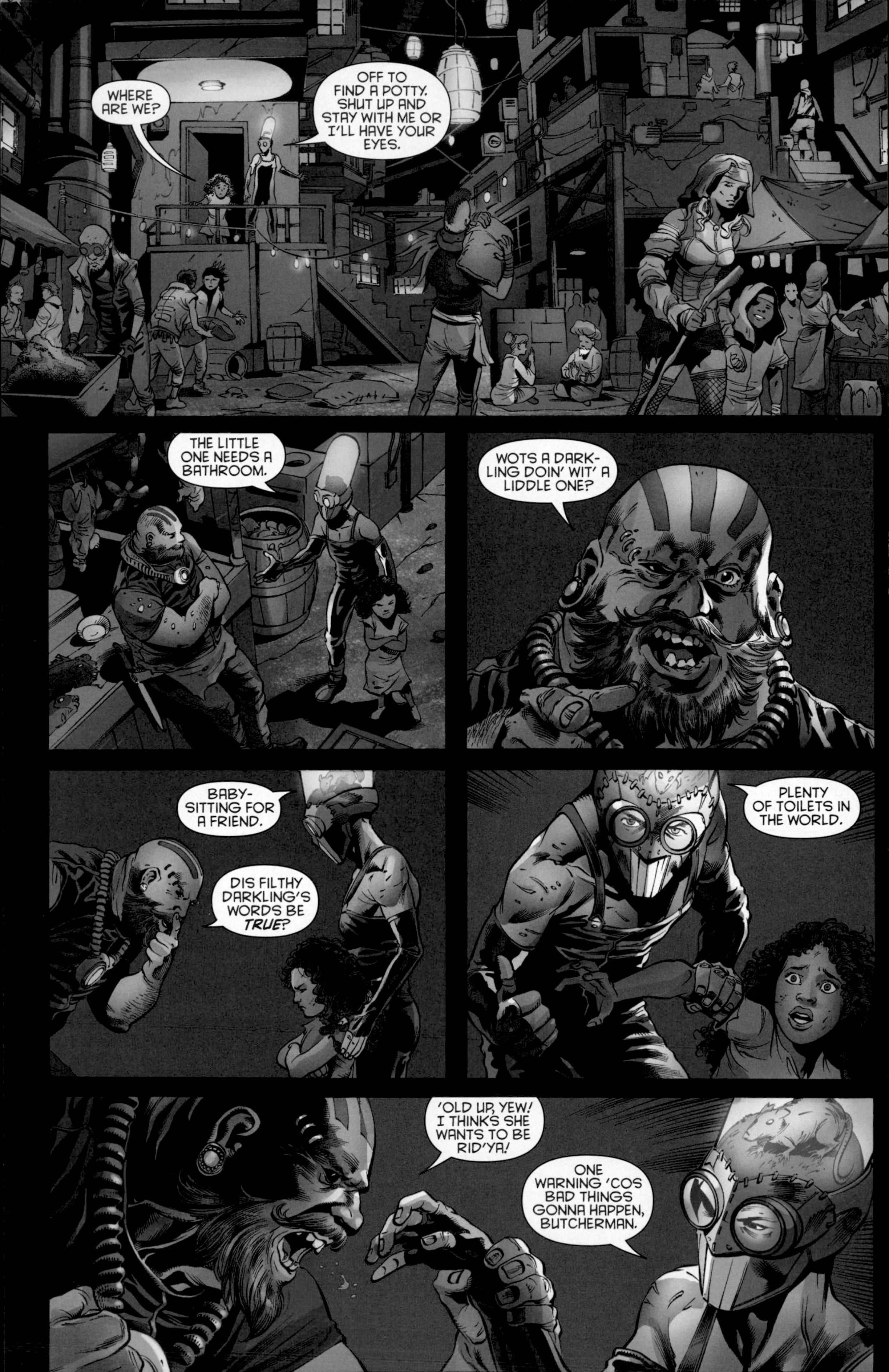
WHERE ARE WE?
OFF TO FIND A POTTY. SHUT UP AND STAY WITH ME OR I'LL HAVE YOUR EYES.
THE LITTLE ONE NEEDS A BATHROOM.
WOTS A DARKLING DOIN' WIT' A LIDDLE ONE?
BABY-SITTING FOR A FRIEND.
DIS FILTHY DARKLING'S WORDS BE *TRUE*?
PLENTY OF TOILETS IN THE WORLD.
'OLD UP, YEW! I THINKS SHE WANTS TO BE RID'YA!
ONE WARNING 'COS BAD THINGS GONNA HAPPEN, BUTCHERMAN.

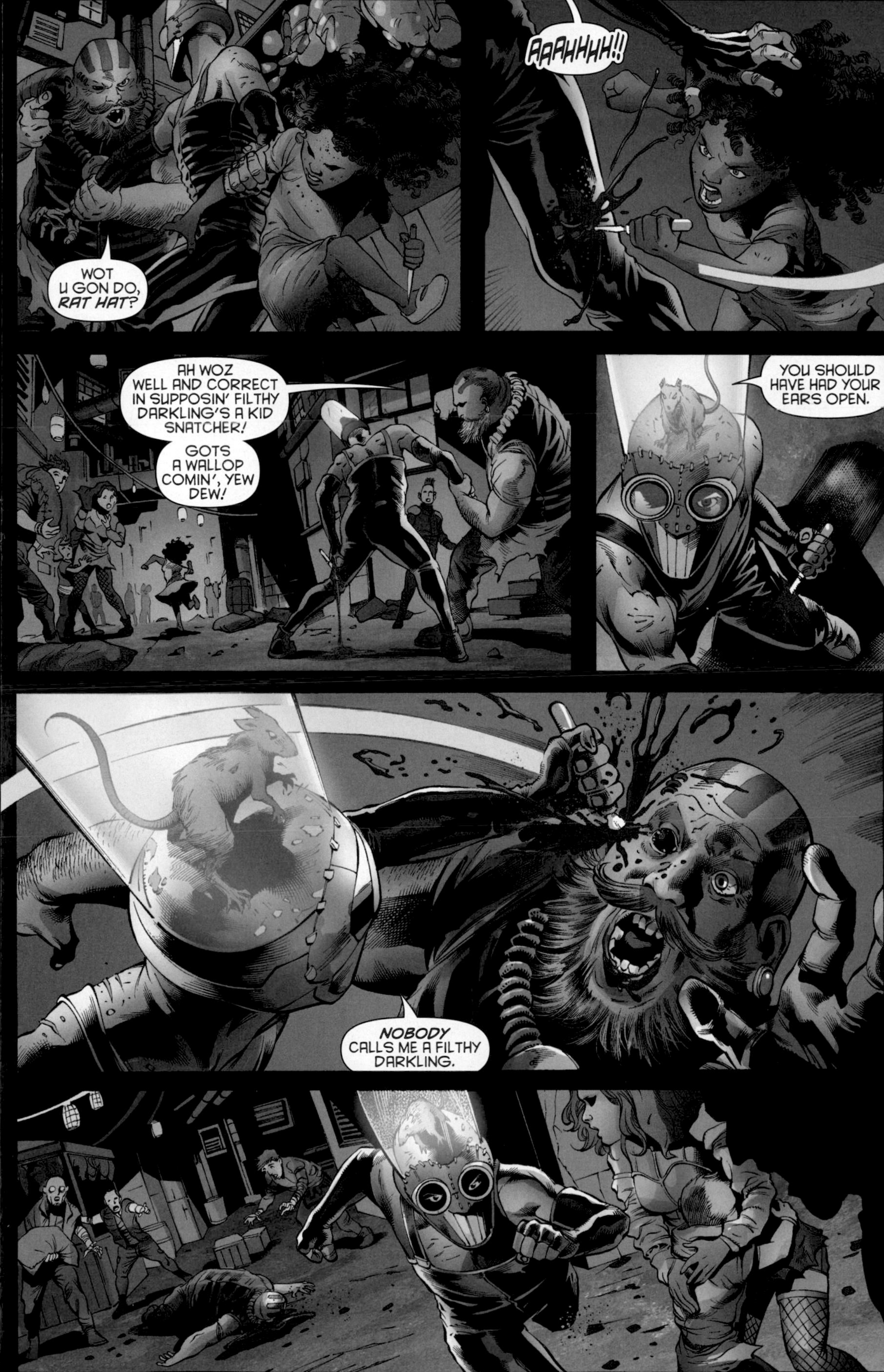
WOT U GON DO, *RAT HAT?*
AAAHHHH!!
AH WOZ WELL AND CORRECT IN SUPPOSIN' FILTHY DARKLING'S A KID SNATCHER!
GOTS A WALLOP COMIN', YEW DEW!
YOU SHOULD HAVE HAD YOUR EARS OPEN.
NOBODY CALLS ME A FILTHY DARKLING.

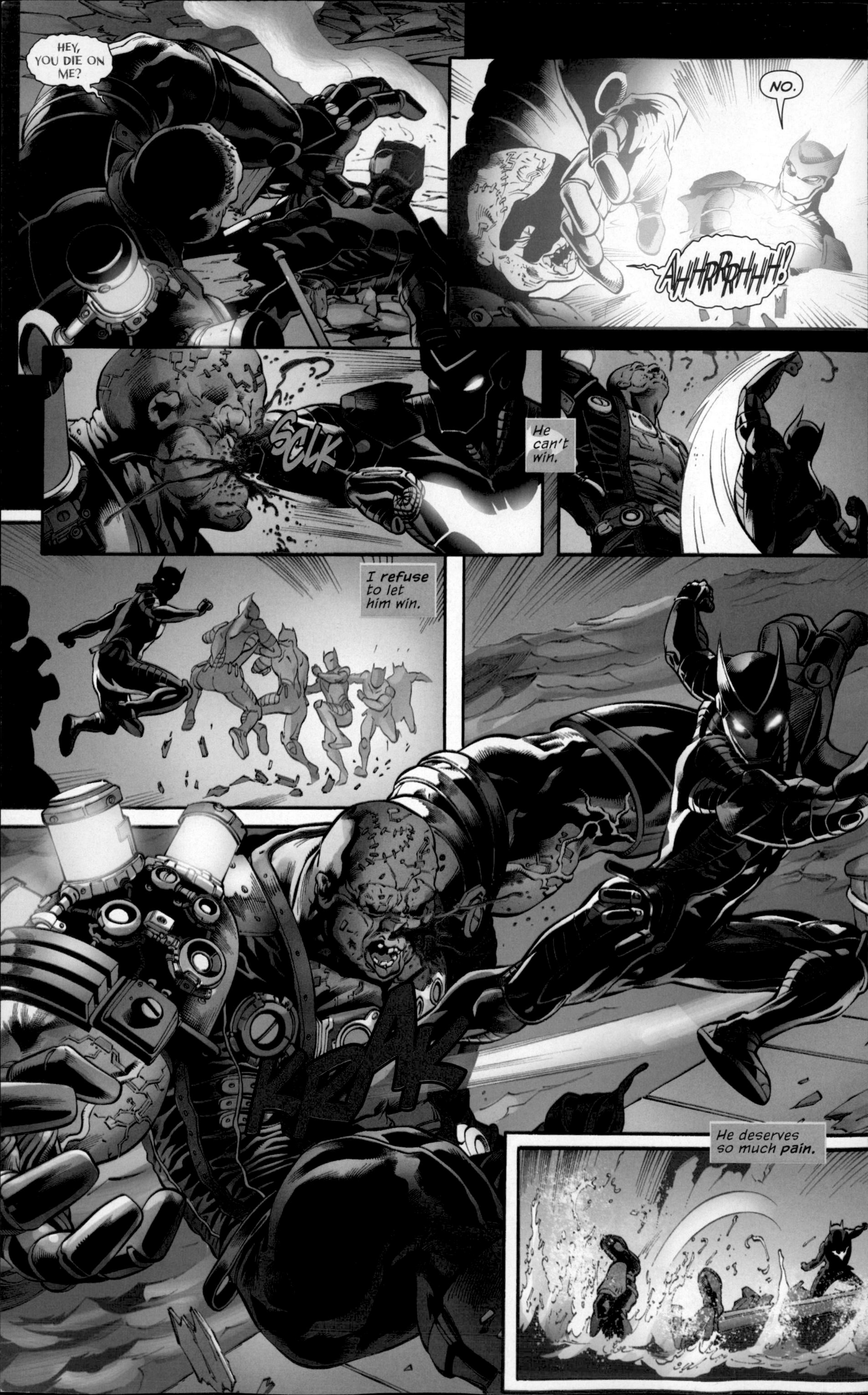

HEY, YOU DIE ON ME?
NO.
AHHRRRHHH!
SCLK
He can't win.
I refuse to let him win.
He deserves so much pain.

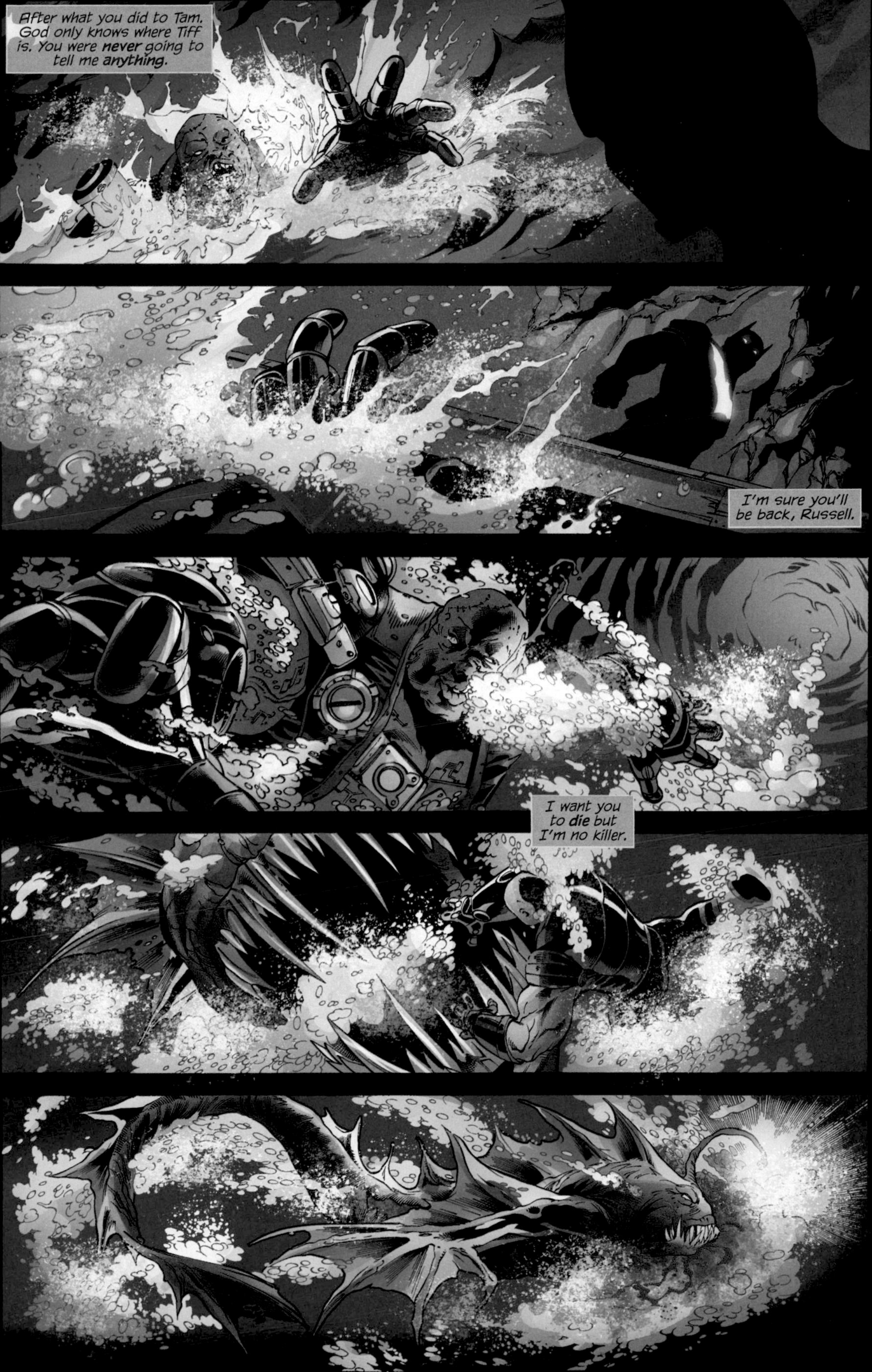
After what you did to Tam. God only knows where Tiff is. You were **never** going to tell me **anything**.
I'm sure you'll be back, Russell.
I want you to **die** but I'm no killer.

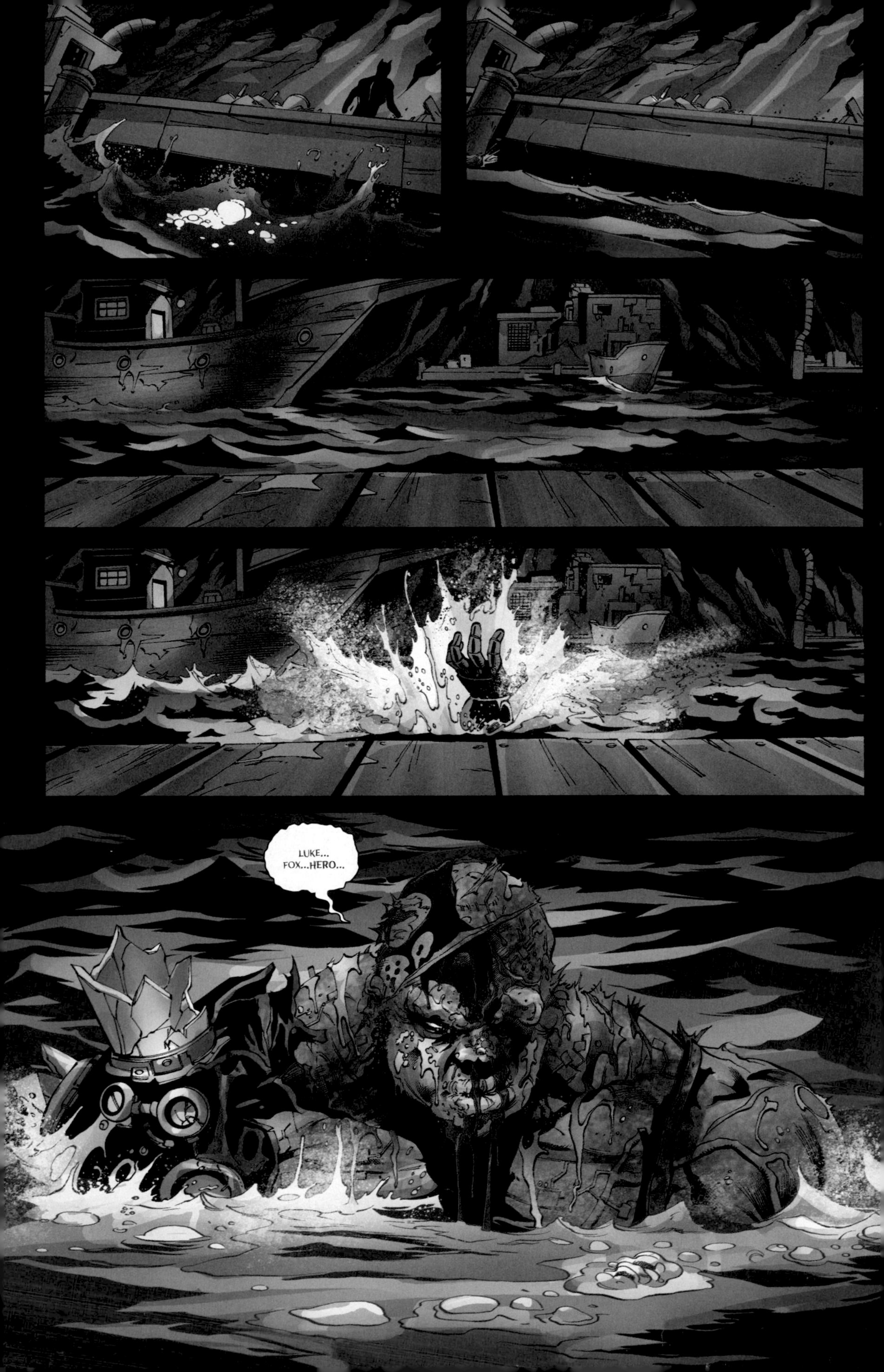
LUKE...
FOX...HERO...

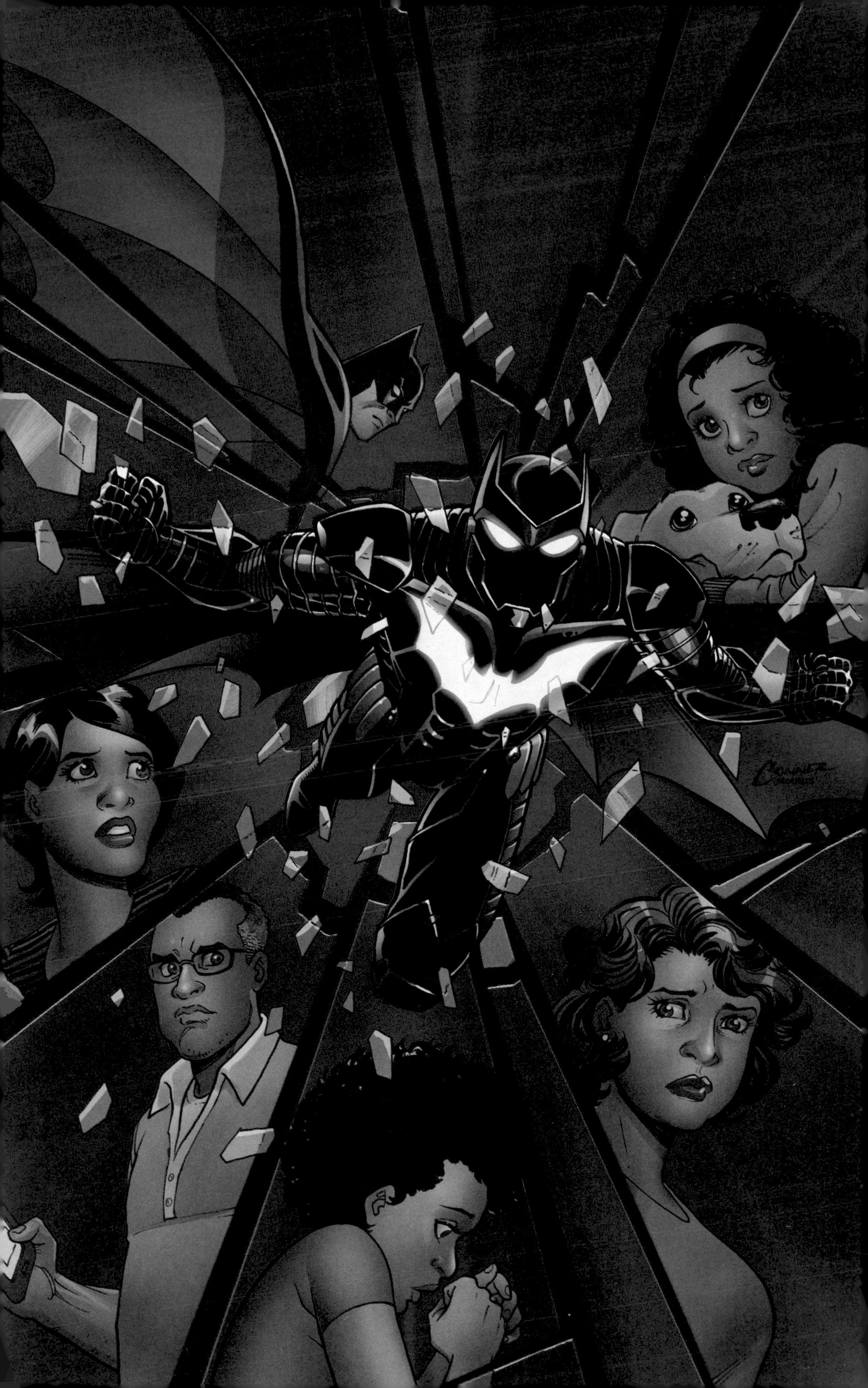

FAMILY IS EVERYTHING

JIMMY PALMIOTTI
JUSTIN GRAY
writers

EDUARDO PANSICA
penciller

JÚLIO FERREIRA
inker

PAUL MOUNTS
colorist

DEZI SIENTY
letterer

cover art by
AMANDA CONNOR and PAUL MOUNTS

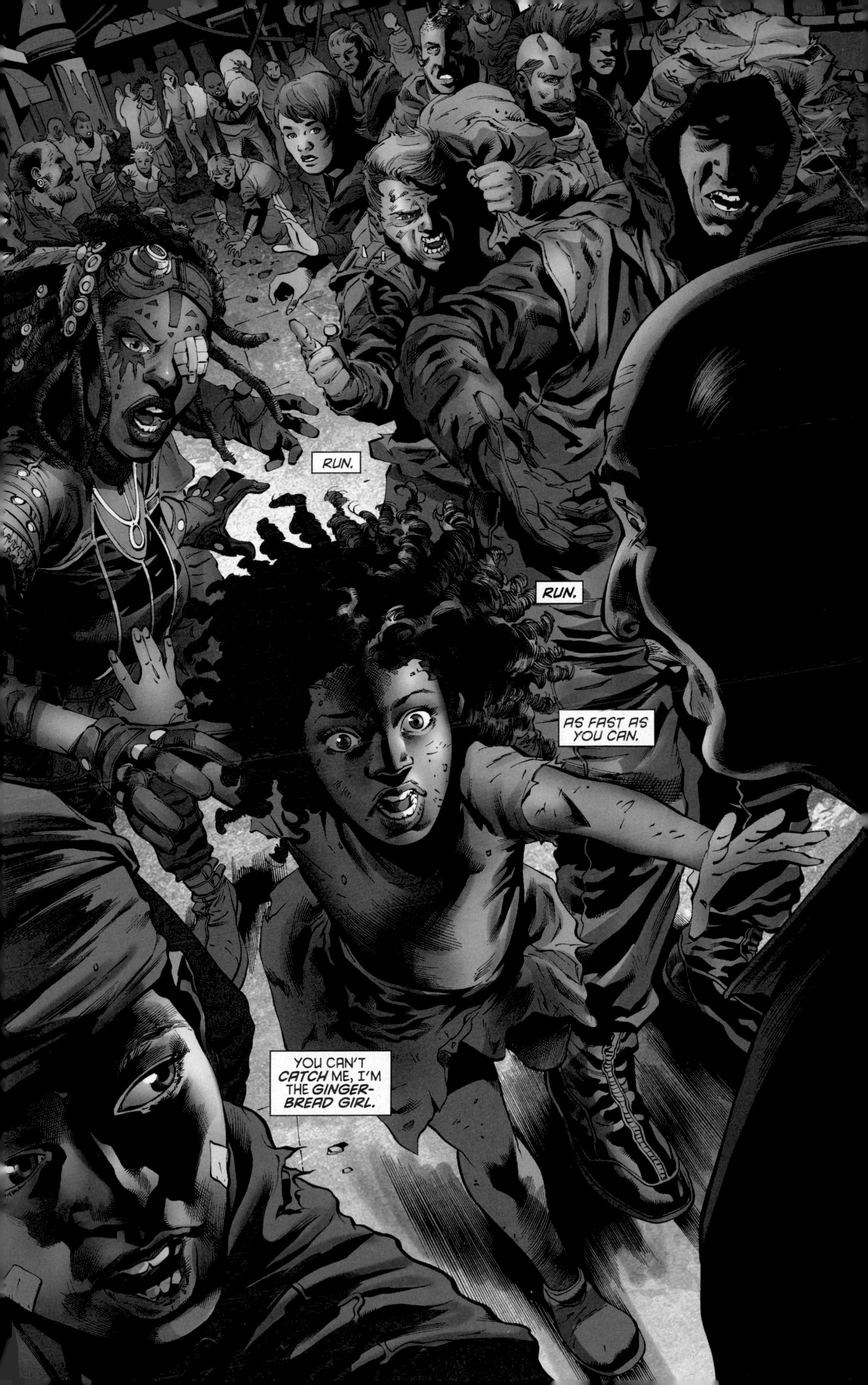
RUN.
RUN.
AS FAST AS YOU CAN.
YOU CAN'T CATCH ME, I'M THE GINGER-BREAD GIRL.

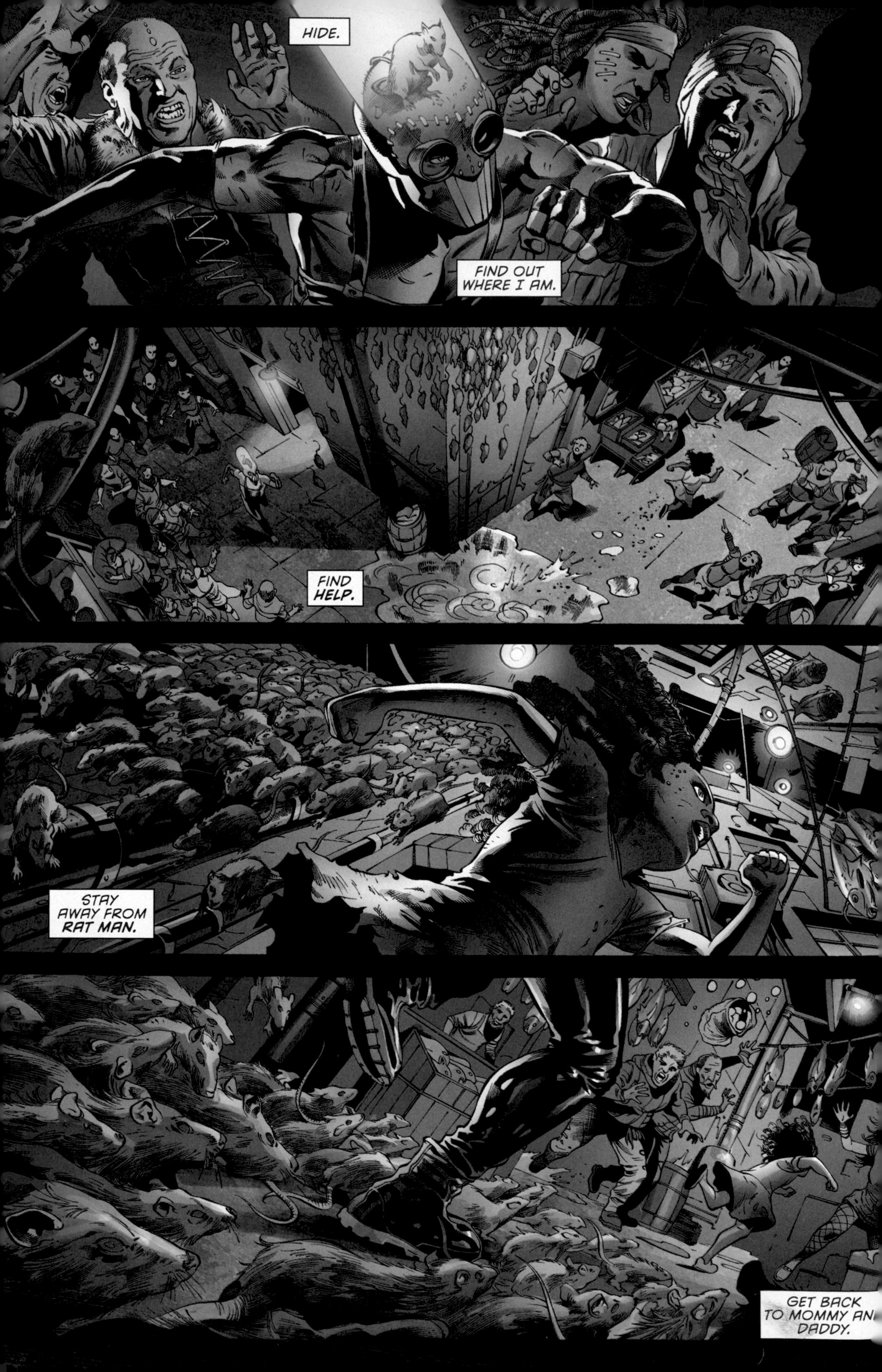
HIDE.
FIND OUT WHERE I AM.
FIND HELP.
STAY AWAY FROM RAT MAN.
GET BACK TO MOMMY AN DADDY.

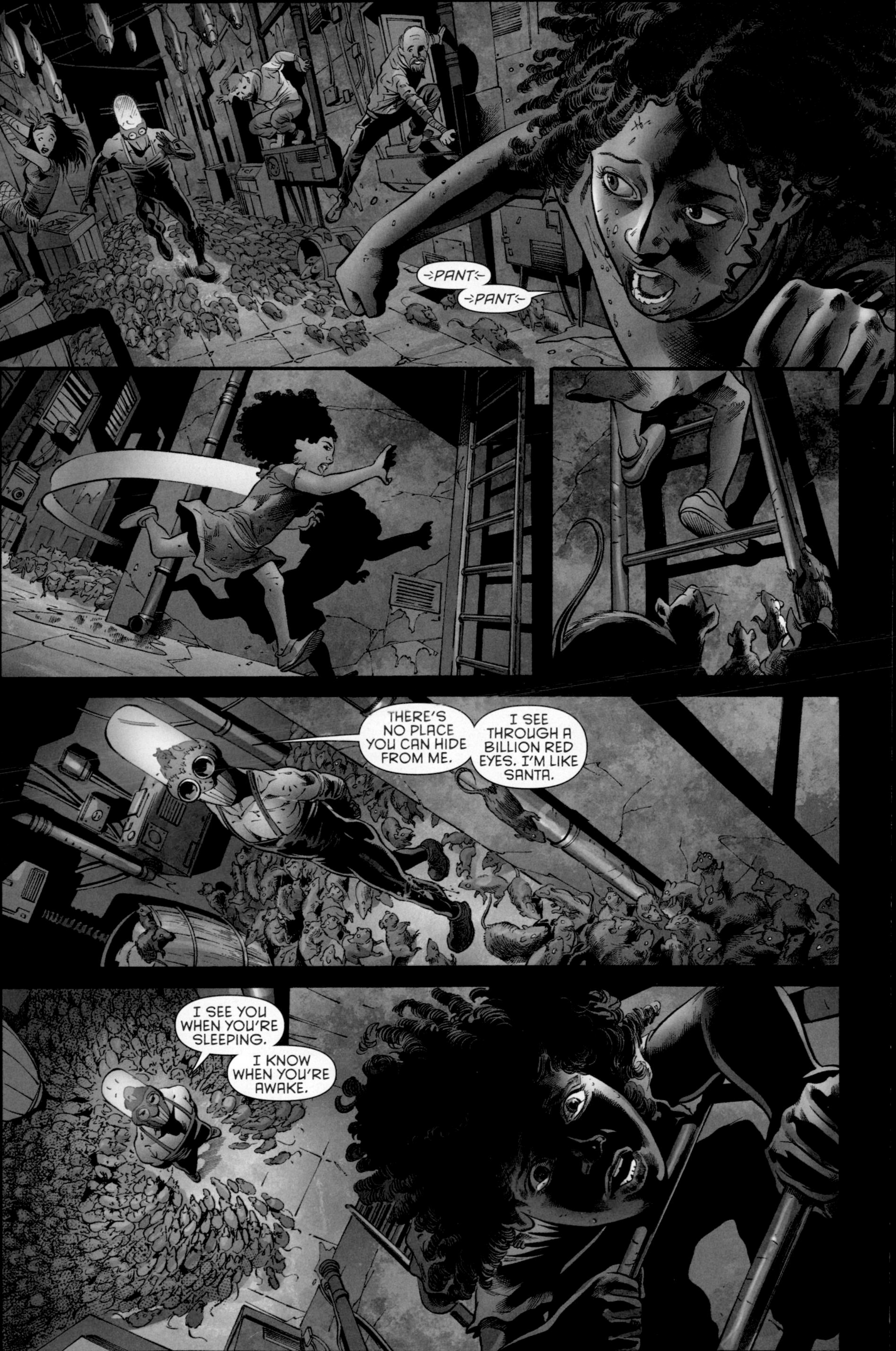

PANT
PANT
THERE'S NO PLACE YOU CAN HIDE FROM ME.
I SEE THROUGH A BILLION RED EYES. I'M LIKE SANTA.
I SEE YOU WHEN YOU'RE SLEEPING.
I KNOW WHEN YOU'RE AWAKE.

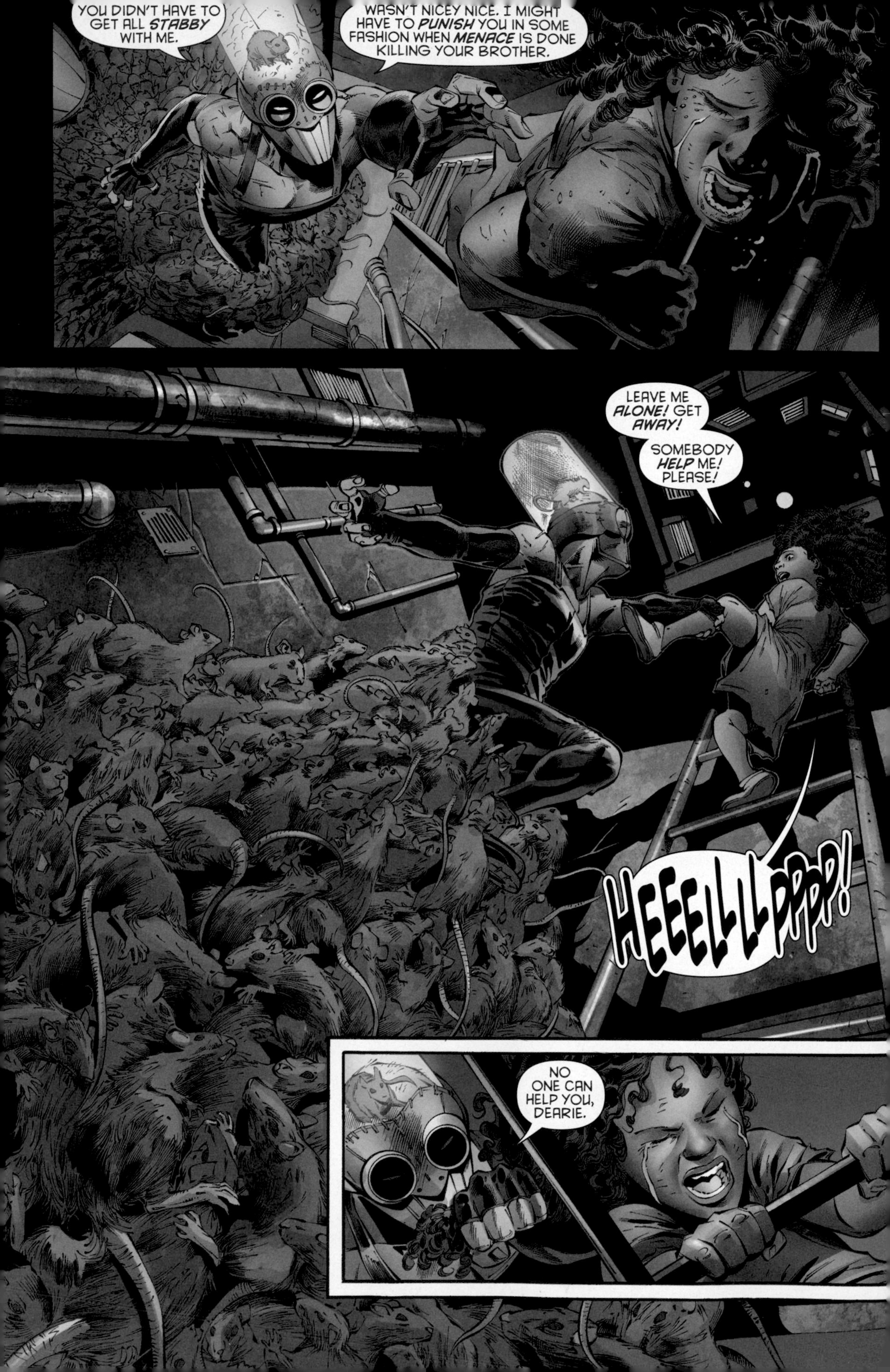
YOU DIDN'T HAVE TO GET ALL STABBY WITH ME.
WASN'T NICEY NICE. I MIGHT HAVE TO PUNISH YOU IN SOME FASHION WHEN MENACE IS DONE KILLING YOUR BROTHER.
LEAVE ME ALONE! GET AWAY!
SOMEBODY HELP ME! PLEASE!
HEEELLLPPPP!
NO ONE CAN HELP YOU, DEARIE.

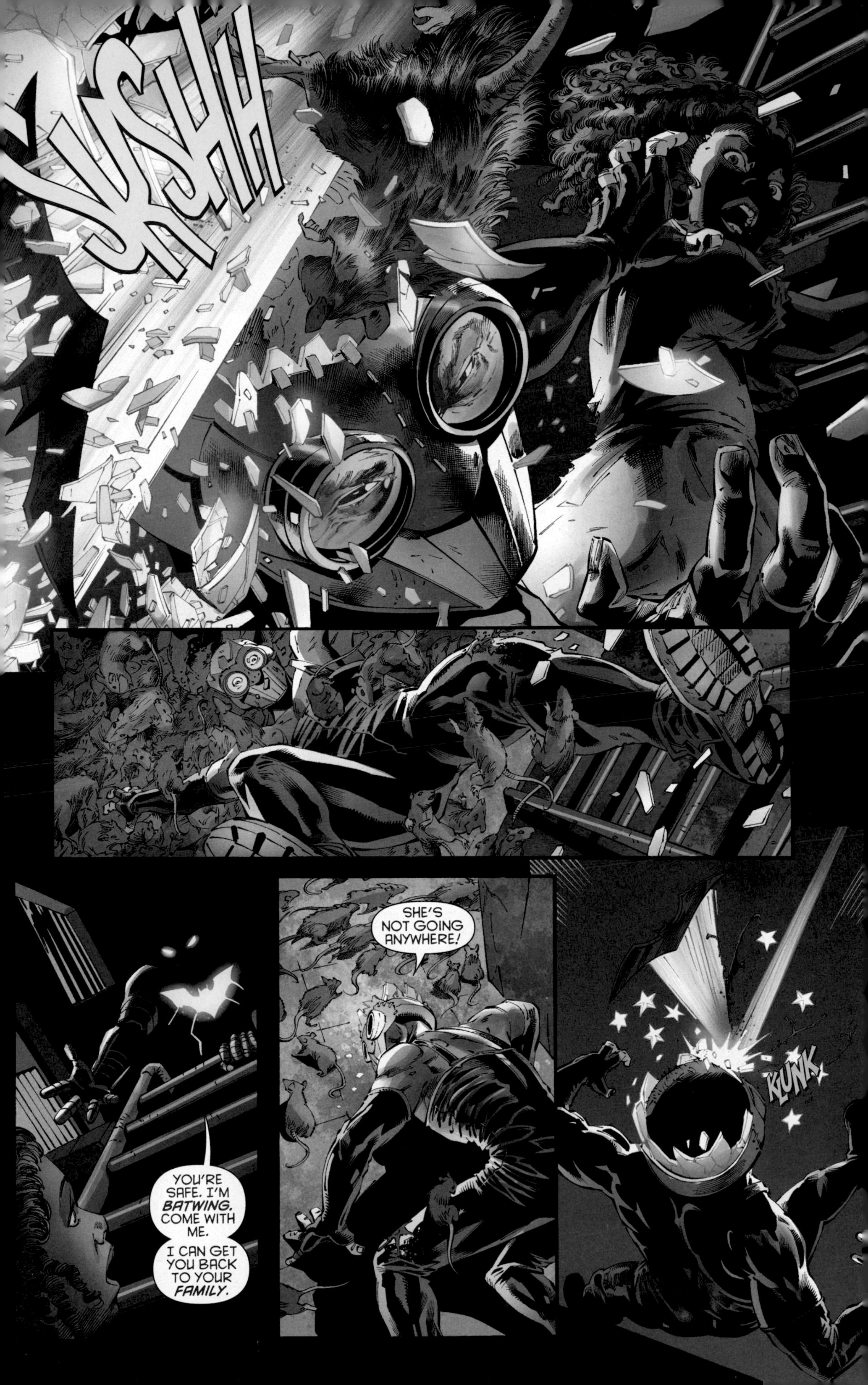

SHHSHH
YOU'RE SAFE. I'M BATWING. COME WITH ME.
I CAN GET YOU BACK TO YOUR FAMILY.
SHE'S NOT GOING ANYWHERE!
KLUNK

MEANWHILE...
WAYNE TOWER.

THE SEARCH IS STILL ON FOR SIX-YEAR-OLD *TIFFANY FOX,* DAUGHTER OF WAYNE ENTERPRISES CEO *LUCIUS FOX.*

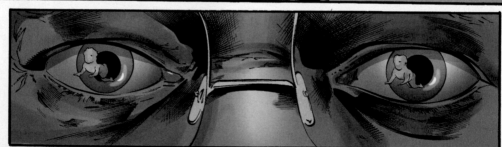

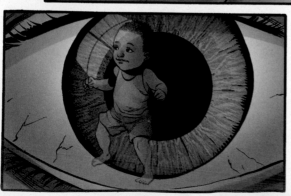

YOU GOT IT, TIFFANY! THAT'S IT... YOU'RE *WALKING...* THAT'S MY BIG GIRL...

DADDY PICKED THE *RIGHT* DAY T WORK FROM HOME, DIDN' HE?

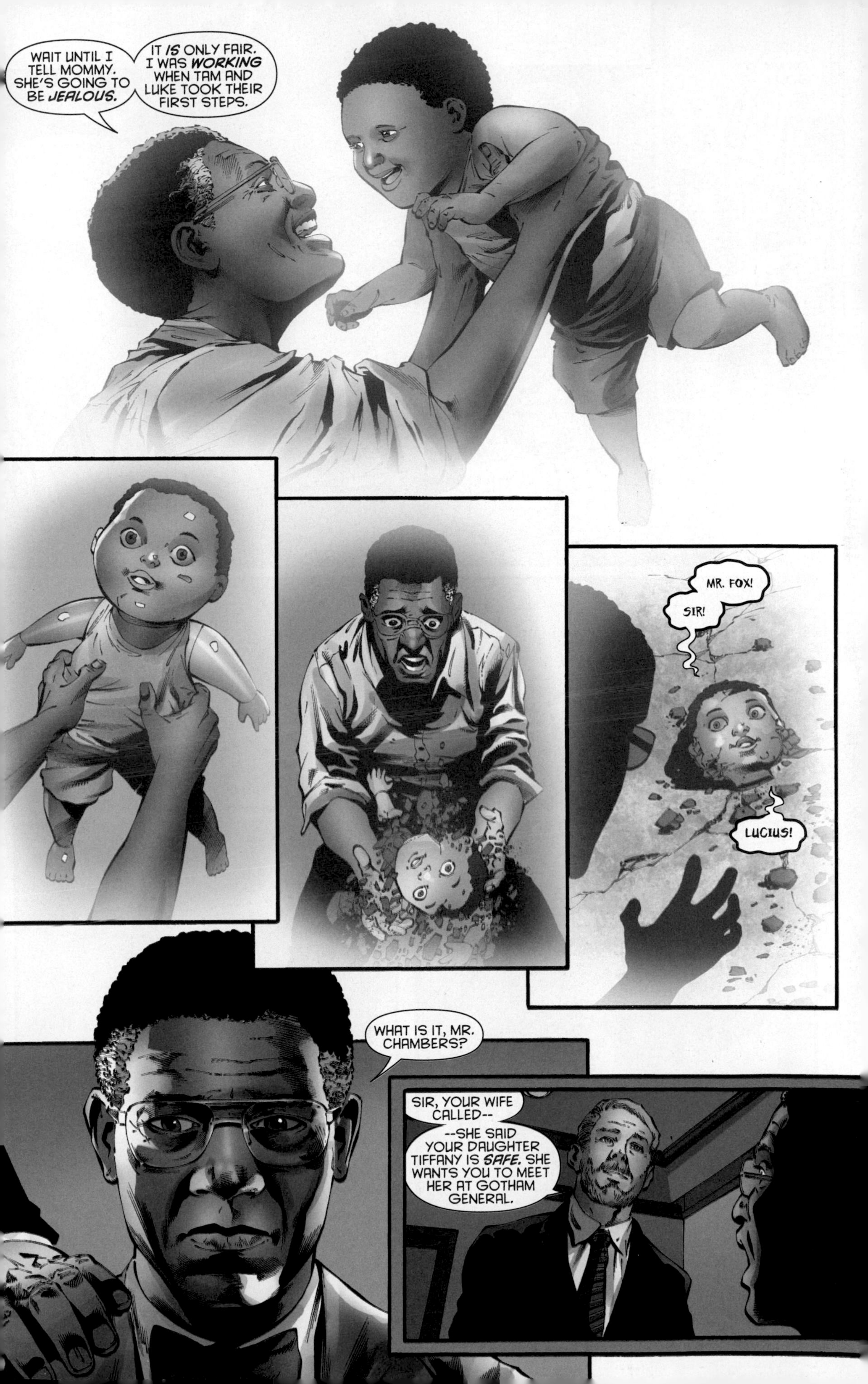
WAIT UNTIL I TELL MOMMY. SHE'S GOING TO BE *JEALOUS.*
IT *IS* ONLY FAIR. I WAS *WORKING* WHEN TAM AND LUKE TOOK THEIR FIRST STEPS.
MR. FOX!
SIR!
LUCIUS!
WHAT IS IT, MR. CHAMBERS?
SIR, YOUR WIFE CALLED--
--SHE SAID YOUR DAUGHTER TIFFANY IS *SAFE.* SHE WANTS YOU TO MEET HER AT GOTHAM GENERAL.

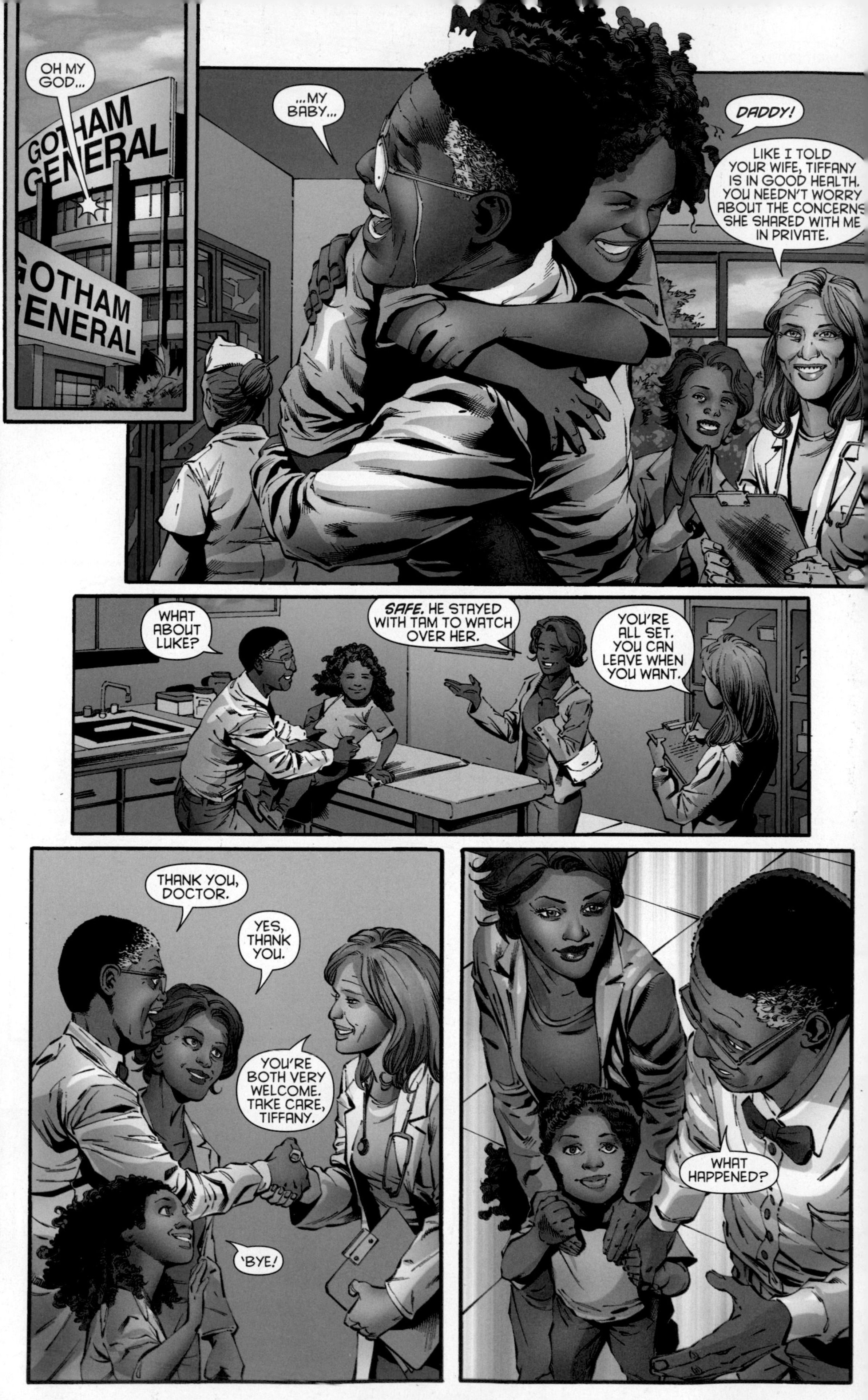
OH MY GOD...
GOTHAM GENERAL
GOTHAM GENERAL
...MY BABY...
DADDY!
LIKE I TOLD YOUR WIFE, TIFFANY IS IN GOOD HEALTH. YOU NEEDN'T WORRY ABOUT THE CONCERNS SHE SHARED WITH ME IN PRIVATE.
WHAT ABOUT LUKE?
SAFE. HE STAYED WITH TAM TO WATCH OVER HER.
YOU'RE ALL SET. YOU CAN LEAVE WHEN YOU WANT.
THANK YOU, DOCTOR.
YES, THANK YOU.
YOU'RE BOTH VERY WELCOME. TAKE CARE, TIFFANY.
'BYE!
WHAT HAPPENED?

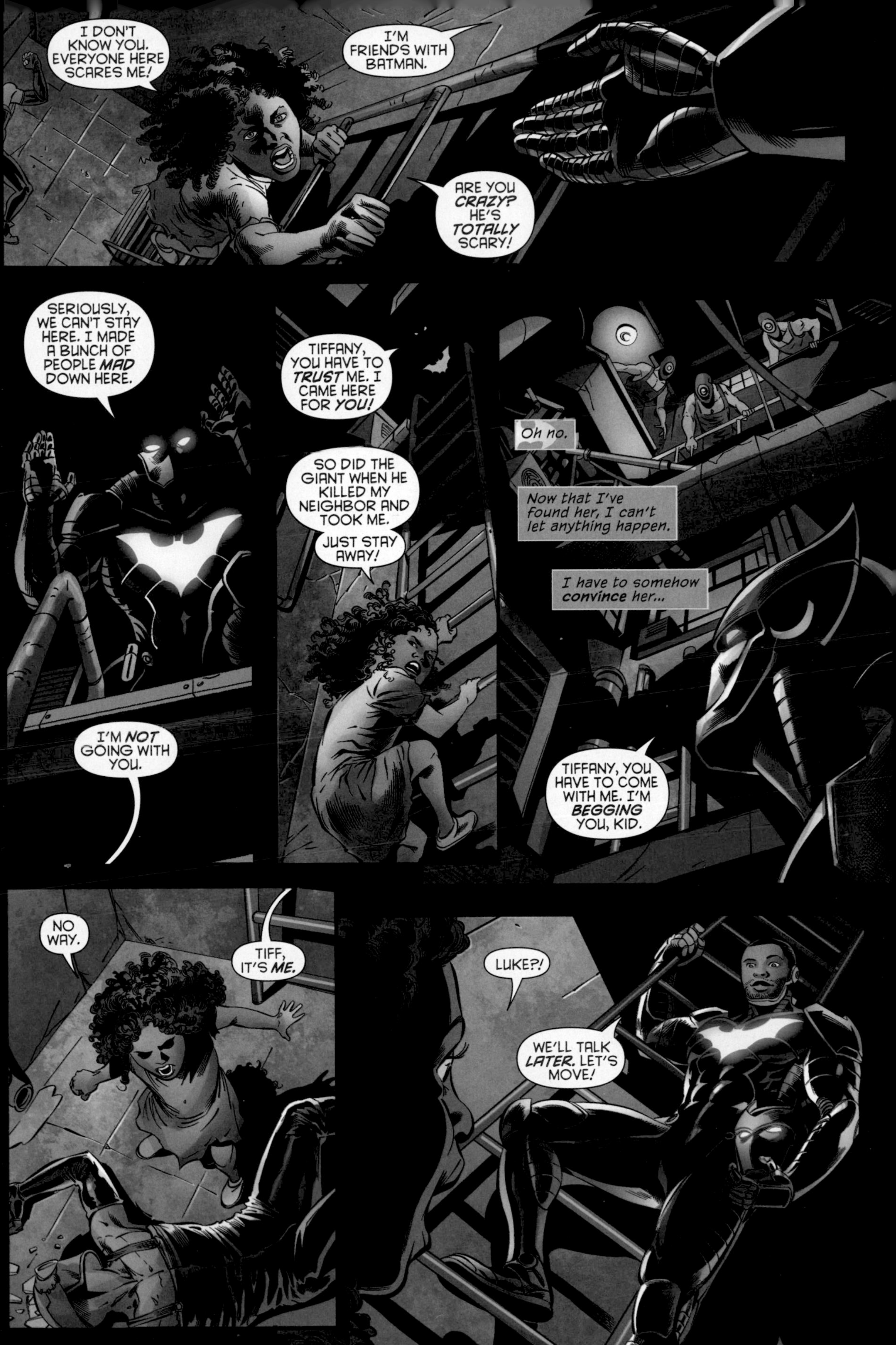
I DON'T KNOW YOU. EVERYONE HERE SCARES ME!
I'M FRIENDS WITH BATMAN.
ARE YOU *CRAZY?* HE'S *TOTALLY* SCARY!
SERIOUSLY, WE CAN'T STAY HERE. I MADE A BUNCH OF PEOPLE *MAD* DOWN HERE.
I'M *NOT* GOING WITH YOU.
TIFFANY, YOU HAVE TO *TRUST* ME. I CAME HERE FOR *YOU!*
SO DID THE GIANT WHEN HE KILLED MY NEIGHBOR AND TOOK ME.
JUST STAY AWAY!
Oh no.
Now that I've found her, I can't let anything happen.
I have to somehow **convince** her...
TIFFANY, YOU HAVE TO COME WITH ME. I'M *BEGGING* YOU, KID.
NO WAY.
TIFF, IT'S *ME.*
LUKE?!
WE'LL TALK *LATER.* LET'S MOVE!

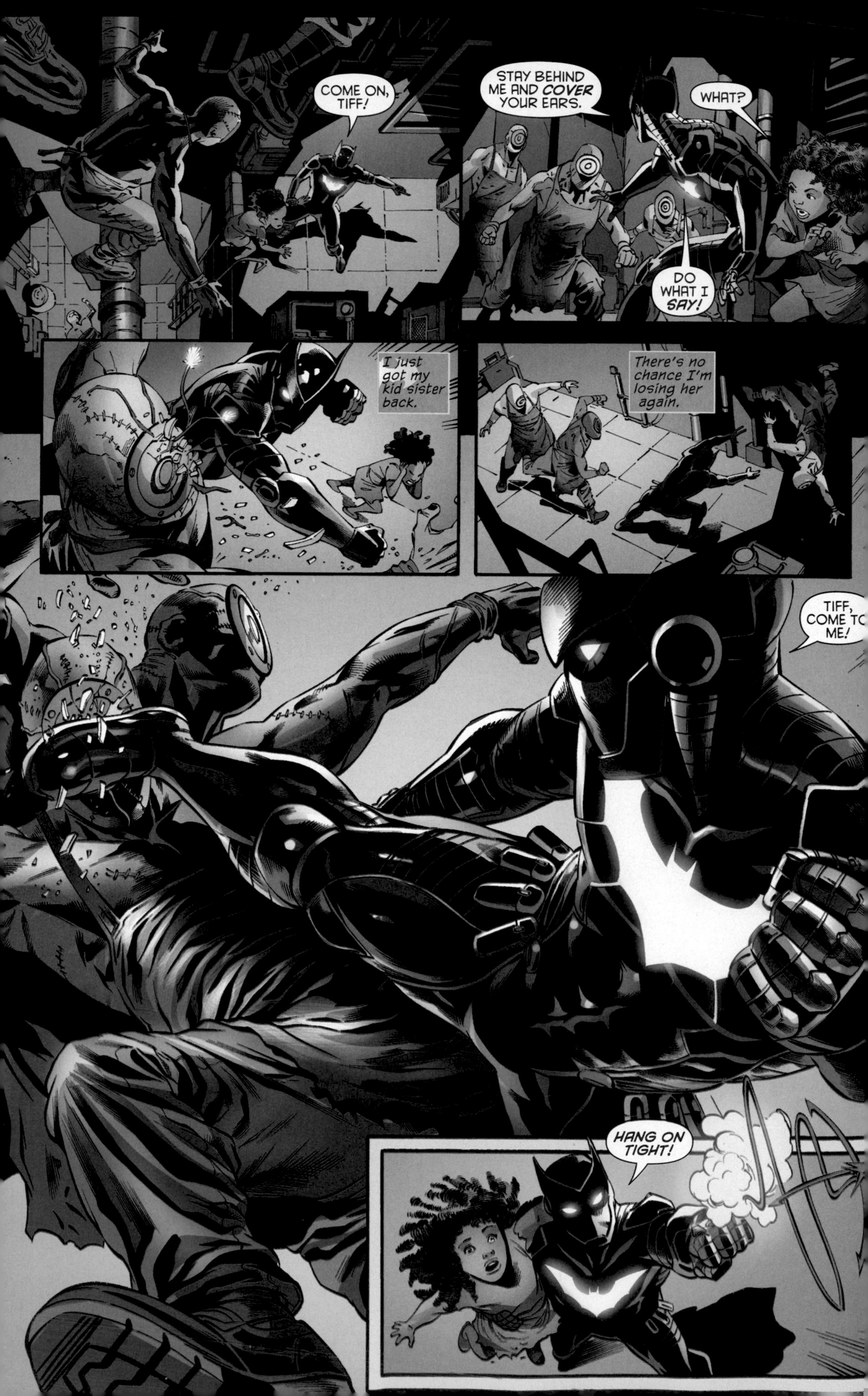
COME ON, TIFF!
STAY BEHIND ME AND COVER YOUR EARS.
WHAT?
DO WHAT I SAY!
I just got my kid sister back.
There's no chance I'm losing her again.
TIFF, COME TO ME!
HANG ON TIGHT!

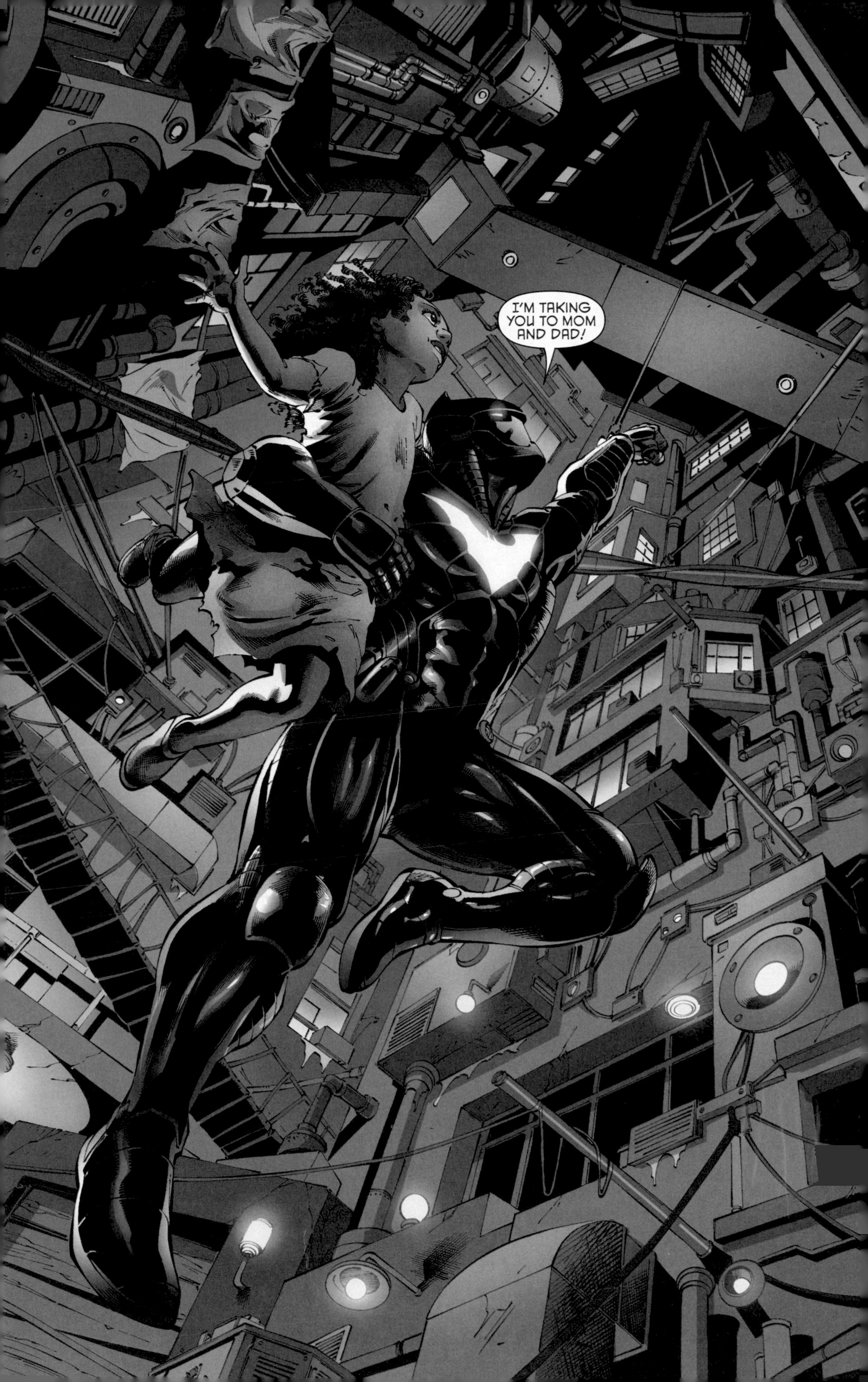
I'M TAKING YOU TO MOM AND DAD!

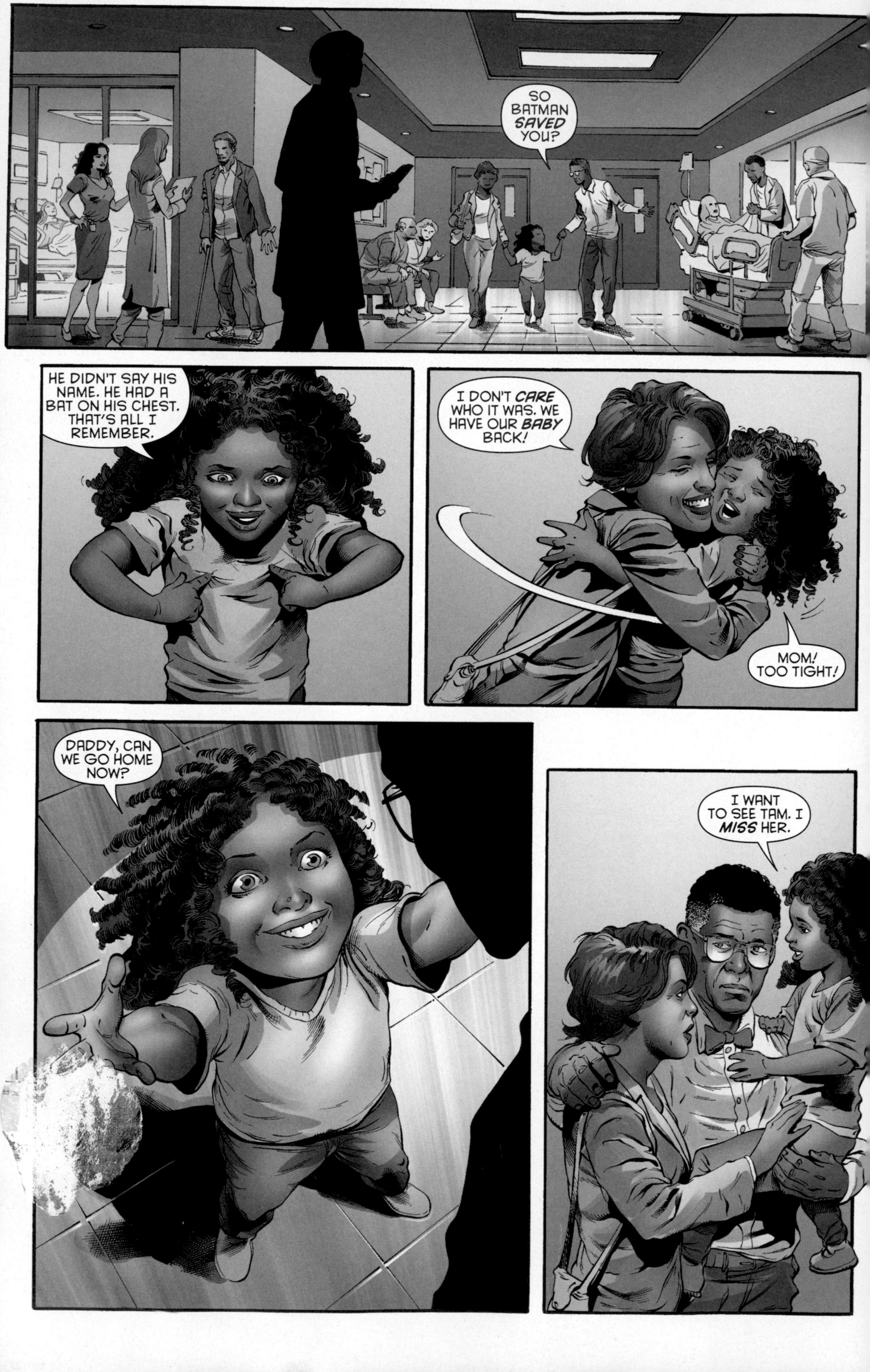
SO BATMAN SAVED YOU?
HE DIDN'T SAY HIS NAME. HE HAD A BAT ON HIS CHEST. THAT'S ALL I REMEMBER.
I DON'T CARE WHO IT WAS. WE HAVE OUR BABY BACK!
MOM! TOO TIGHT!
DADDY, CAN WE GO HOME NOW?
I WANT TO SEE TAM. I MISS HER.

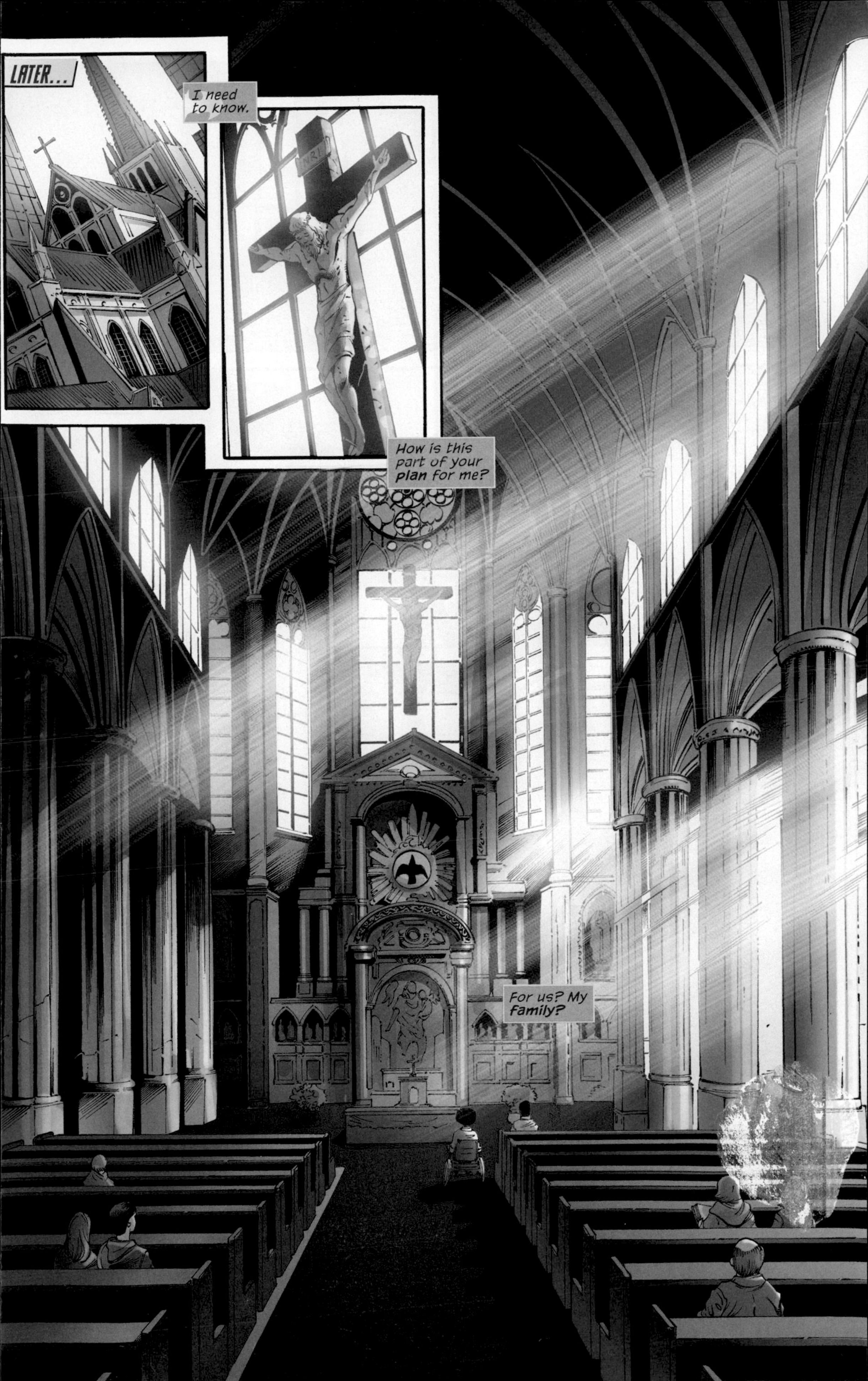
LATER...
I need to know.
INRI
How is this part of your **plan** for me?
For us? My **family?**

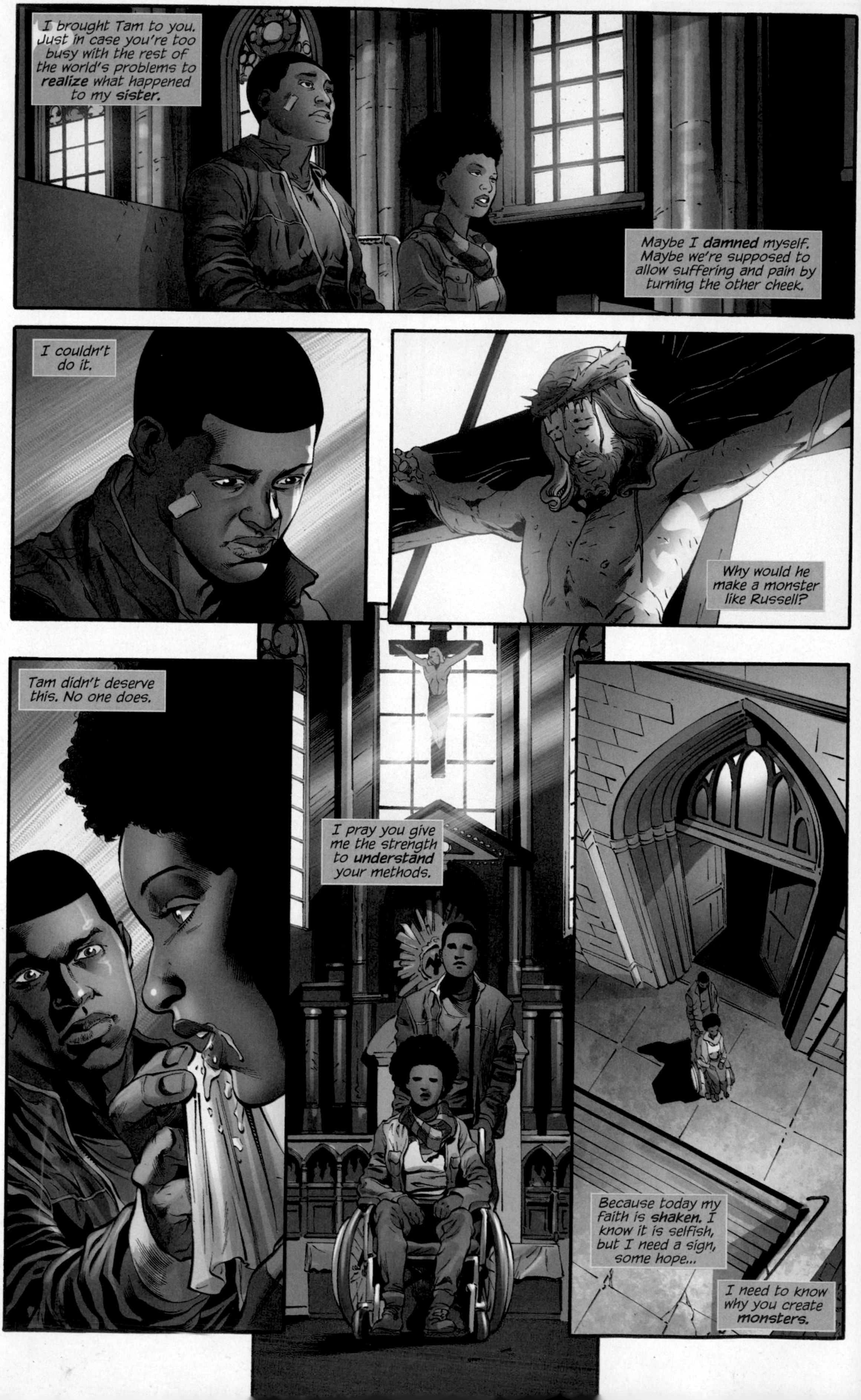
I brought Tam to you. Just in case you're too busy with the rest of the world's problems to **realize** what happened to my **sister.**
Maybe I **damned** myself. Maybe we're supposed to allow suffering and pain by turning the other cheek.
I couldn't do it.
Why would he make a monster like Russell?
Tam didn't deserve this. No one does.
I pray you give me the strength to **understand** your methods.
Because today my faith is **shaken.** I know it is selfish, but I need a sign, some hope...
I need to know why you create **monsters.**

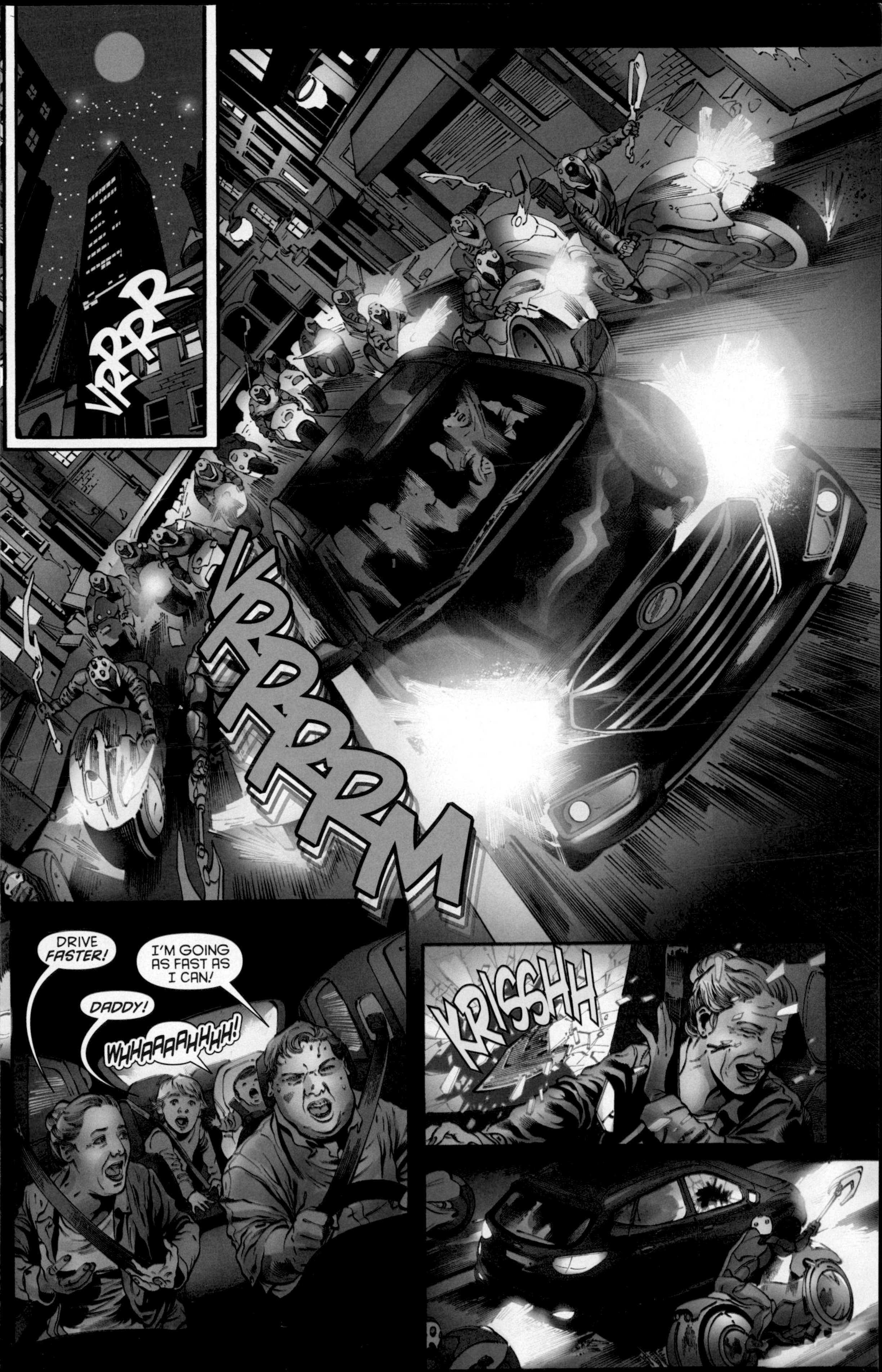

VRRRR
VRRRRM
DRIVE FASTER!
I'M GOING AS FAST AS I CAN!
DADDY!
WHHAAAAAHHHH!
KRISSHH

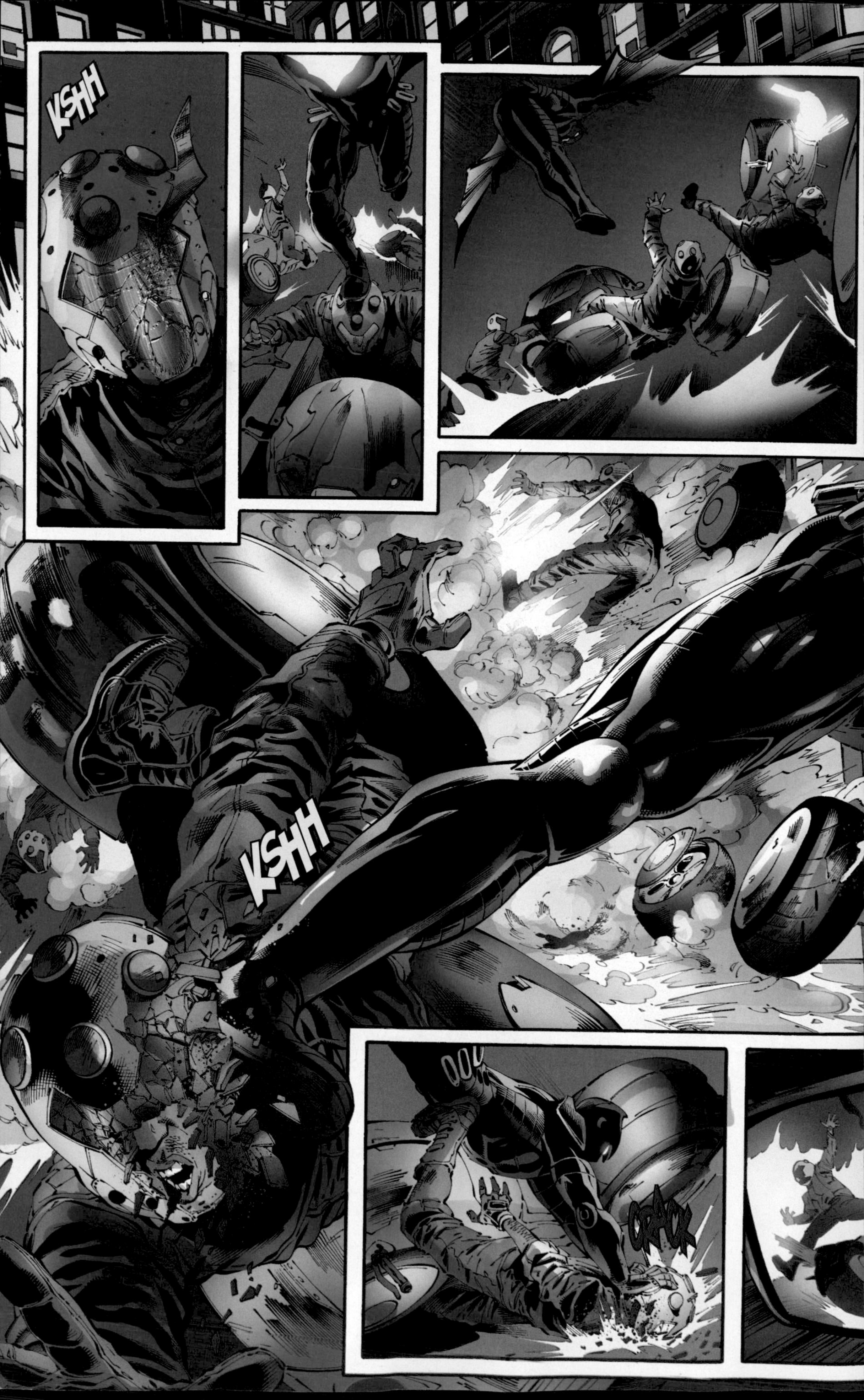
KSHH
KSHH
CRACK

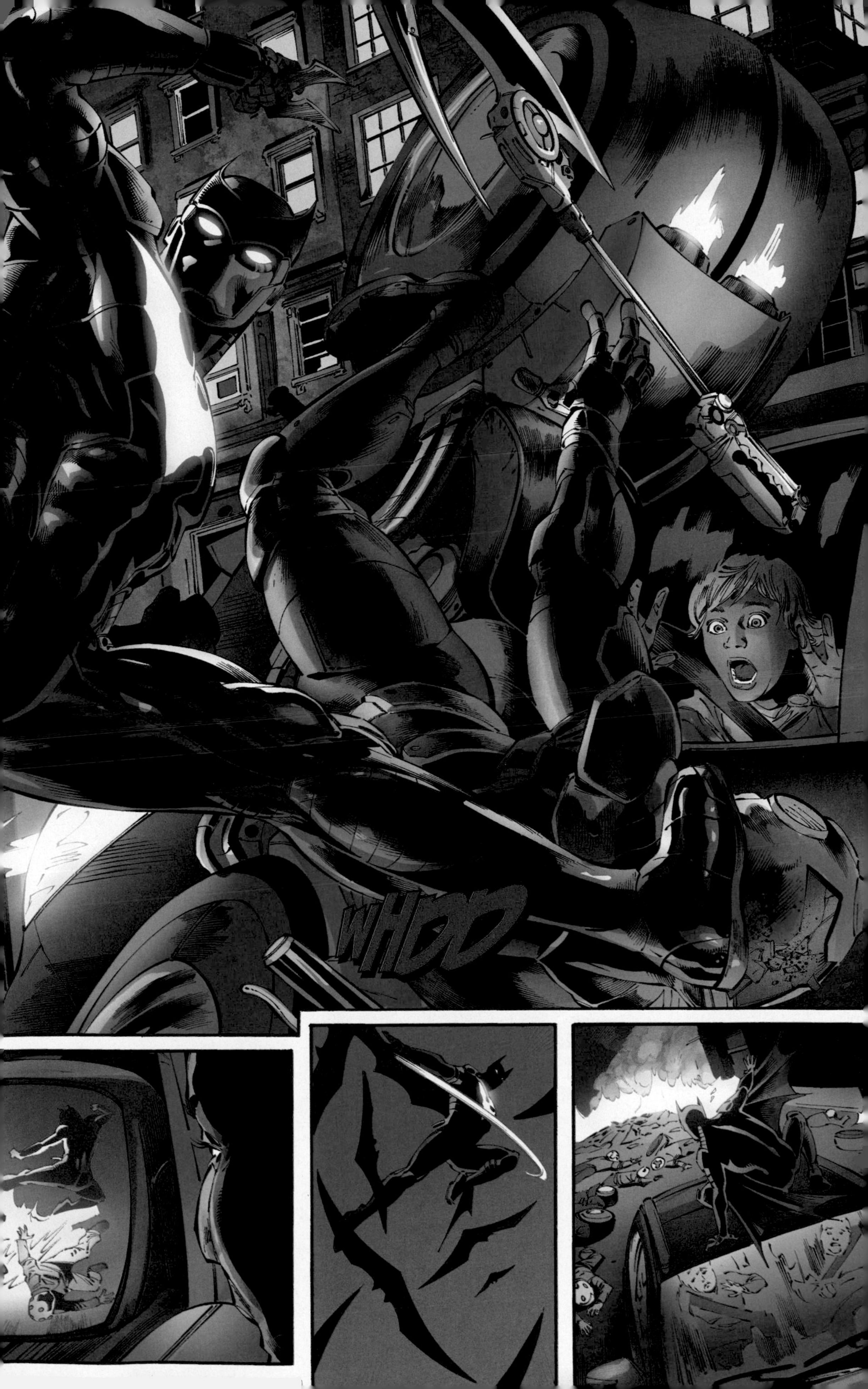
WHOO

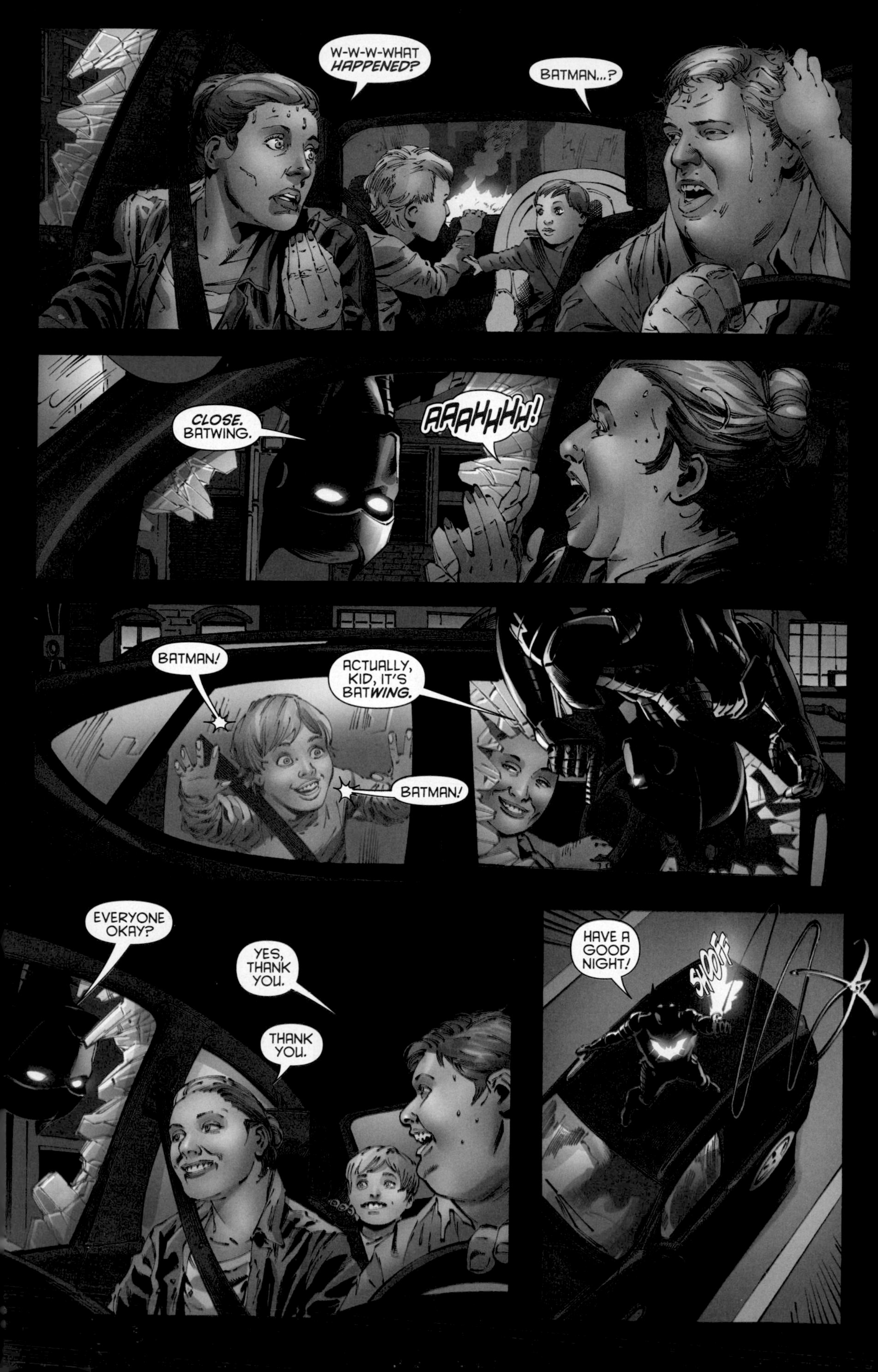
W-W-W-WHAT *HAPPENED?*
BATMAN...?
CLOSE. BATWING.
AAAHHHH!
BATMAN!
ACTUALLY, KID, IT'S BAT*WING.*
BATMAN!
EVERYONE OKAY?
YES, THANK YOU.
THANK YOU.
HAVE A GOOD NIGHT!
SHOOOF

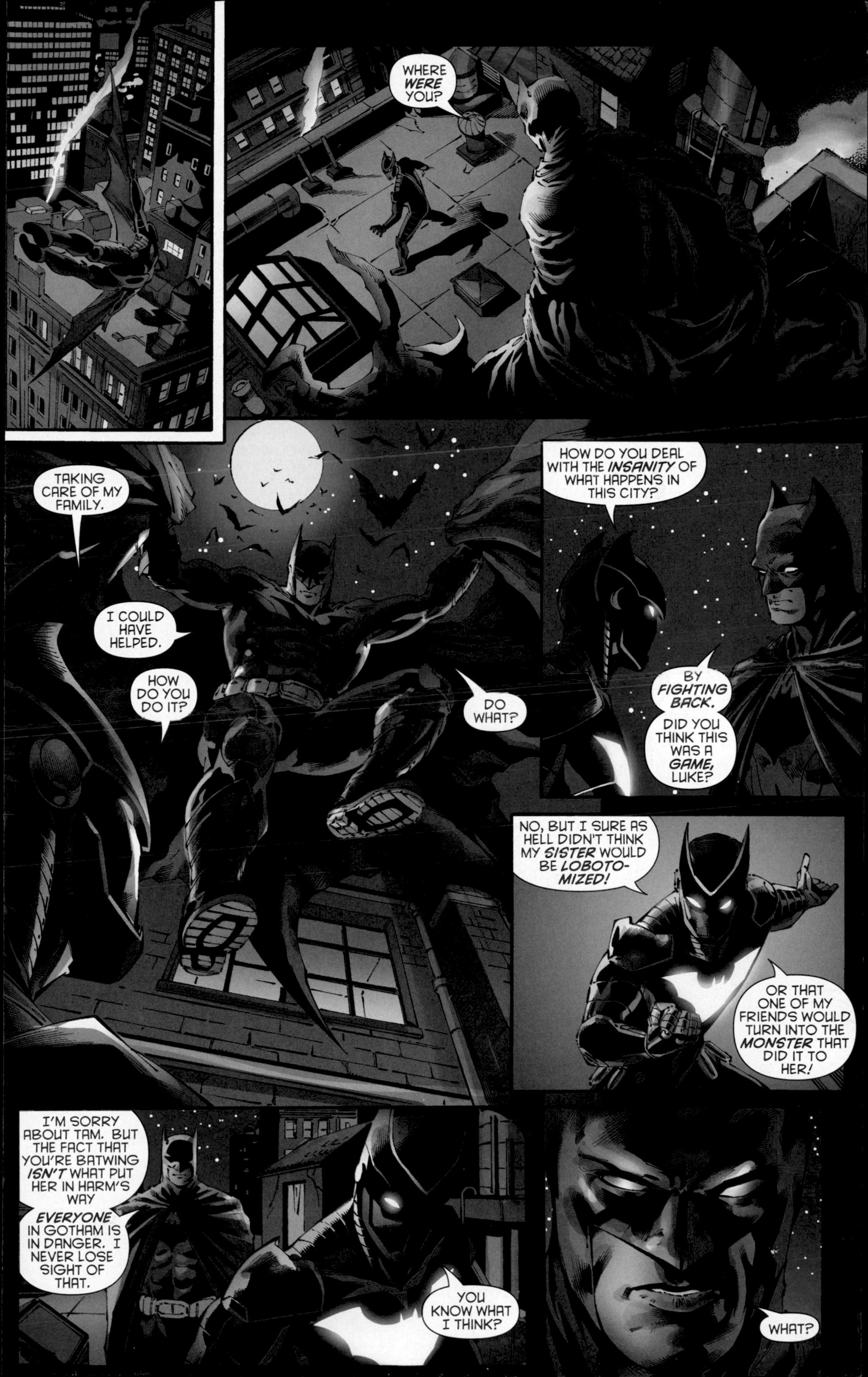
WHERE *WERE* YOU?
TAKING CARE OF MY FAMILY.
I COULD HAVE HELPED.
HOW DO YOU DO IT?
DO WHAT?
HOW DO YOU DEAL WITH THE *INSANITY* OF WHAT HAPPENS IN THIS CITY?
BY *FIGHTING BACK.*
DID YOU THINK THIS WAS A *GAME,* LUKE?
NO, BUT I SURE AS HELL DIDN'T THINK MY *SISTER* WOULD BE *LOBOTO-MIZED!*
OR THAT ONE OF MY FRIENDS WOULD TURN INTO THE *MONSTER* THAT DID IT TO HER!
I'M SORRY ABOUT TAM. BUT THE FACT THAT YOU'RE BATWING *ISN'T* WHAT PUT HER IN HARM'S WAY
EVERYONE IN GOTHAM IS IN DANGER. I NEVER LOSE SIGHT OF THAT.
YOU KNOW WHAT I THINK?
WHAT?

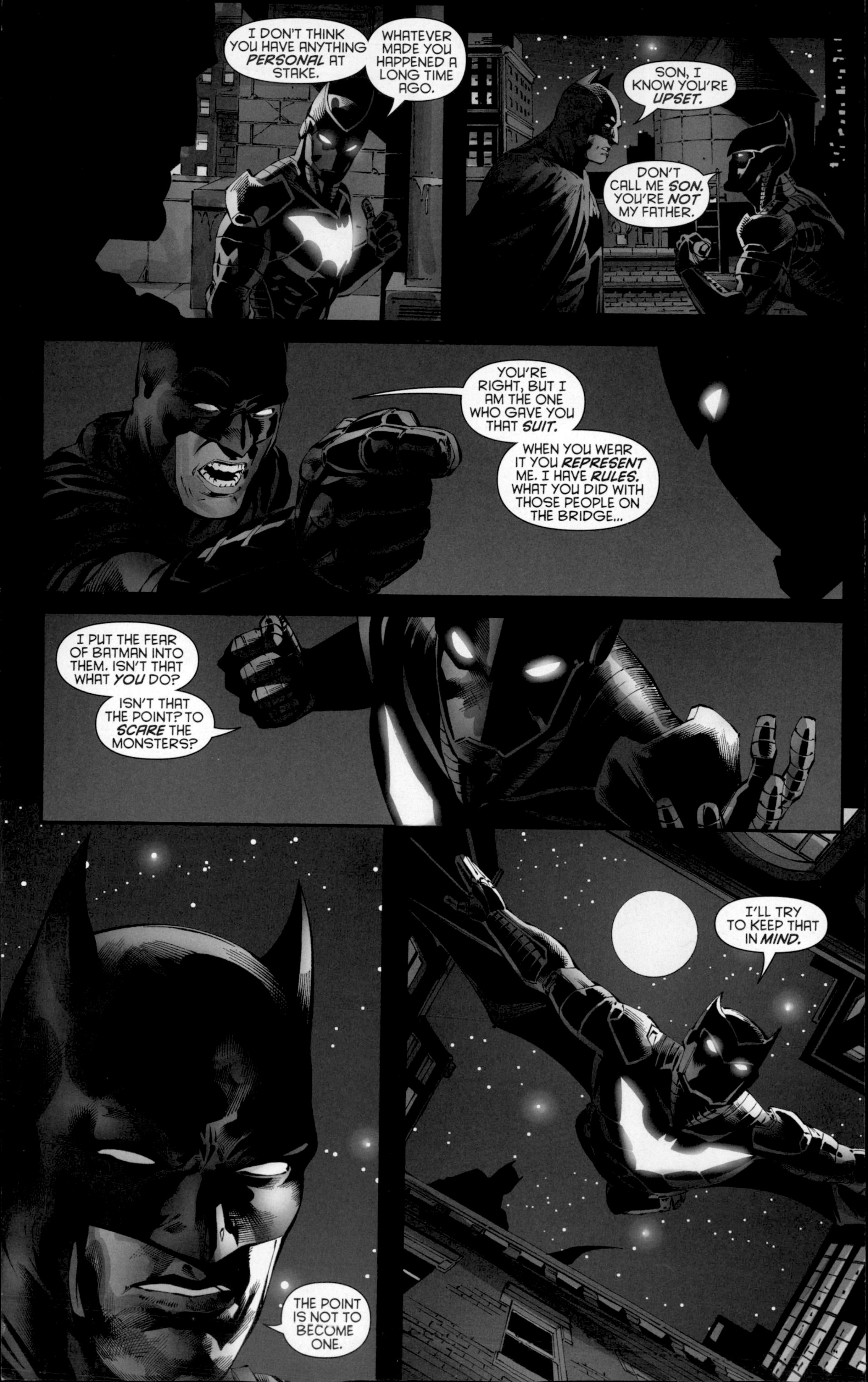
I DON'T THINK YOU HAVE ANYTHING *PERSONAL* AT STAKE.
WHATEVER MADE YOU HAPPENED A LONG TIME AGO.
SON, I KNOW YOU'RE *UPSET.*
DON'T CALL ME *SON.* YOU'RE *NOT* MY FATHER.
YOU'RE RIGHT, BUT I AM THE ONE WHO GAVE YOU THAT *SUIT.*
WHEN YOU WEAR IT YOU *REPRESENT* ME. I HAVE *RULES.* WHAT YOU DID WITH THOSE PEOPLE ON THE BRIDGE...
I PUT THE FEAR OF BATMAN INTO THEM. ISN'T THAT WHAT *YOU* DO?
ISN'T THAT THE POINT? TO *SCARE* THE MONSTERS?
THE POINT IS NOT TO BECOME ONE.
I'LL TRY TO KEEP THAT IN *MIND.*

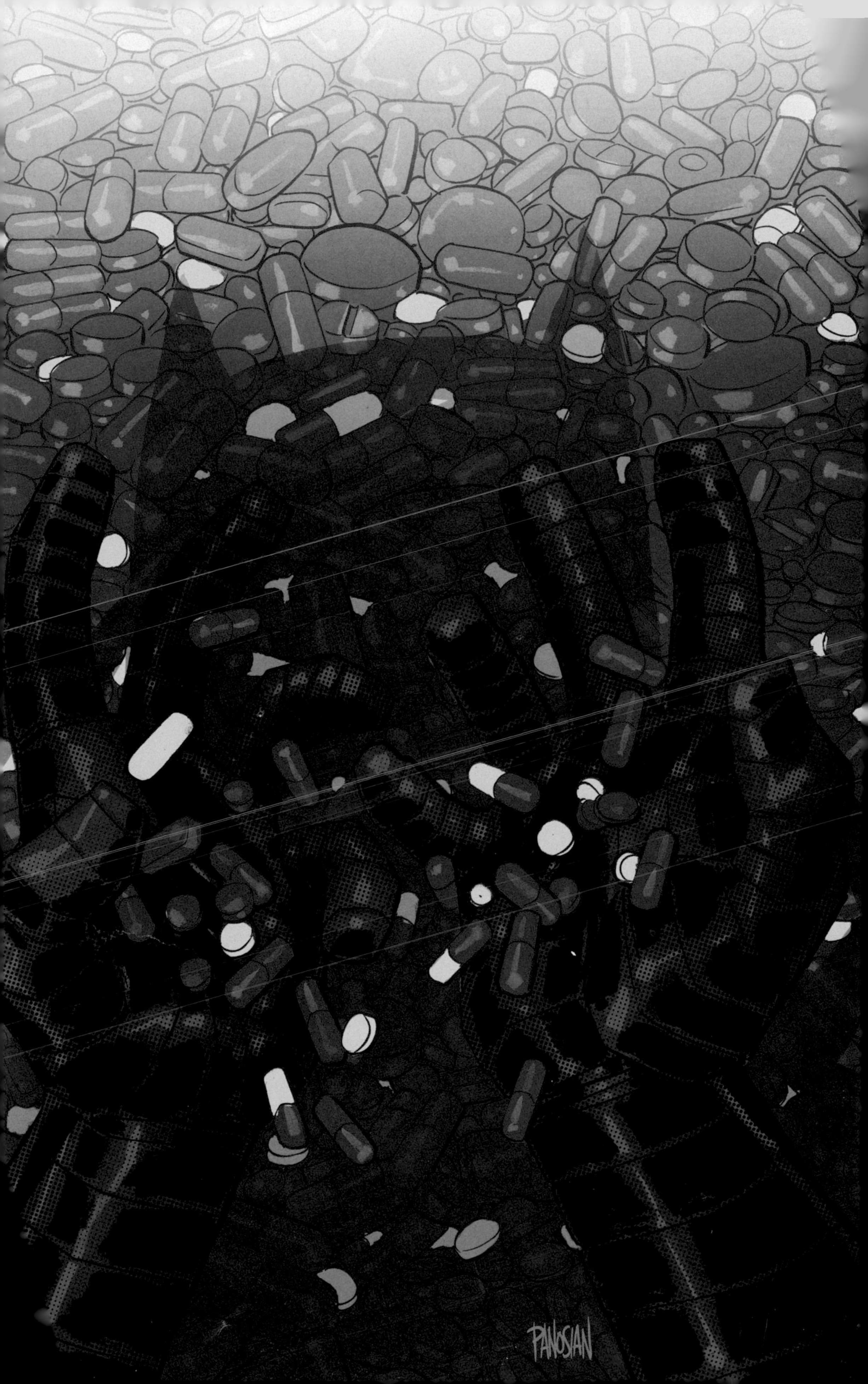
PANOSIAN

GRUESOME GEORGE

JIMMY PALMIOTTI
JUSTIN GRAY
writers

EDUARDO PANSICA
penciller

JÚLIO FERREIRA
inker

PAUL MOUNTS
colorist

TRAVIS LANHAM
letterer

cover art by
DAN PANOSIAN

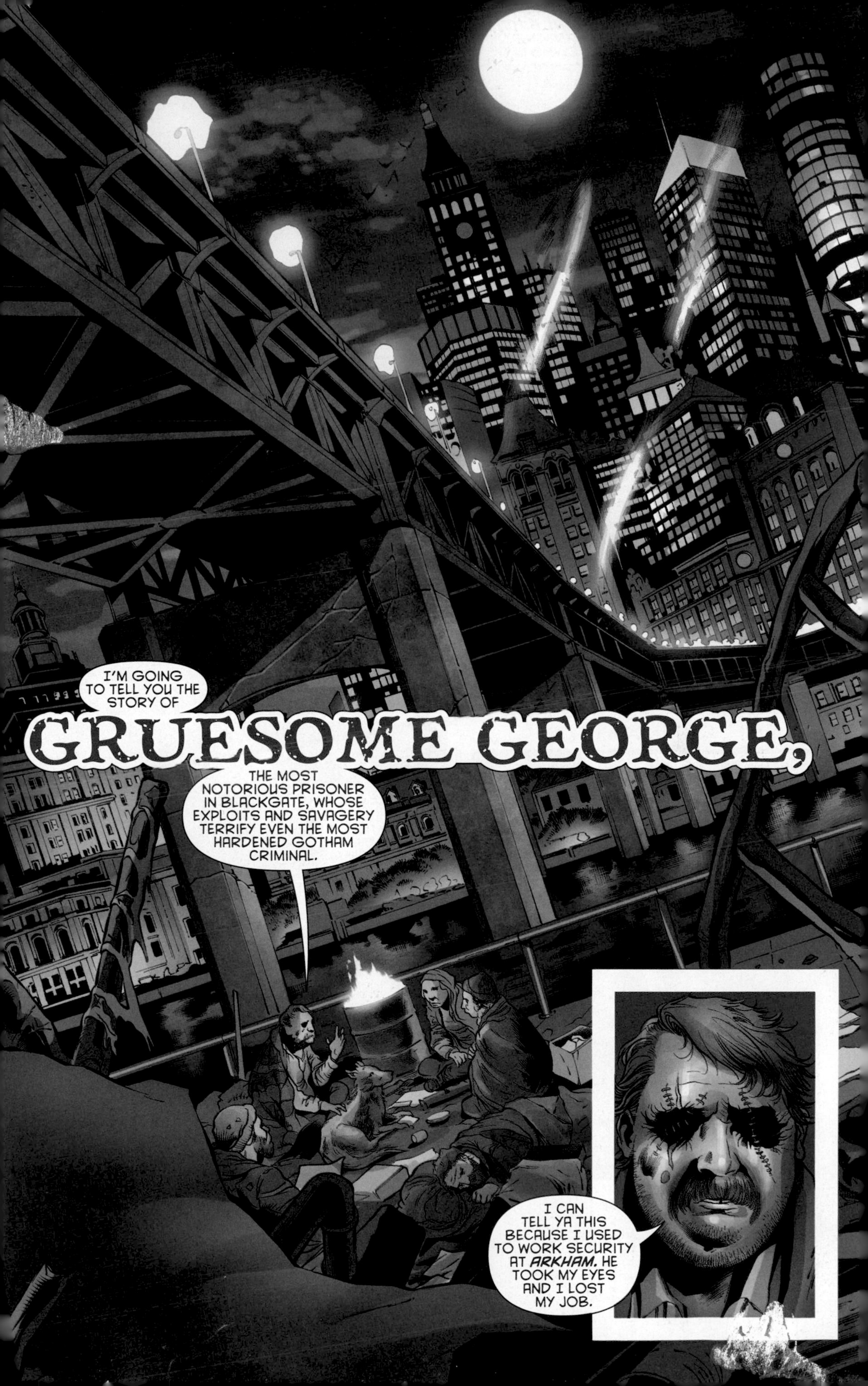
I'M GOING TO TELL YOU THE STORY OF
GRUESOME GEORGE,
THE MOST NOTORIOUS PRISONER IN BLACKGATE, WHOSE EXPLOITS AND SAVAGERY TERRIFY EVEN THE MOST HARDENED GOTHAM CRIMINAL.
I CAN TELL YA THIS BECAUSE I USED TO WORK SECURITY AT ARKHAM. HE TOOK MY EYES AND I LOST MY JOB.

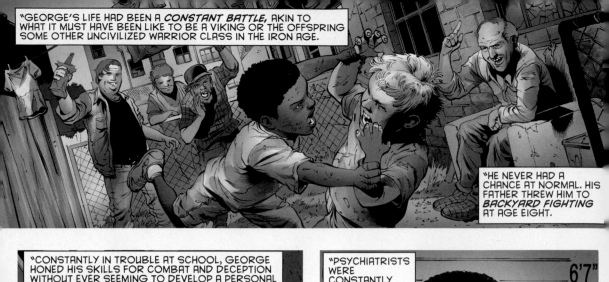

"GEORGE'S LIFE HAD BEEN A *CONSTANT BATTLE*, AKIN TO WHAT IT MUST HAVE BEEN LIKE TO BE A VIKING OR THE OFFSPRING SOME OTHER UNCIVILIZED WARRIOR CLASS IN THE IRON AGE.

"HE NEVER HAD A CHANCE AT NORMAL. HIS FATHER THREW HIM TO *BACKYARD FIGHTING* AT AGE EIGHT.

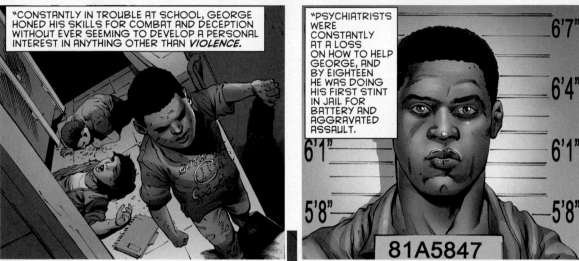

"CONSTANTLY IN TROUBLE AT SCHOOL, GEORGE HONED HIS SKILLS FOR COMBAT AND DECEPTION WITHOUT EVER SEEMING TO DEVELOP A PERSONAL INTEREST IN ANYTHING OTHER THAN *VIOLENCE.*

"PSYCHIATRISTS WERE CONSTANTLY AT A LOSS ON HOW TO HELP GEORGE, AND BY EIGHTEEN HE WAS DOING HIS FIRST STINT IN JAIL FOR BATTERY AND AGGRAVATED ASSAULT.

6'7"

6'4"

6'1"

6'1"

5'8"

5'8"

81A5847

"ONCE INSIDE, HIS REACTION TO PRISON WAS THE COMPLETE OPPOSITE OF ITS INTENDED EFFECT--HE *LOVED* IT.

"HE HAD ACCESS TO CONSTANT CONFLICT AND VIOLENCE.

"IT DIDN'T *MATTER* IF HE WON OR LOST A FIGHT--THE ACT WAS ALL THAT MATTERED. TRADING BLOWS, BLOOD, THE SMELL OF SWEAT AND FEAR--IT WAS HIS *ART FORM.*"

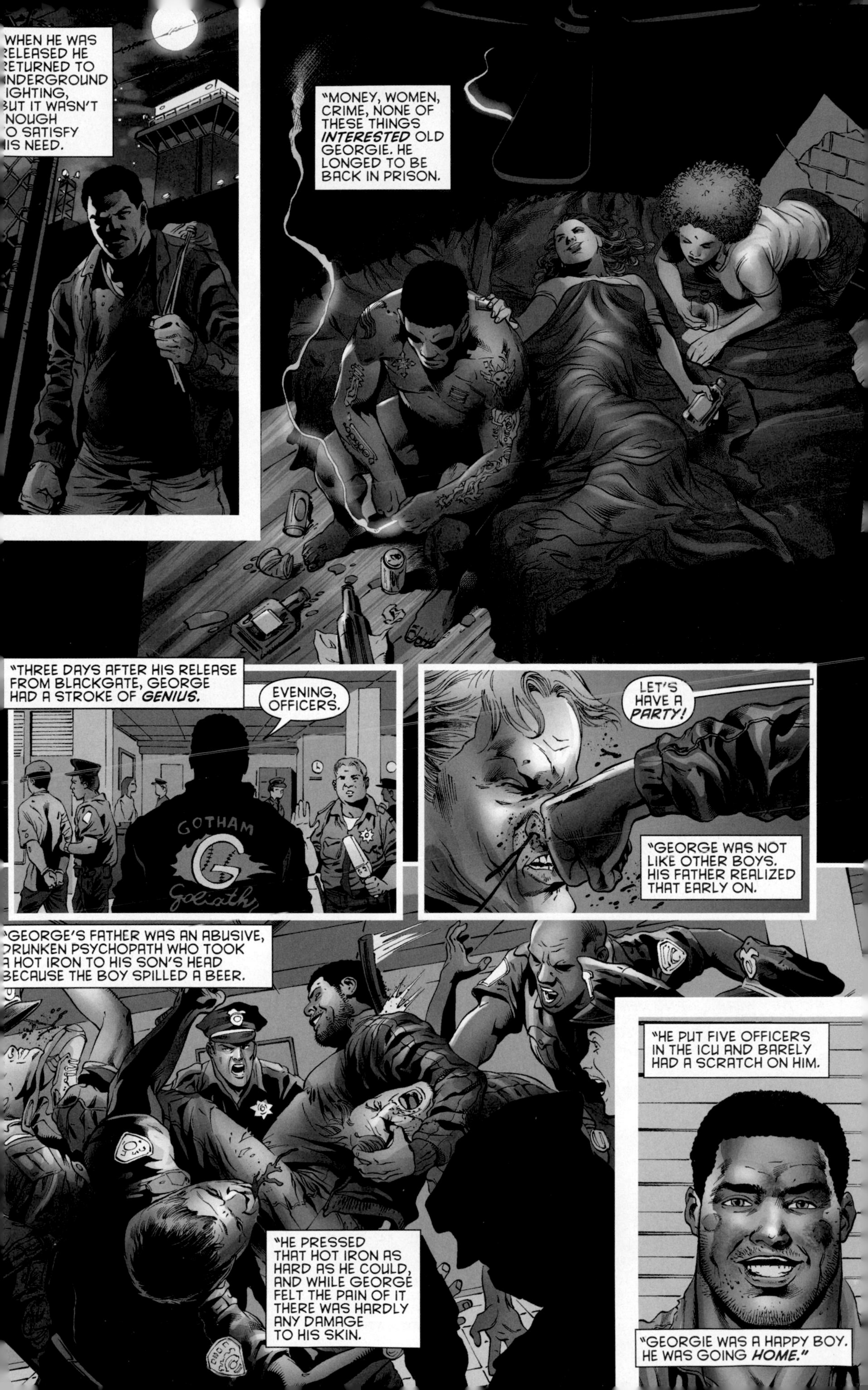
WHEN HE WAS
RELEASED HE RETURNED TO UNDERGROUND FIGHTING,
BUT IT WASN'T ENOUGH TO SATISFY HIS NEED.
"MONEY, WOMEN, CRIME, NONE OF THESE THINGS *INTERESTED* OLD GEORGIE. HE LONGED TO BE BACK IN PRISON.
"THREE DAYS AFTER HIS RELEASE FROM BLACKGATE, GEORGE HAD A STROKE OF *GENIUS.*
EVENING, OFFICERS.
GOTHAM
G
Goliaths
LET'S HAVE A *PARTY!*
"GEORGE WAS NOT LIKE OTHER BOYS. HIS FATHER REALIZED THAT EARLY ON.
"GEORGE'S FATHER WAS AN ABUSIVE, DRUNKEN PSYCHOPATH WHO TOOK A HOT IRON TO HIS SON'S HEAD BECAUSE THE BOY SPILLED A BEER.
"HE PRESSED THAT HOT IRON AS HARD AS HE COULD, AND WHILE GEORGE FELT THE PAIN OF IT THERE WAS HARDLY ANY DAMAGE TO HIS SKIN.
"HE PUT FIVE OFFICERS IN THE ICU AND BARELY HAD A SCRATCH ON HIM.
"GEORGIE WAS A HAPPY BOY. HE WAS GOING *HOME.*"

"BACK HOME, HE ROSE TO THE TOP H'S THE *MOST FEARED* CIVILIAN INMATE. THEY THREW HIM IN SOLITARY OVER AND OVER AGAIN, BUT NO ONE COULD REACH HIS MIND SO THEY SENT HIM *SOMEPLACE ELSE.*"

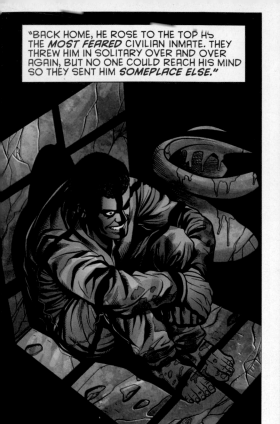

I WANT TO GO *HOME!*

THIS IS NOT FOR ME!

"GEORGIE DIDN'T LIKE ARKHAM ASYLUM ONE BIT. HE COULDN'T TASTE ANYTHING. HE WAS ALWAYS SLEEPY.

"WORST OF ALL, HE COULDN'T *PUNCH* ANYONE.

"HE WAS STILL CAPABLE OF SEEING THROUGH THE HAZE OF HIS MEDICATION CLEARLY ENOUGH TO REALIZE HE NEEDED A PURPOSE.

"SOMETHING TO LIVE FOR."

SEVERAL OF THE MEN TAKEN INTO CUSTODY SAID THEY WERE *ATTACKED* BY A MAN WEARING A BATSUIT.

THIS BATMAN SUBDUED MORE THAN A *DOZEN* GANG MEMBERS SINGLE-HANDEDLY.

"THEN ONE NIGHT HE GETS A *SIGN.* HE GETS THE HOPE FOR A BETTER DAY.

"PROBLEM IS, POOR GEORGIE'S STILL IN THE LOONY BIN.

"THEN, FIVE YEARS LATER, A MIRACLE OF MIRACLES WHEN ONE NIGHT THE WHOLE WORLD GOES TOPSY-TURVY, THE LUNATICS AND SUPER-WACKOS BUST OUT OF THE CUCKOO'S NEST."

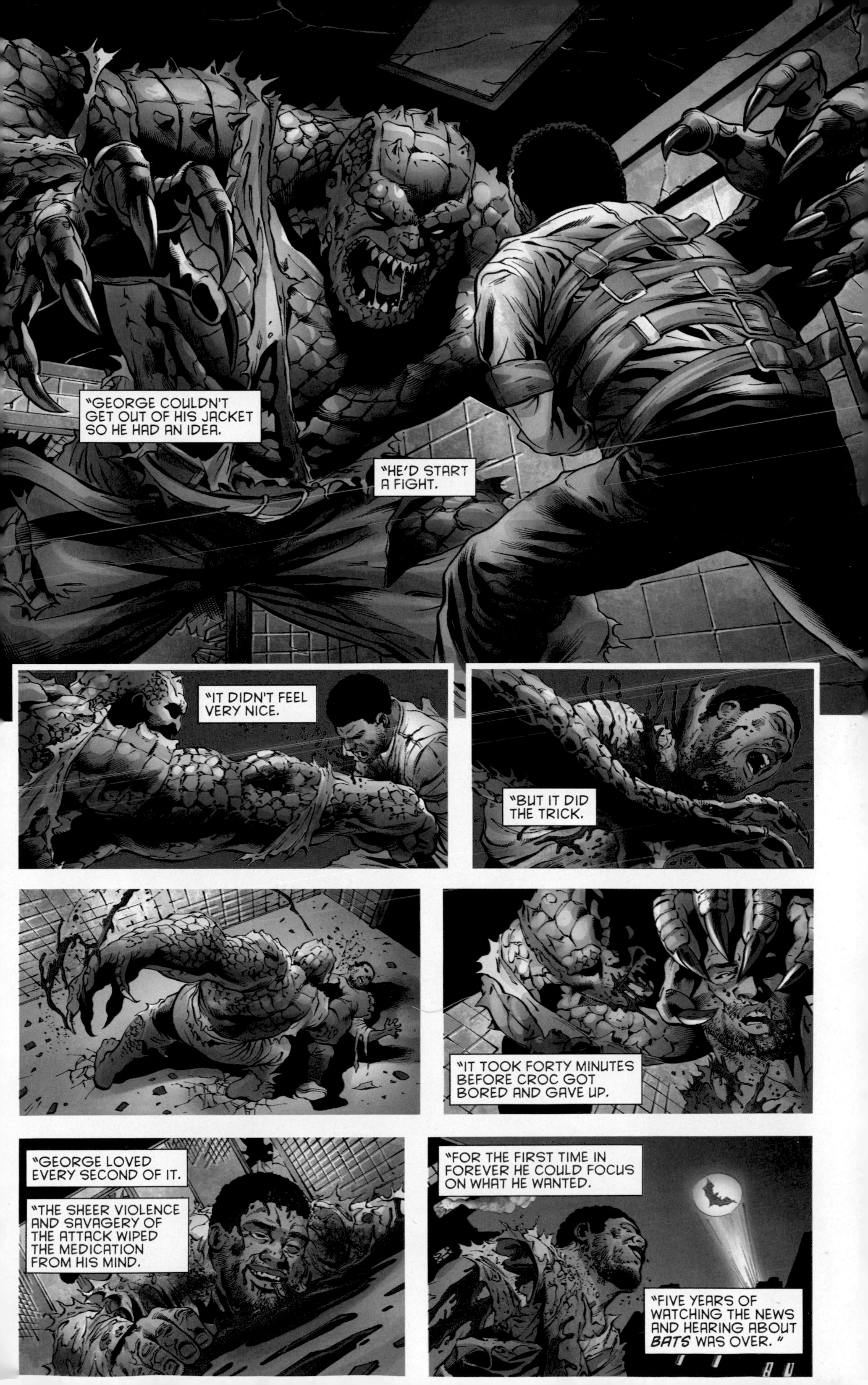

"GEORGE COULDN'T GET OUT OF HIS JACKET SO HE HAD AN IDEA.
"HE'D START A FIGHT.
"IT DIDN'T FEEL VERY NICE.
"BUT IT DID THE TRICK.
"IT TOOK FORTY MINUTES BEFORE CROC GOT BORED AND GAVE UP.
"GEORGE LOVED EVERY SECOND OF IT.
"THE SHEER VIOLENCE AND SAVAGERY OF THE ATTACK WIPED THE MEDICATION FROM HIS MIND.
"FOR THE FIRST TIME IN FOREVER HE COULD FOCUS ON WHAT HE WANTED.
"FIVE YEARS OF WATCHING THE NEWS AND HEARING ABOUT *BATS* WAS OVER."

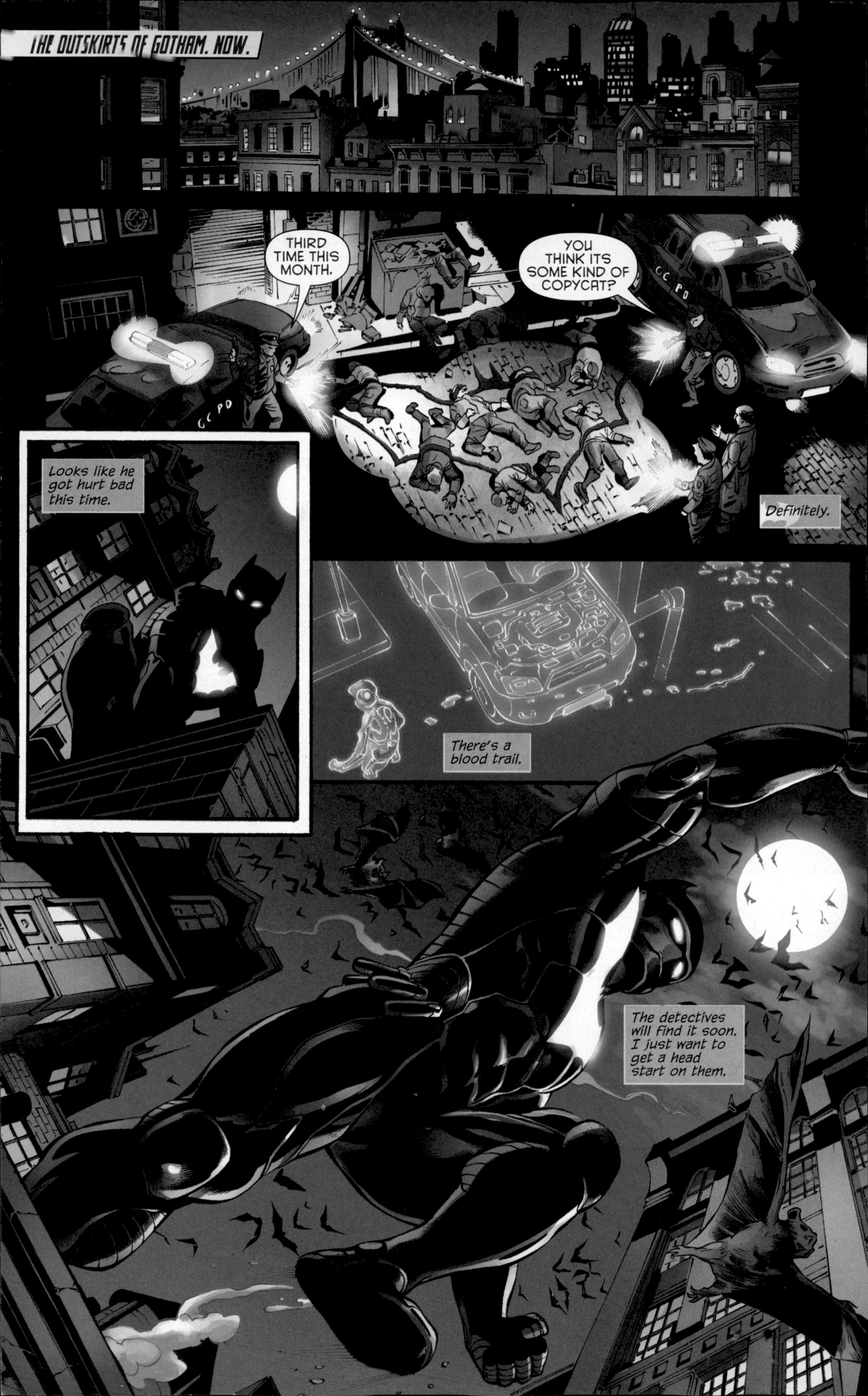
THE OUTSKIRTS OF GOTHAM. NOW.
THIRD TIME THIS MONTH.
YOU THINK ITS SOME KIND OF COPYCAT?
Definitely.
Looks like he got hurt bad this time.
There's a blood trail.
The detectives will find it soon. I just want to get a head start on them.

This guy lost a lot of blood and he was on foot.

Looks like home.

I'm willing to bet you have a record.

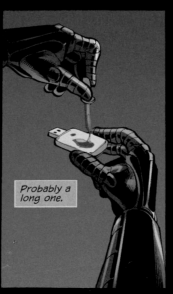

Probably a long one.

Let's see if your DNA pops up in the GCPD database.

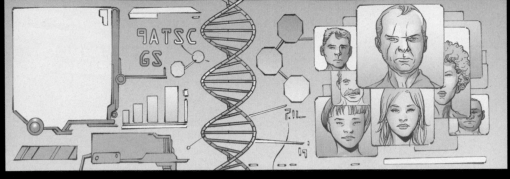

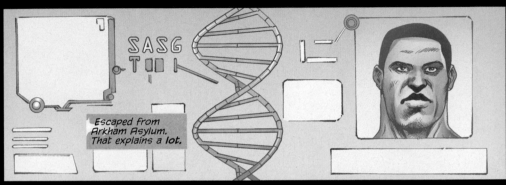

Escaped from Arkham Asylum. That explains a *lot.*

He's wounded and down a few quarts. Shouldn't be too much trouble once I find a way inside.

INCOMING CALL FROM ENCRYPTED PERSONAL CELL PHONE.

CALLER ID?

MOM.

RESTRICT EXTERNAL AUDIO. BROADCAST INSIDE THE HELMET AND ANSWER.

HEY, MOM. WHAT'S UP? WHY ARE YOU CALLING ME IN THE MIDDLE OF THE NIGHT?

HI, BABY. I COULDN'T SLEEP.

I WANTED TO ASK IF YOU'D PICK UP TAM'S *BIRTHDAY CAKE* FROM THE BAKERY.

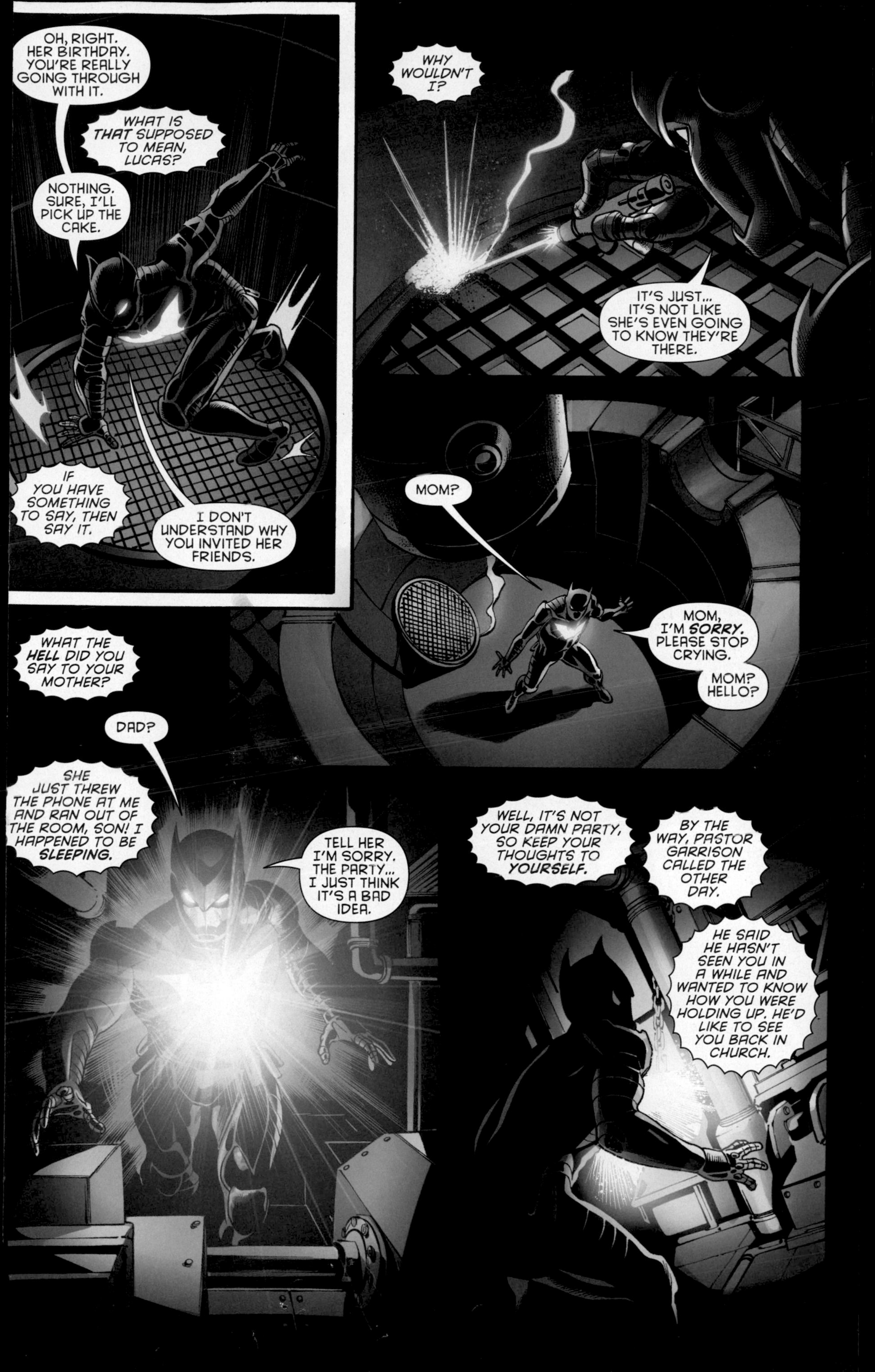
OH, RIGHT. HER BIRTHDAY. YOU'RE REALLY GOING THROUGH WITH IT.
WHAT IS THAT SUPPOSED TO MEAN, LUCAS?
NOTHING. SURE, I'LL PICK UP THE CAKE.
IF YOU HAVE SOMETHING TO SAY, THEN SAY IT.
I DON'T UNDERSTAND WHY YOU INVITED HER FRIENDS.
WHY WOULDN'T I?
IT'S JUST... IT'S NOT LIKE SHE'S EVEN GOING TO KNOW THEY'RE THERE.
MOM?
MOM, I'M SORRY. PLEASE STOP CRYING.
MOM? HELLO?
WHAT THE HELL DID YOU SAY TO YOUR MOTHER?
DAD?
SHE JUST THREW THE PHONE AT ME AND RAN OUT OF THE ROOM, SON! I HAPPENED TO BE SLEEPING.
TELL HER I'M SORRY. THE PARTY... I JUST THINK IT'S A BAD IDEA.
WELL, IT'S NOT YOUR DAMN PARTY, SO KEEP YOUR THOUGHTS TO YOURSELF.
BY THE WAY, PASTOR GARRISON CALLED THE OTHER DAY.
HE SAID HE HASN'T SEEN YOU IN A WHILE AND WANTED TO KNOW HOW YOU WERE HOLDING UP. HE'D LIKE TO SEE YOU BACK IN CHURCH.

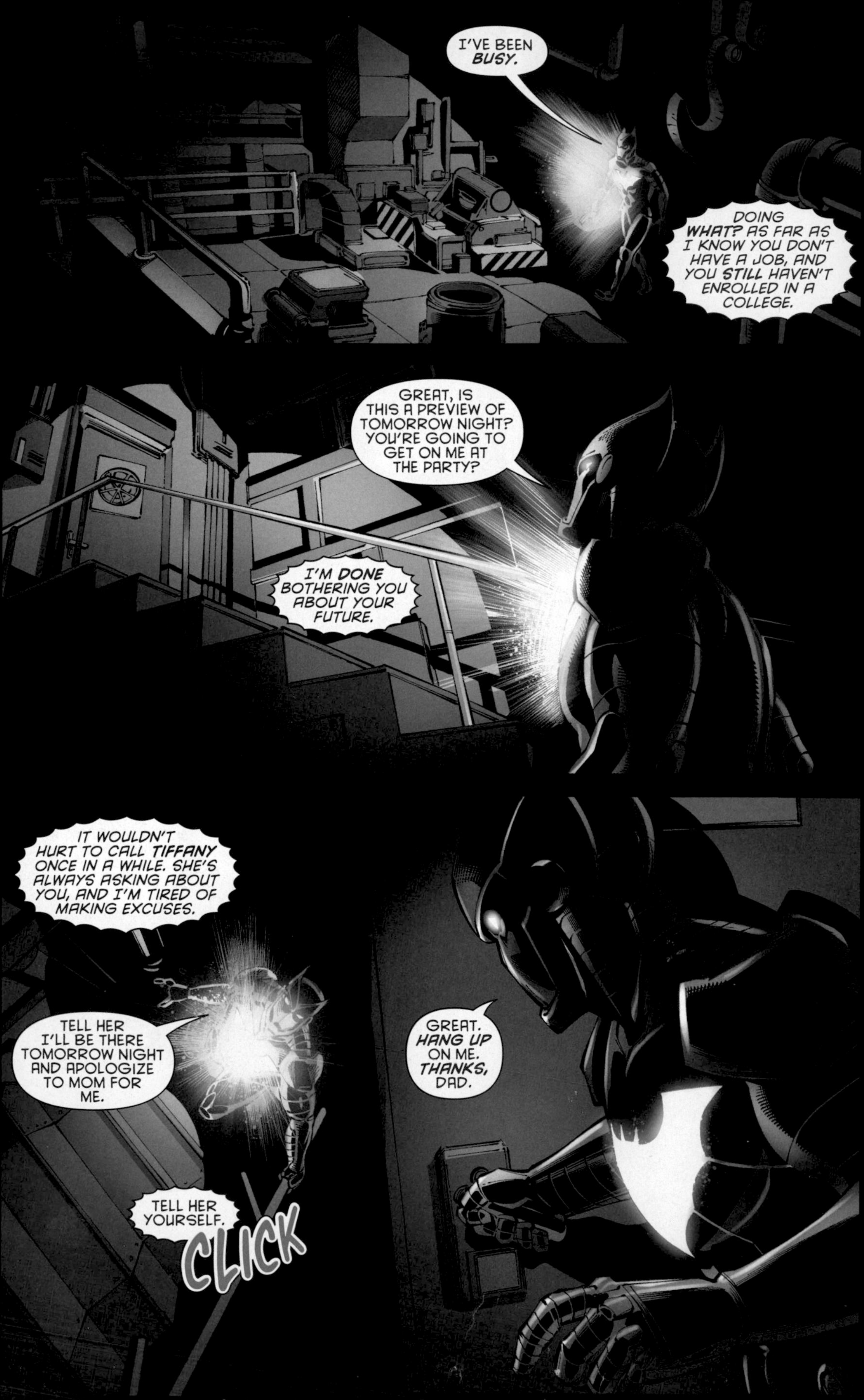
I'VE BEEN BUSY.
DOING WHAT? AS FAR AS I KNOW YOU DON'T HAVE A JOB, AND YOU STILL HAVEN'T ENROLLED IN A COLLEGE.
GREAT, IS THIS A PREVIEW OF TOMORROW NIGHT? YOU'RE GOING TO GET ON ME AT THE PARTY?
I'M DONE BOTHERING YOU ABOUT YOUR FUTURE.
IT WOULDN'T HURT TO CALL TIFFANY ONCE IN A WHILE. SHE'S ALWAYS ASKING ABOUT YOU, AND I'M TIRED OF MAKING EXCUSES.
TELL HER I'LL BE THERE TOMORROW NIGHT AND APOLOGIZE TO MOM FOR ME.
TELL HER YOURSELF.
CLICK
GREAT. HANG UP ON ME. THANKS, DAD.

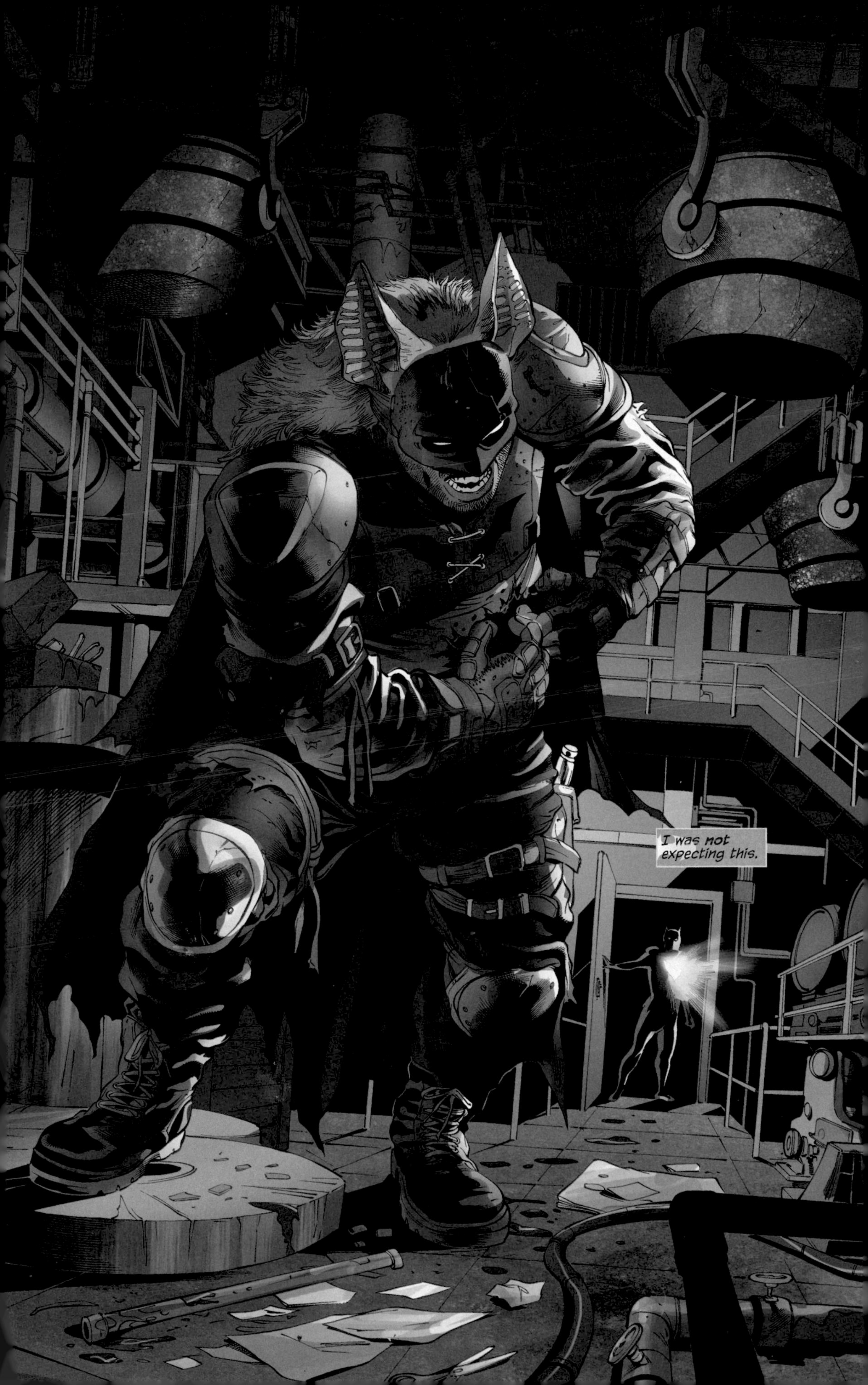
I was not expecting this.

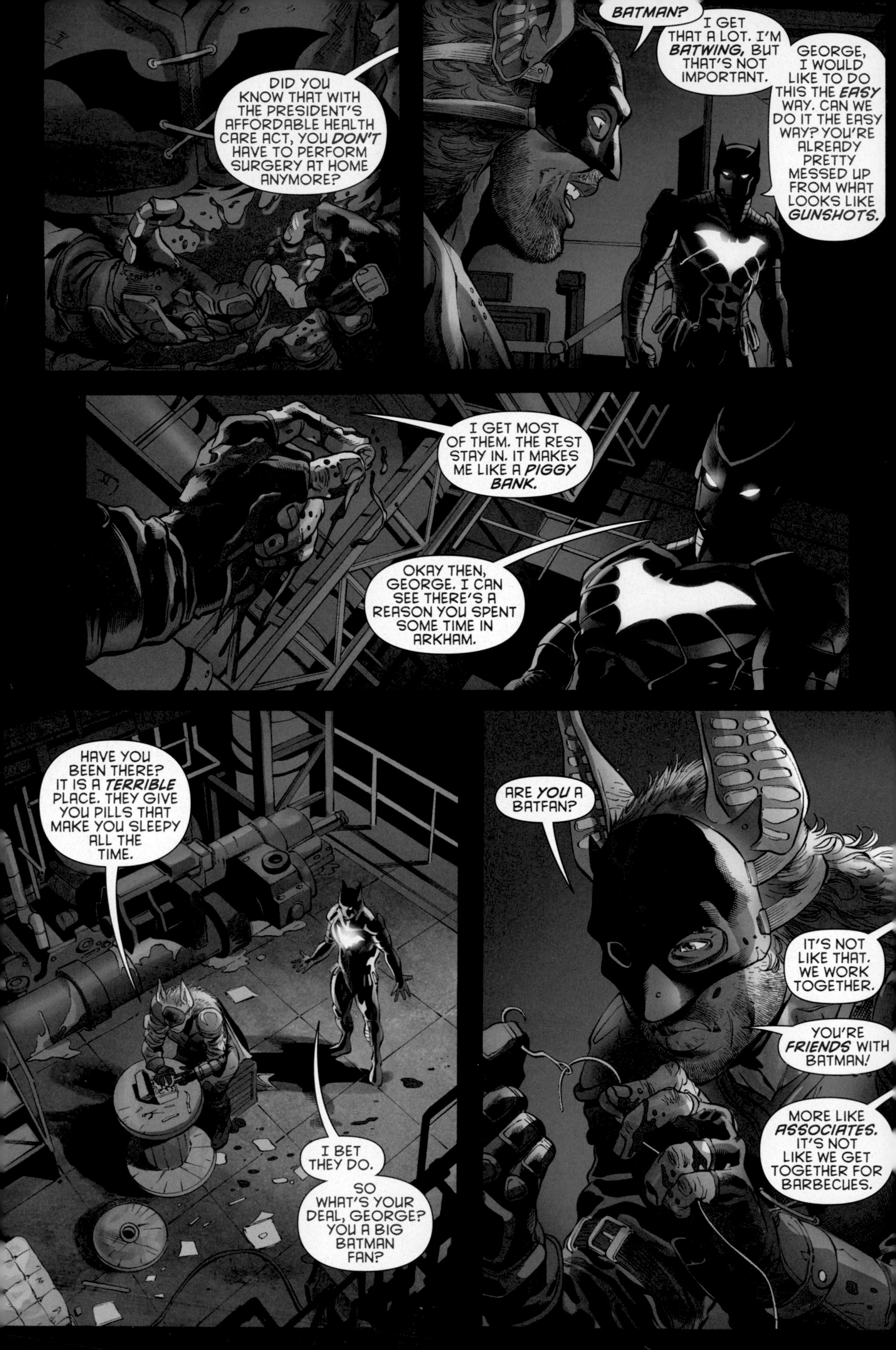
DID YOU KNOW THAT WITH THE PRESIDENT'S AFFORDABLE HEALTH CARE ACT, YOU DON'T HAVE TO PERFORM SURGERY AT HOME ANYMORE?
BATMAN?
I GET THAT A LOT. I'M BATWING, BUT THAT'S NOT IMPORTANT.
GEORGE, I WOULD LIKE TO DO THIS THE EASY WAY. CAN WE DO IT THE EASY WAY? YOU'RE ALREADY PRETTY MESSED UP FROM WHAT LOOKS LIKE GUNSHOTS.
I GET MOST OF THEM. THE REST STAY IN. IT MAKES ME LIKE A PIGGY BANK.
OKAY THEN, GEORGE. I CAN SEE THERE'S A REASON YOU SPENT SOME TIME IN ARKHAM.
HAVE YOU BEEN THERE? IT IS A TERRIBLE PLACE. THEY GIVE YOU PILLS THAT MAKE YOU SLEEPY ALL THE TIME.
I BET THEY DO.
SO WHAT'S YOUR DEAL, GEORGE? YOU A BIG BATMAN FAN?
ARE YOU A BATFAN?
IT'S NOT LIKE THAT. WE WORK TOGETHER.
YOU'RE FRIENDS WITH BATMAN!
MORE LIKE ASSOCIATES. IT'S NOT LIKE WE GET TOGETHER FOR BARBECUES.

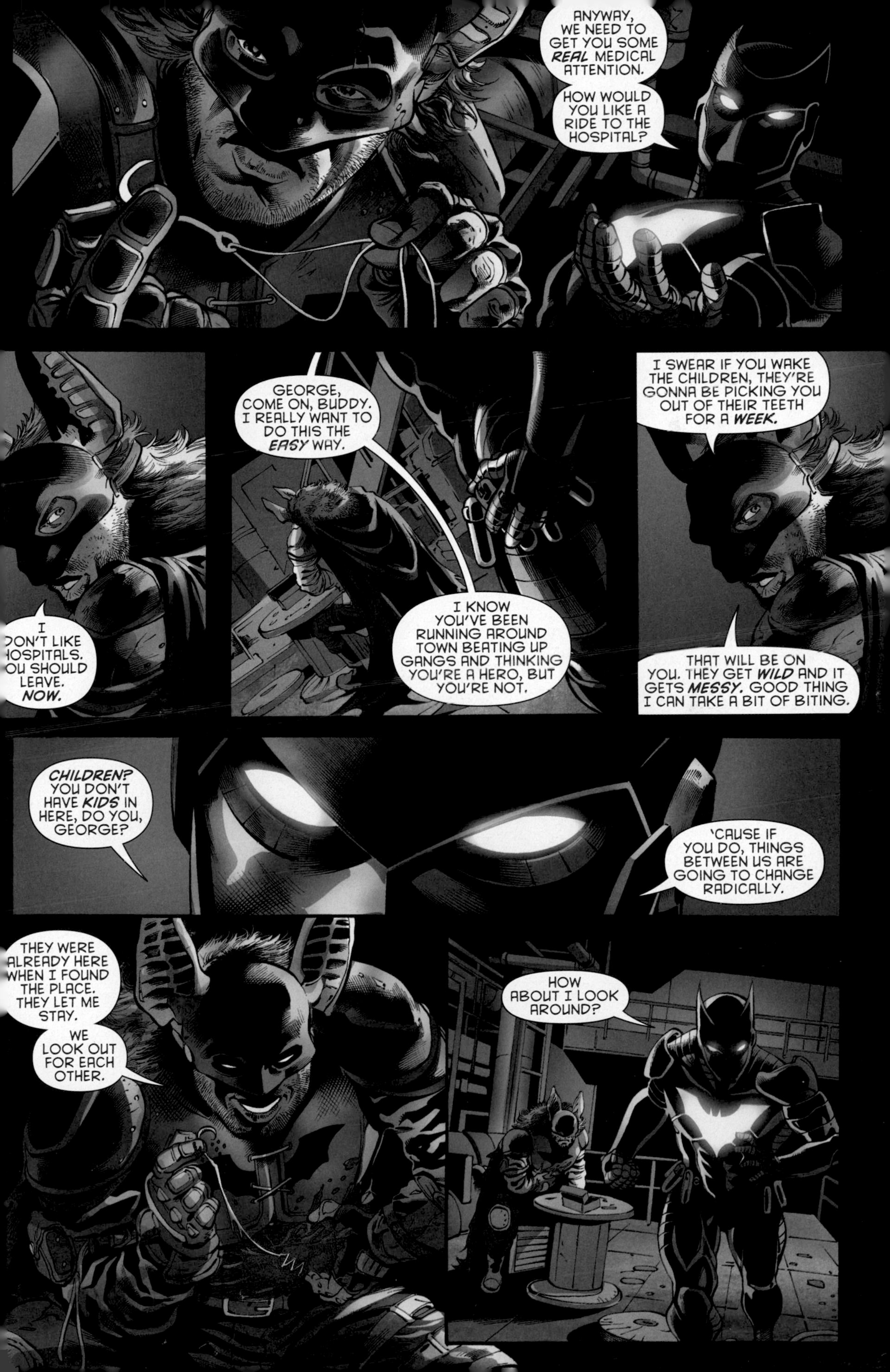
ANYWAY, WE NEED TO GET YOU SOME REAL MEDICAL ATTENTION.
HOW WOULD YOU LIKE A RIDE TO THE HOSPITAL?
I DON'T LIKE HOSPITALS. YOU SHOULD LEAVE. NOW.
GEORGE, COME ON, BUDDY. I REALLY WANT TO DO THIS THE EASY WAY.
I KNOW YOU'VE BEEN RUNNING AROUND TOWN BEATING UP GANGS AND THINKING YOU'RE A HERO, BUT YOU'RE NOT.
I SWEAR IF YOU WAKE THE CHILDREN, THEY'RE GONNA BE PICKING YOU OUT OF THEIR TEETH FOR A WEEK.
THAT WILL BE ON YOU. THEY GET WILD AND IT GETS MESSY. GOOD THING I CAN TAKE A BIT OF BITING.
CHILDREN? YOU DON'T HAVE KIDS IN HERE, DO YOU, GEORGE?
'CAUSE IF YOU DO, THINGS BETWEEN US ARE GOING TO CHANGE RADICALLY.
THEY WERE ALREADY HERE WHEN I FOUND THE PLACE. THEY LET ME STAY.
WE LOOK OUT FOR EACH OTHER.
HOW ABOUT I LOOK AROUND?

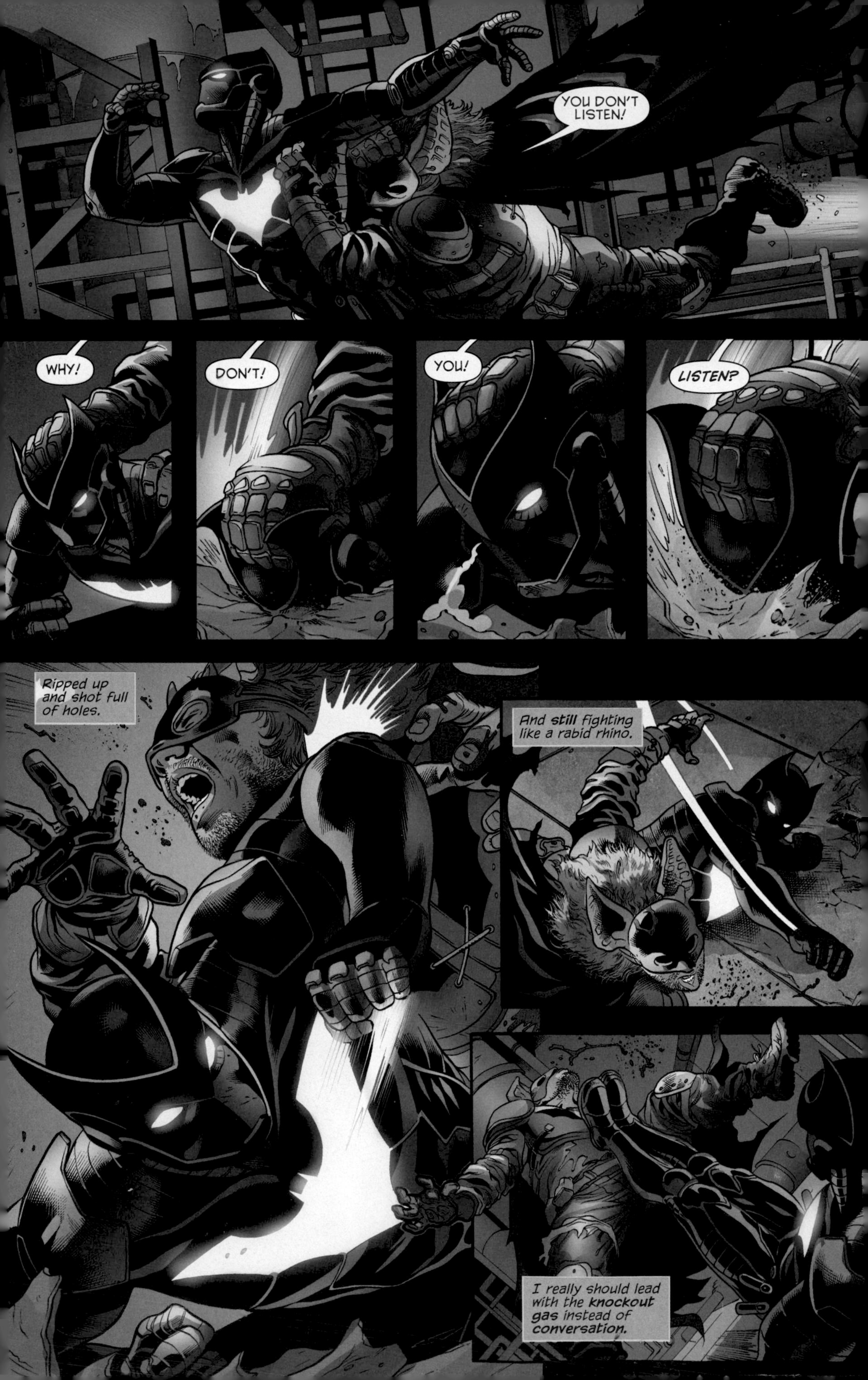
YOU DON'T LISTEN!
WHY!
DON'T!
YOU!
LISTEN?
Ripped up and shot full of holes.
And still fighting like a rabid rhino.
I really should lead with the knockout gas instead of conversation.

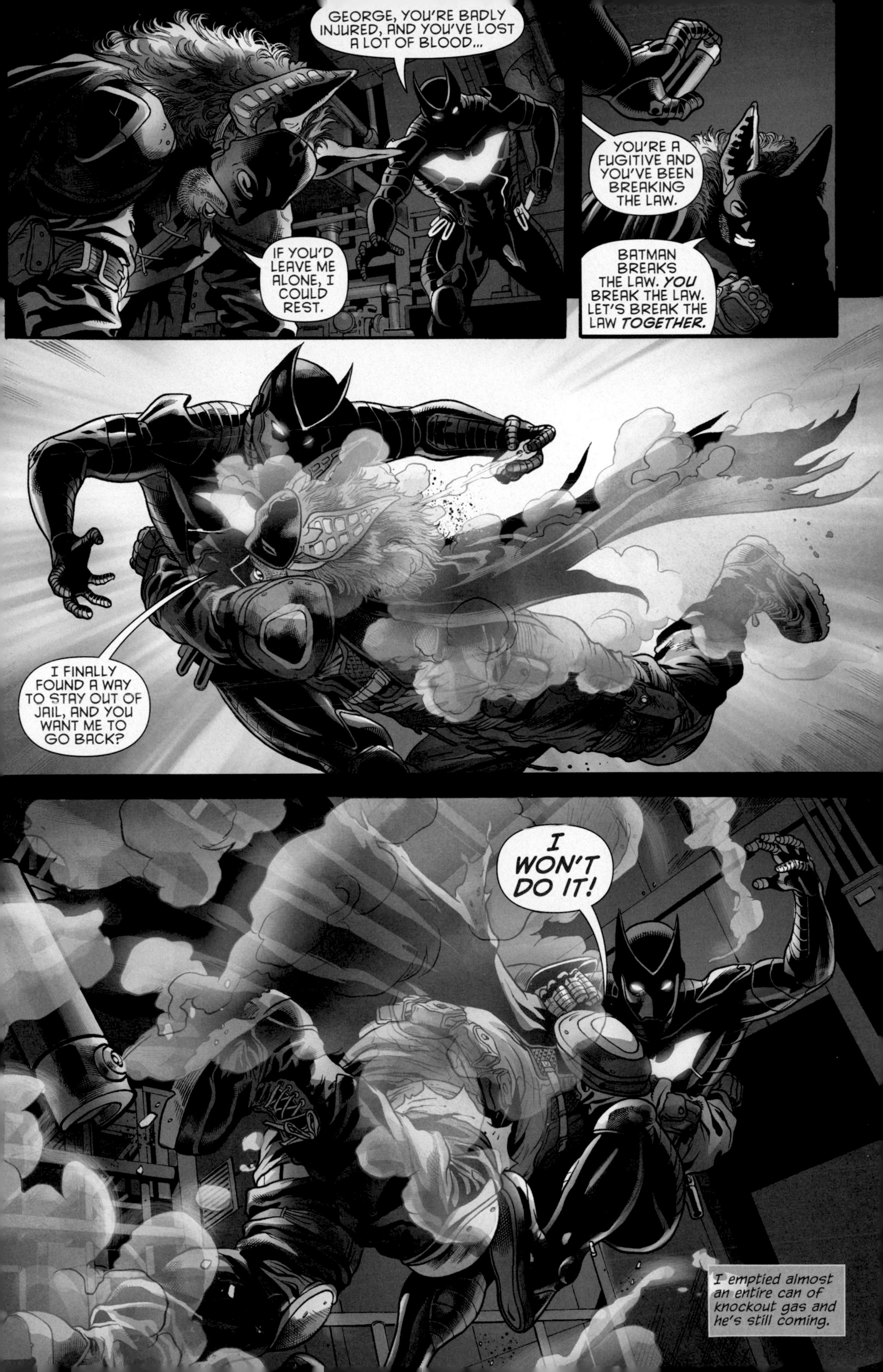
GEORGE, YOU'RE BADLY INJURED, AND YOU'VE LOST A LOT OF BLOOD...
IF YOU'D LEAVE ME ALONE, I COULD REST.
YOU'RE A FUGITIVE AND YOU'VE BEEN BREAKING THE LAW.
BATMAN BREAKS THE LAW. *YOU* BREAK THE LAW. LET'S BREAK THE LAW *TOGETHER.*
I FINALLY FOUND A WAY TO STAY OUT OF JAIL, AND YOU WANT ME TO GO BACK?
I WON'T DO IT!
I emptied almost an entire can of knockout gas and he's still coming.

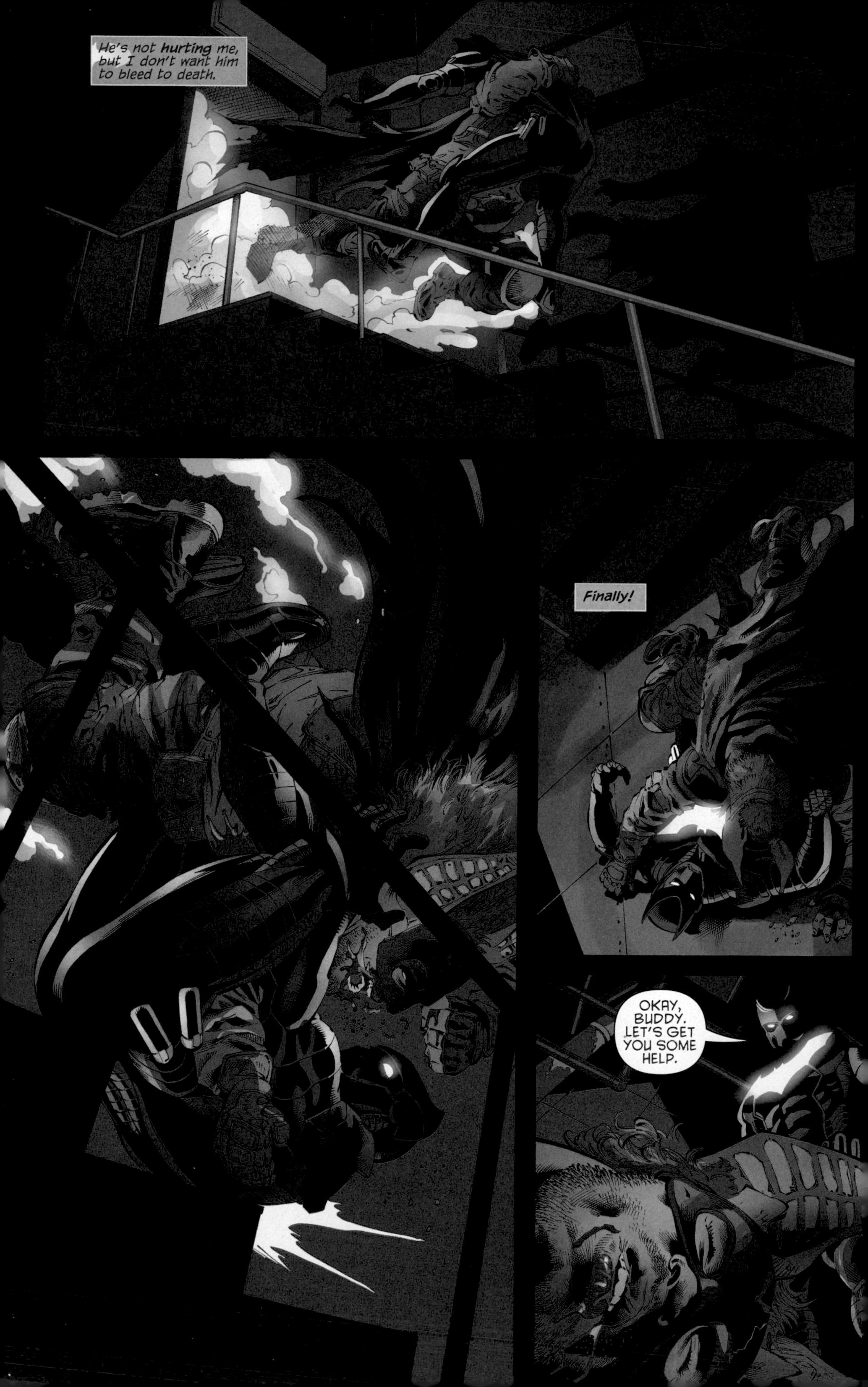
He's not **hurting** me, but I don't want him to bleed to death.
Finally!
OKAY, BUDDY. LET'S GET YOU SOME HELP.

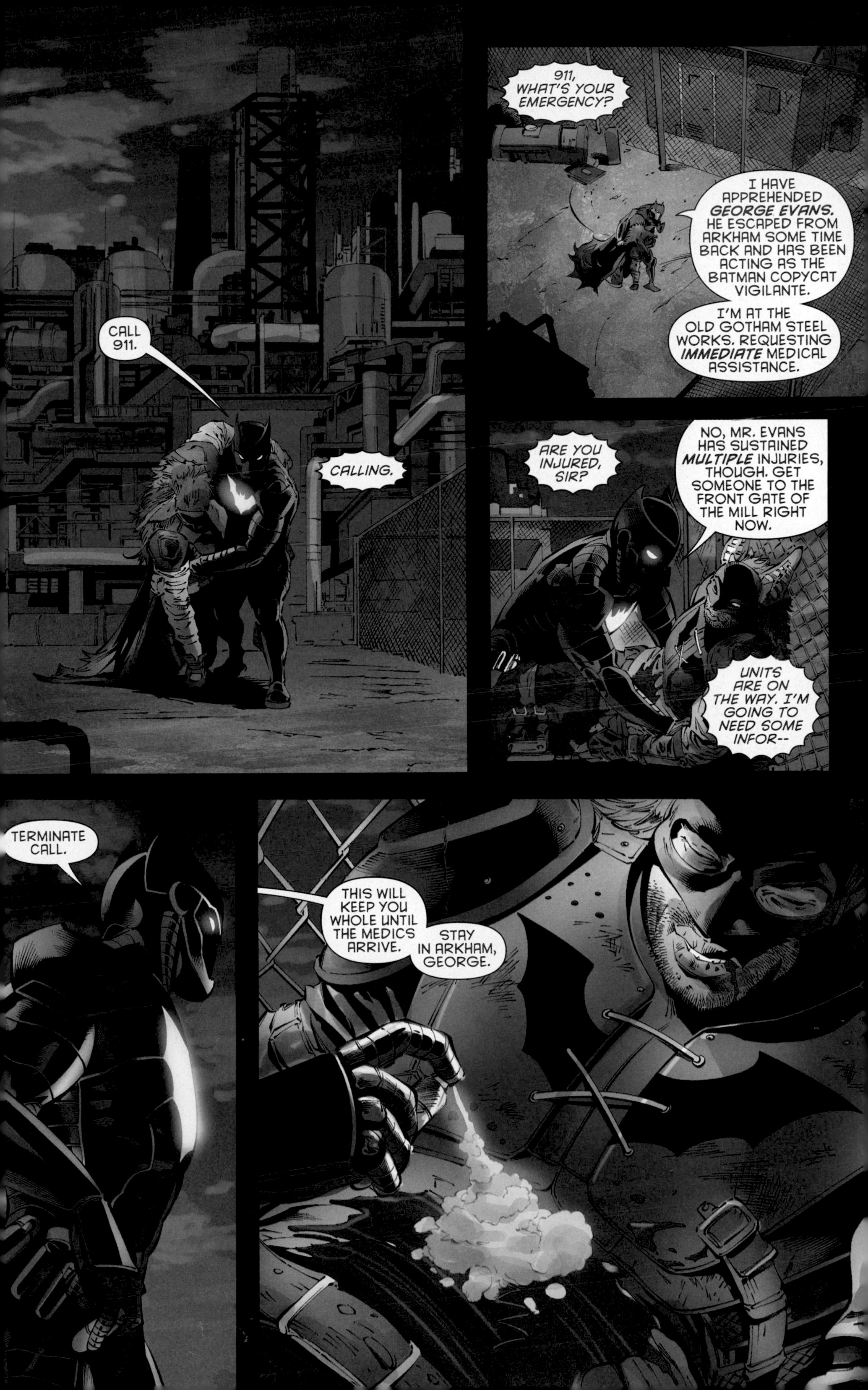
CALL 911.
CALLING.
911, WHAT'S YOUR EMERGENCY?
I HAVE APPREHENDED GEORGE EVANS. HE ESCAPED FROM ARKHAM SOME TIME BACK AND HAS BEEN ACTING AS THE BATMAN COPYCAT VIGILANTE.
I'M AT THE OLD GOTHAM STEEL WORKS. REQUESTING IMMEDIATE MEDICAL ASSISTANCE.
ARE YOU INJURED, SIR?
NO, MR. EVANS HAS SUSTAINED MULTIPLE INJURIES, THOUGH. GET SOMEONE TO THE FRONT GATE OF THE MILL RIGHT NOW.
UNITS ARE ON THE WAY. I'M GOING TO NEED SOME INFOR--
TERMINATE CALL.
THIS WILL KEEP YOU WHOLE UNTIL THE MEDICS ARRIVE.
STAY IN ARKHAM, GEORGE.

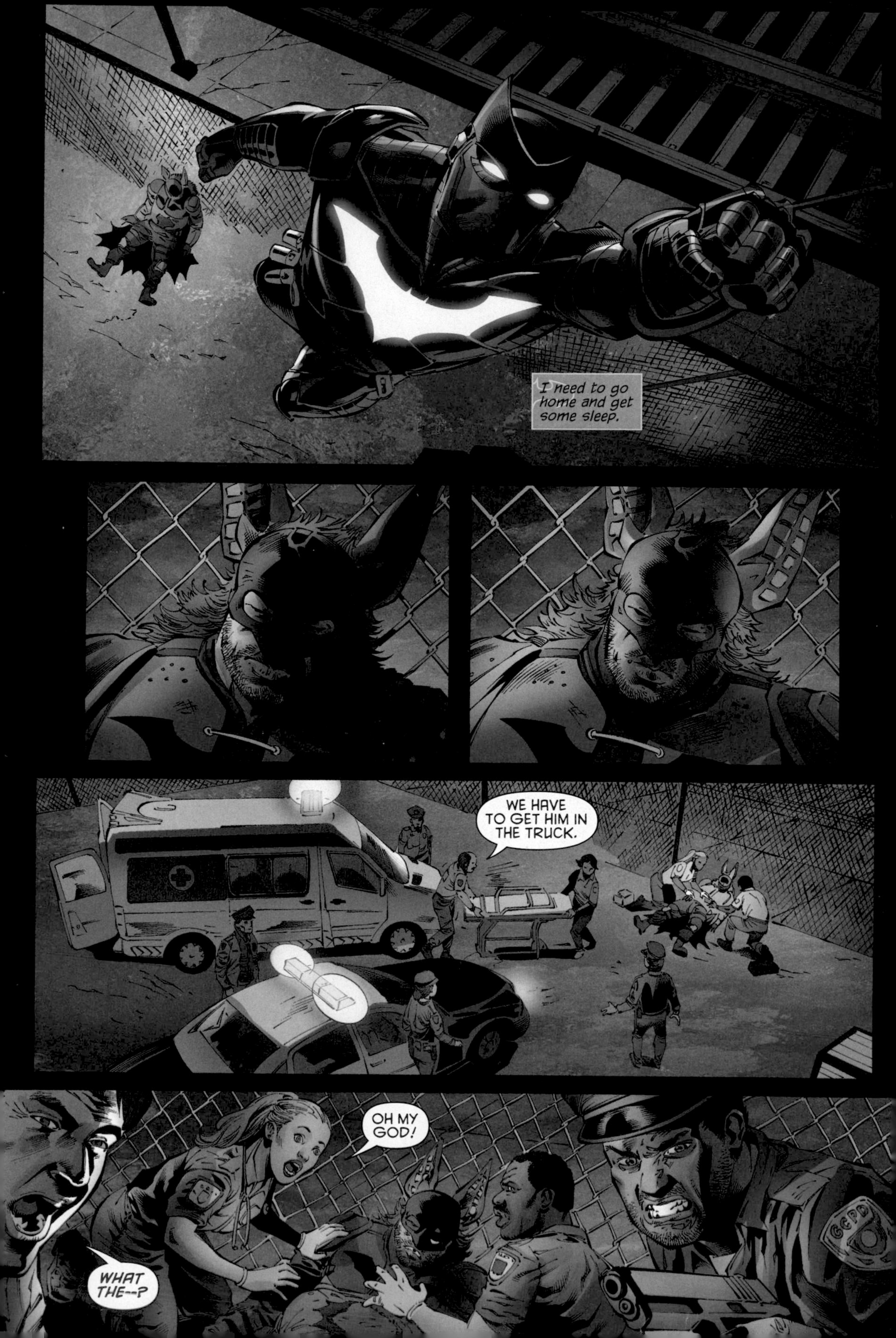
I need to go home and get some sleep.
WE HAVE TO GET HIM IN THE TRUCK.
OH MY GOD!
WHAT THE--?

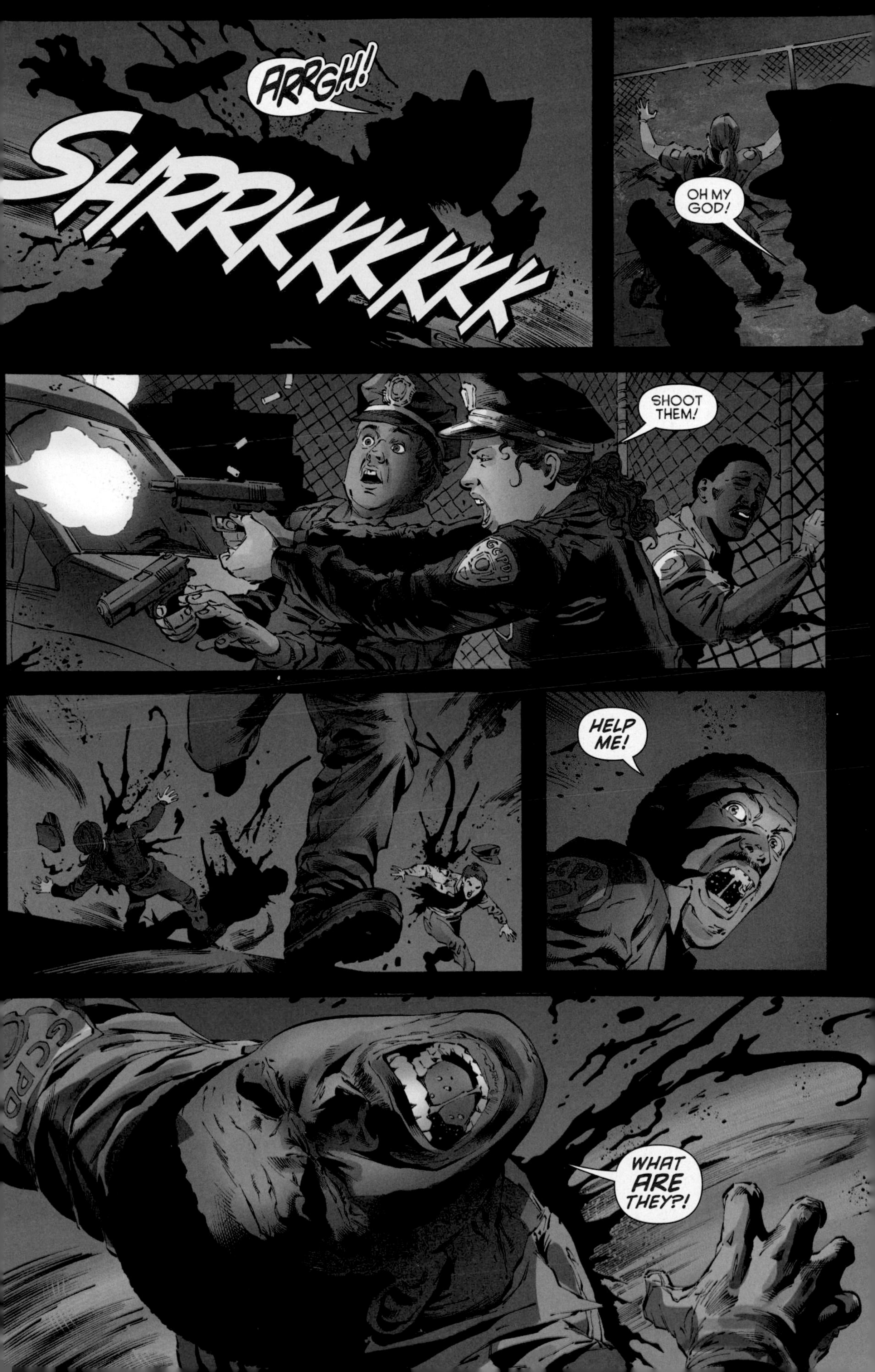
ARRGH!
SHRRKKKKKK
OH MY GOD!
SHOOT THEM!
HELP ME!
WHAT ARE THEY?!

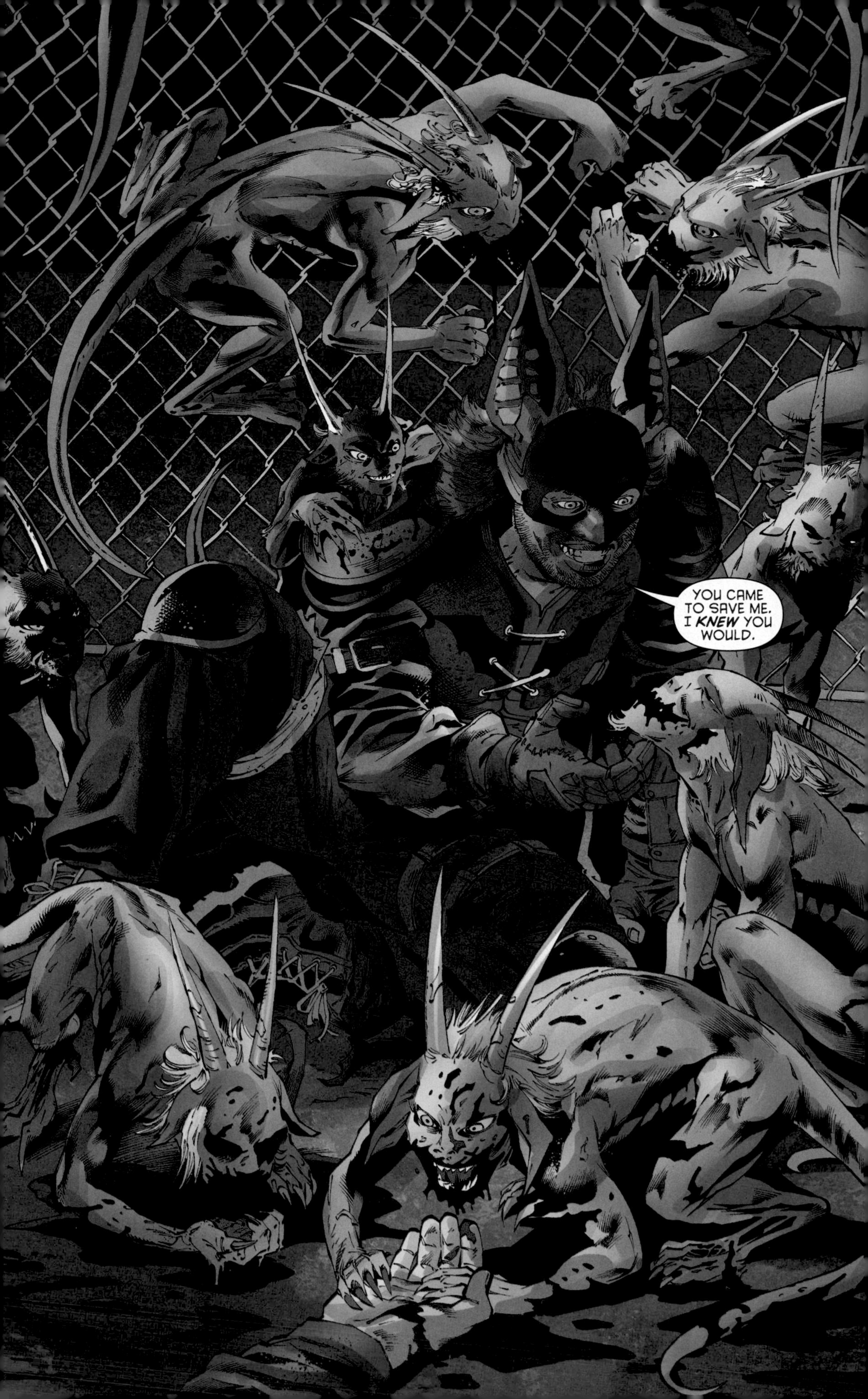
YOU CAME TO SAVE ME. I KNEW YOU WOULD.

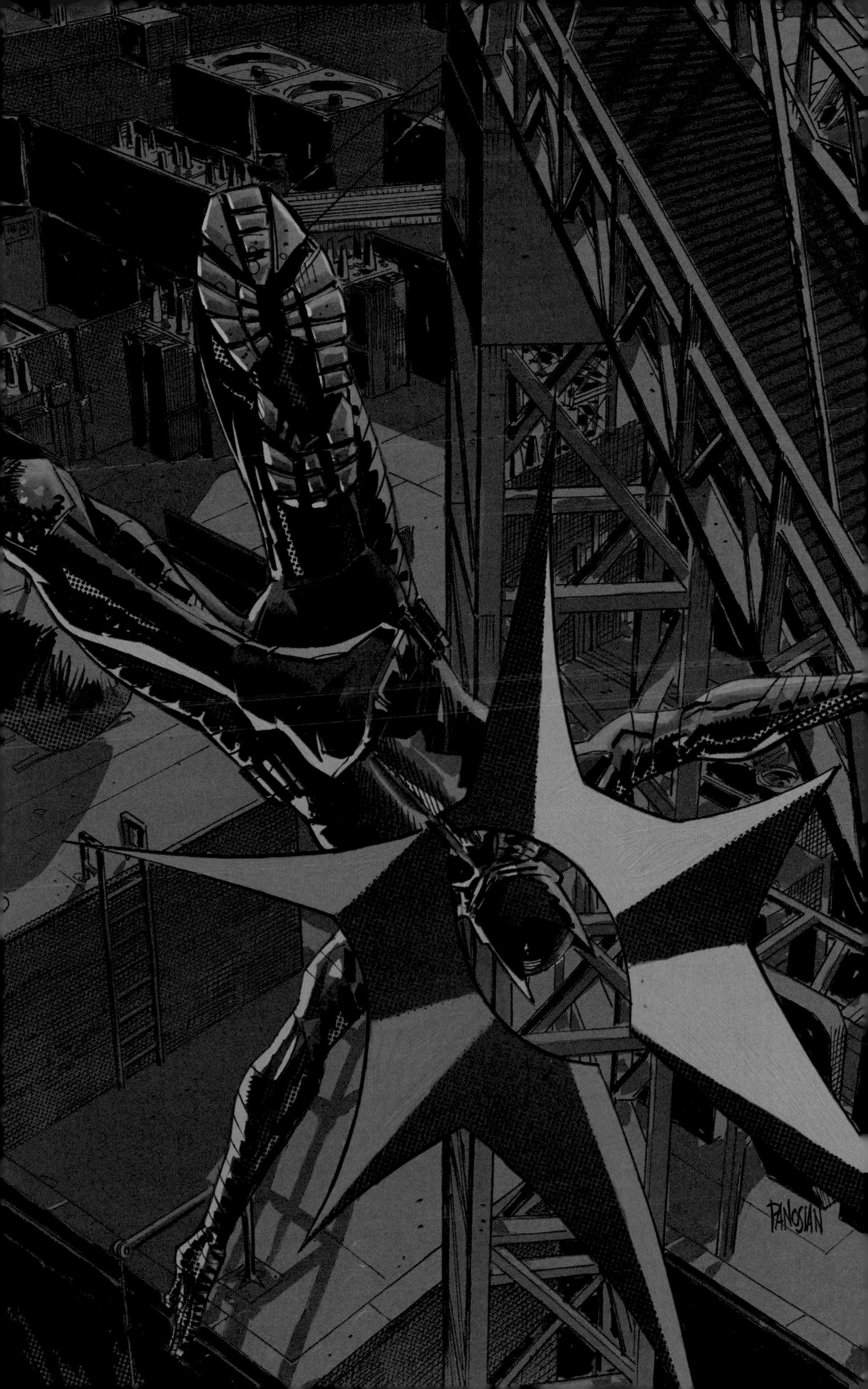
PANOSIAN

PURPOSE

JIMMY PALMIOTTI
JUSTIN GRAY
writers

EDUARDO PANSICA
penciller

JÚLIO FERREIRA
inker

CHRIS SOTOMAYOR
colorist

DEZI SIENTY
letterer

cover art by
DAN PANOSIAN

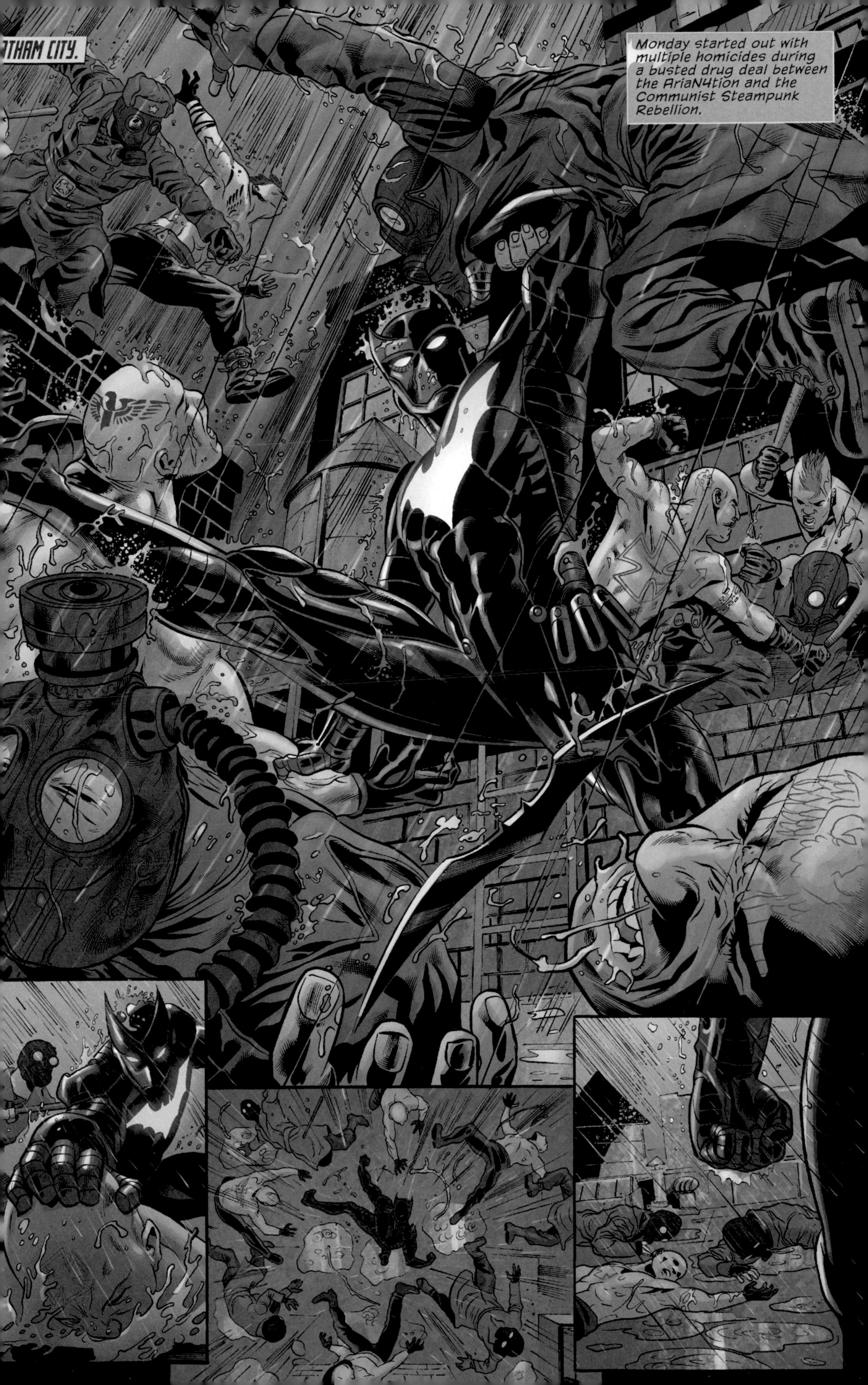

OTHAM CITY.
Monday started out with multiple homicides during a busted drug deal between the AriaN4tion and the Communist Steampunk Rebellion.

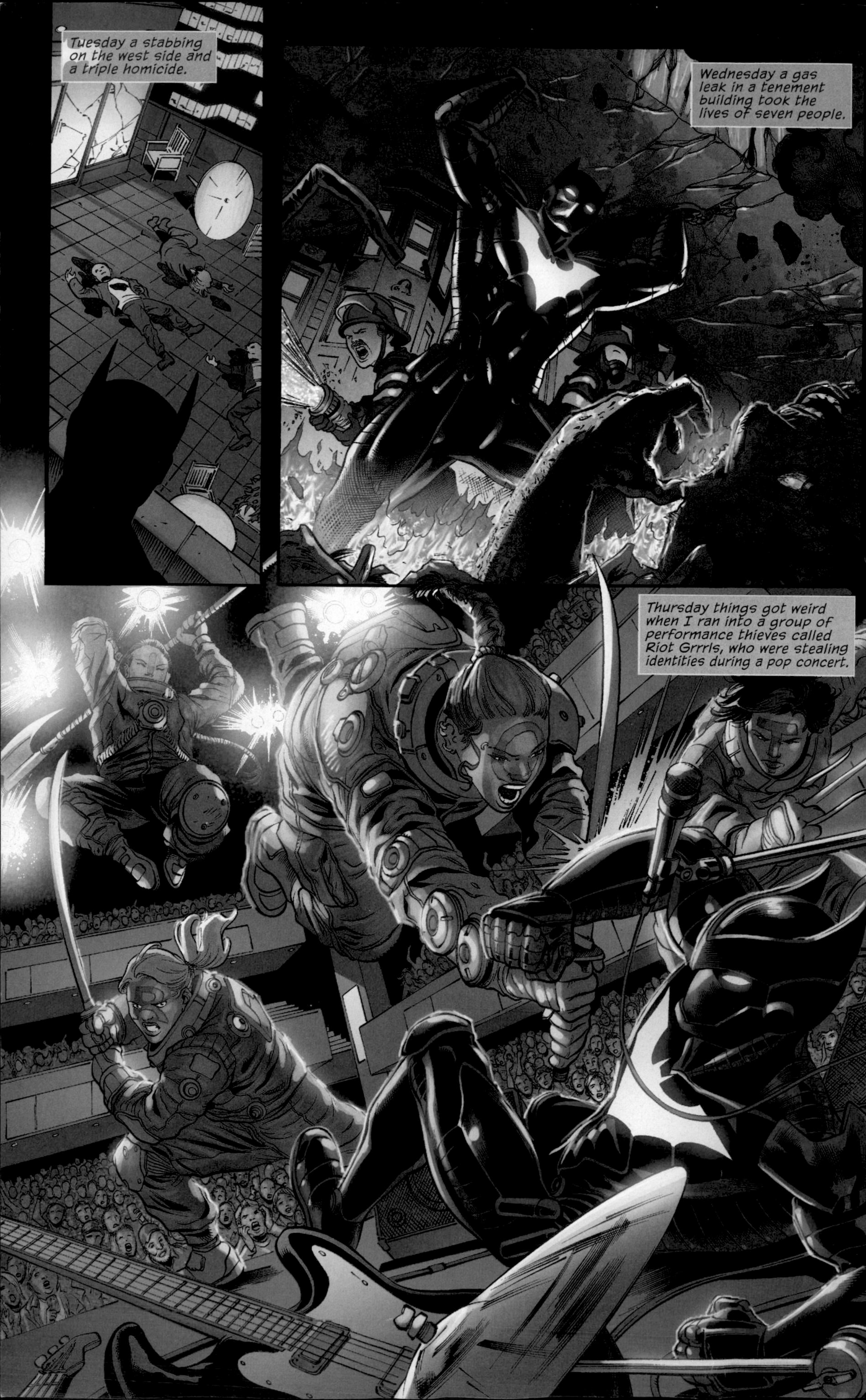
Tuesday a stabbing on the west side and a triple homicide.
Wednesday a gas leak in a tenement building took the lives of seven people.
Thursday things got weird when I ran into a group of performance thieves called Riot Grrrls, who were stealing identities during a pop concert.

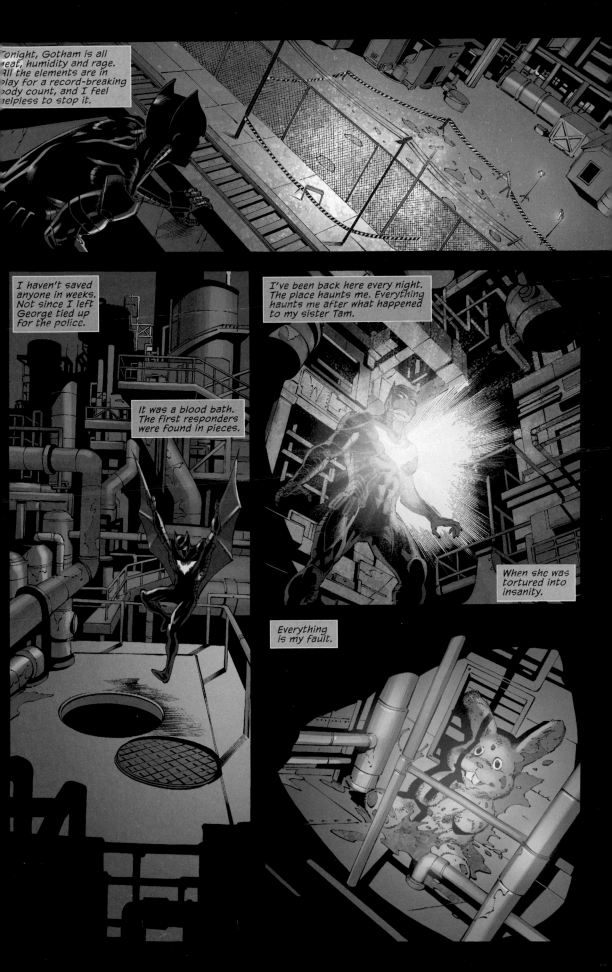

Tonight, Gotham is all heat, humidity and rage. All the elements are in play for a record-breaking body count, and I feel helpless to stop it.

I haven't saved anyone in weeks. Not since I left George tied up for the police.

It was a blood bath. The first responders were found in pieces.

I've been back here every night. The place haunts me. Everything haunts me after what happened to my sister Tam.

When she was tortured into insanity.

Everything is my fault.

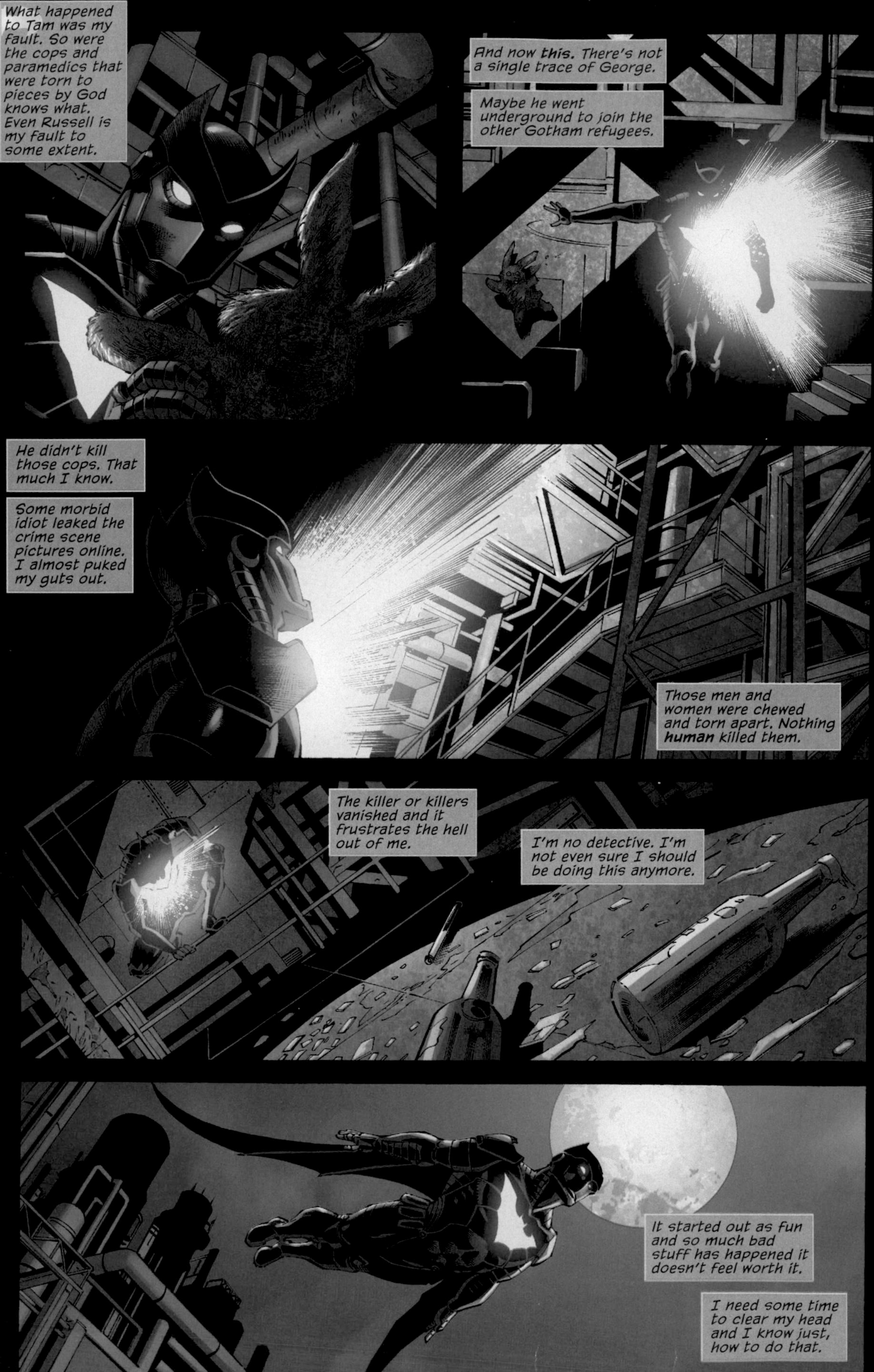
What happened to Tam was my fault. So were the cops and paramedics that were torn to pieces by God knows what. Even Russell is my fault to some extent.
And now **this**. There's not a single trace of George.
Maybe he went underground to join the other Gotham refugees.
He didn't kill those cops. That much I know.
Some morbid idiot leaked the crime scene pictures online. I almost puked my guts out.
Those men and women were chewed and torn apart. Nothing **human** killed them.
The killer or killers vanished and it frustrates the hell out of me.
I'm no detective. I'm not even sure I should be doing this anymore.
It started out as fun and so much bad stuff has happened it doesn't feel worth it.
I need some time to clear my head and I know just how to do that.

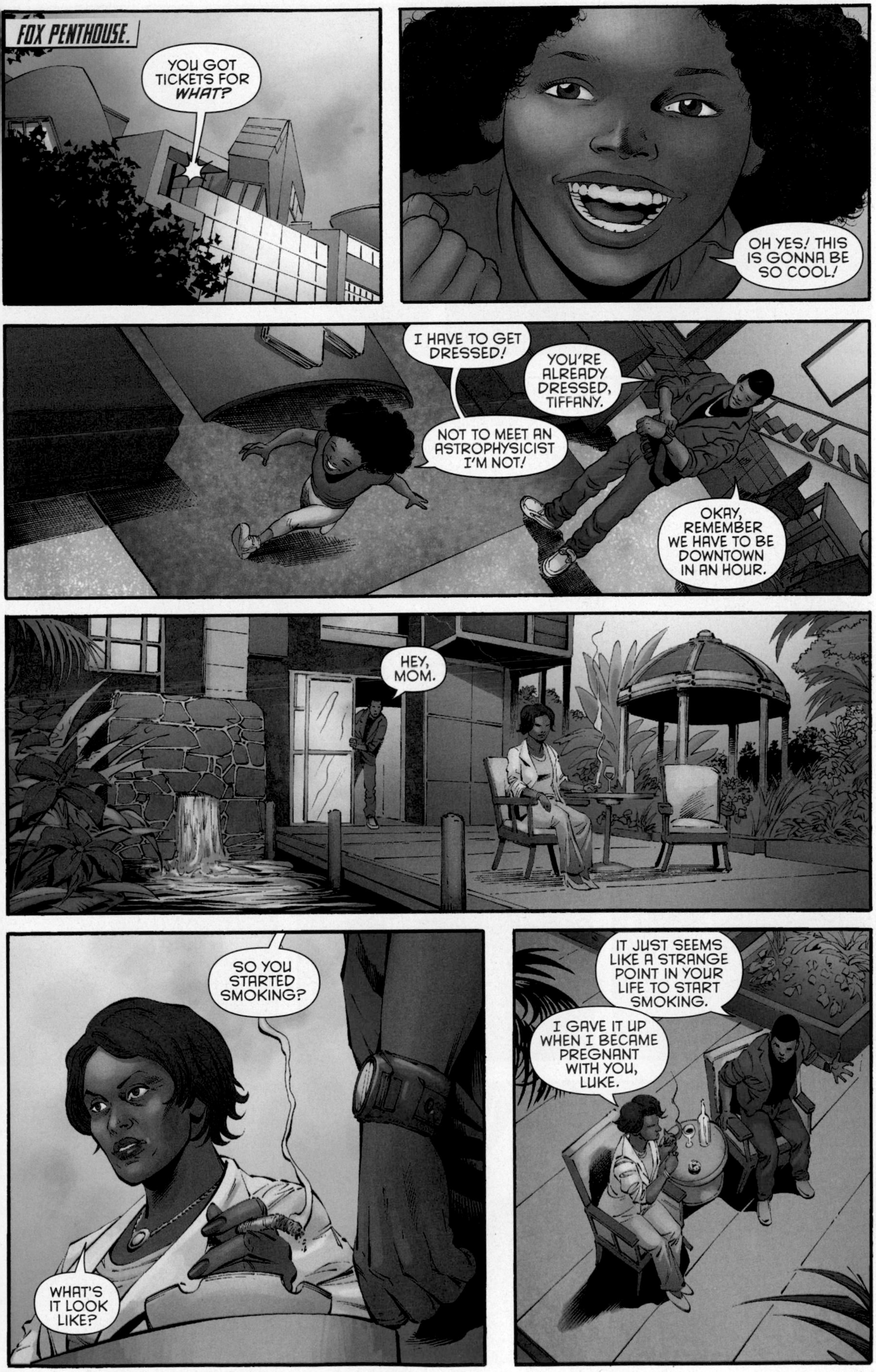
FOX PENTHOUSE.
YOU GOT TICKETS FOR WHAT?
OH YES! THIS IS GONNA BE SO COOL!
I HAVE TO GET DRESSED!
YOU'RE ALREADY DRESSED, TIFFANY.
NOT TO MEET AN ASTROPHYSICIST I'M NOT!
OKAY, REMEMBER WE HAVE TO BE DOWNTOWN IN AN HOUR.
HEY, MOM.
SO YOU STARTED SMOKING?
WHAT'S IT LOOK LIKE?
IT JUST SEEMS LIKE A STRANGE POINT IN YOUR LIFE TO START SMOKING.
I GAVE IT UP WHEN I BECAME PREGNANT WITH YOU, LUKE.

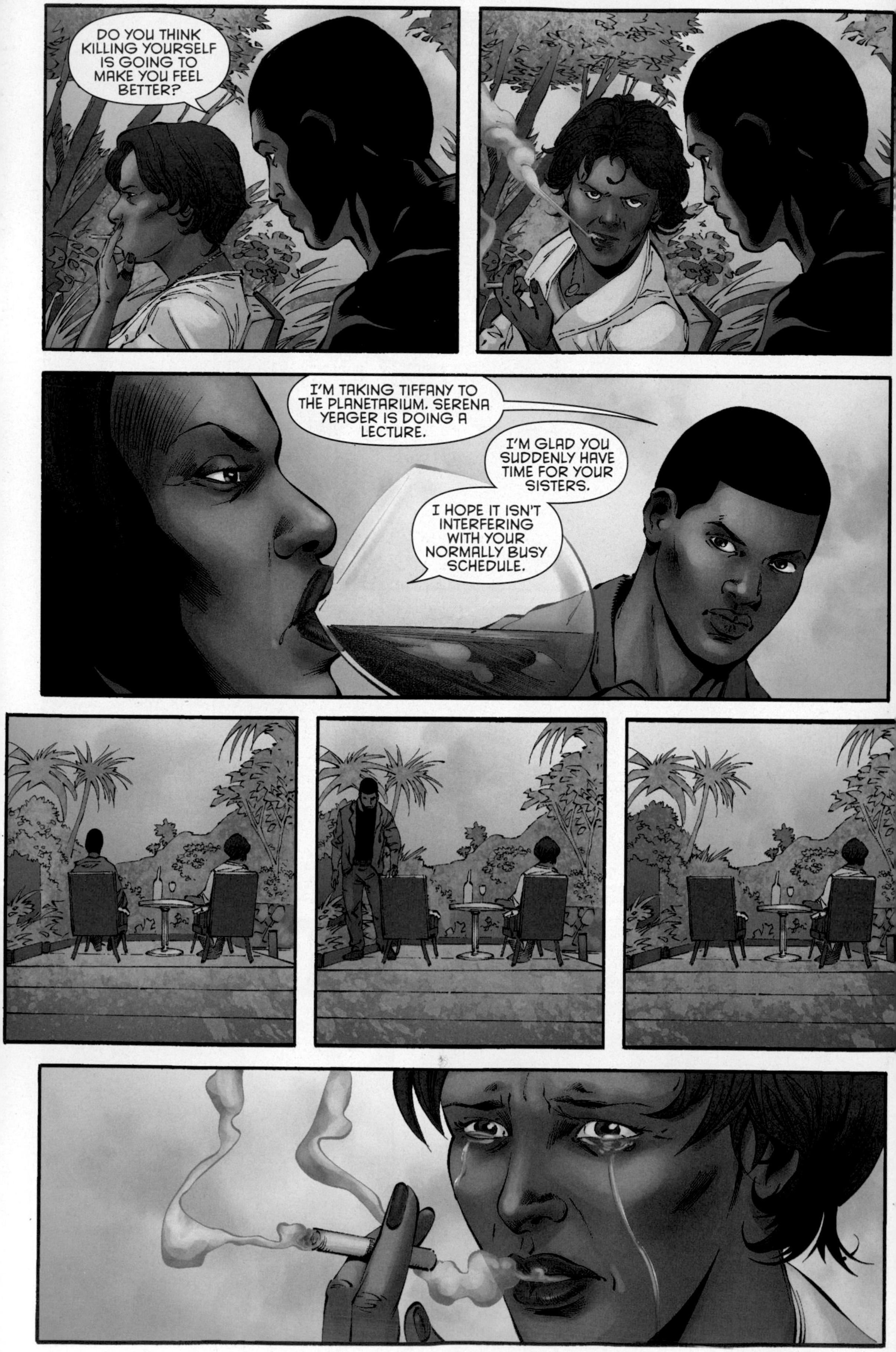
DO YOU THINK KILLING YOURSELF IS GOING TO MAKE YOU FEEL BETTER?
I'M TAKING TIFFANY TO THE PLANETARIUM. SERENA YEAGER IS DOING A LECTURE.
I'M GLAD YOU SUDDENLY HAVE TIME FOR YOUR SISTERS.
I HOPE IT ISN'T INTERFERING WITH YOUR NORMALLY BUSY SCHEDULE.

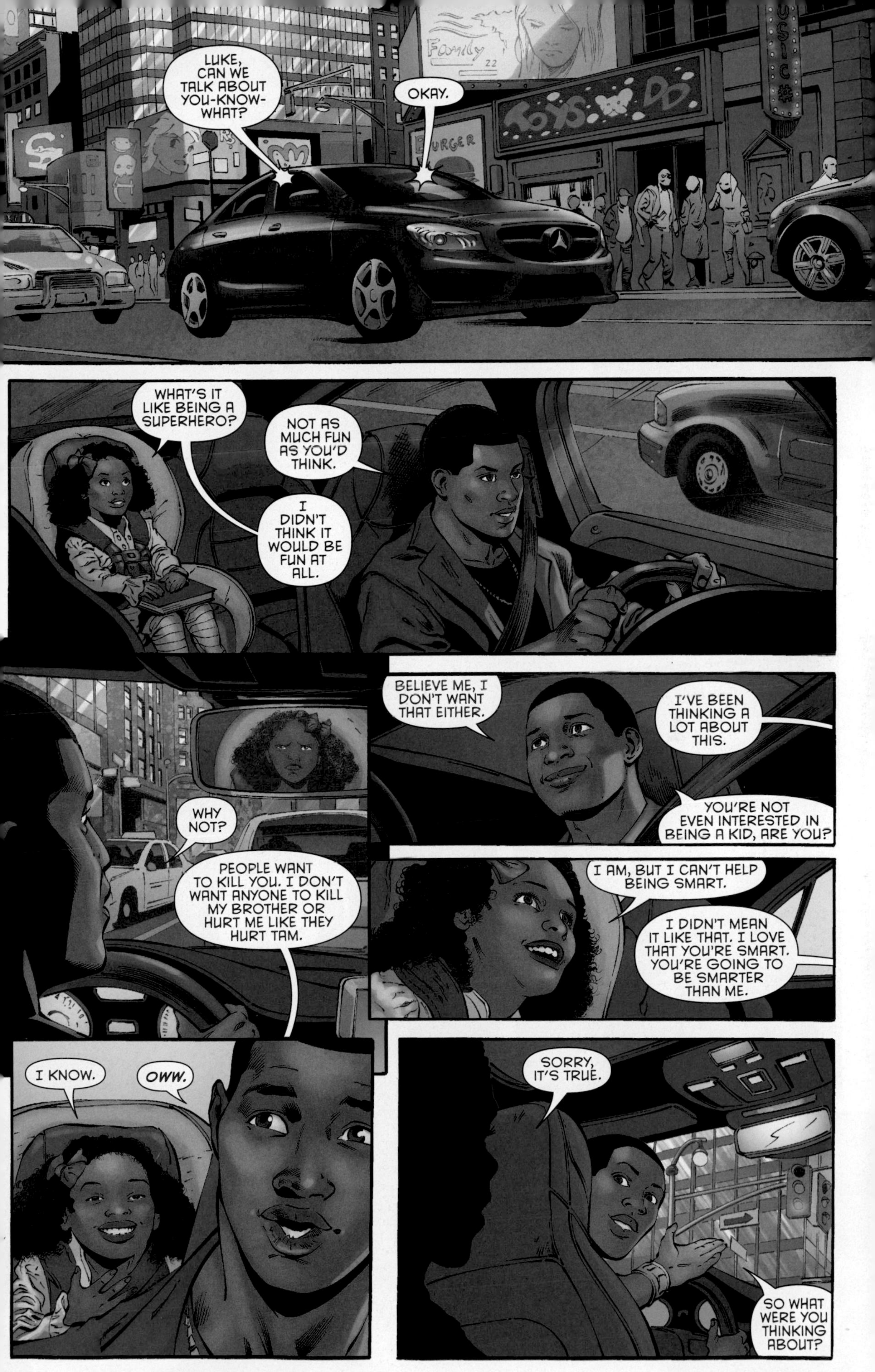
LUKE, CAN WE TALK ABOUT YOU-KNOW-WHAT?
OKAY.
TOYS DO
BURGER
WHAT'S IT LIKE BEING A SUPERHERO?
NOT AS MUCH FUN AS YOU'D THINK.
I DIDN'T THINK IT WOULD BE FUN AT ALL.
WHY NOT?
PEOPLE WANT TO KILL YOU. I DON'T WANT ANYONE TO KILL MY BROTHER OR HURT ME LIKE THEY HURT TAM.
BELIEVE ME, I DON'T WANT THAT EITHER.
I'VE BEEN THINKING A LOT ABOUT THIS.
YOU'RE NOT EVEN INTERESTED IN BEING A KID, ARE YOU?
I AM, BUT I CAN'T HELP BEING SMART.
I DIDN'T MEAN IT LIKE THAT. I LOVE THAT YOU'RE SMART. YOU'RE GOING TO BE SMARTER THAN ME.
I KNOW.
OWW.
SORRY, IT'S TRUE.
SO WHAT WERE YOU THINKING ABOUT?

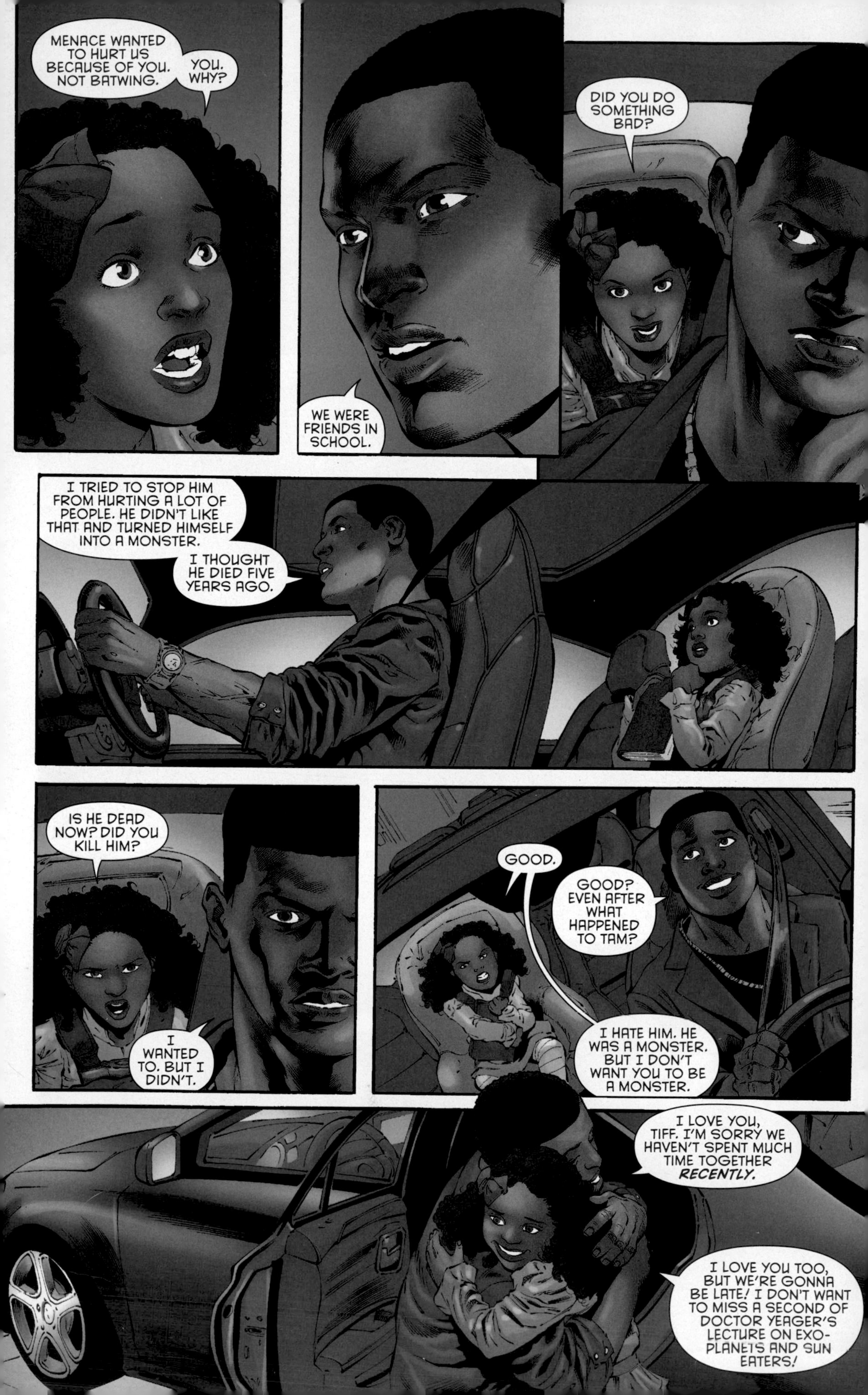
MENACE WANTED TO HURT US BECAUSE OF YOU. NOT BATWING.
YOU. WHY?
WE WERE FRIENDS IN SCHOOL.
DID YOU DO SOMETHING BAD?
I TRIED TO STOP HIM FROM HURTING A LOT OF PEOPLE. HE DIDN'T LIKE THAT AND TURNED HIMSELF INTO A MONSTER.
I THOUGHT HE DIED FIVE YEARS AGO.
IS HE DEAD NOW? DID YOU KILL HIM?
I WANTED TO. BUT I DIDN'T.
GOOD.
GOOD? EVEN AFTER WHAT HAPPENED TO TAM?
I HATE HIM. HE WAS A MONSTER. BUT I DON'T WANT YOU TO BE A MONSTER.
I LOVE YOU, TIFF. I'M SORRY WE HAVEN'T SPENT MUCH TIME TOGETHER *RECENTLY.*
I LOVE YOU TOO, BUT WE'RE GONNA BE LATE! I DON'T WANT TO MISS A SECOND OF DOCTOR YEAGER'S LECTURE ON EXO-PLANETS AND SUN EATERS!

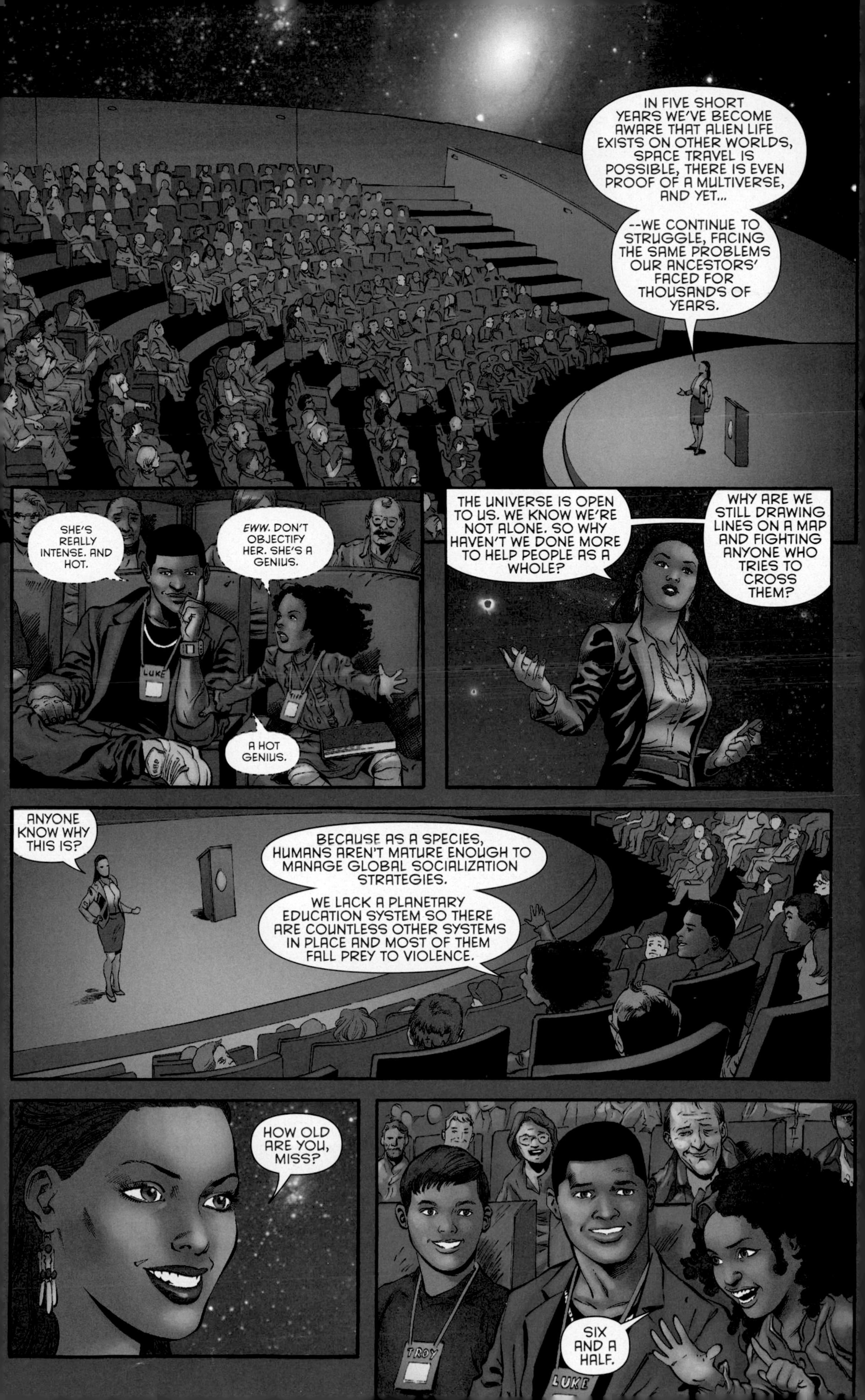
IN FIVE SHORT YEARS WE'VE BECOME AWARE THAT ALIEN LIFE EXISTS ON OTHER WORLDS, SPACE TRAVEL IS POSSIBLE, THERE IS EVEN PROOF OF A MULTIVERSE, AND YET...
--WE CONTINUE TO STRUGGLE, FACING THE SAME PROBLEMS OUR ANCESTORS' FACED FOR THOUSANDS OF YEARS.
SHE'S REALLY INTENSE. AND HOT.
EWW. DON'T OBJECTIFY HER. SHE'S A GENIUS.
A HOT GENIUS.
LUKE
THE UNIVERSE IS OPEN TO US. WE KNOW WE'RE NOT ALONE. SO WHY HAVEN'T WE DONE MORE TO HELP PEOPLE AS A WHOLE?
WHY ARE WE STILL DRAWING LINES ON A MAP AND FIGHTING ANYONE WHO TRIES TO CROSS THEM?
ANYONE KNOW WHY THIS IS?
BECAUSE AS A SPECIES, HUMANS AREN'T MATURE ENOUGH TO MANAGE GLOBAL SOCIALIZATION STRATEGIES.
WE LACK A PLANETARY EDUCATION SYSTEM SO THERE ARE COUNTLESS OTHER SYSTEMS IN PLACE AND MOST OF THEM FALL PREY TO VIOLENCE.
HOW OLD ARE YOU, MISS?
SIX AND A HALF.
TROY
LUKE

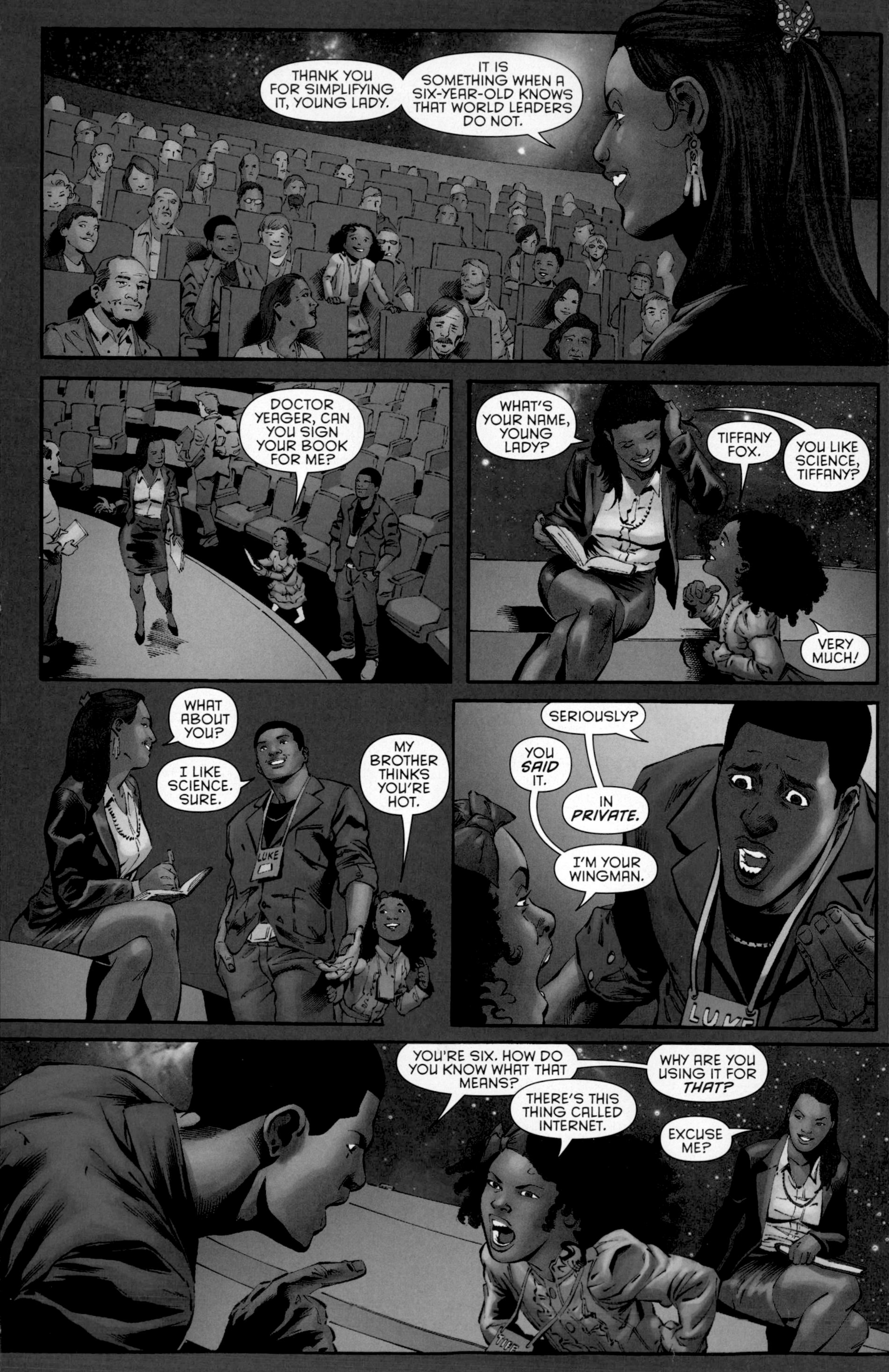
THANK YOU FOR SIMPLIFYING IT, YOUNG LADY.
IT IS SOMETHING WHEN A SIX-YEAR-OLD KNOWS THAT WORLD LEADERS DO NOT.
DOCTOR YEAGER, CAN YOU SIGN YOUR BOOK FOR ME?
WHAT'S YOUR NAME, YOUNG LADY?
TIFFANY FOX.
YOU LIKE SCIENCE, TIFFANY?
VERY MUCH!
WHAT ABOUT YOU?
I LIKE SCIENCE. SURE.
MY BROTHER THINKS YOU'RE HOT.
LUKE
SERIOUSLY?
YOU *SAID* IT.
IN *PRIVATE.*
I'M YOUR WINGMAN.
LUKE
YOU'RE SIX. HOW DO YOU KNOW WHAT THAT MEANS?
THERE'S THIS THING CALLED INTERNET.
WHY ARE YOU USING IT FOR *THAT?*
EXCUSE ME?

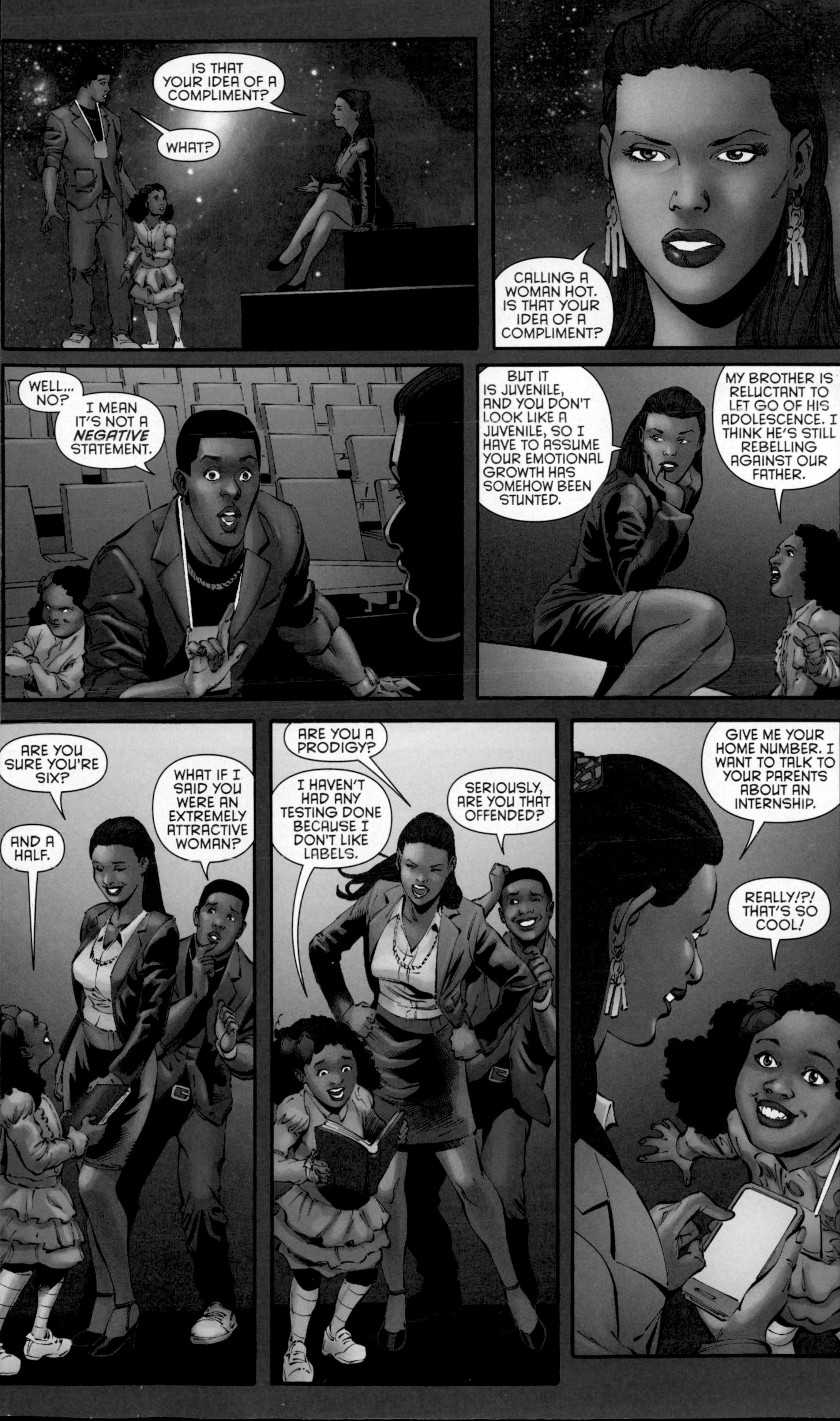
IS THAT YOUR IDEA OF A COMPLIMENT?
WHAT?
CALLING A WOMAN HOT. IS THAT YOUR IDEA OF A COMPLIMENT?
WELL... NO?
I MEAN IT'S NOT A *NEGATIVE* STATEMENT.
BUT IT IS JUVENILE, AND YOU DON'T LOOK LIKE A JUVENILE, SO I HAVE TO ASSUME YOUR EMOTIONAL GROWTH HAS SOMEHOW BEEN STUNTED.
MY BROTHER IS RELUCTANT TO LET GO OF HIS ADOLESCENCE. I THINK HE'S STILL REBELLING AGAINST OUR FATHER.
ARE YOU SURE YOU'RE SIX?
AND A HALF.
WHAT IF I SAID YOU WERE AN EXTREMELY ATTRACTIVE WOMAN?
ARE YOU A PRODIGY?
I HAVEN'T HAD ANY TESTING DONE BECAUSE I DON'T LIKE LABELS.
SERIOUSLY, ARE YOU THAT OFFENDED?
GIVE ME YOUR HOME NUMBER. I WANT TO TALK TO YOUR PARENTS ABOUT AN INTERNSHIP.
REALLY!?! THAT'S SO COOL!

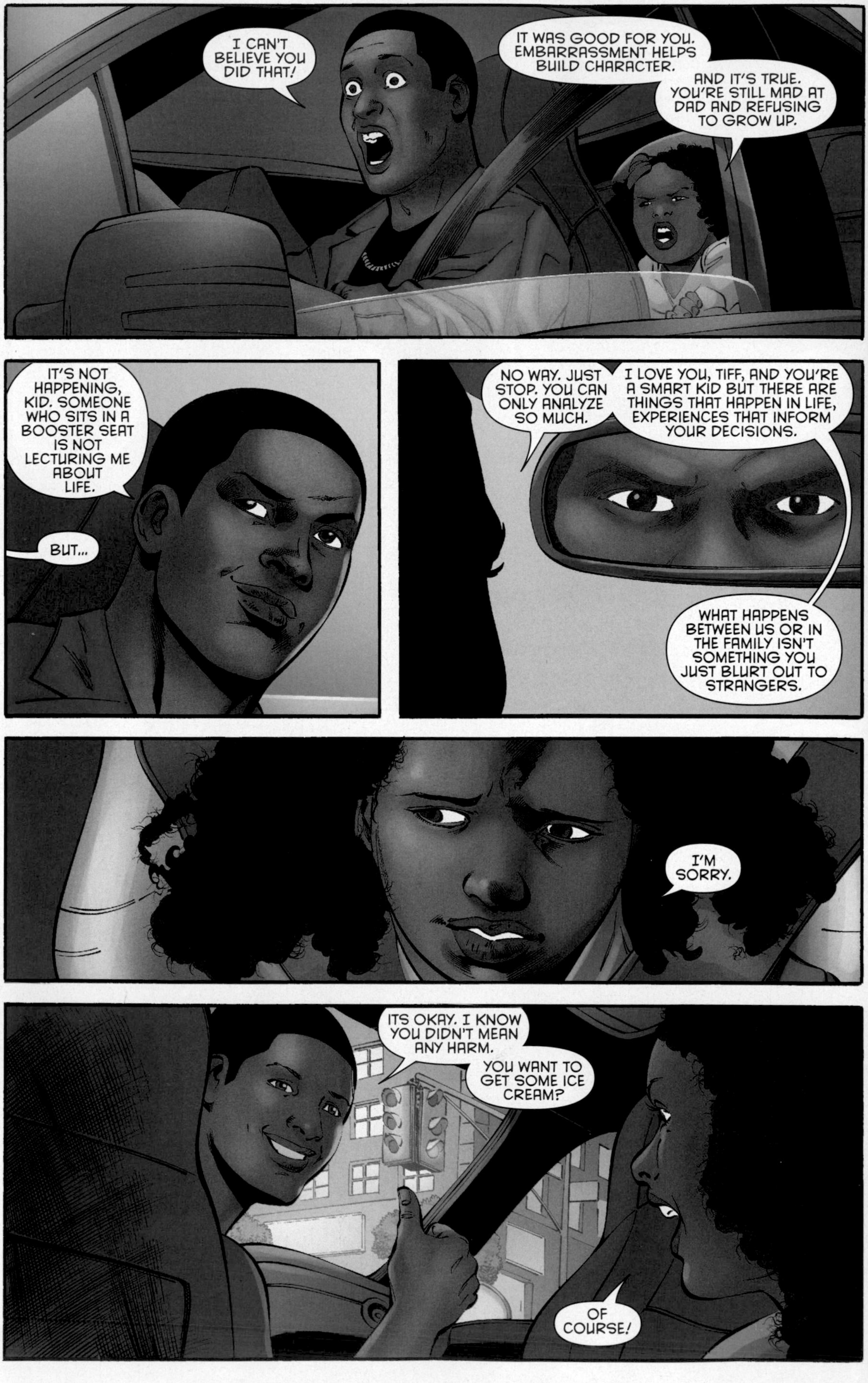

I CAN'T BELIEVE YOU DID THAT!
IT WAS GOOD FOR YOU. EMBARRASSMENT HELPS BUILD CHARACTER.
AND IT'S TRUE. YOU'RE STILL MAD AT DAD AND REFUSING TO GROW UP.
IT'S NOT HAPPENING, KID. SOMEONE WHO SITS IN A BOOSTER SEAT IS NOT LECTURING ME ABOUT LIFE.
BUT...
NO WAY. JUST STOP. YOU CAN ONLY ANALYZE SO MUCH.
I LOVE YOU, TIFF, AND YOU'RE A SMART KID BUT THERE ARE THINGS THAT HAPPEN IN LIFE, EXPERIENCES THAT INFORM YOUR DECISIONS.
WHAT HAPPENS BETWEEN US OR IN THE FAMILY ISN'T SOMETHING YOU JUST BLURT OUT TO STRANGERS.
I'M SORRY.
ITS OKAY. I KNOW YOU DIDN'T MEAN ANY HARM.
YOU WANT TO GET SOME ICE CREAM?
OF COURSE!

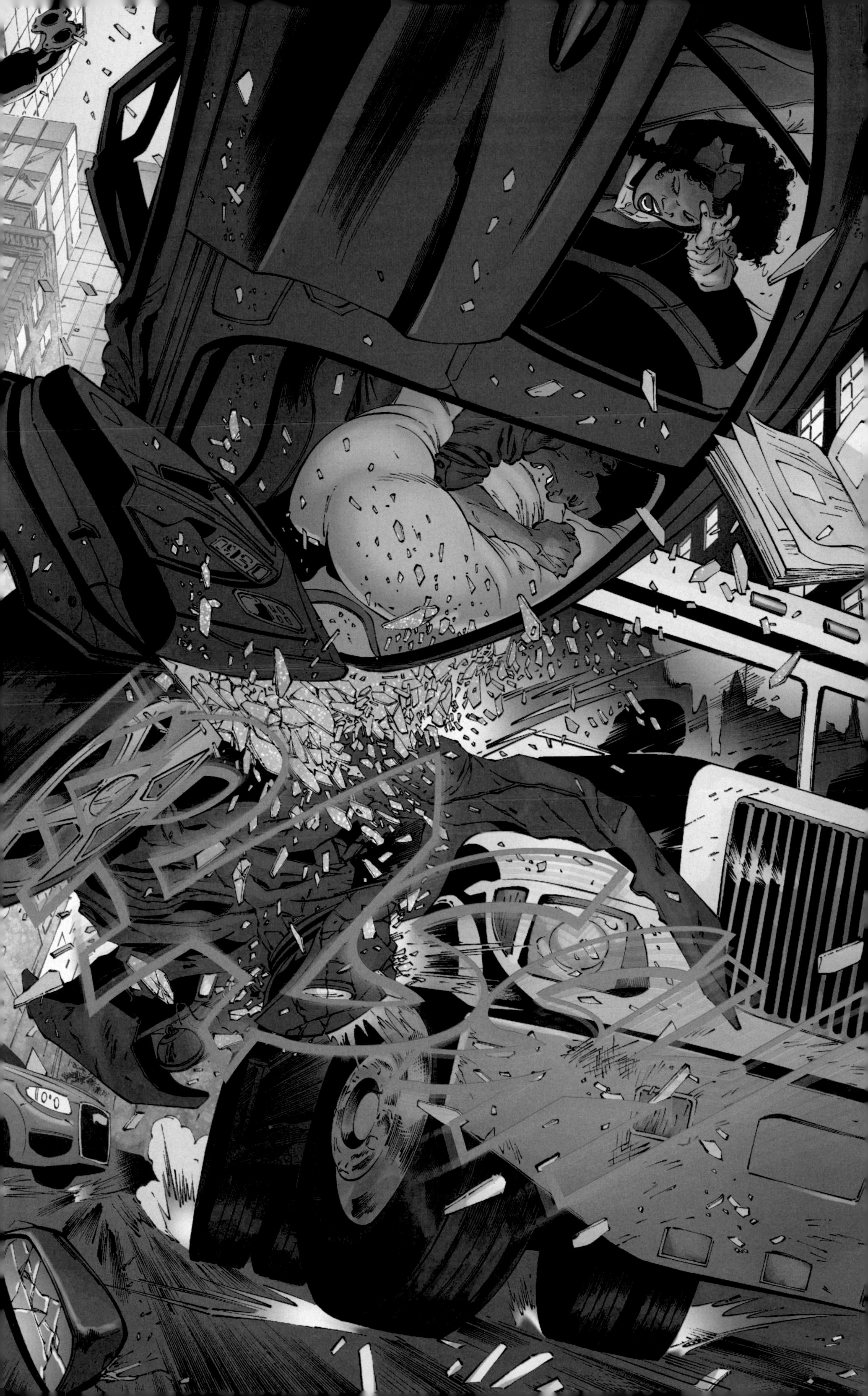

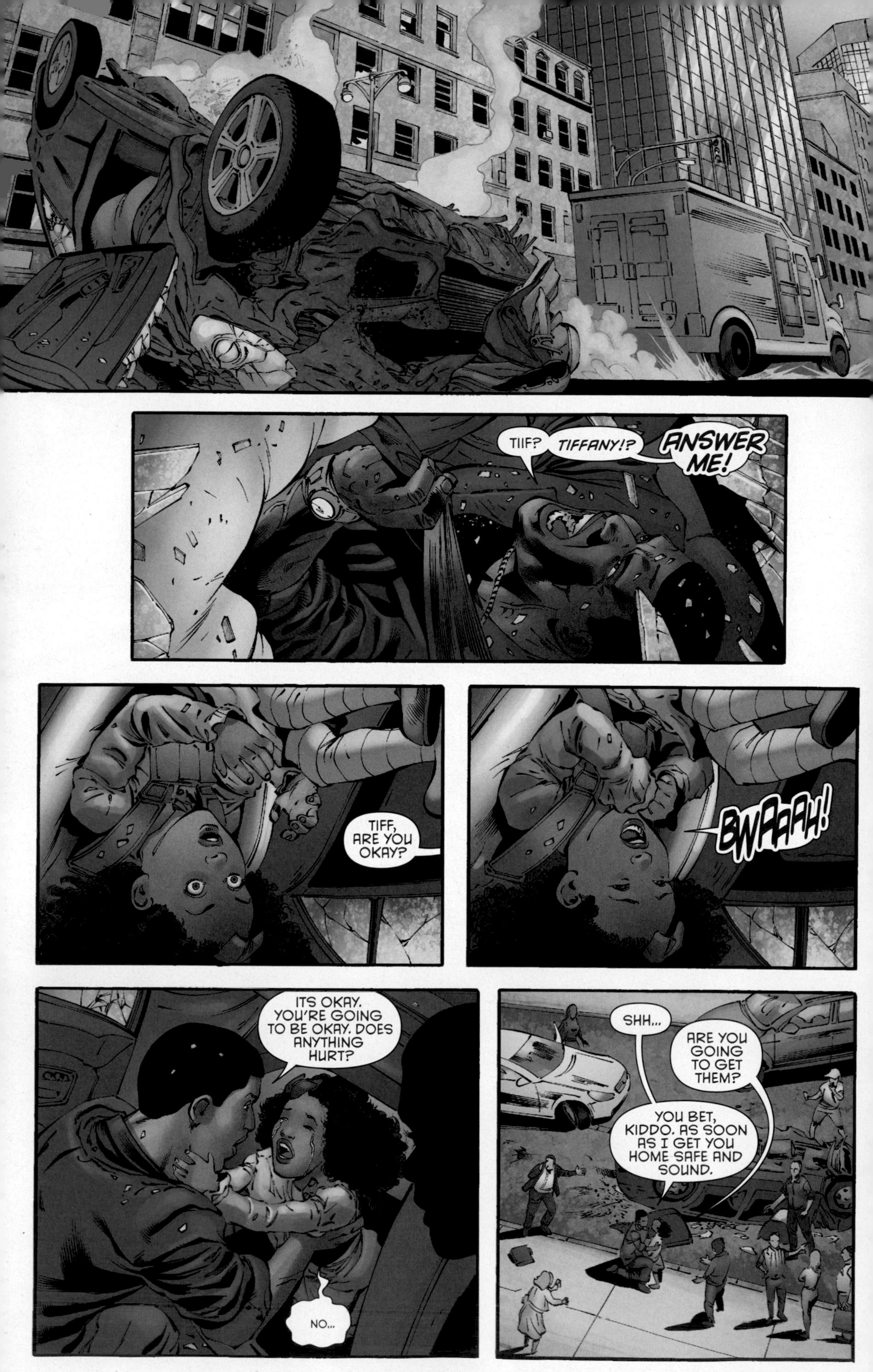
TIIF?
TIFFANY!?
ANSWER ME!
TIFF, ARE YOU OKAY?
BWAAAH!
ITS OKAY. YOU'RE GOING TO BE OKAY. DOES ANYTHING HURT?
NO...
SHH...
ARE YOU GOING TO GET THEM?
YOU BET, KIDDO. AS SOON AS I GET YOU HOME SAFE AND SOUND.

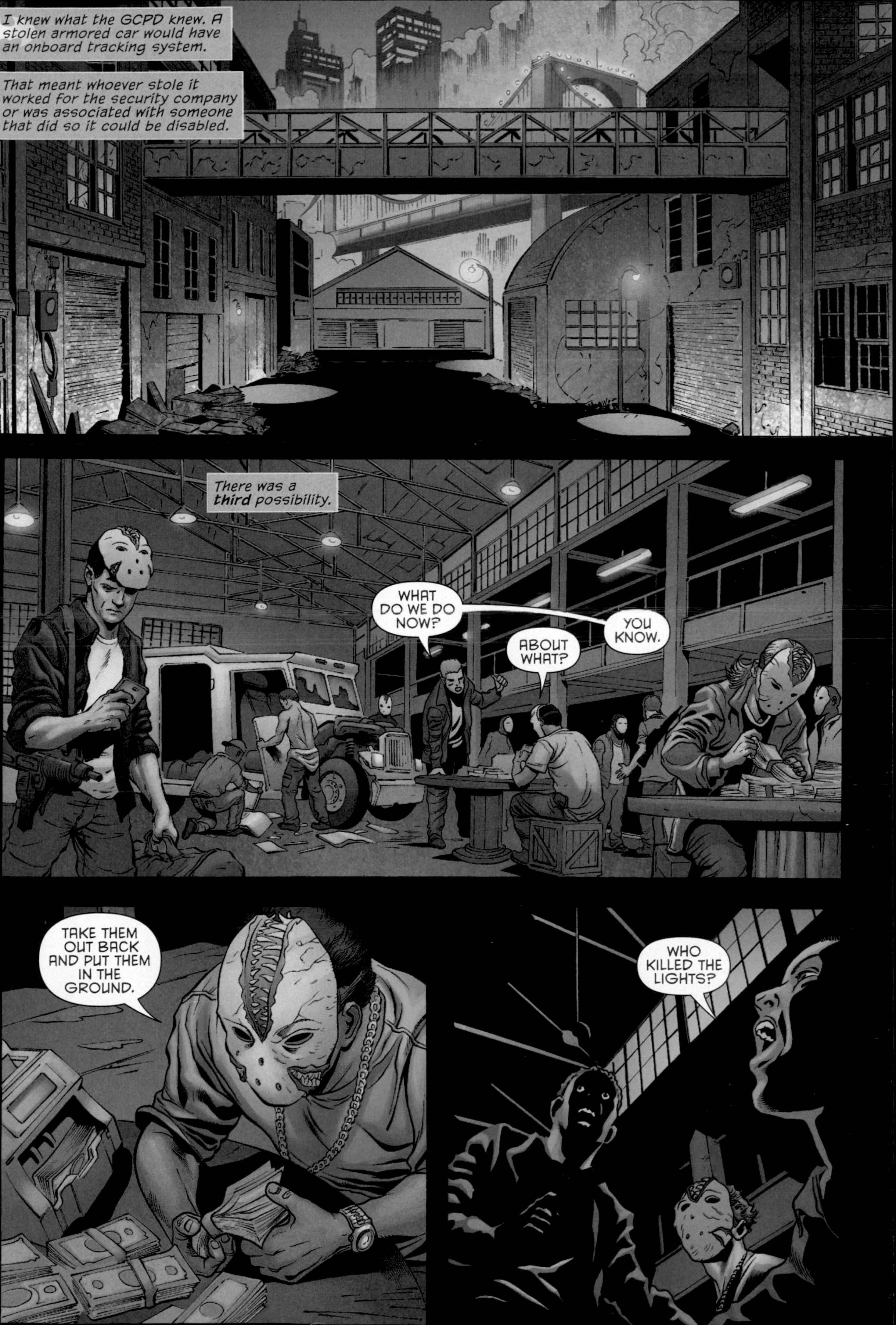
I knew what the GCPD knew. A stolen armored car would have an onboard tracking system.
That meant whoever stole it worked for the security company or was associated with someone that did so it could be disabled.
There was a **third** possibility.
WHAT DO WE DO NOW?
YOU KNOW.
ABOUT WHAT?
TAKE THEM OUT BACK AND PUT THEM IN THE GROUND.
WHO KILLED THE LIGHTS?

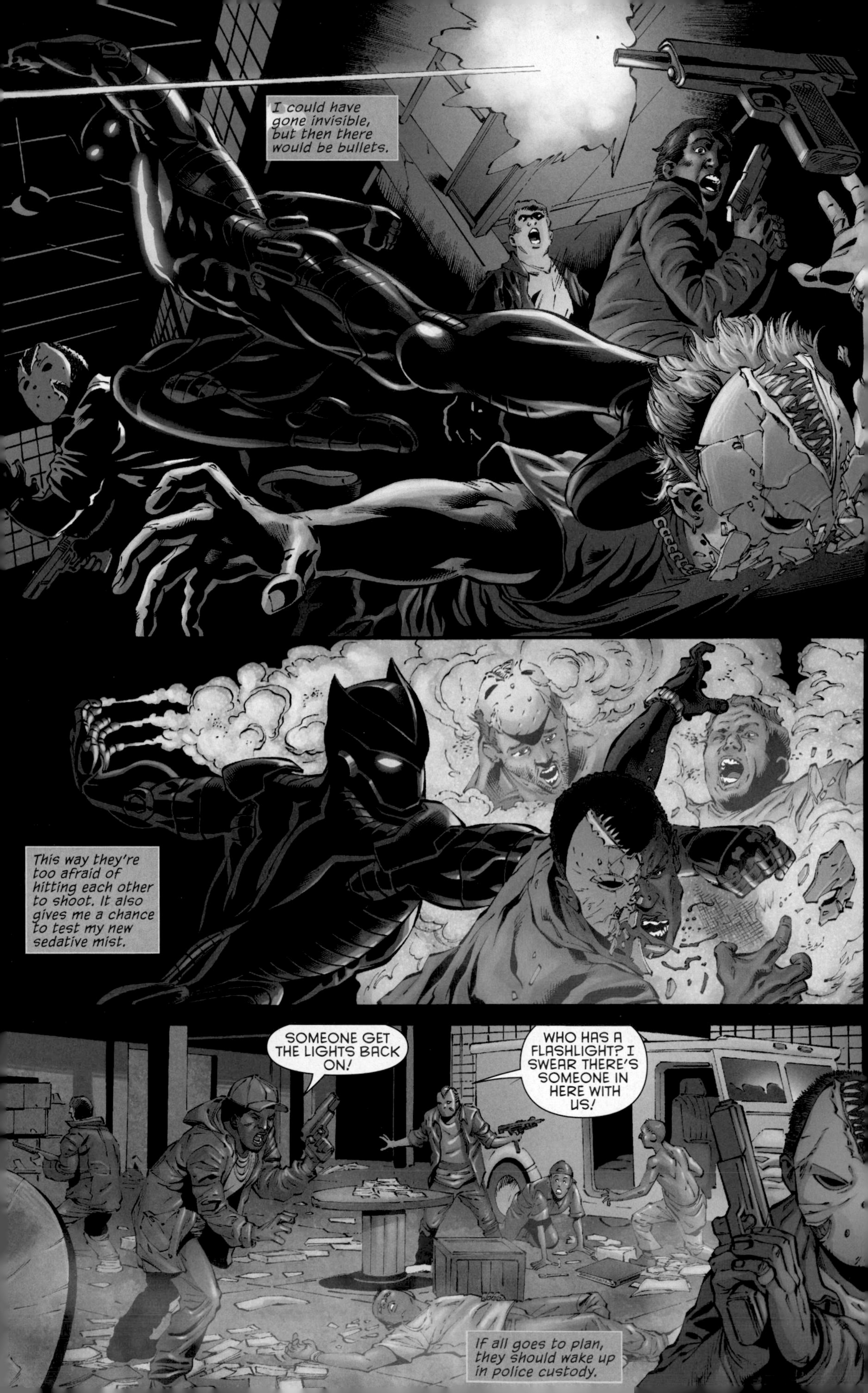

I could have gone invisible, but then there would be bullets.
This way they're too afraid of hitting each other to shoot. It also gives me a chance to test my new sedative mist.
SOMEONE GET THE LIGHTS BACK ON!
WHO HAS A FLASHLIGHT? I SWEAR THERE'S SOMEONE IN HERE WITH US!
If all goes to plan, they should wake up in police custody.

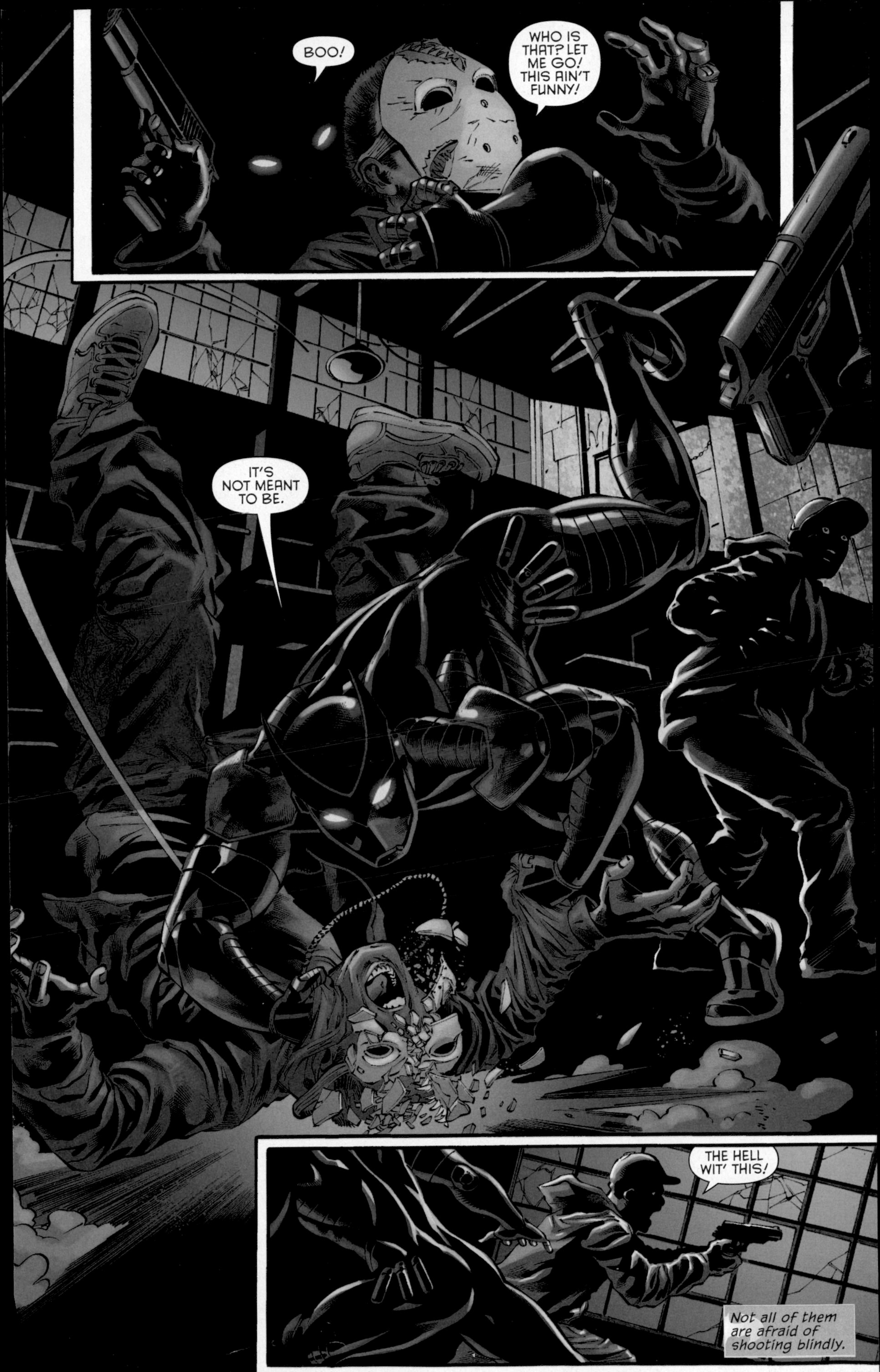
BOO!
WHO IS THAT? LET ME GO! THIS AIN'T FUNNY!
IT'S NOT MEANT TO BE.
THE HELL WIT' THIS!
Not all of them are afraid of shooting blindly.

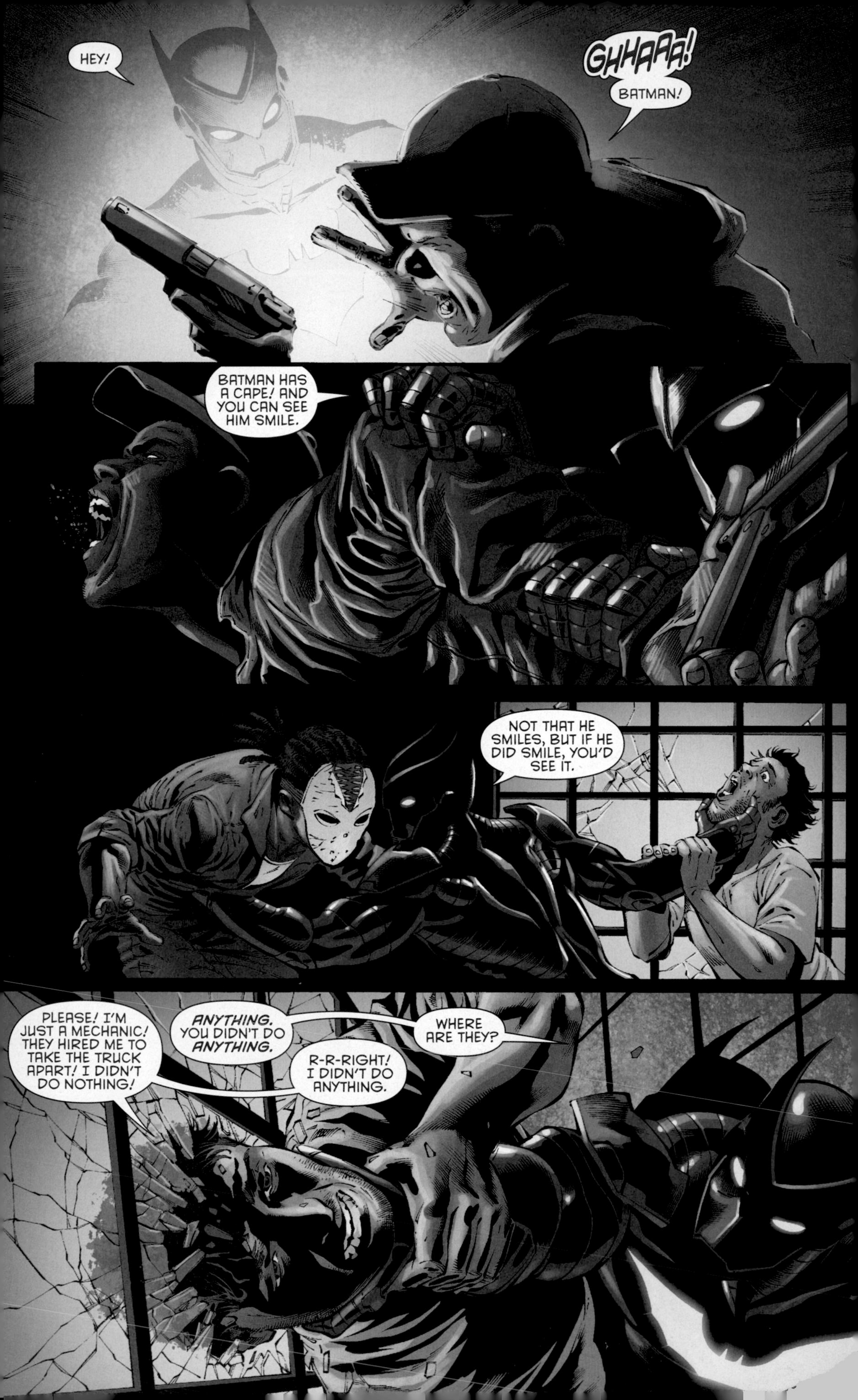
HEY!
GHHAAA!
BATMAN!
BATMAN HAS A CAPE! AND YOU CAN SEE HIM SMILE.
NOT THAT HE SMILES, BUT IF HE DID SMILE, YOU'D SEE IT.
PLEASE! I'M JUST A MECHANIC! THEY HIRED ME TO TAKE THE TRUCK APART! I DIDN'T DO NOTHING!
ANYTHING. YOU DIDN'T DO ANYTHING.
R-R-RIGHT! I DIDN'T DO ANYTHING.
WHERE ARE THEY?

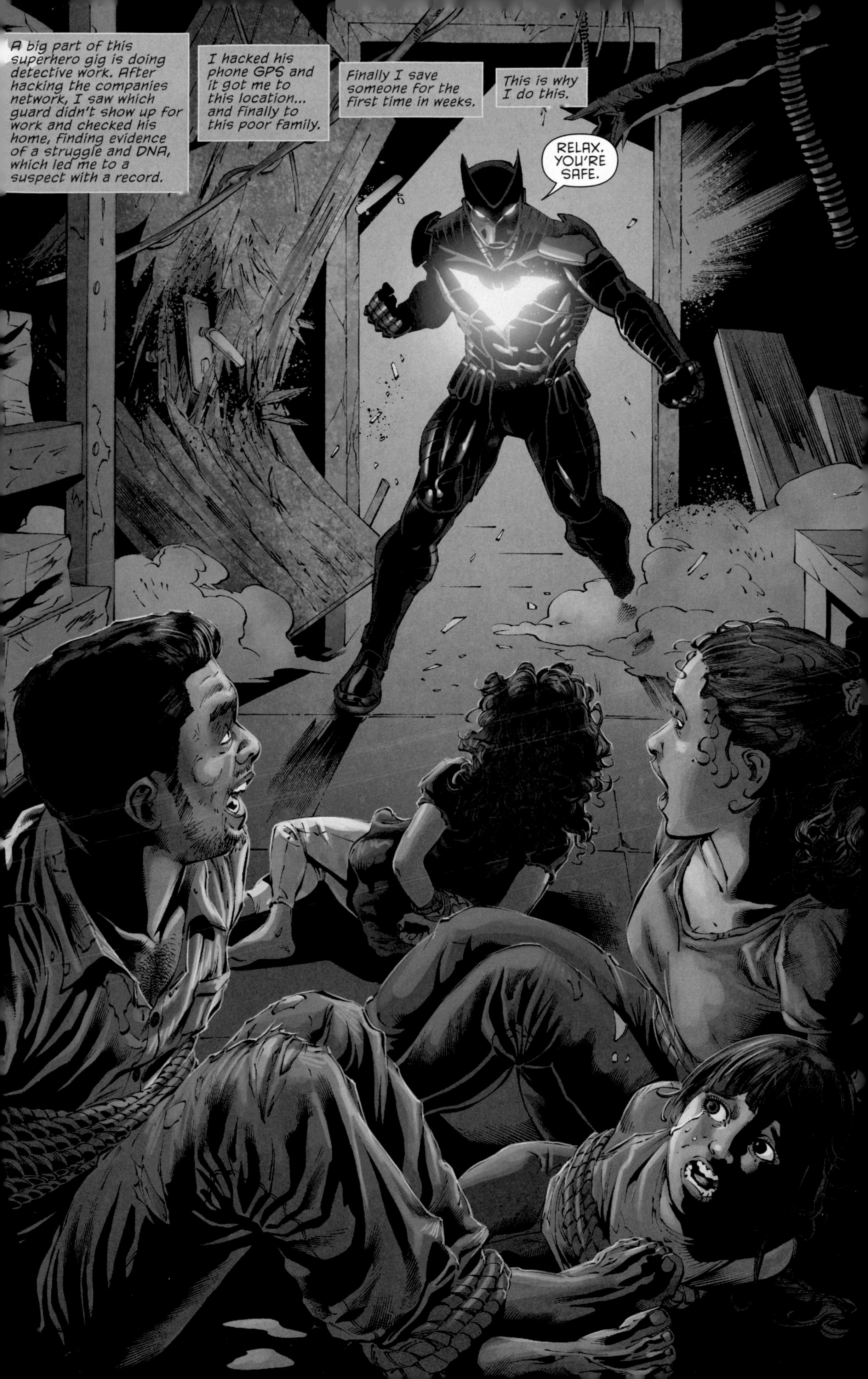

A big part of this superhero gig is doing detective work. After hacking the companies network, I saw which guard didn't show up for work and checked his home, finding evidence of a struggle and DNA, which led me to a suspect with a record.
I hacked his phone GPS and it got me to this location... and finally to this poor family.
Finally I save someone for the first time in weeks.
This is why I do this.
RELAX. YOU'RE SAFE.

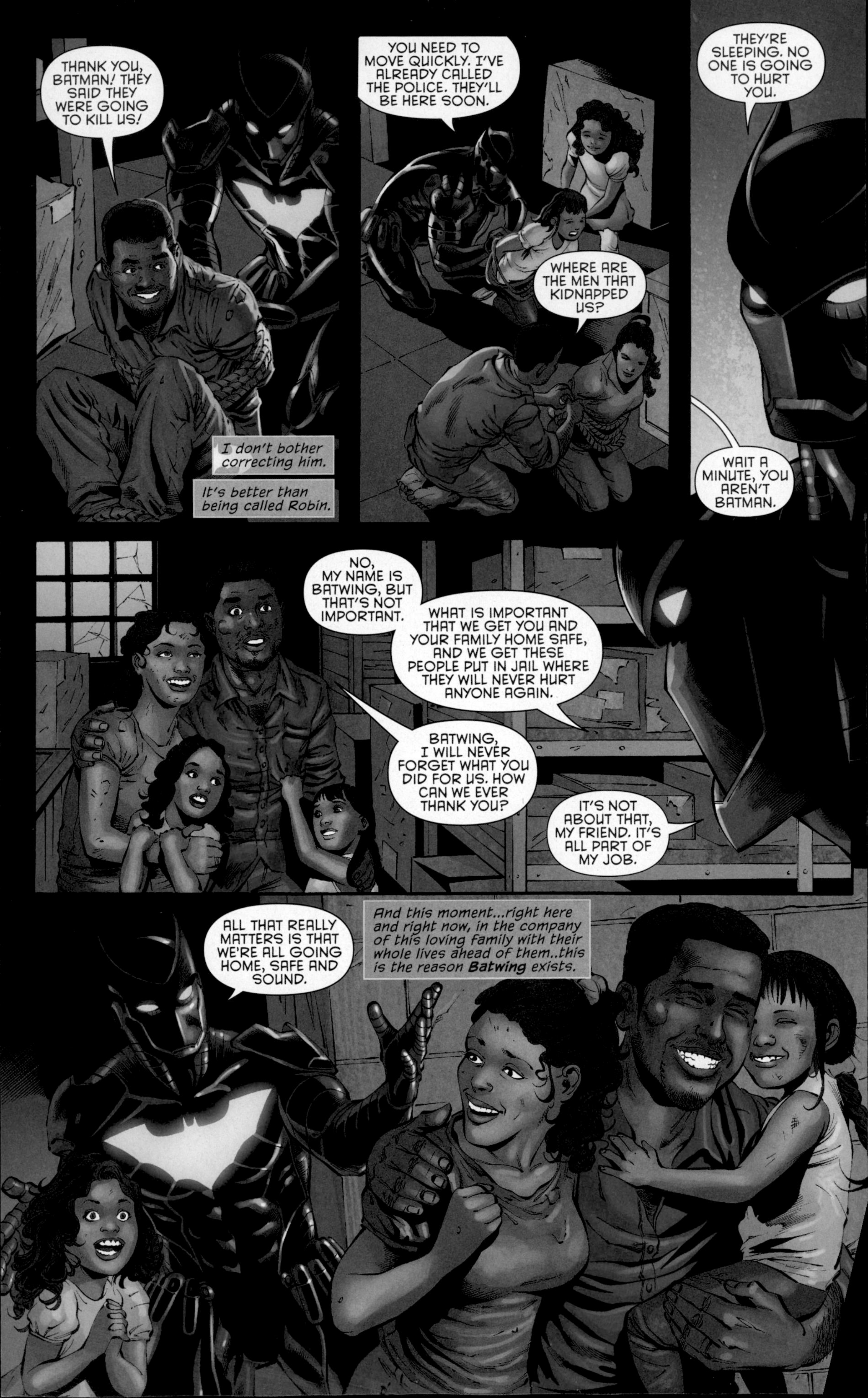
THANK YOU, BATMAN! THEY SAID THEY WERE GOING TO KILL US!
I don't bother correcting him.
It's better than being called Robin.
YOU NEED TO MOVE QUICKLY. I'VE ALREADY CALLED THE POLICE. THEY'LL BE HERE SOON.
WHERE ARE THE MEN THAT KIDNAPPED US?
THEY'RE SLEEPING. NO ONE IS GOING TO HURT YOU.
WAIT A MINUTE, YOU AREN'T BATMAN.
NO, MY NAME IS BATWING, BUT THAT'S NOT IMPORTANT.
WHAT IS IMPORTANT THAT WE GET YOU AND YOUR FAMILY HOME SAFE, AND WE GET THESE PEOPLE PUT IN JAIL WHERE THEY WILL NEVER HURT ANYONE AGAIN.
BATWING, I WILL NEVER FORGET WHAT YOU DID FOR US. HOW CAN WE EVER THANK YOU?
IT'S NOT ABOUT THAT, MY FRIEND. IT'S ALL PART OF MY JOB.
ALL THAT REALLY MATTERS IS THAT WE'RE ALL GOING HOME, SAFE AND SOUND.
And this moment...right here and right now, in the company of this loving family with their whole lives ahead of them..this is the reason Batwing exists.

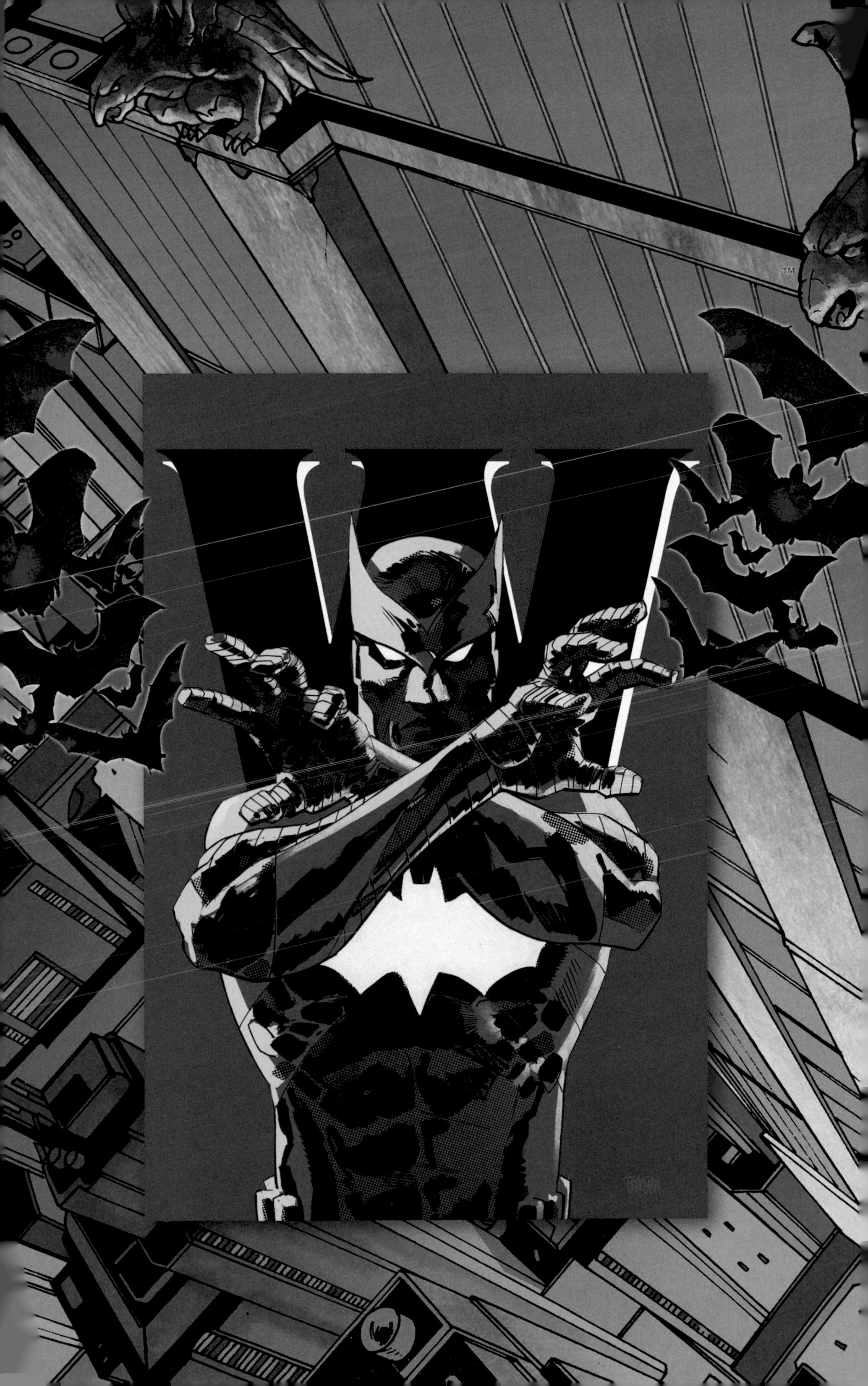
W

LEVIATHAN RISES

JIMMY PALMIOTTI
JUSTIN GRAY
writers

EDUARDO PANSICA
penciller

JÚLIO FERREIRA
JP MAYER (pgs 17-18)
inkers

CHRIS SOTOMAYOR
colorist

DEZI SIENTY
letterer

cover art by
DAN PANOSIAN

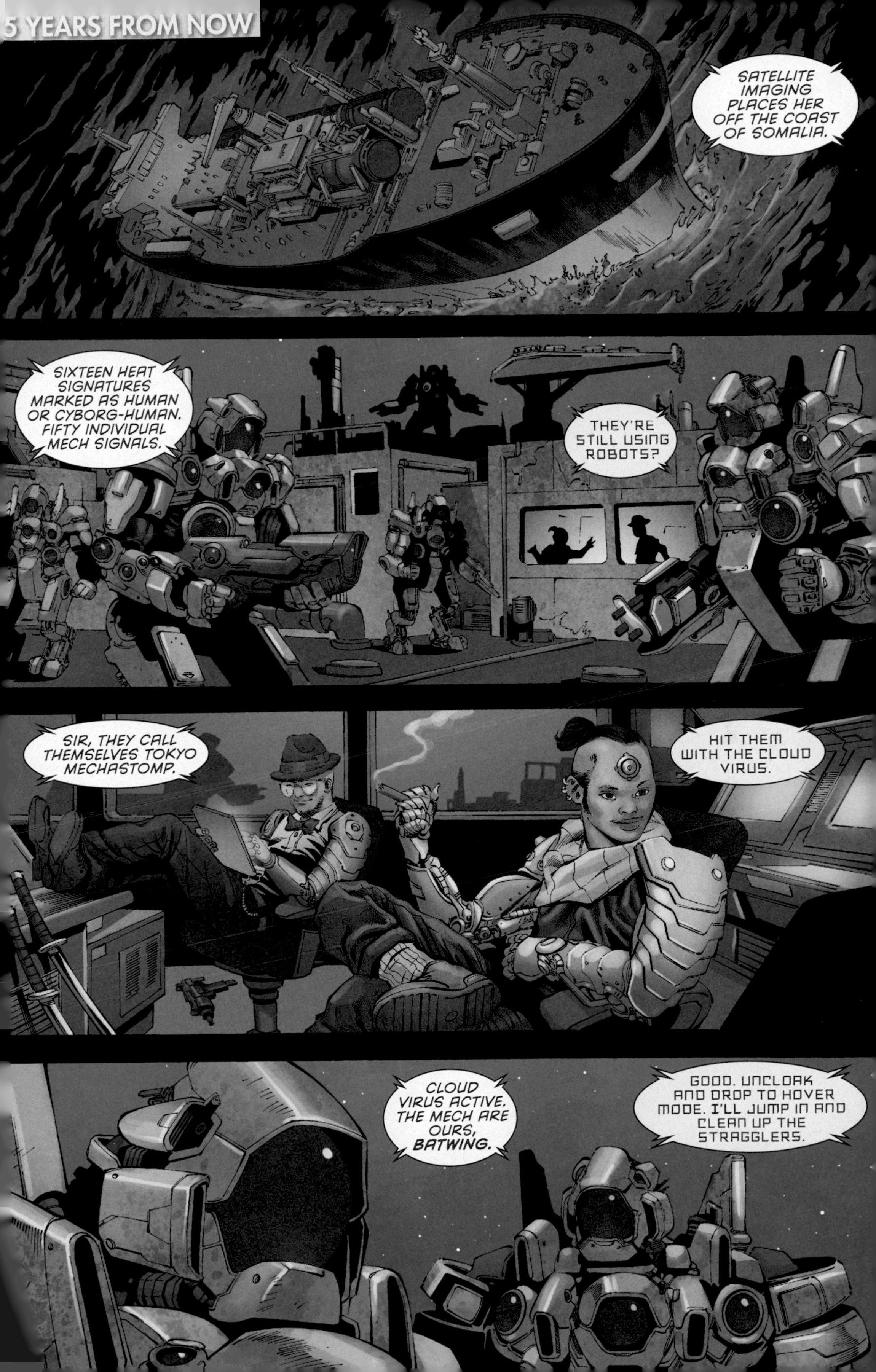
5 YEARS FROM NOW
SATELLITE IMAGING PLACES HER OFF THE COAST OF SOMALIA.
SIXTEEN HEAT SIGNATURES MARKED AS HUMAN OR CYBORG-HUMAN. FIFTY INDIVIDUAL MECH SIGNALS.
THEY'RE STILL USING ROBOTS?
SIR, THEY CALL THEMSELVES TOKYO MECHASTOMP.
HIT THEM WITH THE CLOUD VIRUS.
CLOUD VIRUS ACTIVE. THE MECH ARE OURS, BATWING.
GOOD. UNCLOAK AND DROP TO HOVER MODE. I'LL JUMP IN AND CLEAN UP THE STRAGGLERS.

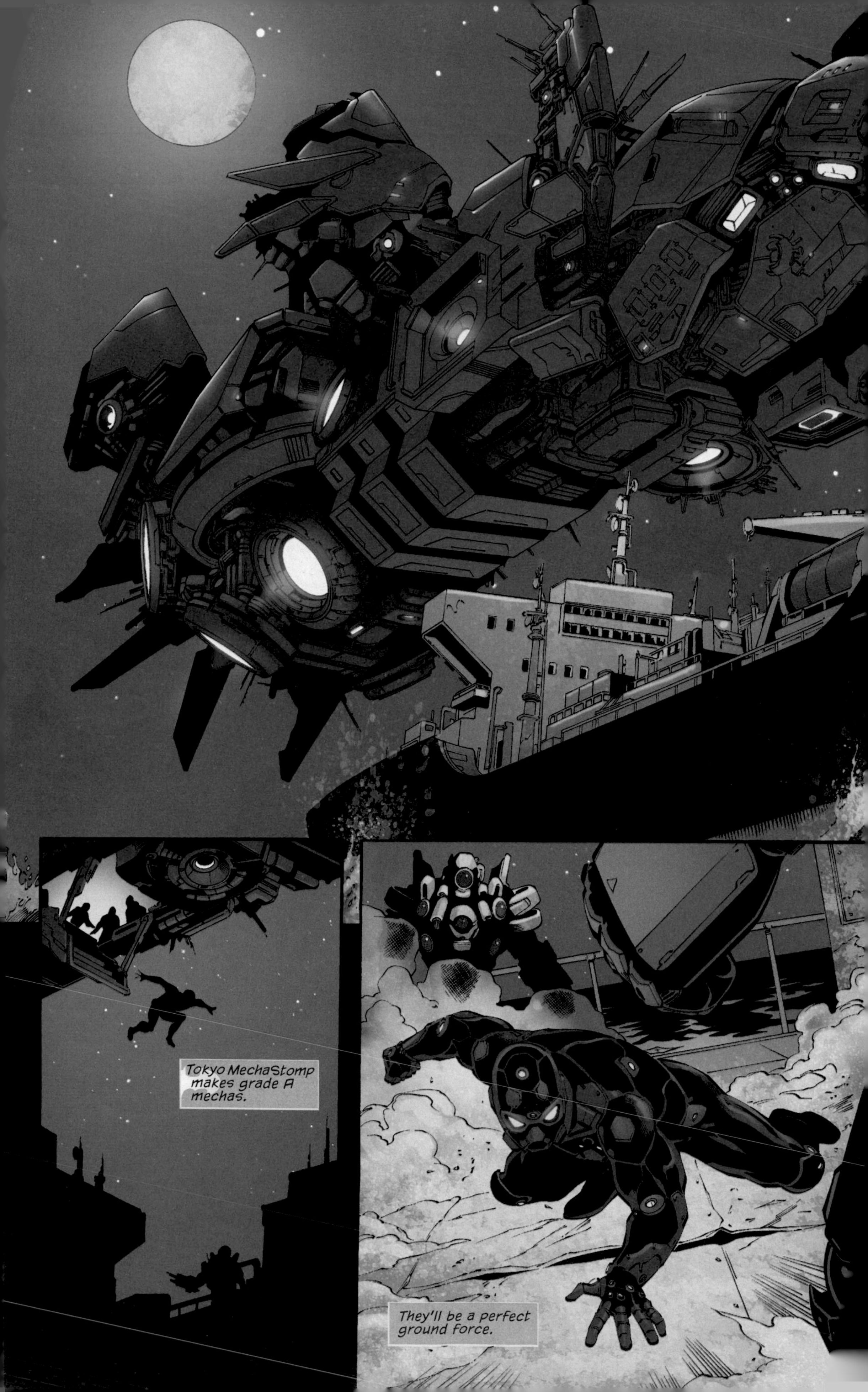
Tokyo MechaStomp makes grade A mechas.
They'll be a perfect ground force.

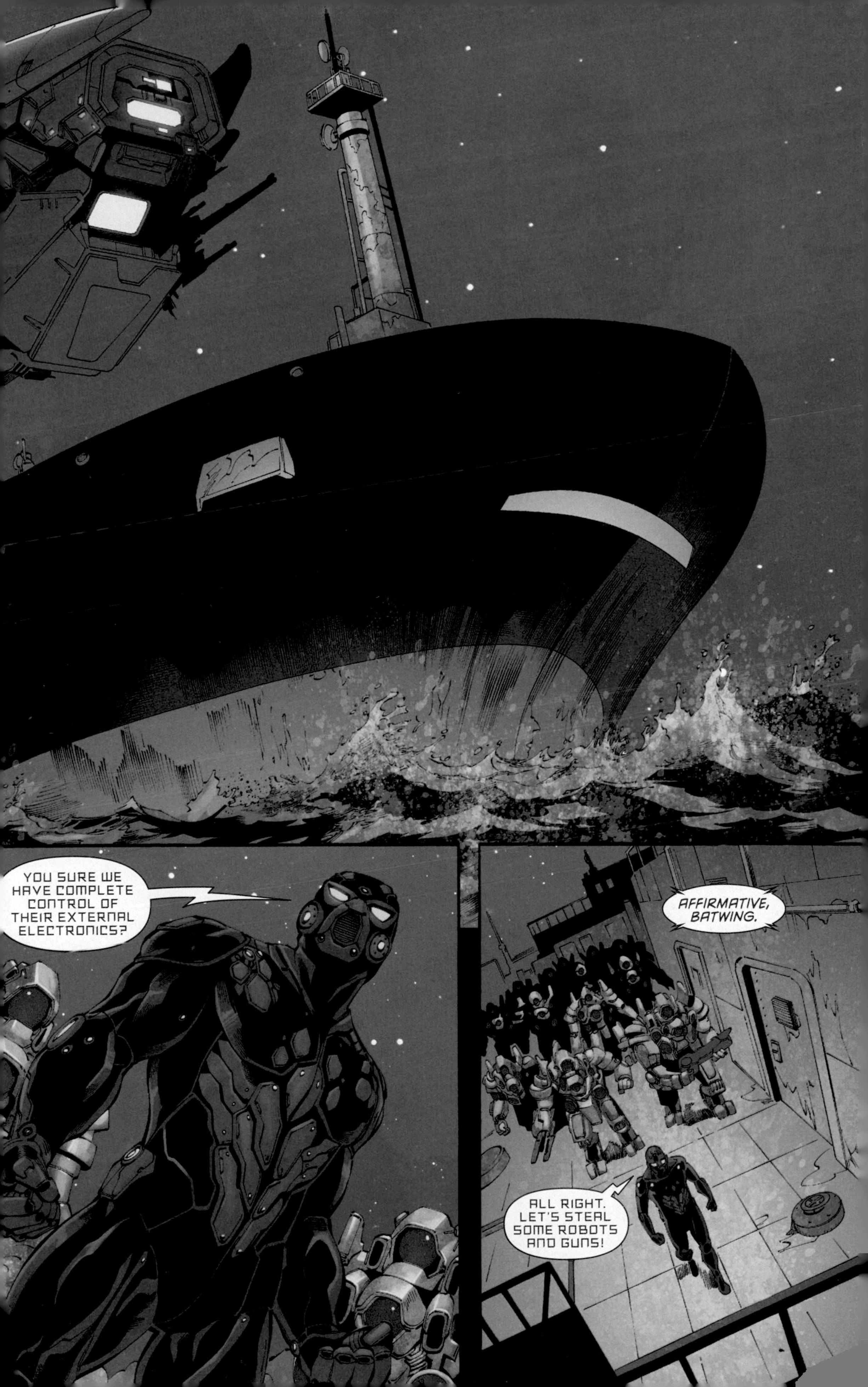
YOU SURE WE HAVE COMPLETE CONTROL OF THEIR EXTERNAL ELECTRONICS?
AFFIRMATIVE, BATWING.
ALL RIGHT. LET'S STEAL SOME ROBOTS AND GUNS!

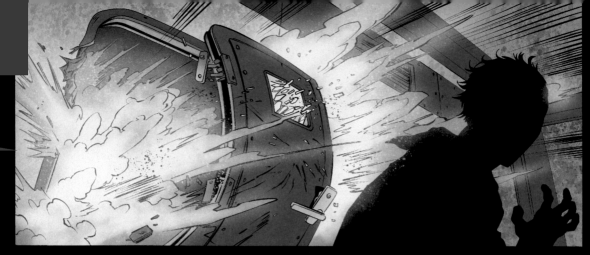

GENTLEMEN OF TOKYO MECHASTOMP, THIS SHIP AND ALL HER CONTENTS ARE BEING CONFISCATED.

JOIN US OR YOUR ROBOTS, WHICH ARE NOW MY ROBOTS, WILL ESCORT YOU TO THE LIFEBOATS.

WHO THE HELL DO YOU THINK YOU ARRRREEEE!?!?

WE ARE LEVIATHAN.

WE ARE LEVIATHAN.

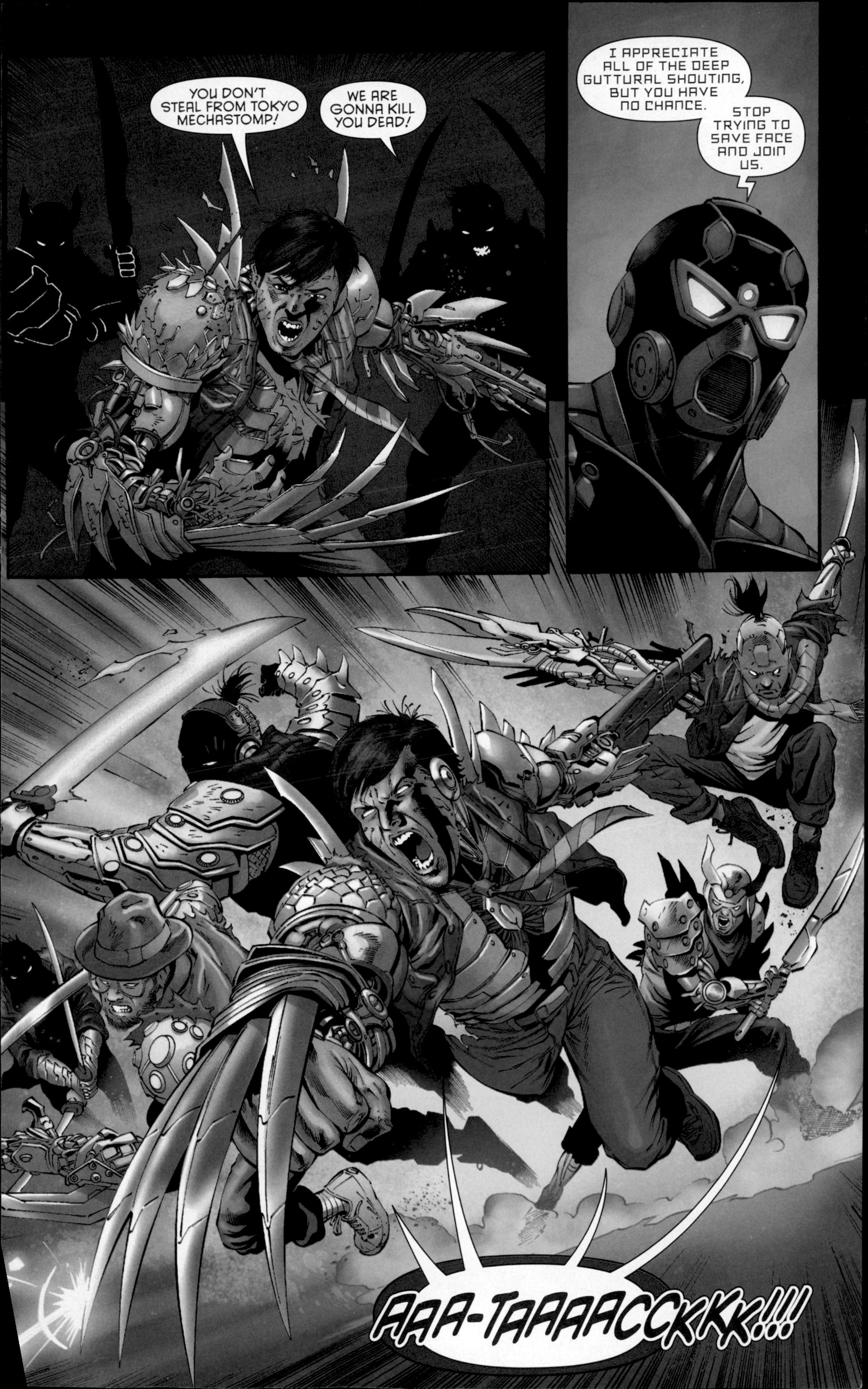
YOU DON'T STEAL FROM TOKYO MECHASTOMP!
WE ARE GONNA KILL YOU DEAD!
I APPRECIATE ALL OF THE DEEP GUTTURAL SHOUTING, BUT YOU HAVE NO CHANCE.
STOP TRYING TO SAVE FACE AND JOIN US.
AAA-TAAAACCKKK!!!

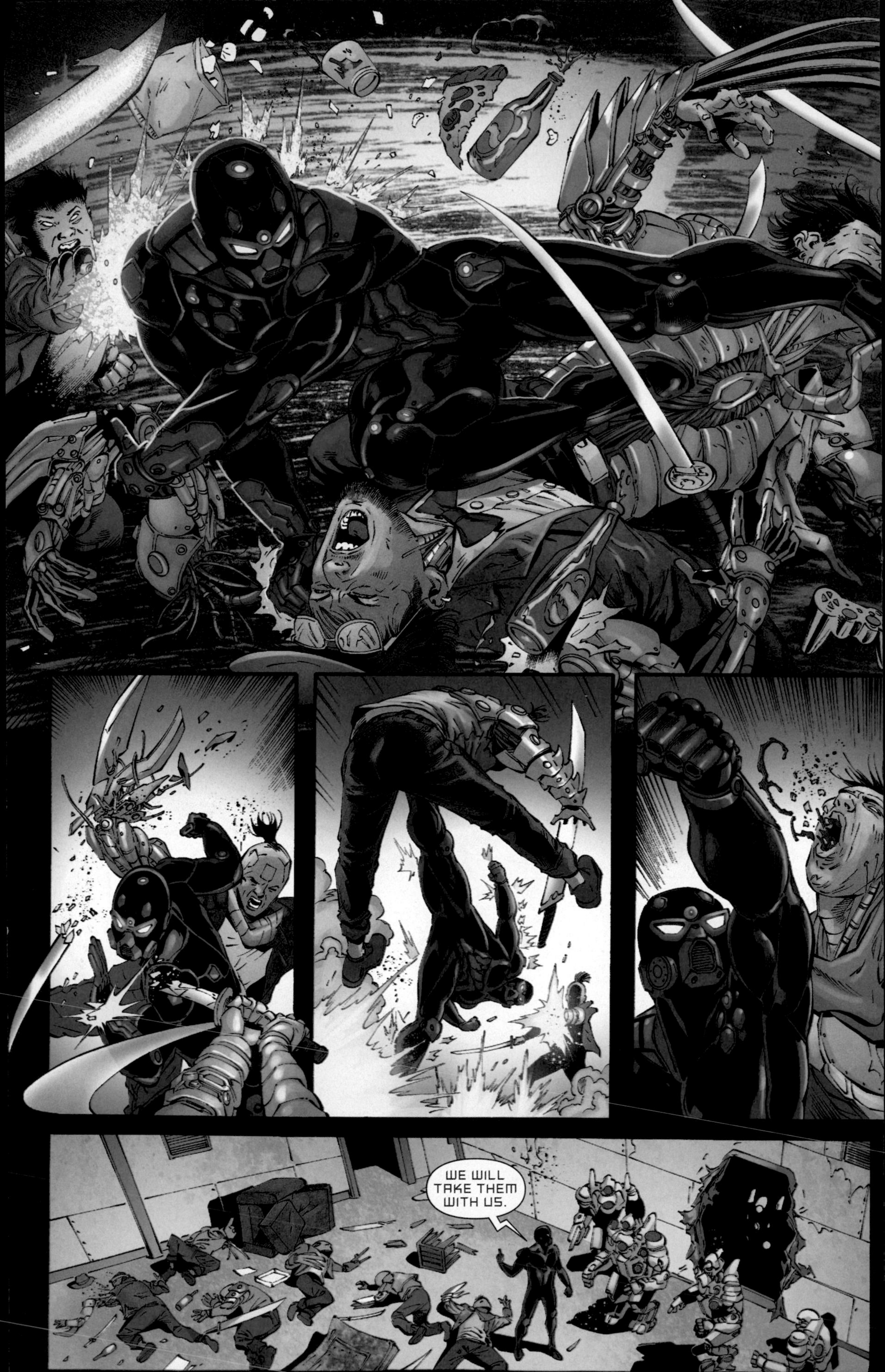
WE WILL TAKE THEM WITH US.

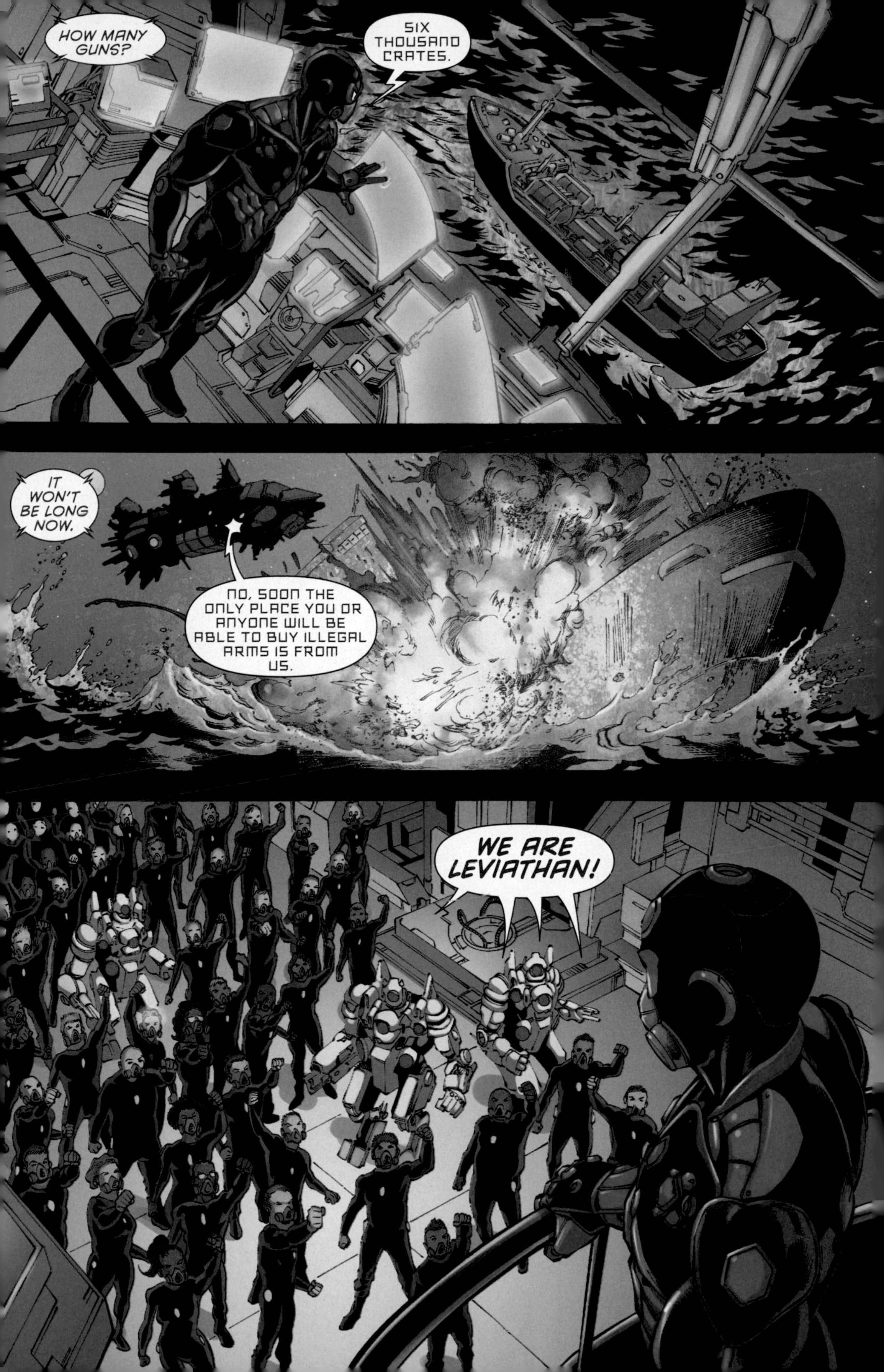
HOW MANY GUNS?
SIX THOUSAND CRATES.
IT WON'T BE LONG NOW.
NO, SOON THE ONLY PLACE YOU OR ANYONE WILL BE ABLE TO BUY ILLEGAL ARMS IS FROM US.
WE ARE LEVIATHAN!

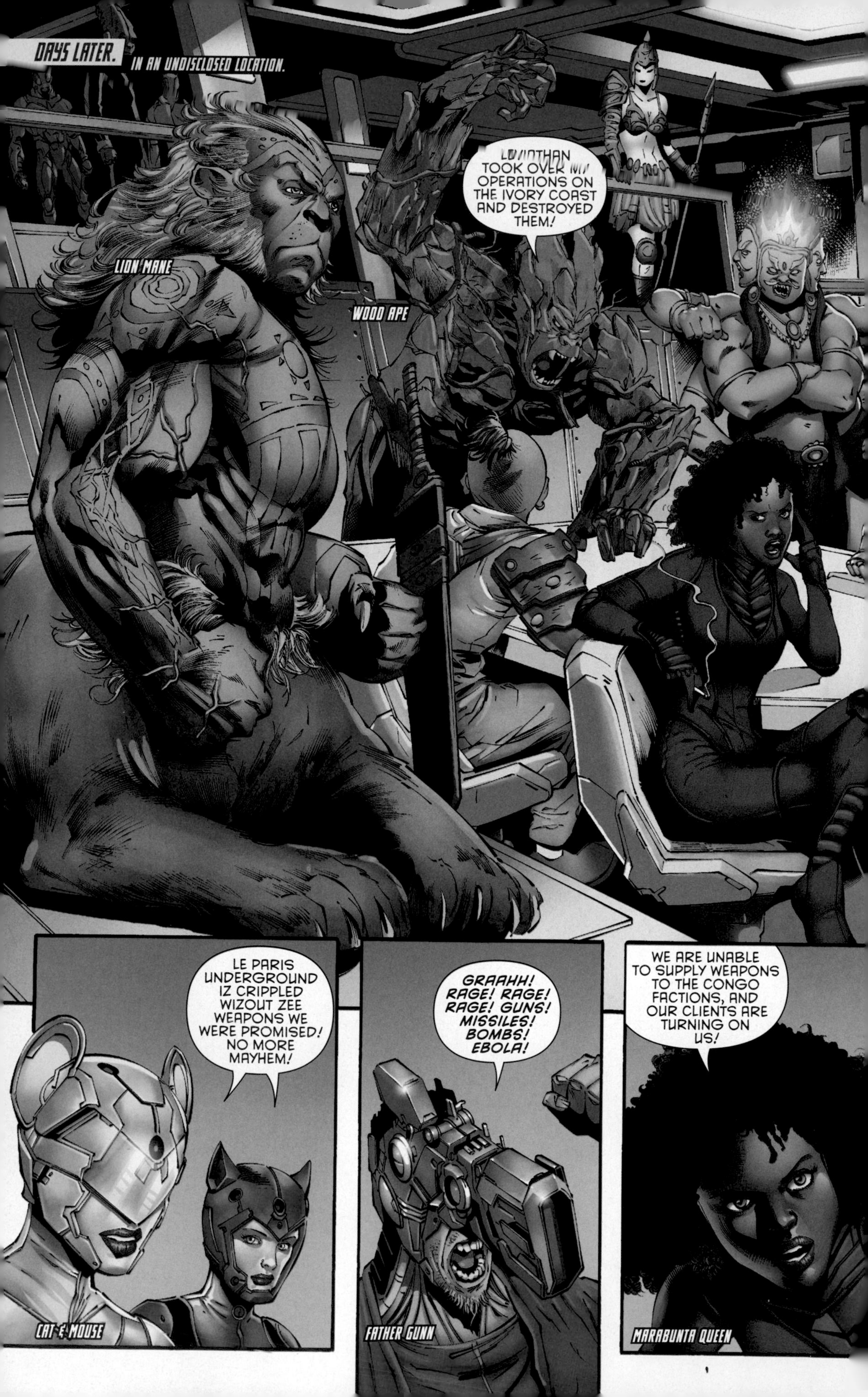
DAYS LATER.
IN AN UNDISCLOSED LOCATION.
LEVIATHAN TOOK OVER MY OPERATIONS ON THE IVORY COAST AND DESTROYED THEM!
LION MANE
WOOD APE
LE PARIS UNDERGROUND IZ CRIPPLED WIZOUT ZEE WEAPONS WE WERE PROMISED! NO MORE MAYHEM!
CAT & MOUSE
GRAAHH! RAGE! RAGE! RAGE! GUNS! MISSILES! BOMBS! EBOLA!
FATHER GUNN
WE ARE UNABLE TO SUPPLY WEAPONS TO THE CONGO FACTIONS, AND OUR CLIENTS ARE TURNING ON US!
MARABUNTA QUEEN

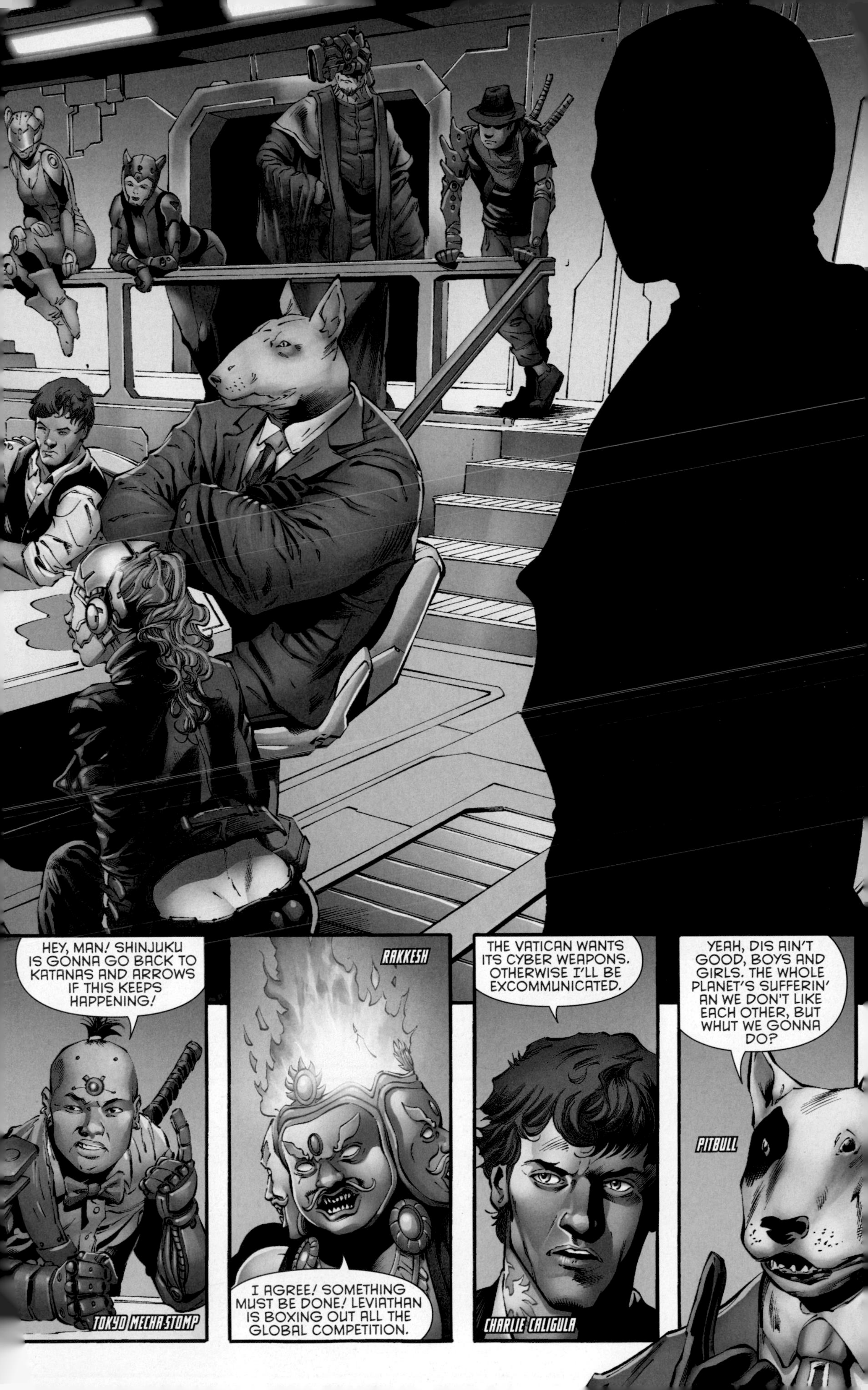
HEY, MAN! SHINJUKU IS GONNA GO BACK TO KATANAS AND ARROWS IF THIS KEEPS HAPPENING!
TOKYO MECHA-STOMP
RAKKESH
I AGREE! SOMETHING MUST BE DONE! LEVIATHAN IS BOXING OUT ALL THE GLOBAL COMPETITION.
THE VATICAN WANTS ITS CYBER WEAPONS. OTHERWISE I'LL BE EXCOMMUNICATED.
CHARLIE CALIGULA
YEAH, DIS AIN'T GOOD, BOYS AND GIRLS. THE WHOLE PLANET'S SUFFERIN' AN WE DON'T LIKE EACH OTHER, BUT WHUT WE GONNA DO?
PITBULL

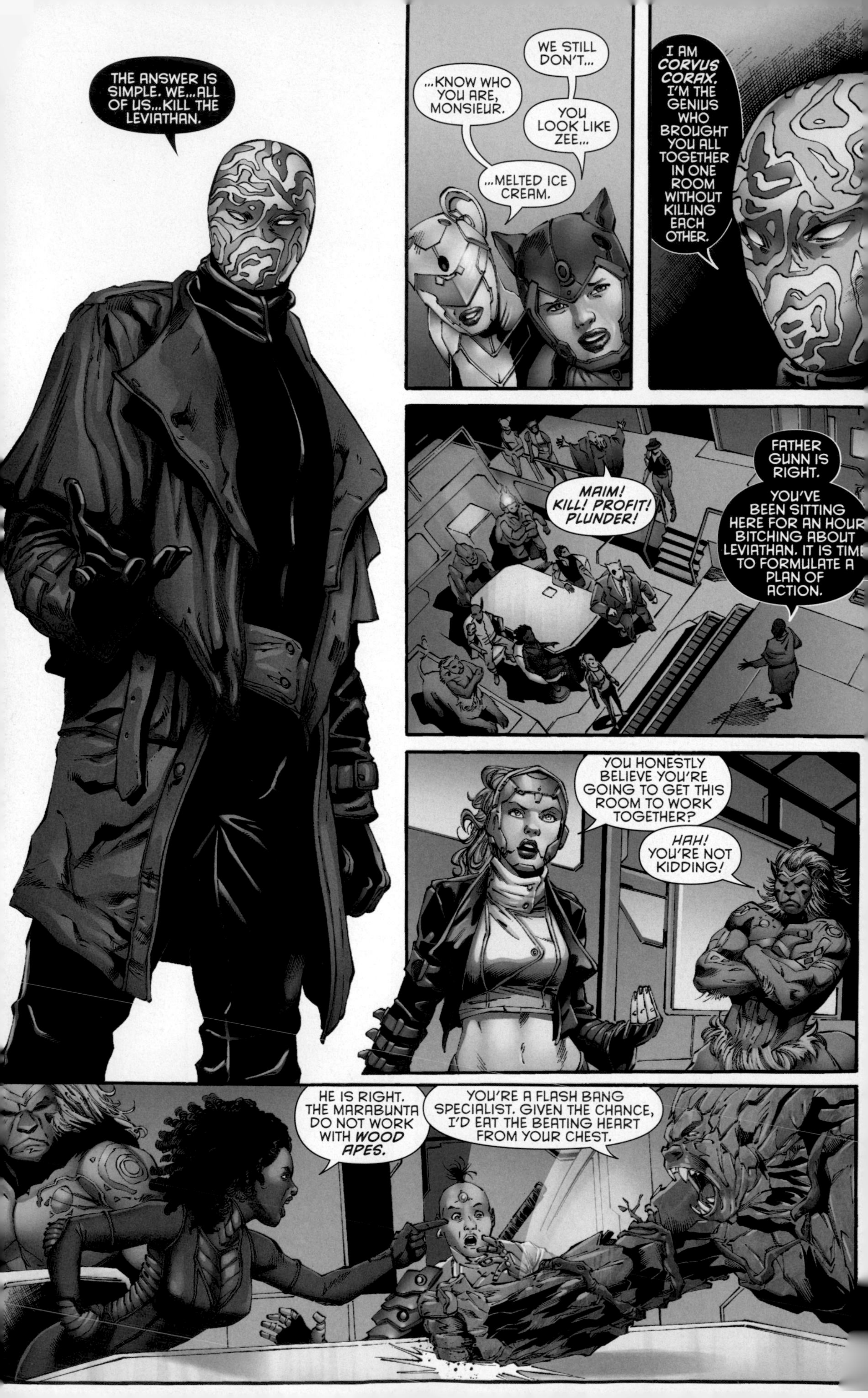
THE ANSWER IS SIMPLE. WE...ALL OF US...KILL THE LEVIATHAN.
WE STILL DON'T...
...KNOW WHO YOU ARE, MONSIEUR.
YOU LOOK LIKE ZEE...
...MELTED ICE CREAM.
I AM *CORVUS CORAX.* I'M THE GENIUS WHO BROUGHT YOU ALL TOGETHER IN ONE ROOM WITHOUT KILLING EACH OTHER.
MAIM! KILL! PROFIT! PLUNDER!
FATHER GUNN IS RIGHT.
YOU'VE BEEN SITTING HERE FOR AN HOUR BITCHING ABOUT LEVIATHAN. IT IS TIME TO FORMULATE A PLAN OF ACTION.
YOU HONESTLY BELIEVE YOU'RE GOING TO GET THIS ROOM TO WORK TOGETHER?
HAH! YOU'RE NOT KIDDING!
HE IS RIGHT. THE MARABUNTA DO NOT WORK WITH *WOOD APES.*
YOU'RE A FLASH BANG SPECIALIST. GIVEN THE CHANCE, I'D EAT THE BEATING HEART FROM YOUR CHEST.

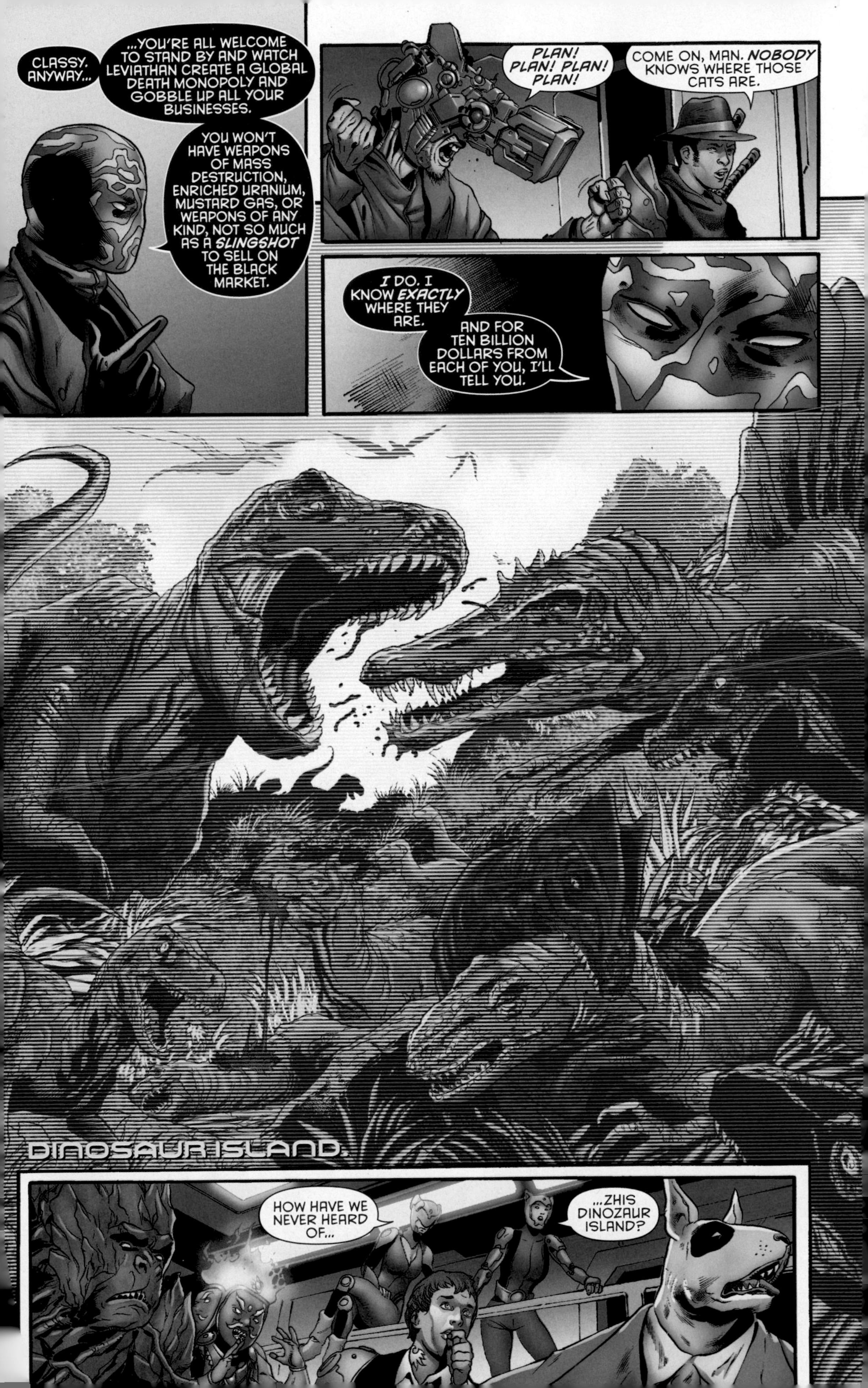
CLASSY. ANYWAY...
...YOU'RE ALL WELCOME TO STAND BY AND WATCH LEVIATHAN CREATE A GLOBAL DEATH MONOPOLY AND GOBBLE UP ALL YOUR BUSINESSES.
YOU WON'T HAVE WEAPONS OF MASS DESTRUCTION, ENRICHED URANIUM, MUSTARD GAS, OR WEAPONS OF ANY KIND, NOT SO MUCH AS A SLINGSHOT TO SELL ON THE BLACK MARKET.
PLAN! PLAN! PLAN! PLAN!
COME ON, MAN. NOBODY KNOWS WHERE THOSE CATS ARE.
I DO. I KNOW EXACTLY WHERE THEY ARE.
AND FOR TEN BILLION DOLLARS FROM EACH OF YOU, I'LL TELL YOU.
DINOSAUR ISLAND.
HOW HAVE WE NEVER HEARD OF...
...ZHIS DINOZAUR ISLAND?

WHY WOULD YOU? IT IS REMOTE, EXTREMELY DANGEROUS, AND TWO DECADES AGO, THE UNITED NATIONS BLOCKED ALL TRAVEL TO THE ISLAND.

THAT'S WHERE THEIR MAIN HUB OF OPERATIONS IS. DEEP UNDERGROUND.

THERE ARE THREE ENTRY POINTS.

HOW DO YOU KNOW SO MUCH ABOUT IT?

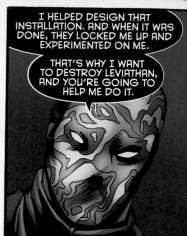

I HELPED DESIGN THAT INSTALLATION. AND WHEN IT WAS DONE, THEY LOCKED ME UP AND EXPERIMENTED ON ME.

THAT'S WHY I WANT TO DESTROY LEVIATHAN, AND YOU'RE GOING TO HELP ME DO IT.

NOT BUYING IT! NOT BUYING!

CH'OOM

I'M NOT STUPID AND NEITHER ARE MOST OF YOU.

YOU DON'T HAVE TO TRUST ME, OR EACH OTHER, BUT I'LL GIVE YOU ONE WEEK TO DECIDE IF YOU'RE GOING TO HELP DESTROY LEVIATHAN.

HE'S A HOLOGRAM?

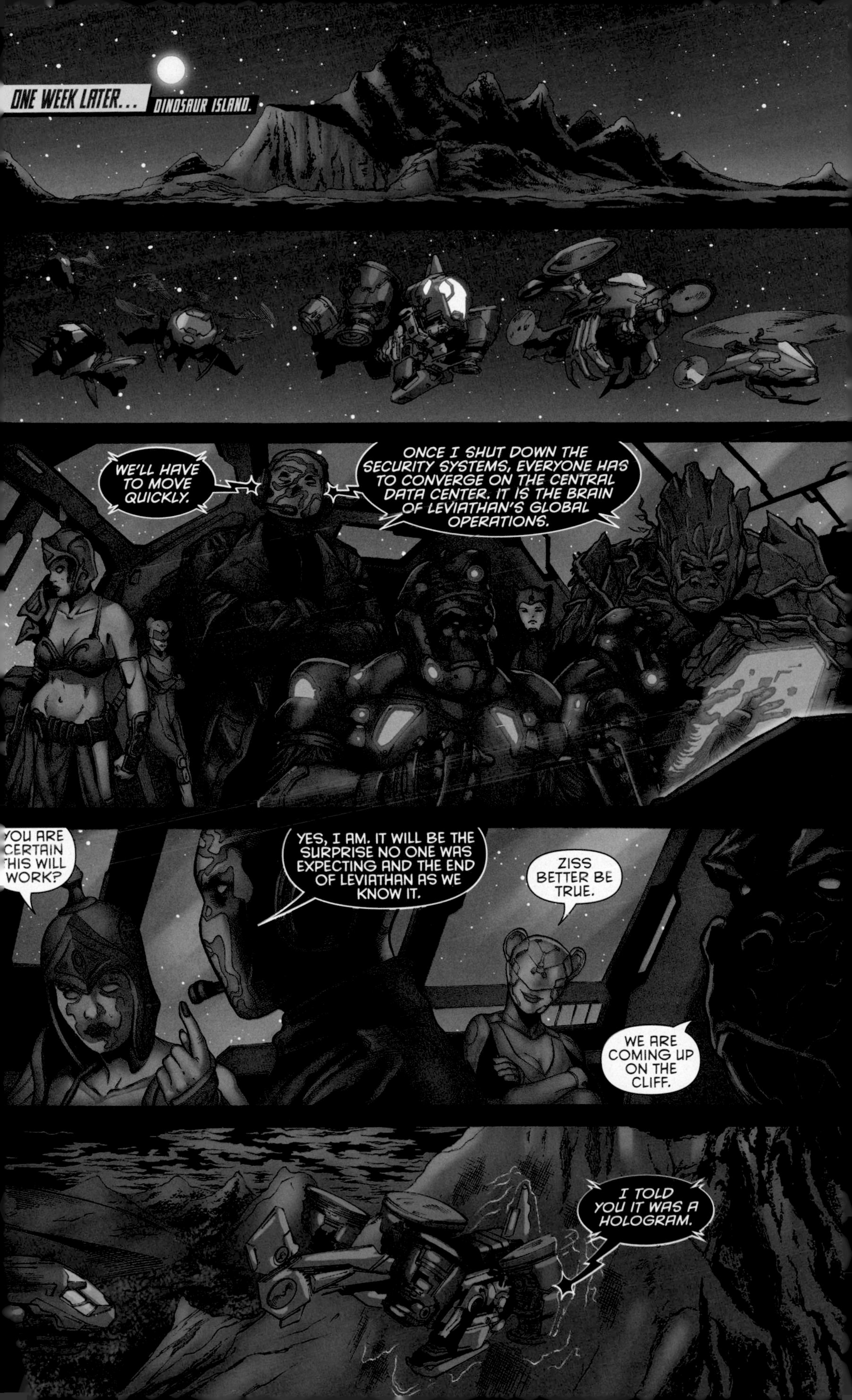

ONE WEEK LATER...
DINOSAUR ISLAND.
WE'LL HAVE TO MOVE QUICKLY.
ONCE I SHUT DOWN THE SECURITY SYSTEMS, EVERYONE HAS TO CONVERGE ON THE CENTRAL DATA CENTER. IT IS THE BRAIN OF LEVIATHAN'S GLOBAL OPERATIONS.
YOU ARE CERTAIN THIS WILL WORK?
YES, I AM. IT WILL BE THE SURPRISE NO ONE WAS EXPECTING AND THE END OF LEVIATHAN AS WE KNOW IT.
ZISS BETTER BE TRUE.
WE ARE COMING UP ON THE CLIFF.
I TOLD YOU IT WAS A HOLOGRAM.

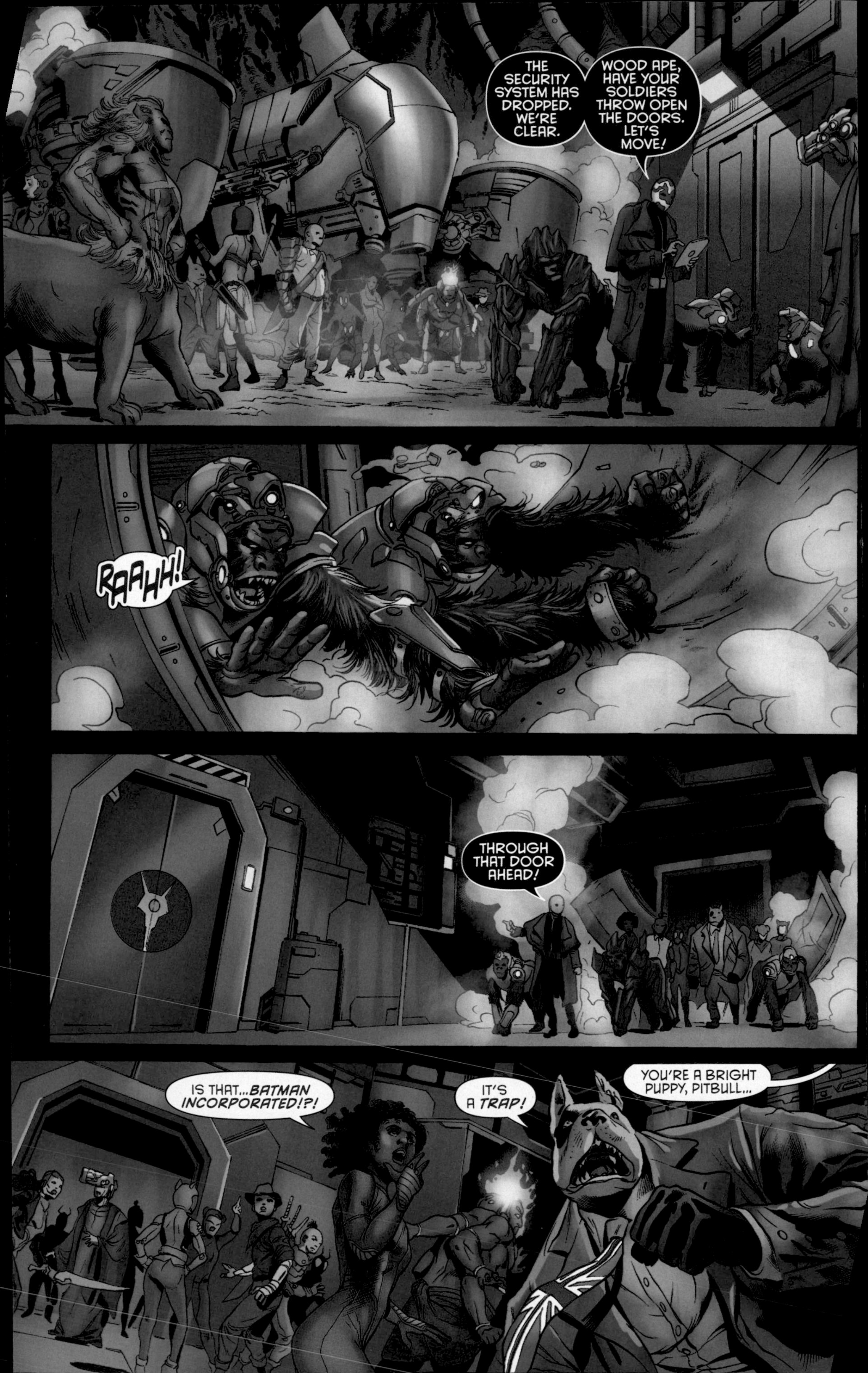
THE SECURITY SYSTEM HAS DROPPED. WE'RE CLEAR.
WOOD APE, HAVE YOUR SOLDIERS THROW OPEN THE DOORS. LET'S MOVE!
RAAHH!
THROUGH THAT DOOR AHEAD!
IS THAT...BATMAN INCORPORATED!?!
IT'S A TRAP!
YOU'RE A BRIGHT PUPPY, PITBULL...

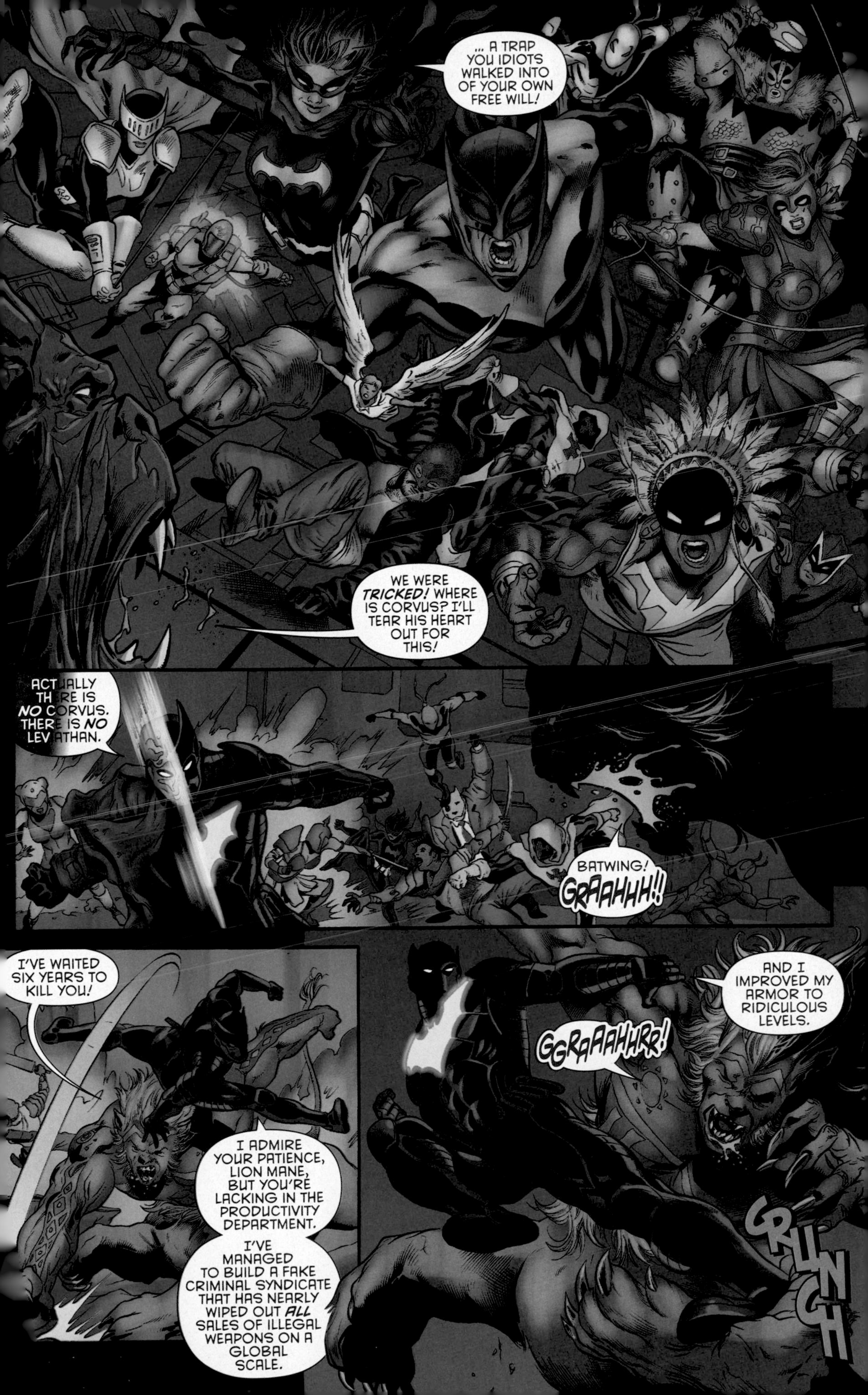
... A TRAP YOU IDIOTS WALKED INTO OF YOUR OWN FREE WILL!
WE WERE *TRICKED!* WHERE IS CORVUS? I'LL TEAR HIS HEART OUT FOR THIS!
ACTUALLY THERE IS *NO* CORVUS. THERE IS *NO* LEVIATHAN.
BATWING! GRAAHHH!!
I'VE WAITED SIX YEARS TO KILL YOU!
I ADMIRE YOUR PATIENCE, LION MANE, BUT YOU'RE LACKING IN THE PRODUCTIVITY DEPARTMENT.
I'VE MANAGED TO BUILD A FAKE CRIMINAL SYNDICATE THAT HAS NEARLY WIPED OUT *ALL* SALES OF ILLEGAL WEAPONS ON A GLOBAL SCALE.
GGRAAAHHRR!
AND I IMPROVED MY ARMOR TO RIDICULOUS LEVELS.
CRUNCH

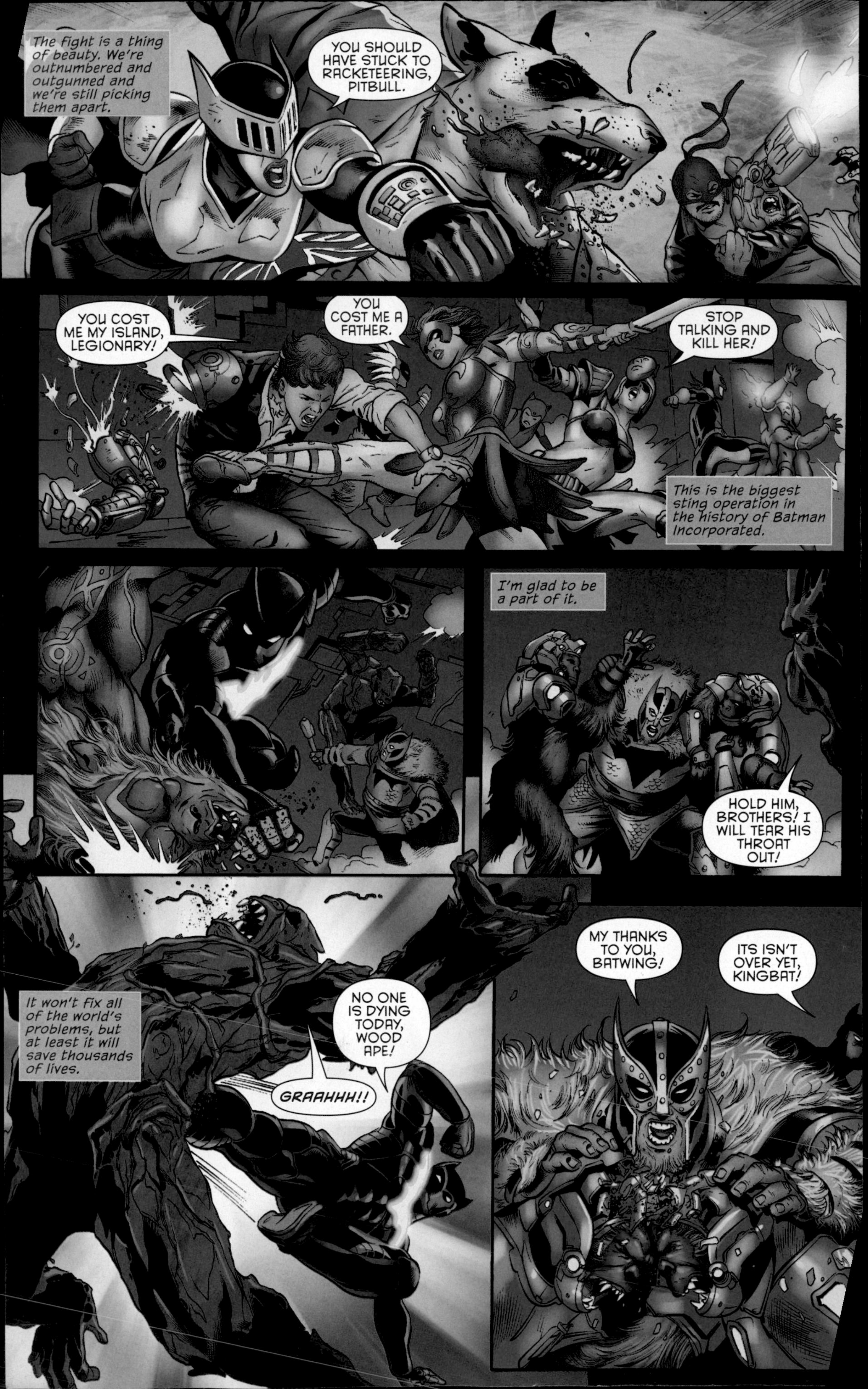
The fight is a thing of beauty. We're outnumbered and outgunned and we're still picking them apart.
YOU SHOULD HAVE STUCK TO RACKETEERING, PITBULL.
YOU COST ME MY ISLAND, LEGIONARY!
YOU COST ME A FATHER.
STOP TALKING AND KILL HER!
This is the biggest sting operation in the history of Batman Incorporated.
I'm glad to be a part of it.
HOLD HIM, BROTHERS! I WILL TEAR HIS THROAT OUT!
It won't fix all of the world's problems, but at least it will save thousands of lives.
NO ONE IS DYING TODAY, WOOD APE!
GRAAHHH!!
MY THANKS TO YOU, BATWING!
ITS ISN'T OVER YET, KINGBAT!

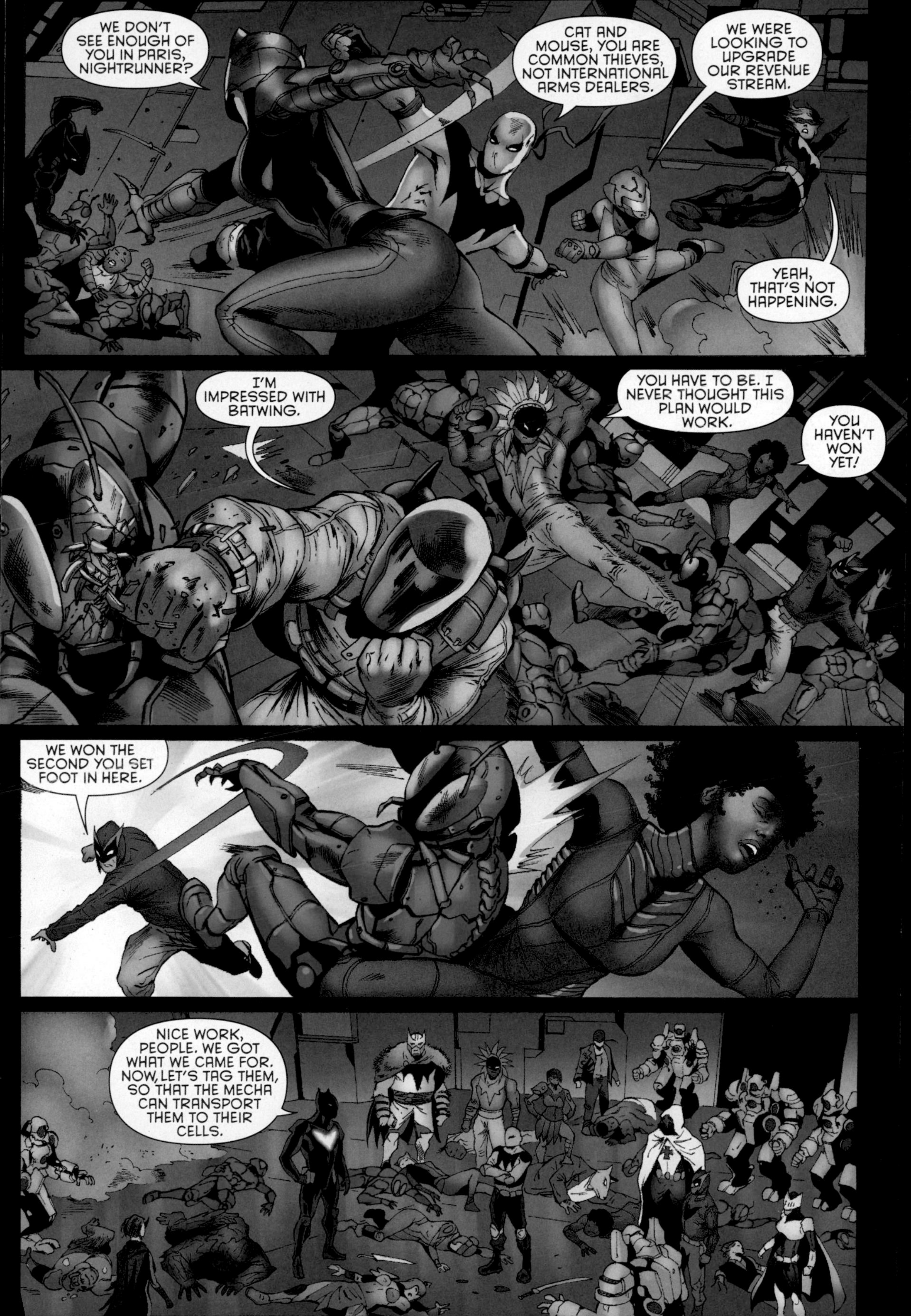
WE DON'T SEE ENOUGH OF YOU IN PARIS, NIGHTRUNNER?
CAT AND MOUSE, YOU ARE COMMON THIEVES, NOT INTERNATIONAL ARMS DEALERS.
WE WERE LOOKING TO UPGRADE OUR REVENUE STREAM.
YEAH, THAT'S NOT HAPPENING.
I'M IMPRESSED WITH BATWING.
YOU HAVE TO BE. I NEVER THOUGHT THIS PLAN WOULD WORK.
YOU HAVEN'T WON YET!
WE WON THE SECOND YOU SET FOOT IN HERE.
NICE WORK, PEOPLE. WE GOT WHAT WE CAME FOR. NOW, LET'S TAG THEM, SO THAT THE MECHA CAN TRANSPORT THEM TO THEIR CELLS.

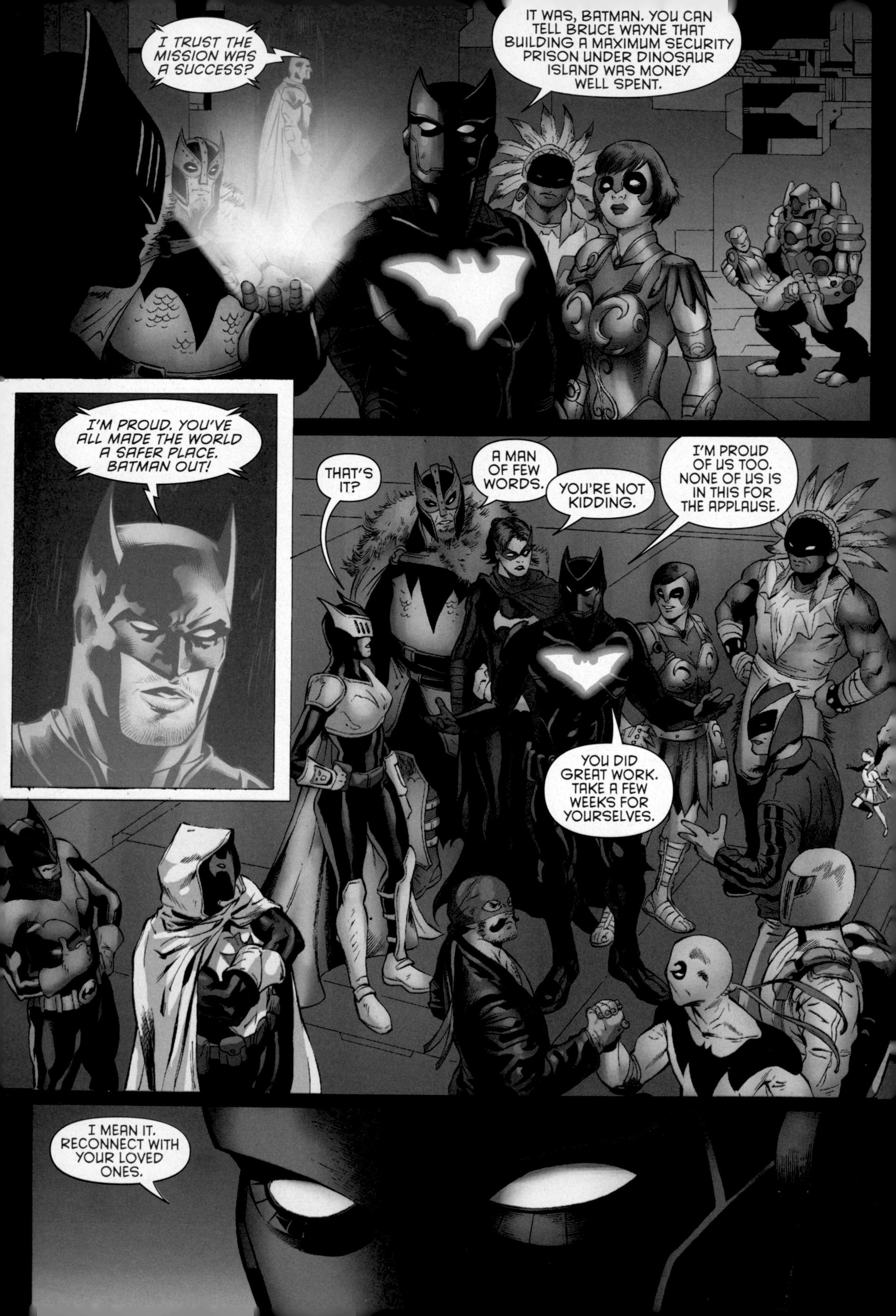

I TRUST THE MISSION WAS A SUCCESS?
IT WAS, BATMAN. YOU CAN TELL BRUCE WAYNE THAT BUILDING A MAXIMUM SECURITY PRISON UNDER DINOSAUR ISLAND WAS MONEY WELL SPENT.
I'M PROUD. YOU'VE ALL MADE THE WORLD A SAFER PLACE. BATMAN OUT!
THAT'S IT?
A MAN OF FEW WORDS.
YOU'RE NOT KIDDING.
I'M PROUD OF US TOO. NONE OF US IS IN THIS FOR THE APPLAUSE.
YOU DID GREAT WORK. TAKE A FEW WEEKS FOR YOURSELVES.
I MEAN IT. RECONNECT WITH YOUR LOVED ONES.

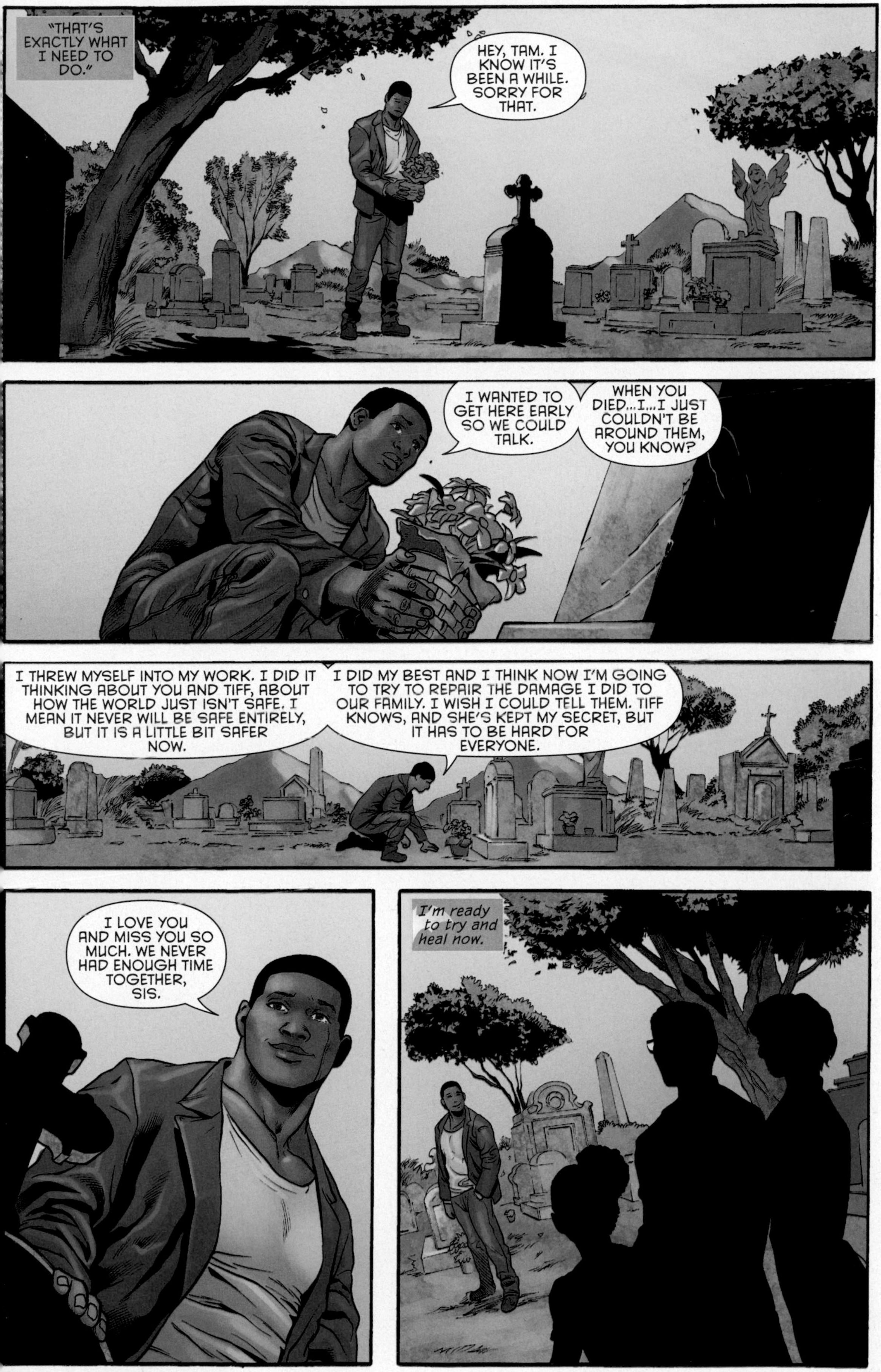
"THAT'S EXACTLY WHAT I NEED TO DO."
HEY, TAM. I KNOW IT'S BEEN A WHILE. SORRY FOR THAT.
I WANTED TO GET HERE EARLY SO WE COULD TALK.
WHEN YOU DIED...I...I JUST COULDN'T BE AROUND THEM, YOU KNOW?
I THREW MYSELF INTO MY WORK. I DID IT THINKING ABOUT YOU AND TIFF, ABOUT HOW THE WORLD JUST ISN'T SAFE. I MEAN IT NEVER WILL BE SAFE ENTIRELY, BUT IT IS A LITTLE BIT SAFER NOW.
I DID MY BEST AND I THINK NOW I'M GOING TO TRY TO REPAIR THE DAMAGE I DID TO OUR FAMILY. I WISH I COULD TELL THEM. TIFF KNOWS, AND SHE'S KEPT MY SECRET, BUT IT HAS TO BE HARD FOR EVERYONE.
I LOVE YOU AND MISS YOU SO MUCH. WE NEVER HAD ENOUGH TIME TOGETHER, SIS.
I'm ready to try and heal now.

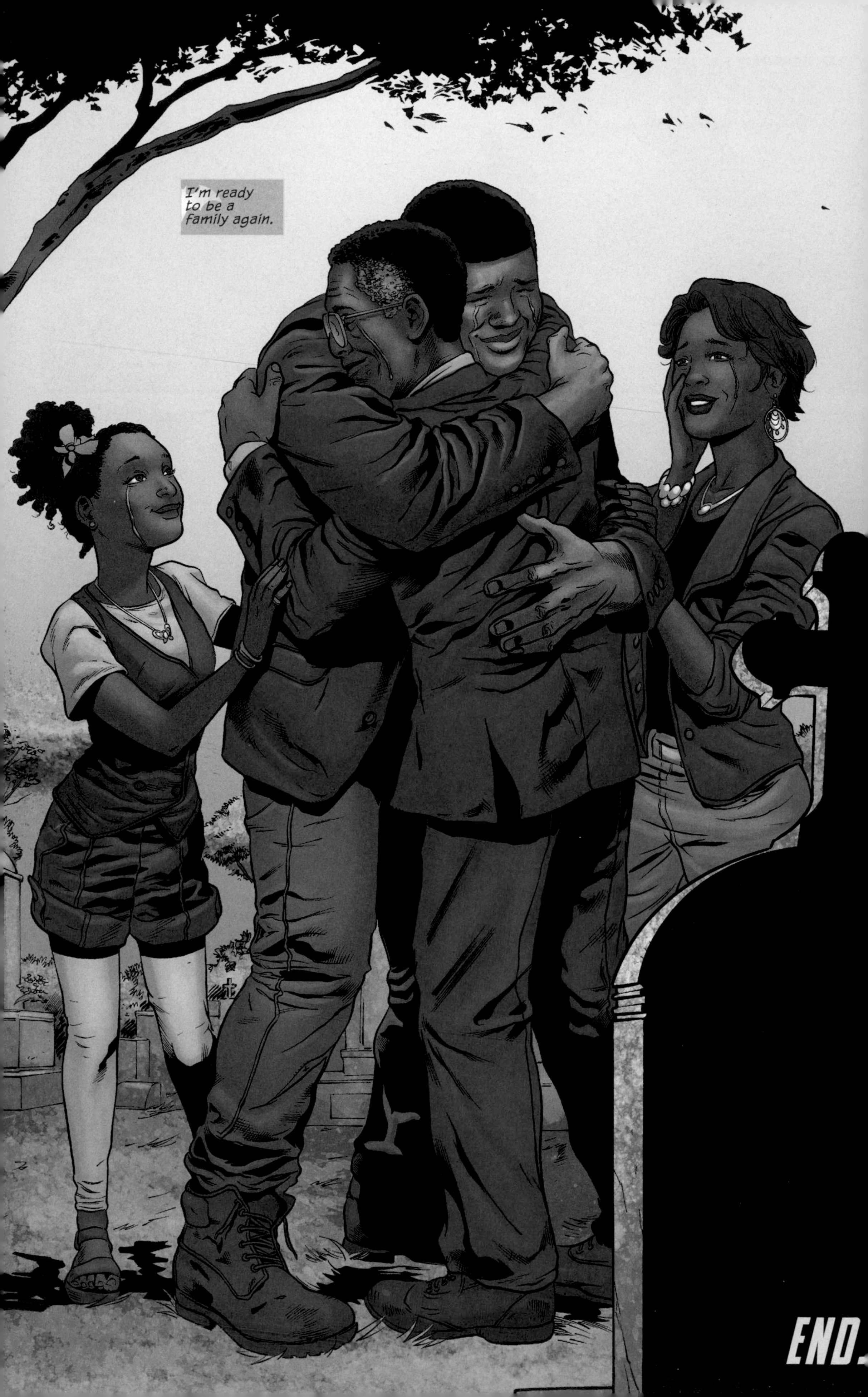
I'm ready to be a family again.
END.

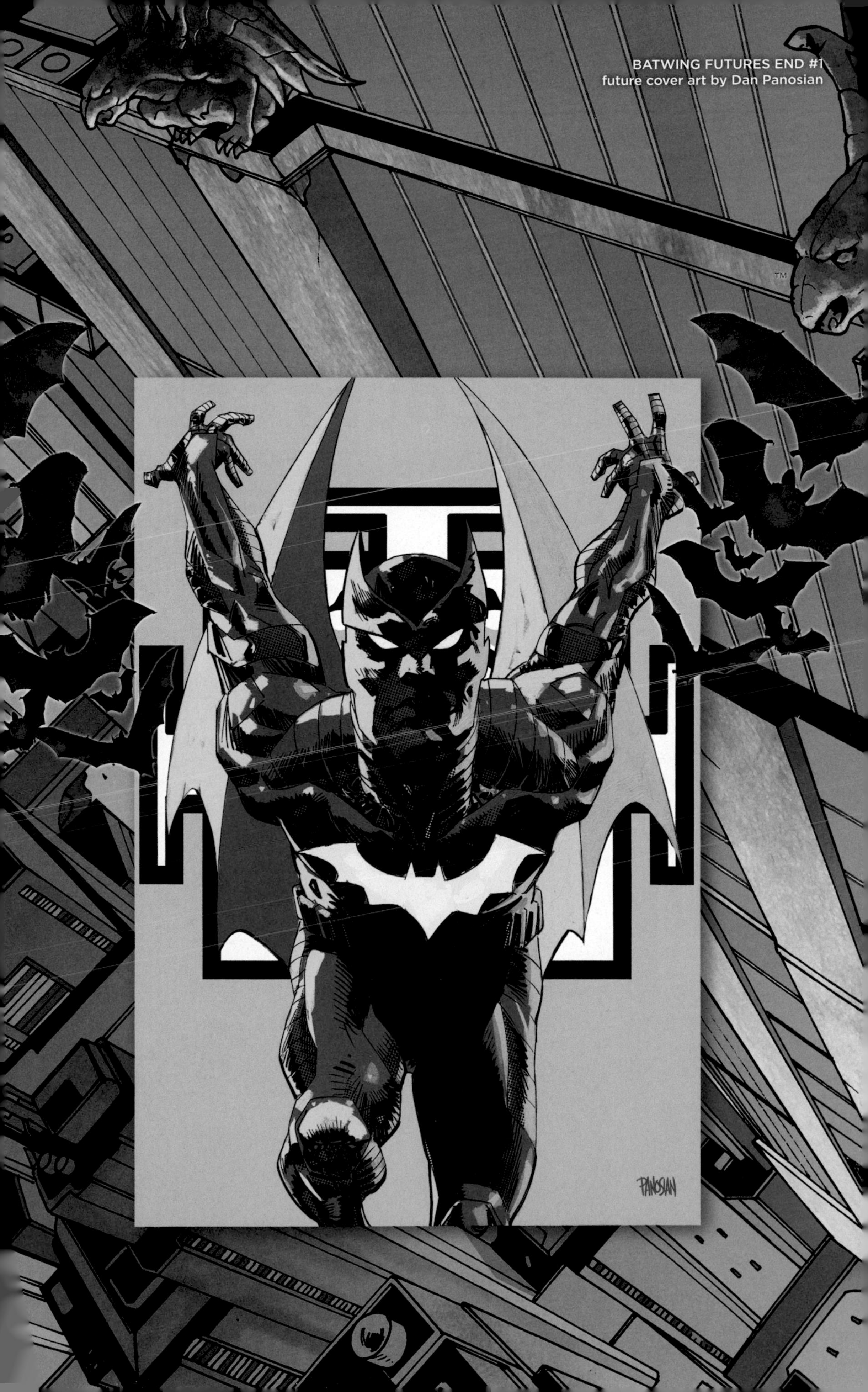
PANOSIAN

BATWING FUTURES END #1
future cover art by Dan Panosian

"[Writer Scott Snyder] pulls from the oldes aspects of the Batman myth, combines it with sinister-comi elements from the series' best period, and gives the whole thing terrific forward-spin."—ENTERTAINMENT WEEKL

START AT THE BEGINNING!

BATMAN VOLUME 1: THE COURT OF OWLS

BATMAN VOL. 2: THE CITY OF OWLS

with SCOTT SNYDER and GREG CAPULLO

BATMAN VOL. 3: DEATH OF THE FAMILY

with SCOTT SNYDER and GREG CAPULLO

BATMAN: NIGHT OF THE OWLS

with SCOTT SNYDER and GREG CAPULLO

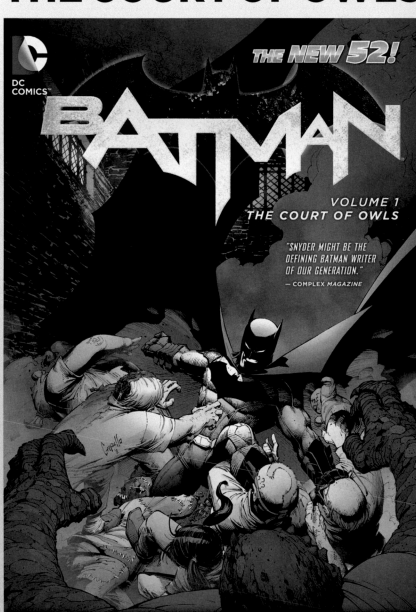

THE NEW 52!

DC COMICS™

BATMAN

VOLUME 1
THE COURT OF OWLS

"SNYDER MIGHT BE THE DEFINING BATMAN WRITER OF OUR GENERATION."
— COMPLEX MAGAZINE

SCOTT **SNYDER** GREG **CAPULLO** JONATHAN **GLAPION**

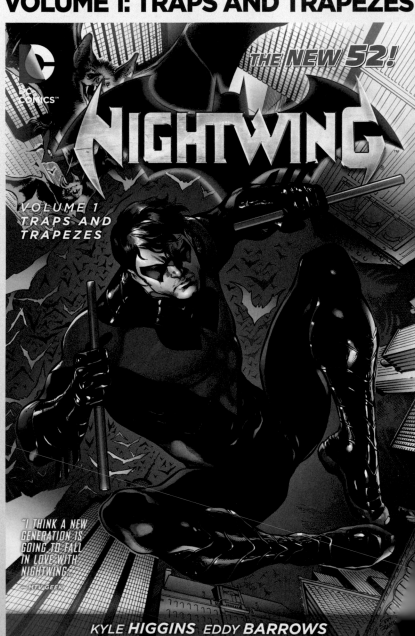

FROM THE *NEW YORK TIMES* BEST-SELLING WRITERS
ED BRUBAKER
& GREG RUCKA
with MICHAEL LARK

**GOTHAM CENTRAL
BOOK TWO:
JOKERS AND MADMEN**

**GOTHAM CENTRAL
BOOK THREE:
ON THE FREAK BEAT**

**GOTHAM CENTRAL
BOOK FOUR:
CORRIGAN**

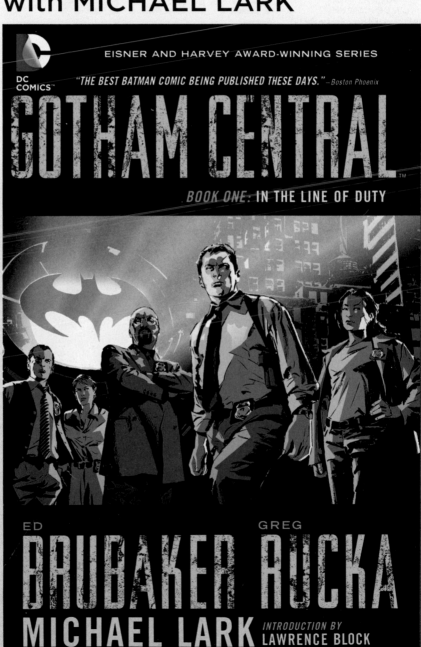

"Simone and artist Ardian Syaf not only do justice to Babs' legacy, but build in a new complexity that is the starting point for a future full of new storytelling possibilities. A hell of a ride." —IGN

START AT THE BEGINNING!

BATGIRL
VOLUME 1: THE DARKEST REFLECTION

"THIS IS A MUST-BUY SERIES." — THE NEW YORK TIMES

THE NEW 52!

DC COMICS

BATGIRL

VOLUME 1
THE DARKEST
REFLECTION

GAIL SIMONE   ARDIAN SYAF   VICENTE CIFUENTES